Monty Canto

AQA A-level History

Tsarist and Communist Russia

1855–1964

Chris Corin

Terry Fiehn

Approval message from AQA

This textbook has been approved by AQA for use with our qualification. This means that we have checked that it broadly covers the specification and we are satisfied with the overall quality. Full details of our approval process can be found on our website.

We approve textbooks because we know how important it is for teachers and students to have the right resources to support their teaching and learning. However, the publisher is ultimately responsible for the editorial control and quality of this book.

Please note that when teaching the **AQA A-level History** course, you must refer to AQA's specification as your definitive source of information. While this book has been written to match the specification, it cannot provide complete coverage of every aspect of the course. Please also note that the practice questions in this title are written to reflect the question styles of the AS and A-level papers. They are designed to help students become familiar with question types and practise exam skills. AQA has published specimen papers and mark schemes online and these should be consulted for definitive examples.

A wide range of other useful resources can be found on the relevant subject pages of our website: www.aqa.org.uk.

HODDER EDUCATION
AN HACHETTE UK COMPANY

Photo credits

p.v *l* © Heritage Image Partnership Ltd/Alamy, *r* © RIA Novosti/TopFoto; **p.vi** © Sovfoto/UIG via Getty Images; **p.vii** © Maksim Dmitriev/FotoSoyuz/Getty Images; **p.viii** © FineArt/Alamy; **p.1** © Heritage Image Partnership Ltd/Alamy; **p.10** © Heritage Image Partnership Ltd/Alamy; **p.37** © TopFoto; **p.43** © Heritage Image Partnership Ltd/Alamy; **p.54** © Library of Congress Prints and Photographs Division Washington [LC-USZ62-128298]; **p.62** © TopFoto; **p.65** © Maksim Dmitriev/FotoSoyuz/Getty Images; **p.71** © Sovfoto/UIG via Getty Images; **p.78** V. Filimonov/©RIA Novosti/TopFoto; **p.79** © Illustrated London News; **p.81** © Illustrated London News; **p.86** © Photos.com/Thinkstock Images; **p.89** © Photos.com/Thinkstock Images; **p.90** © Illustrated London News; **p.93** V. Filimonov/©RIA Novosti/TopFoto; **p.121** Detail from The Storming of the Winter Palace, 7th November 1917 (oil on canvas), Russian School, (20th century)/Private Collection/RIA Novosti/Bridgeman Images; **p.130** © Fine Art Images/Heritage Images/Getty Images; **p.137** Detail from The Storming of the Winter Palace, 7th November 1917 (oil on canvas), Russian School, (20th century)/Private Collection/RIA Novosti/Bridgeman Images; **p.157** Fine Art Images/Heritage Images/Getty Images; **p.168** © Photos.com/Thinkstock Images; **p.172** Fine Art Images/ Heritage Images/Getty Images; **p.176** Fine Art Images/Heritage Images/TopFoto; **p.177** © Illustrated London News; **p.178** *t* General Photographic Agency/Getty Images, *b* Hulton Archive/Getty Images; **p.179** *t* © RIA Novosti/ Alamy, *b* Hulton-Deutsch Collection/CORBIS; **p.188** © Photos 12/Alamy; **p.194** © Stoyanov/Fotolia; **p.199** © RIA Novosti/TopFoto; **p.212** © RIA Novosti/Alamy; **p.219** © FineArt/Alamy; **p.220** *t* © Stoyanov/Fotolia, *b* Fine Art Images/Superstock; **p.221** *tl* © Heritage Image Partnership Ltd/Alamy, *bl* © ITAR-TASS Photo Agency/Alamy, *r* © Illustrated London News; **p.231** Sovfoto/UIG via Getty Images; **p.238** Fine Art Images/SuperStock/Getty Images; **p.245** Sovfoto/UIG via Getty Images; **p.252** Fine Art Images/Heritage Images/TopFoto; **p.260** © ITAR-TASS Photo Agency/Alamy; **p.262** © RIA Novosti/Alamy; **p.263** Carl Mydans/The LIFE Picture Collection/Getty Images; **p.271** © ITAR-TASS Photo Agency/Alamy.

Text acknowledgements

pp.80, 96, 131, 152: Orlando Figes: from *A People's Tragedy: The Russian Revolution 1891–1924* (Pimlico, 1997), reproduced by permission of the publisher; **p.83, 92: Marc Ferro:** from *Nicholas II, The Last of the Tsars* (OUP, 1990); **p.129: John Reed:** tables: 'The cost of living before and during the Revolution' from *Ten Days that Shook the World* (Penguin, 1977); **p.170: E.H. Carr:** from *What is History?* (Palgrave Macmillan, 2002); **p.175: Jim Grant:** diagram (adapted): 'Stalin's Power Base' from *Stalin and the Soviet Union* (Longman, 1988); **p.212:** A Soviet account of Yezhov from *Komsomolskaya Pravda* (*Komsomolskaya Pravda*, 1988); **p.235: John Barber:** from 'The Image of Stalin in Soviet Propaganda' (St. Martin's Press, 1993); **p.247: Dmitri Shepilov:** from *The Kremlin's Scholar: A Memoir of Soviet Politics Under Stalin and Khrushchev* (Yale University Press, 2014); **p.276: Yevgeny Yevtushenko:** from 'The Heirs of Stalin', originally published in *Pravda* (*Pravda*, 21st October 1962).

The Routledge Atlas of Russian History, Sir Martin Gilbert, © 2007, published by Routledge, reproduced by permission of Taylor & Francis Books UK, for map on p. 239.

AQA material is reproduced by permission of AQA.

Every effort has been made to trace or contact all copyright holders, but if any have been inadvertently overlooked the Publishers will be pleased to make the necessary arrangements at the first opportunity.

Although every effort has been made to ensure that website addresses are correct at time of going to press, Hodder Education cannot be held responsible for the content of any website mentioned in this book. It is sometimes possible to find a relocated web page by typing in the address of the home page for a website in the URL window of your browser.

Hachette UK's policy is to use papers that are natural, renewable and recyclable products and made from wood grown in well-managed forests and other controlled sources. The logging and manufacturing processes are expected to conform to the environmental regulations of the country of origin.

Orders: please contact Hachette UK Distribution, Hely Hutchinson Centre, Milton Road, Didcot, Oxfordshire, OX11 7HH. Telephone: +44 (0)1235 827827. Email education@hachette.co.uk Lines are open from 9 a.m. to 5 p.m., Monday to Friday. You can also order through our website: www.hoddereducation.co.uk

© Terry Fiehn, Chris Corin 2015
First published in 2015 by
Hodder Education,
An Hachette UK Company,
Carmelite House,
50 Victoria Embankment,
London EC4Y 0DZ

Impression number   11

Year   2022

Cover photo © RIA Novosti/TopFoto

Illustrations by Integra Software Services

Typeset in 10.5/12.5pt ITC Berkeley Oldstyle Std Book by Integra Software Services Pvt. Ltd., Pondicherry, India

Printed in India

A catalogue record for this title is available from the British Library

ISBN 9781471837807

Contents

Part 2: The Soviet Union, 1917–64

Section 1: The emergence of Communist dictatorship, 1917–41

Section 2: The Stalinist dictatorship and reaction, 1941–64

Introduction

This book on Russian history is written to support the Tsarist and Communist option of AQA's A-level History Breadth Study specification. It is a fascinating period in world history, including one of the most important events of the twentieth century – the Russian Revolution – which led to the creation of the first socialist state. This not only brought about enormous changes in Russia itself but also had a huge impact on the rest of the world. Communist Russia represented a philosophy and world view which terrified the West and gave rise to the idea of the totalitarian state which provided the model for George Orwell's *1984* and Aldous Huxley's *Brave New World*. This period is full of intriguing characters, great art and artists, and dramatic events. It is the Russia of Tolstoy and Chekhov, of the disreputable monk Rasputin and the last Tsar Nicholas II, his wife Alexandra and their five children who were tragically murdered in 1918. It is the Russia of Lenin, Trotsky and Stalin – the great figures of world revolution. They were responsible for the death of millions of their subjects and left their mark on countries around the globe. Studying this period of Russian history is essential if you want to make sense of the events in the twentieth century and also understand better Russia's actions in the world today.

▲ Portrait of Alexander III, 1875.

v

The key content

'Tsarist and Communist Russia, 1855–1964 ' is one of the breadth studies offered by AQA, and as such covers over 100 years. The content is divided into two parts.

Part 1 (1855–1917) is studied by those taking the AS examination.

Parts 1 and 2 (1917–1964) are studied by those taking the full A-level examination.

Each part is subdivided into two sections.

PART 1: AUTOCRACY, REFORM AND REVOLUTION: RUSSIA, 1855–1917

This covers the reigns of the last three tsars – Alexander II, Alexander III and Nicholas II.

During this period Russia changed enormously as a result of the emancipation of the serfs in 1861 and the industrialisation and modernisation of the Russian economy. Russian cities grew rapidly, particularly St Petersburg and Moscow which flourished as centres of culture.

The tsarist autocracy had to decide whether to keep on ruling in the way it was or to engage with the population through reform of its institutions.

Trying to preserve autocracy, 1855–94

The Crimean War exposed the backwardness of Russia and Alexander II realised he had to drag Russia into the modern age if it was to remain a world power. He sought to strengthen and preserve the Russian autocracy by reforming some of its major institutions – serfdom, the army, the legal system, local government and education. However, the result of this reform process was a surge in opposition to the regime and the rise of a revolutionary movement which culminated in Alexander's assassination in 1881. His son, Alexander III, reacted to this by introducing a raft of counter-reforms and repressive measures which gave Russia thirteen years of peace and stability. However, many of the underlying problems remained when Alexander III died unexpectedly in 1894.

The collapse of autocracy, 1894–1917

Nicholas II took over as tsar and carried on his father's policies. This included a drive to industrialise and modernise Russia. But the process of modernisation created problems for the regime, notably a growing and resentful working class who lived and worked in appalling conditions and a middle class who wanted greater participation in government. After the government's incompetent handling of the Russo-Japanese war, discontent exploded into revolution in 1905. Nicholas survived this by conceding a parliament or *duma* and repressing workers and peasants. However, he wanted to retain the autocracy in all its power and never really wanted to reform the regime. Under the pressure of the First World War, its weaknesses were exposed and the autocracy collapsed.

PART 2: THE SOVIET UNION, 1917–64

This covers the first three leaders of the Soviet Union – Lenin, Stalin and Khrushchev. Once the communists were established in power the pace of change accelerated, particularly under Stalin. The Stalin revolution resulted in millions of deaths and irreversible developments as forced collectivisation accelerated the transformation into an urbanised country. However, the Soviet Union played a massive part in the defeat of Hitler which made Stalin's position impregnable. His system solidified after the war and Khrushchev found it very difficult to reform.

The emergence of communist dictatorship, 1917–41

Lenin was determined on one-party government. Civil war and dictatorship flowed from this decision. The civil war was only one of many challenges the communists had to overcome between 1917 and 1921 and Lenin's health collapsed at the end of 1922. Stalin was successful in the power struggle which ensued. His 'revolution' consisting of collectivisation, industrialisation and the Great Terror transformed the Soviet Union. His dictatorship grew more and more repressive and permeated all aspects of life. It came at a huge cost in human terms but the economy, with its emphasis on heavy industry, placed the country in a position, eventually, to throw back the German invasion.

The Stalinist dictatorship and reaction, 1941–64

Stalin's position was enormously strengthened by victory over Germany. It was a victory for the heroic resistance of the Russian people in a war of annihilation. Stalin saw it as vindicating his system and, instead of the post-war relaxation the people hoped for, High Stalinism – the final phase of his rule – was an attempt to reimpose the same structures on a society that had changed. Khrushchev emerged as Stalin's successor and in his 20th Party Congress speech in 1956 he denounced Stalin's crimes. This was the time of 'the thaw' and there was an easing in cultural life and living standards improved. By 1964 the unpredictable Khrushchev had alienated too many interest groups. He was ousted, but it was a mark of the changes that he had brought in that he was allowed to retire into obscurity.

Key concepts

The study of history does not just include narrative – interesting though the stories often are! There are four concepts which steer our thinking and our understanding of the past. These are important in your study, and questions are likely to involve assessing these concepts.

- Change and continuity: To what extent did things change? What are the similarities and differences over time?
- Cause and consequence: What were the factors that led to change? How did the changes affect individuals and groups within society, as well as the country as a whole?

In relation to these concepts, the essay questions you will face will be asking you to assess, for example:

- the extent you agree with a statement
- the validity of a statement
- the importance of a particular factor relating to a key question
- how much something changed or to what extent something was achieved.

In addition, you will be learning about different interpretations: how and why events have been portrayed in different ways over time by historians. In the first section of both the AS and A-level examination you will be tested on this skill with a selection of contrasting extracts.

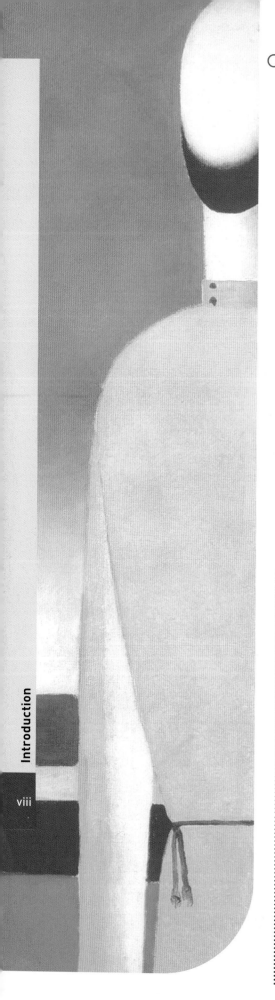

The key questions

The specification lists six key questions around which the study is based. These are wide-ranging in scope and can be considered across the whole period. They reflect the broadly based questions (covering twenty years or more) that will be set in the examination.

1 How was Russia governed and how did political authority change and develop?

You will learn about how Russia was governed by an autocracy under the tsars until 1917 and the principles and practices which underpinned its political authority. Then you will learn about how this changed under the Bolsheviks and how Lenin, Stalin and Khrushchev differed as rulers of Russia – though Stalin told his mother that he was like a tsar! You will examine the nature of Stalinism.

2 Why did opposition develop and how effective was it?

You will study the growth of the revolutionary movement in Russia in the late nineteenth century and the spread of Marxism; also how opposition to the regime came from the workers, peasants and middle classes. The Bolshevik takeover provoked a civil war, but opposition under the communists was generally short-lived and under Stalin more imaginary than real. Khrushchev, though, was actually overthrown.

3 How and with what results did the economy develop and change?

You will learn about the impressive growth rates of Russian industry and about developments in agriculture in the tsarist period. You will examine the different economic policies of the Bolsheviks and assess the impact of Stalin's Great Turn to rapid industrialisation.

4 What was the extent of social and cultural change?

Industrialisation and modernisation in the late nineteenth and early twentieth centuries led to the rapid growth of cities with their attendant problems. Life in the countryside changed more slowly but population growth and city culture had a significant impact on the lives of peasants. You will learn about the dramatic impact collectivisation had on the peasants and how the Soviet Union became an urbanised society. There was an attempt to create a New Soviet Person, and culture and the arts were strictly controlled.

5 How important were ideas and ideology?

You will consider the differences and importance of ideas and ideology throughout the period. The principles of autocracy, orthodoxy and nationalism formed the core of the ideology which supported the tsarist regime and gave the tsar the God-given right to lead the Russian people without any constraints on his power. Marxism–Leninism was the ideology which underpinned the communist regime. It was particularly important to Lenin and Stalin and at different times class struggle loomed very large.

6 How important was the role of individuals and groups and how were they affected by developments?

The powerful role of the Tsar at the very heart of the Russian state meant that individuals, their personalities and their attributes were central to the decisions and actions that determined the course of events in the tsarist period. You will learn about statesmen of great stature such as Sergei Witte and Peter Stolypin as well as revolutionaries such as Lenin and Trotsky who arguably changed the course of history by their interventions. Stalin's importance was undeniable too. Groups like the Kronstadt sailors and organisations like the secret police were also influential.

How this book is designed to help your studies

1 With the facts, concepts and key questions of the specification

At the beginning of each chapter the book flags up the elements of the specification and the key questions that are being covered.

Activities are provided, helping you to create notes, and enabling you to consider the main areas of interpretation throughout the book.

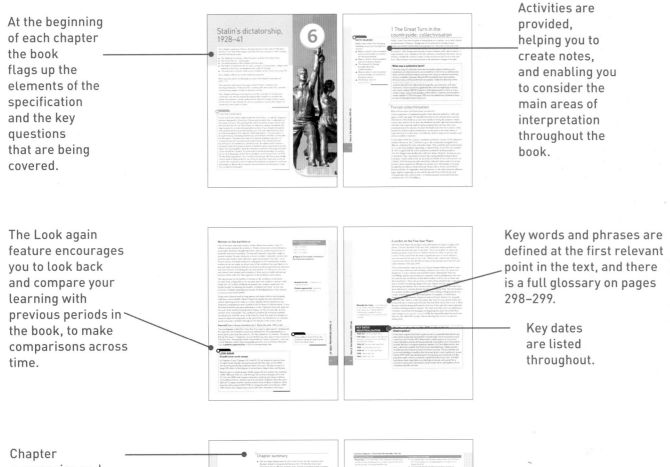

The Look again feature encourages you to look back and compare your learning with previous periods in the book, to make comparisons across time.

Key words and phrases are defined at the first relevant point in the text, and there is a full glossary on pages 298–299.

Key dates are listed throughout.

Chapter summaries and diagrams are provided to help consolidate your learning.

2 With the skills needed to answer examination questions

The book provides guidance in answering different types of examination questions in the form of a separate 'skills' section at the end of each chapter.

Interpretation skills are developed through the analysis of extended pieces of writing by leading academics.

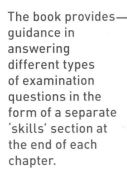

3 With the skills in reading, understanding and making notes from the book

Note-making

Good note-making is really important. Your notes are an essential revision resource. What is more, the process of making notes will help you understand and remember what you are reading.

How to make notes

Most note-making styles reflect the distinction between key points and supporting evidence. Below is advice on a variety of different note-making styles. Throughout each section in the book are note-making activities for you to carry out.

The important thing is that you understand your notes. Therefore, you don't have to write *everything* down, and you don't have to write in full sentences.

While making notes you can use abbreviations:

Full text	Abbreviation
Provisional Government	PG
Russia	Ru
Development	Devt
Alexander II	AII

You can develop your own abbreviations. Usually it is only yourself who has to understand them!

You can use arrows instead of words:

Full text	Abbreviation
Increased	↑
Decreased	↓

You can use mathematical notation:

Equals	=
plus, and	+
Because	∵
Therefore	∴

Note-making styles

There are a large number of note-making styles. However you prefer to make notes, by hand or on a laptop or tablet, the principles are the same. You can find examples of three popular styles below. All of them have their strengths; it is a good idea to try them all and work out which style suits you.

Style 1: Bullet points

Bullet points can be a useful method of making notes:

- They encourage you to write in note form, rather than in full sentences.
- They help you to organise your ideas in a systematic fashion.
- They are easy to skim read later.
- You can show relative importance visually by indenting less important or supporting points.

Usually it is easier to write notes with bullet points after you have skim-read a section or a paragraph first in order to get the overall sense in your head.

Style 2: The 1–2 method

The 1–2 method is a variation on bullet points. The method is based on dividing your page into two columns: the first for the main point, the second for supporting detail. This allows you to see the structure of the information clearly. To do this, you can create a chart to complete, as follows:

Main point	Supporting detail

Style 3: Spider diagrams

Spider diagrams or mind maps can be a useful method of making notes:

- They will help you to categorise factors: each of the main branches coming from the centre should be a new category.
- They can help you see what is most important: often the most important factors will be close to the centre of the diagram.
- They can help you see connections between different aspects of what you are studying. It is useful to draw lines between different parts of your diagram to show links.
- They can also help you with essay planning: you can use them to quickly get down the main points and develop a clear structure in response to an essay question.
- You can set out the spider diagram in any way that seems appropriate for the task, but usually, as with a spider's web, you would start with the title or central issue in the middle with connecting lines radiating outwards.

Alexander II, the Tsar Liberator

1

This chapter introduces Russian society in the middle of the nineteenth century and covers the reign of Alexander II from 1855 to 1881. It deals with the following areas:

- The political, social, cultural and economic condition of Russia in the mid-nineteenth century and the impact of the Crimean War
- Nobles, landowners and the position of the peasantry
- Alexander II – emancipation of the serfs and attempts at domestic and military reform
- Opposition – ideas and ideologies, individuals, radical groups and the tsarist reaction

This chapter will focus on the following question:

How successful were the great reforms of Alexander II?

This question will help you to think about why reforms were needed in Russia, the reforms themselves, whether Alexander II implemented these effectively, and the results of the reforms.

This chapter will have a strong focus on the concepts of cause and consequence. You will be invited throughout the chapter to consider the reasons for events and developments and the consequences these had for subsequent developments in Russia. The key issues covered are those concerning the change and development of political authority, the role of individuals and groups, and the growth of opposition.

CHAPTER OVERVIEW

Tsarist Russia was a huge and diverse country ruled by an autocracy led by a tsar. Its size and poor communications made it difficult to govern. The tsar ruled with the support of the nobility. In return for this support the nobles had been given land and the people to work it – serfs who were owned by the nobles and whose position was little better than that of slaves. Defeat in the Crimean War was a huge shock to the Russian regime for which military power was central to its world power status and control of Russia itself. Russia's backwardness was held responsible so Tsar Alexander II set in motion a series of reforms to remedy this. The most important reform was the emancipation of the serfs but its terms displeased peasants and nobles. Other reforms included changes to local government, the justice system, the military and education. The result of the reforms was mounting criticism of the regime and the growth of revolutionary activity. So, after 1866, Alexander brought in more reactionary policies but these did not stop the Populists in the 1870s 'going to the people' to spread the message of socialism and peaceful revolution. This failed, but the regime's reaction of arrests, punishment and harassment of young revolutionaries led to increasing violence and terrorism, in the course of which Alexander II was assassinated.

1 Russian society in the middle of the nineteenth century

This section looks at the size, geographical divisions and diversity of the Russian Empire in the middle of the nineteenth century. It introduces the main groups that made up Russian society and provides an overview of the way Russia was governed.

NOTE-MAKING

Throughout this section make your own notes on:
- the problems Russia's size and diversity created for its rulers
- the social structure of Russia
- the way tsarist Russia governed this huge area.

Russia: the land, people and social structure

What were the main physical features of Russia and what did Russian society look like?

Tsarist Russia in the mid-nineteenth century occupied a vast area across two continents – Europe and Asia – covering about one-sixth of the world's total landmass. Its boundaries stretched some 6,000km from the west to the Pacific Ocean and some 3,000km from the Baltic Sea in the north to the Black Sea in the south. The USA could fit into it two and a half times and Britain over ninety times. Large parts were (and still are) either uninhabited or sparsely populated. The northern part of Russia, the tundra, is frozen for most of the year and only supports scrub vegetation. South of the tundra lies endless miles of forest, a huge resource of wood but impenetrable in places. Then comes the steppes – open plains and grassland. It is here that the most fertile land for agriculture can be found, particularly the Black Earth region. To the far south there are deserts. The climate of Russia has had a huge impact on its people. It has made agriculture difficult with unpredictable rainfall patterns and droughts that can ruin harvests.

The size and inhospitable geography of Russia has created problems for its rulers. Communications across this huge area were poor. There were few paved roads except in the big cities. Most of the roads were hard packed earth, which turned to mud in heavy rain and became impassable in winter. For longer journeys, rivers were used. Most of Russia's major cities had grown up along important river routes. The other major form of travel – railways – was undeveloped by the 1850s. The Moscow to St Petersburg railway was only opened in 1851. All this made it difficult to administer the Empire from the centre.

The people

Tsarist Russia in the middle of the nineteenth century was a vast, sprawling empire containing a patchwork quilt of different national groups. From the fifteenth century onwards, the Russians who lived in the area around Moscow had conquered the peoples around them. The land they controlled expanded and developed into the Russian Empire (see Figure 1). Large areas were added only in the middle of the nineteenth century. Vladivostok and the most easterly part on the Pacific Ocean became part of the Empire in 1859. The Caucasus region, which included the Georgian and Chechen people, was secured as late as 1864, and the central Asian area of Russia including Turkestan was conquered in the 1860s and 1870s. This late expansion brought over 100 different nationalities under the control of the Russian state.

The Russians themselves formed about half of the population, the vast majority of whom lived in the European part of Russia west of the Ural mountains. The diversity of culture, religion, ethnicity and language throughout the Empire was

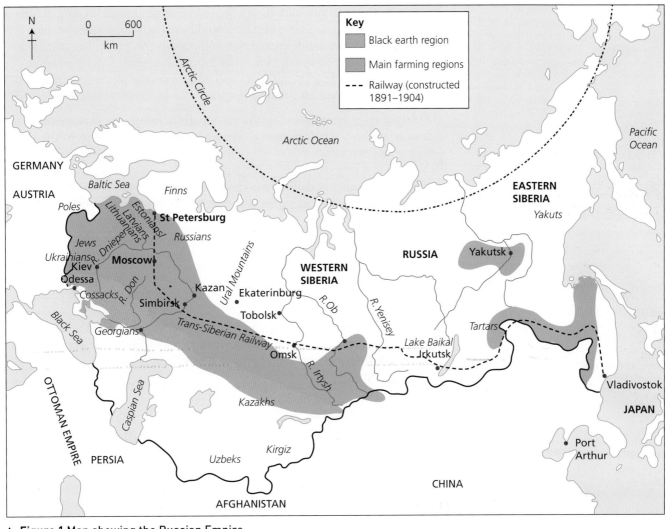

▲ **Figure 1** Map showing the Russian Empire.

astonishing, from sophisticated European Russians living in St Petersburg to nomadic Muslim peoples living in the desert areas of the south, to the tribes who wandered the vast spaces of Siberia, living and dressing very much like Native Americans. You can read more about the nationalities and their position in the Russian Empire in Chapter 2.

The social structure of Russia

The population in 1859 was around 70 million. Over 90 per cent were peasants living and working in the countryside.

Nobility

Nobles made up less than one per cent of the population. In the seventeenth century they had been given landed estates by the tsars. In return for the land the nobles would provide services for the tsar, most usually as officers in the armed forces or as public officials in the capital or the provinces. This established a system of military officers and civil servants who had a vested interest in supporting the tsar. It was based on the idea of rewards for services. The nobles were not only given land but were given serfs – people who worked the land and provided their masters with food and revenue.

[handwritten annotations:] Social economic + political — The country was massive

Population of modern day britain, but 90 times as big.

The nobility had another important role – administration and keeping order. Russia covered such a vast area that it would have been impossible for the central authority to provide enough state officials to cover it. In fact there were far fewer officials in Russia than in other European countries. So the nobility filled this role, acting as the judiciary and administrative officials running regions and local areas on behalf of the tsar.

There were huge variations of wealth among the nobility. The most wealthy estate owners were a tiny minority, owning large numbers of serfs. In the 1850s Count Sergei Seremetev, one of the richest, owned nearly 150,000 male serfs. He also owned large amounts of property in Moscow. Other rich nobles profited from owning timber or distilleries. The vast majority, around three-quarters of the nobility, owned fewer than 100 serfs which meant their estates did not generate sufficient income to support a lavish lifestyle. Some nobles were downright poor which meant that they had to seek income in other areas or live in relative poverty. As the nineteenth century progressed many of these sold up their estates and moved to the towns and cities.

A significant number of nobles lived away from their estates either because of state service or personal choice, preferring to live in the cities, particularly St Petersburg. Here the rich and powerful enjoyed a life of luxury and power, taking important positions in the government or dominating the army. Many middle-ranking nobles worked as government officials earning a salary.

The nobility was not necessarily conservative. An active minority in the middle of the century were looking to reform aspects of Russian society, particularly the institution of serfdom. Some even questioned the notion that the nobility should not pay taxes or automatically hold key positions in state service. Others felt that Russia needed a more representative government and looked to ideas of liberalism to be found in Western Europe.

The middle classes

This was a small group in mid-century Russia, due largely to the absence of industry on a large scale. There were merchants who played an important part in Russia's trade with the rest of the world and some of these were wealthy and influential. There were entrepreneurs and businessmen but it was not until the second part of the century that they became a more dynamic force in society (see Chapter 2). Probably most could be found in bureaucratic clerical roles in central and provincial government and running shops and stores.

Peasants

In the mid-nineteenth century over 90 per cent of the Russian population was peasants, most of whom supported themselves by farming. There was a huge amount of variation among peasants across Russia but we can make some general observations. Broadly they can be divided into two groups:

1 Around half were serfs who were tied to the landowning nobility. They were found mainly in central Russia and the western provinces. Serfdom ensured that the nobility had labour and income. The key features of serfdom were:
   - Serfs were bound to the landed estates of the nobles and could not leave the estates without the land-owner's permission.
   - They were required to provide labour, usually three days a week on the noble's land (more at harvest time), or pay **dues** in cash or produce, or sometimes all three. The amount of work to be done was sometimes worked out for a whole village, sometimes for individual households. Some landowners paid serfs for extra work at busy times, some set it against their labour obligation. There was variation between estates and between regions.

Who paid taxes in tsarist Russia?

The nobility and the clergy were exempt from direct taxation. So it was the peasants who largely bore the burden of a poll tax. Indirect taxes on everyday items like kerosene and tobacco also bore most heavily on poorer Russians.

Dues – Payments in cash or kind (for example, produce) made by serfs to nobles.

- In return they could use a plot of land for their own use, to grow food to feed themselves or sell locally.
- The nobles acted as police, judge and jury in respect of serfs on their] — *political* estates. Serfs had no access to the legal system.
- They had almost no rights as individuals and could be sold, traded or forbidden to marry.
- Some serfs, around seven per cent, worked as domestic servants. They had no land and were not paid and consequently led the worst lives.

Labour service was most common in the Black Earth regions to the south and east of Moscow where the land was fertile and agriculture was the main activity. Dues were more common in less fertile central and northern regions. Where estates were near large cities, nobles used serf labour to produce foodstuffs for the urban market. They also hired out serfs to work in industry. Some landowners treated their serfs well and even educated them. Others were brutal: whipping was common and troublesome peasants could be shipped off to the army.

2 State peasants formed the other half. They lived on estates owned by the state, Church or the tsar. They paid rent to the state for the use of the land they farmed. Legally free, they were still under the control of state administrators and there were restrictions on their travel. Generally, they were better off than serfs, had larger landholdings and could get more involved in rural handicrafts or get work in factories to supplement their income.

The *Mir*

Peasants were subject to controls exercised by the village commune, the *Mir*, an assembly of households. It was run by the peasants themselves and village meetings allowed discussion of issues. It had distinct advantages and drawbacks. It provided security and support and ensured an equitable distribution of land. But it controlled its members in important areas:

- It allocated land, deciding who should get what. The amount of land depended on the size of the household. So that everybody had a share of good and bad land it was divided up into strips in fields. In some villages there were periodic redistributions as the size of households changed. Pastureland and meadows were held in common.
- On private estates it was responsible for making sure that serfs fulfilled their obligations in labour or payments.

> *Mir* – The peasant commune.
>
> **Three-field rotation system** – Crops were grown in two fields while one field was left fallow each year to recover.

Although egalitarian, the allocation and redistribution of strips was inefficient with time wasted moving between strips and no incentive to improve strips if they changed hands. Arable decisions had to be co-ordinated so there was little scope for enterprising peasants who wished to try something different. The commune tended to be dominated by older peasants who resisted change. They could punish people who did not conform; for instance, they chose the conscripts for the army. On the one hand the *Mir* could be a model of co-operation and mutual support, on the other it was a source of petty jealousies and rivalries where violence, communal and domestic, was not uncommon.

Farming was generally organised around a three-field rotation system with wheat, rye and oats being the main crops, depending on the region. Peasants also had the household plots – land on which their houses were built – and garden plots where they grew vegetables and kept domestic livestock. Vegetables formed a large part of the diet, depending on the area: cabbage soup was common in the north and centre of Russia, beetroot soup in the south. Little meat was eaten but fish was common. Beer was the main drink, with vodka drunk at festivals and celebrations.

Typically Russian villages consisted of a line of unpainted wooden huts with thatched roofs along each side of an unpaved main street. Most peasants were poor and illiterate. Their lives were hard and unremitting, slogged out on their small patches of land. They got by in the good years and suffered greatly when the harvests were poor. In famine years many thousands died of starvation. Many peasants lived in squalor, prone to drunkenness and sexually transmitted diseases, especially syphilis.

Workers

Russia had not experienced an industrial revolution like Britain and Germany so there were few large-scale industrial works by the 1850s. The closest they got to factory industry were the spinning mills around St Petersburg. There were iron-ore mines in the Urals but the iron industry was technologically backward. Most other industry was carried out in peasants' cottages (handicrafts, weaving) or in small-scale workshops. The conditions in which people worked were generally appalling: in smaller enterprises, workers and their families might live and sleep alongside their workbenches in stinking, filthy surroundings. The hours of work were long. At this time the workers formed a relatively small proportion of the population.

The Russian Orthodox Church

The Russian Orthodox Church was the established Church in the Russian Empire. It was part of the wider Eastern Orthodox branch of Christianity and was independent of the Pope and Catholic Europe. Russia had not experienced the Reformation or Renaissance although there were divisions in the Orthodox Church, notably between the mainstream Church and the Old Believers. The Russians believed that they kept the true faith and this gave them a belief that they were somehow special – hence the expression 'Holy Russia'. The Orthodox Church was intimately bound up with the autocracy since the tsar was God's lieutenant on earth.

A large majority, about 70 per cent of the population, were members of the Russian Orthodox Church. The Church was staffed by 100,000 clerics who played a significant role in Russian society and exerted a huge amount of influence over the peasants. Priests lived in the villages and so were involved in the lives and struggles of the peasants, especially as it was the villagers who supported them. Religious observance played a significant role in the life of the peasant, especially in the rites and rituals connected with birth, death and marriage. Most peasant huts had an icon in one corner of the room. The Church was also the means by which peasants, for the most part illiterate, got information. For instance, the terms and details of the emancipation of the serfs were read out in churches.

The Old Believers

The Old Believers remained true to the old customs of the Orthodox Church before the reforms by Patriarch Nikon in the mid-seventeenth century, and to an ideal of Russianness which harked back to before Peter the Great. They faced persecution, which continued up until 1905. They had a deep religious faith and a strict work ethic.

Autocracy – System of government in which there are no constraints on the power of the ruler.

Icon – A religious painting, usually of a holy figure, often on wood and used as an aid to devotion.

Tsarist government

How was Russia governed under the tsars?

The tsar was an autocrat, an absolute ruler, who had supreme power over his subjects. As far as the tsars were concerned they had been appointed by God and rejected any hint that their power rested on the consent of the people – their role was to lead and guide the people. The autocrat could rule the country without constraints. You can read more about the nature of the autocracy and the tsarist state in Chapter 2.

The tsar had an Imperial Council (see page 40), made up of nobles to advise him, and a cabinet of ministers who ran the various government departments. But they were responsible to him alone, not to a parliament or prime minister. They reported directly to the tsar and took instructions from him. This meant that the tsar was the pivot at the centre of the system.

There was a huge bureaucracy of civil servants and officials who ran the Empire. The top ranks were dominated by the nobility. In the 1850s and 1860s an elite of bureaucratic officials was developing alongside a more professional civil service. Some of these had liberal reforming tendencies and wanted to bring about changes in the way Russia was run. The lower ranks that had contact with the people were generally badly paid and there was a culture of corruption in which bribery was common. This, together with the arbitrary nature of decision-making, undermined respect for the authorities. The bureaucracy was virtually impenetrable for ordinary citizens who rarely found that their interests were served properly.

The different regions of the Empire were under the control of governors who had their own local bureaucracies. Poor communications meant that it was hard to get decisions from the centre carried out. The regional governors often acted like independent rulers in their own fiefdoms. They were supported in districts by nobles, who controlled judicial and police functions.

The government made use of the secret police, the 'Third Section', to root out people likely to cause trouble. There was a system of surveillance with an extensive network of agents. Strict censorship was imposed on newspapers, periodicals and books to stop the spread of ideas deemed dangerous to the regime. Those who fell foul of the regime faced tough punishments – execution, floggings, imprisonment or exile. Large-scale disturbances or riots were suppressed by the army. Tsarist Russia was an oppressive regime.

The role of the army

The Russian army was the largest in Europe and an important element in Russia's status as a world power. Most officers were from noble backgrounds. Ordinary soldiers were conscripts taken from the villages who were required to serve for 25 years, reduced to 15 for those with good service records. The government kept them for so long because it was worried that peasants returning home might use their training to promote discontent. Soldiers had to be completely subservient to officers and had few rights, for instance they could be flogged and were not allowed to enter most restaurants and cafes. Pay was extremely poor and most soldiers grew their own food and lived mainly on soup, tea and bread.

Tsar Nicholas I, 1825–55

Nicholas I established a centralised and authoritarian state. He believed in a personal autocracy in which the tsar exercised a God-given right to rule his subjects. He exercised great personal control over the details of government. Worried by the prospect of revolution, he set up the Third Section of Personal Chancery – the secret police. His approach was centred in military discipline and he used its language: 'I am a sentry at an outpost on guard, to see all and observe all. I must stay there until relieved.'

The army was crucial to the survival of the tsarist regime. Not only was it required to defend Russia's long borders, it was also used to suppress internal disturbances and revolts. This was particularly important because its officials and police were spread very thinly over the huge expanse of Russia. So the loyalty of the army and its willingness to follow orders was of paramount importance to the tsarist regime. One section of the army the regime could rely on was the Cossacks who came from the Don area of Russia and had been incorporated into the army in the early nineteenth century. They were fiercely loyal to the tsar and could be trusted to act against other peoples in the Empire, including Russians. They were feared because they could be brutal and ruthless.

The Crimean War, 1853–56

The Crimean War was fought mainly on the Crimean peninsula between Russia on one side and Britain, France, Sardinia and the Ottoman Empire (modern-day Turkey) on the other. The immediate cause was a dispute over control of Christian sites in the Holy Land and the protection of Christians in the Ottoman Empire. But the British and French thought the Russians were trying to move in on the weak Ottoman Empire and gain a strategic advantage in this part of the world. They did not want to see Russian warships with easy access to the Eastern Mediterranean from the Black Sea. So they landed troops on the Crimea to attack the Russian Black Sea fleet at its base in Sevastopol. After two years of heavy fighting the Russians were forced to sue for peace.

Romanovs – Michael Romanov was chosen to be tsar in 1613. His descendants were to rule Russia for the next 300 years until the last Romanov, Nicholas II, abdicated in 1917.

Great power status and the Crimean War

How was Russia shocked into reform?

In 1815 Russia was the leading power in Europe. Napoleon's invasion in 1812 had been repulsed and the Russian army, the most powerful in the world, had liberated Europe. In 1814, Alexander I had ridden through Paris in triumph and had dominated the Congress of Vienna, which produced a settlement for Europe after twenty years of war. Maintaining great power status was a high priority for the Russians. Therefore defeat in the Crimean War (1853–56) was a huge shock to the Russian regime, especially as it had been fighting on its own territory. The defeat revealed a number of worrying deficiencies:

1 It highlighted Russia's poor communications and its inability to harness and deploy human and material resources effectively. There was no railway south of Moscow, so troops, armaments and supplies had to be moved along bumpy roads which turned to mud in wet weather.
2 The army's rifles and artillery were hopelessly outclassed by the weapons of the British and French which could fire further and more accurately.
3 Serious questions were raised about the efficiency of the army and the quality of the leadership (see military reforms).

In short it cast doubt on Russia's continued status as a major power and this was damaging to the Romanov dynasty which was identified with military power and now appeared ineffective and unable to defend Russia's own territory. It also showed that the sheer size of Russia made it vulnerable: ships and troops had had to be kept away from the war zone to counter any attacks by the British and French in the Baltic or rebellious uprisings in the Caucasus.

It was clear that Russia did not have adequate resources to fight a major European power. Western European countries had undergone industrial revolutions and industrial might was equated to military might. Many in the top echelons of the tsarist government were convinced that Russia's backwardness had caused its defeat. The case for reform looked unanswerable.

2 The reforms of Alexander II

This section will look at the reforms of Alexander II and the move from reform to reaction in the second part of his reign. It will consider the reasons for the reforms and the consequences for the people involved and for the regime.

After the Crimean War, even conservative statesmen in Russia accepted that the tsarist system needed major reform since it was lagging far behind its European neighbours. Liberal reformers and conservatives alike agreed that the institution of serfdom lay at the heart of the system's perceived backwardness and that other reforms, especially reform of the military, could not take place unless it was abolished. This was a daunting proposition because it would involve making major changes in the way rural Russia was organised and administered, and the tsar was likely to offend the very people – the nobility – on whom his regime depended.

Westernisers and Slavophiles

From the 1840s there had been a debate among intellectuals on the way forward for Russia. 'Westernisers' believed that Russia should adopt certain values and political and economic institutions from the West including individual rights and parliamentary democracy. They thought that Russia needed to industrialise and urbanise like the West or be left behind.

'Slavophiles', on the other hand, believed that Russia had its own distinctive rich culture and traditions that were special and superior to those of the West. This culture was transmitted by the Orthodox Church and institutions like the village commune, which they held in special regard because of its emphasis on 'togetherness' which they saw as a Slavic value. Slavophiles rejected Western parliamentarianism, individualism, rationalism and atheism. They believed that autocracy, and the relationship between tsar and people, conveyed Russian order and stability that was lacking in Western countries. Some embraced Panslavism – the notion that the Slav peoples could be united under the leadership of Russia.

These two positions do not represent two distinct groups. Love of Russia was common to both, as was concern about the dominance of Western European countries. Both thought changes were necessary, for instance, many Slavophiles supported the emancipation of the serfs and both thought the tsar had become divorced from his people by an insensitive bureaucracy. But whereas the Westernisers thought a constitution and parliament was the best option, Slavophiles wanted the tsar to convene a consultative assembly that represented the different estates (social groups) of Russia to bridge the gap that had opened up between the imperial elite and ordinary Russians.

These intellectuals did not touch the mass of the people but their views did influence the debates and discussion being held at higher levels about government policies and particularly the nature of reforms.

Alexander II, 1818–81

How important were the experiences and personality of Alexander II in promoting reform?

Source A *Behind the Veil at the Russian Court* by Count Paul Vassili, (Cassell and Co. Ltd), 1913, p17.

[Alexander II] at heart was really more autocratic than his father, but having been brought up with immense care and by people imbued with Liberalism as it was understood at the time in Russia, he exhibited a curious mixture of despotic and revolutionary ideas.

Alexander assumed power in February 1855. He had been well prepared for his role as tsar in the years leading up to his accession. His father, Nicholas I, instilled in him the value of duty and obedience. As a young man he enjoyed military life and taking part in ceremonies. But he was also given a well-rounded education in history, sciences and languages. Among his tutors was the poet Zhukovsky who believed a sovereign must be raised as a 'human being' and win the love of his subjects. Despite this thorough preparation, Alexander told one of his tutors in 1829 that 'I wish I hadn't been born a grand Duke'. It seems he often felt inadequate and unable to live up to his father. David Saunders says that Alexander was not very bright, not a strong character and not very good at making decisions.

In 1837, with Zhukovsky, he went on a tour of 29 Russian provinces which took him to places no other members of the imperial family had visited, including Siberia where he encountered prisoner exiles. The tour, which was designed to build a bond between the future tsar and his people, was an enormous success. The tall handsome *tsarevich* (the tsar's heir) made a good impression. It also affected Alexander and he became the first tsar to consider that the people's approval was an important part of autocratic rule. In 1839 he embarked on a European tour during which he gained

▶ A painting of Alexander II by Yegor Bottman, 1875.

knowledge of Western ideas and traditions. He also met the German princess, Princess Marie of Hesse-Darmstadt, whom he married in 1841. She was of delicate health but their marriage produced eight children.

Nicholas believed that the tsar should take a personal hand in all aspects of government and passed this on to his son. He had placed Alexander on a number of committees (for example, peasant reform and the development of the railways) and councils including the Council of State, giving him knowledge of the workings of the state. He was also left in charge of routine state affairs when Nicholas was absent.

So Alexander seemed well-fitted for the role of tsar when his coronation took place in 1856. It ushered in a more optimistic period after the tight control of Nicholas I. Alexander had a humane perspective on the world and was more sensitive than his father. He wished to see himself in the ranks of the modern Western monarchs and he knew that Russia needed to become part of the modern world which meant changing some of its institutions. But he was no liberal. He was a firm believer in autocracy and Russia's special identity. He was a conservative who intended to preserve what was best of the old system.

Nevertheless he drove the reform process forward and appointed more enlightened officials to carry out the reforms. In this he was supported by his liberal-minded brother, Grand Duke Constantine, who played an important role in assembling talented and able younger officials to work on the reforms. Also important was his aunt, the Grand Duchess Elena Pavlovna, who provided a forum for liberal thinkers who met at the salon in her palace.

The emancipation of the serfs, 1861

What were the causes and consequences of the emancipation of the serfs?

On 30 March 1856 Alexander II made a speech to the Marshalls of the Nobility in which he signalled the start of the process that led to the abolition of serfdom in 1861. As far as Alexander and his advisers were concerned modern statehood and serfdom were incompatible.

Source B Alexander II's speech to the Marshalls of the Nobility, 30 March 1856.

My intention is to abolish serfdom ... you yourself understand that the present order of owning souls (serfs) cannot remain unchanged. It is better to abolish serfdom from above, than to wait for that time when it starts to abolish itself from below. I ask you to think about the best way to carry this out.

Reasons for abolishing serfdom

A number of reasons have been put forward to explain why the Tsar decided to emancipate the serfs but historians differ as to which were the most important.

The moral case

Members of the royal family dating from Catherine the Great (1762–96) had considered that serfdom was morally and ethically wrong. Nicholas I himself had admitted that serfdom was 'an evil, palpable and obvious to all'. Enlightened nobles and liberal state officials had come to accept the view that it was wrong to own someone like a possession or an object and that it demeaned the serf owner as well as the serf. They had been affected by writers such as Turgenev who had drawn attention to the plight of the serf and the need to improve the condition of peasants. A radical intelligentsia was growing who were opposed to serfdom.

NOTE-MAKING

Use a spider diagram to note down the reasons for emancipating the serfs.

What do you think Alexander meant by this (Source B) and why do you think he added the last sentence?

Nevertheless, the majority of nobles did not accept this position. They thought that the abolition of serfdom would be damaging to the Russian state as well as their own livelihoods.

Risk of revolt

Many historians have cited concern for social stability as one of the main reasons for the emancipation. There had been serious peasant revolts in the past and disturbances had been increasing since the 1840s. As we saw above, Alexander told the nobles that it was better to abolish serfdom from above than to wait for it to abolish itself from below and he had been unsettled by the 1848 revolutions in Europe. Particularly worrying was the fact that the army was made up mainly of peasants so it might be difficult for the government to contain a major peasant uprising. There was also a significant spike in disturbances between 1857 and 1859. The Tsar was worried enough to order weekly reports on the mood of the peasantry from December 1857.

However, other historians have maintained that the scale of peasant unrest had been exaggerated, especially as the main sources of data are unreliable tsarist police records. Also, some nobles feared that major reform might actually provoke serious revolt because the peasants would see it as sign of weakness or might be disappointed by the reform.

The Crimean War

The Crimean War had drawn attention to the state of the army which was mainly comprised of peasants, many of whom were serfs. They were compulsorily enlisted for periods of up to 25 years (reduced to 15 years for those of 'good character') but at the end of that period, if they survived, were given their freedom. Military reformers (see page 22) thought that Russia needed a smaller, better trained army with a reserve like those in other European countries. This entailed conscripting peasants to serve a shorter period of time before going on to the reserve. This would mean that thousands of freed serfs with military training would be released back to their villages, a risky proposition. So officials became convinced that military reform could only be carried out if serfdom was abolished. There was also a question of loyalty: for how long would serfs remain loyal if nothing was done to improve their conditions and accommodate their aspirations?

Economic reasons

Many enlightened government officials and intellectuals in Russia at the time were convinced that it was necessary to abolish serfdom if the Russian economy was to advance. This was expressed clearly by Nicholas Milyutin, an official in the Ministry of Interior Affairs, in a memorandum he wrote in 1847:

Serfdom serves as the main – even the only – hindrance to the development in Russia at the present time … Only with the emancipation of the serfs will the betterment of our rural economy become possible.

(Quoted in *The Abolition of Serfdom in Russia* by David Moon, (Longman), 2001, p23.)

Some of these officials and intellectuals accepted the arguments of economists like Adam Smith that free labour was more productive than forced labour; further that forced labour impoverished the population and stopped the growth of domestic demand which was essential for economic growth. They believed that you needed a free labour market where peasants could move around to where they could be most productive whether in agriculture or industry.

There is disagreement among historians about whether economic motives were a decisive factor in the decision to abolish serfdom. Some, like Olga Crisp, have argued that other factors such as the poor transport system were more significant in preventing economic development. Also, they point to the fact that immediately after emancipation there was a move on the part of the government to restrict the movement of peasants by introducing internal passports. This suggests that freeing labour to allow capitalist growth was not the government's priority.

Summing up

Historians give different weight to the various reasons put forward for the decision to emancipate the serfs. David Moon does not think that the economic argument – freeing up labour to promote economic growth – is convincing. Lindsey Hughes agrees that it was not the main aim; she says that Alexander and his contemporaries did not think in such terms. She maintains that it was done 'rather to improve the condition of the peasants and reduce the risk of rural revolts'. There seems little doubt that there was a strong moral imperative to end the evil of the ownership of other human beings. Moon, however, believes that it was the military factor that prompted Alexander to start the process. What we can say is that, although the need to reform the military was a powerful motive, humanitarian considerations, economic factors and concerns about social stability did influence intellectuals, nobles, state officials and the tsar himself in reaching a decision about serfdom.

The process of emancipation

It took thousands of officials and numerous committees to draft plans for the abolition of serfdom. Provincial committees submitted plans for the emancipation in their areas. The main discussions revolved around:

- whether the serfs should be freed with or without land
- how much land should be given to each household
- how it would be paid for
- how much compensation would be given to landowners
- whether the nobility should retain judicial and economic control over the former serfs.

An Editing Commission was created in 1859 to turn their recommendations into legislation. This resulted in the Emancipation Statutes (22 of them) of 19 February 1861. Alexander declared in his proclamation that the basic aim of emancipation was to satisfy serfs and landowners alike. The main terms of the emancipation can be summed up as follows:

- Serfdom was abolished and serfs were now legally free. They could marry whom they liked, travel, vote in local elections and trade freely.
- Peasants would have land to go with their freedom. They would be allowed to keep their houses and the land immediately around it but would have to buy the other land (strips) they worked at the time of the emancipation.
- They would have to make annual payments for the land they were buying. The government purchased the land and the peasants had to make redemption payments over a period of 49 years.
- Peasants were still under the control of the *Mir*, whose power would be strengthened.
- The nobility would continue to play a role in policing.
- Landowners would be compensated for the loss of their land in government bonds but not for the loss of their rights over their serfs.

In 1866, state peasants were given the right to buy land in the same way as the former serfs or to remain tenants.

Implementing the emancipation

Emancipation did not happen overnight. Some 23 million serfs belonging to the nobility were involved. Sorting out the complexity of the land settlement and compensation package took years. There was a huge variation between regions and the final transfer of land took a long time.

After the 19 February proclamation there was a two-year transitional period during which the obligations to the land owner remained as they had been under serfdom but the serfs were now legally free so they could not be sold, sent to other estates, etc. This was to allow time to work out the amount of land in each area that should be handed over to the peasants and how this should be done. Local committees worked out the area allocated per peasant. But the stock of land was given to the village and it was the village community who actually allocated parcels of land to individual peasants. The peasants would not own the land until the last redemption payment had been made.

Three key aspects of the arrangements

1 Most peasants received slightly less land than they had worked before. Since the supply of affordable, good quality land available to the peasants was limited, many received strips of land that proved difficult to maintain and which yielded little food or profit. In the populous Black Earth region the allocation was well below the average so it was difficult to make ends meet. As a result most peasants had to work for much of the year as hired labour on the noble's remaining land.

2 The landowners received above the market value for the land they were handing over to the peasants. The high valuation meant the peasants were paying more for it. Moreover, the landowners were allowed to decide which part of their holdings they would hand over and, not surprisingly, they kept the best land for themselves. It has been estimated that the landlords retained two-thirds of the land while the peasants received only one-third.

3 The powers of the *Mir* were strengthened. This was for administrative reasons and as a mechanism for keeping order in the countryside. The *Mir* was made responsible for collecting redemption payments and the other taxes peasants had to pay. If the peasant left the area, the land would revert to the *Mir*; the peasant could not sell it. Also the *Mir* issued internal passports allowing peasants to travel. The aim was to make sure that thousands of freed peasants did not start to move around the countryside with the potential for disorder this would bring. Instead of being tied to the lord, the peasant was now tied to the village. On the one hand the peasants were more self-governing but for the individual peasant it was renewed dependence.

The consequences of emancipation

The emancipation had some far-reaching consequences:

● The peasants felt they had been cheated. They had always believed that the land belonged to those who worked it. Now they still did not own the land outright and they had to pay for it – over 49 years! This was a cause of deep resentment. There were over 1,000 disturbances during 1861, one involving 10,000 peasants. The army had to be brought in to restore order on over 300 estates. However, this diminished quickly and most simply got on with the emancipation process.

NOTE-MAKING

Draw a diagram to show the key arrangements and consequences of emancipation for different groups. Then develop your diagram to show their response. Use the academic essay by Christopher Read (see page 16) to help you do this.

Disbelief

When the terms of the emancipation were read out to the serfs, often in churches, they did not believe them and thought the nobility was trying to hoodwink them. The serfs thought the nobles had substituted documents more advantageous to themselves (the nobles). Some tried to search for the 'real freedom' but to no avail. In the village of Bezdna, Anton Petrov claimed that the statutes really did grant immediate freedom for all with land. Peasants flocked to support him. Troops, who were brought in to deal with the situation, opened fire on the peasants.

- Nobles were disgruntled because they felt they had not been compensated for the loss of their rights over the serfs. Also they were losing power, status and influence. A small minority wanted gentry representatives to form a national commission to prevent bureaucrats riding roughshod over their interests again. Some of the more liberal members of the nobility wanted elected representatives from all over Russia to be assembled. Emancipation stirred up a lot of criticism of the regime from the gentry.
- Much of the money paid to the nobles went to pay off existing debts and mortgages. Many nobles who could not afford or did not want to make the adaptation to hired labour moved to towns and simply rented out their land to peasants or went to live in the cities and become absentee landlords. Some just sold up over the following years. From 1862 to 1905 their landholdings fell from 87 million to 50 million *desyatiny*.
- The radical intelligentsia reacted badly to the terms of the emancipation as they felt the emancipation had protected the nobles and betrayed the peasants: this led to the growth of opposition to the regime (see page 28).
- Some go-ahead peasants started buying the land of poorer neighbours, renting land from the nobility and hiring labour. These were known as *kulaks*.

Desyatina (plural, *desyatiny*) – Russian measurement of land, equivalent to 2.7 acres.

Kulak – Better-off peasant who owned animals and hired labour.

Assessing the emancipation

Soon after the emancipation proclamation Nicholas Milyutin, its architect, was sacked by the Tsar. Alexander did this to appease the conservative nobility who did not want serfdom abolished, not because he was unhappy with Milyutin. And in this lies the problem with the emancipation – the Tsar did not want to offend, damage or destroy the ruling class on whom his regime depended for its survival. So in the end, as Christopher Read explains in his essay on pages 16–17, nobody was satisfied by the arrangements set out in the Emancipation Statutes. The nobles, who were the real beneficiaries, did not see it that way. As for the peasants, their resentment, especially over redemption payments, did not diminish over time.

The peasants were supposed to be free to own property, go to law, enter the market on their own account and participate in political life. But at the end of the emancipation they remained a segregated class tied to the commune with their own law courts, unable to move around freely. Christopher Read suggests that the effects of this were long lasting and contributed to the revolutions in 1905 and 1917.

KEY DATES: THE EMANCIPATION OF THE SERFS, 1861

1856 Alexander told the Marshalls of the Nobility that it was better to abolish serfdom from above.

1857 Committee set up to consider how to abolish serfdom.

Provincial nobles elect committee to consider reform.

1857–9 Peasant disturbances on news of emancipation.

Key decision in December that freed serfs would acquire land.

1859 Editing Commission established to draw up the statutes including 'enlightened bureaucrats' like Nicholas Milyutin.

1861 19 February Alexander signed into law the proclamation and statutes abolishing serfdom.

As well as studying the facts of an event in history, historians also use these facts in order to reach conclusions on, for example, why something happened. In other words, they have to interpret the facts in order to reach their conclusions. Often the evidence does not point in just one direction. There is scope for historians reaching different conclusions and producing different interpretations.

In this chapter, as well as Chapters 3, 6 and 8, there is one, longer interpretation to read, followed by some questions that are designed to help you build up your skills as well as helping you to consolidate your knowledge of each chapter.

Working on interpretation skills: extended reading

The impact of the emancipation

Professor Christopher Read analyses the impact of the emancipation of the serfs across Russian society.

It took the tsarist authorities five years to plan and draft the 1861 legislation that made up the Emancipation of the Serfs in Russia. It should be remembered that only about one-third of peasants in the Russian Empire were still serfs by then and in some regions legislation was enacted later but, even so, emancipation had an impact in all areas of Russian society.

The preparation was conducted in secret for fear of the reaction of rising expectations that would ensue if word got out. Before the Emancipation Manifesto was officially announced, rumours had been enough to trigger off hundreds, probably thousands, of peasant rebellions. Once it became public many more extreme reactions burst out in response, including mass support for forged 'Golden Charters' said to contain the real terms of emancipation which had been suppressed or falsified by the landowners.

What had upset them so much? Above all they resented the provision that they were supposed to pay 'redemption payments' for the land they were given as part of the settlement. Since they believed all the land should be theirs as of right, on the grounds that the person who works the land should own it, they could see no reason for paying for it. Secondly, 'cut-offs', comprising up to twenty per cent of what had been common land, was handed to the landowners.

A third feature of emancipation had important but less easily traced consequences. In preparing the legislation the Ministry of the Interior was deeply concerned that former serfs would become vagabonds who might undermine order in rural and urban areas. Therefore, steps were taken to help ensure that, even though they were free of attachment to the land, they would instead be tied to their village community. To achieve this the village as a whole, through the commune (the village committee, in essence), was made into the tax-paying body responsible collectively for redemption payments. It was also given control over granting permission to villagers who wanted to leave. As a result, the communes were unwilling to give permission because the commune as a whole would have to take on the repayments left behind by any peasant who left.

Landowners also felt deprived by the emancipation settlement. In their eyes, the peasants had worked their land in exchange for farming their own communal, village land. If the peasants were no longer obliged to work the landowners' land, the landowners believed all the land should be handed to them, not the peasantry. Even though landowners were compensated for the loss of peasant labour through state bonds, many of them simply cashed them in and spent frivolously on wine, women and gambling. Within twenty years, many were bankrupt. Despite the population rise, between 1877 and 1905 the total number of landowners in Russia fell from around 115,000 to 107,000. Their total landholding fell from approximately 200 million to 144 million acres.

Disillusion with emancipation helped bring into existence a revolutionary intelligentsia, driven by sympathy with the plight of the peasants. It was from these small beginnings that the great revolutionary and opposition movements of the early twentieth century had their origin. But even a significant minority of the landowning gentry were also critical of tsarism after 1861 and called for a constitution, pointing to another defect of the settlement – the failure to fully reform other antiquated parts of the autocratic system. Reforms of the legal system, local government (the *zemstvo*) and army service only scratched the surface of the problem. Russia remained governed by a medieval tyranny and desperately needed a more modern system of government.

Ironically, faced with peasant revolutionary activity in 1905, the Ministry of the Interior attributed it to the solidarity engendered by the commune system. Having striven to preserve it in 1861, after 1905 its top priority was to disband it. The government also abolished the remaining redemption payments. In 1917 there were also echoes of 1861. Peasants had long collective memories and, when the great drive to seize land began, it was often the 1861 'cut-offs' which were among the first pieces retaken by the commune peasants. Many other factors ultimately contributed to revolution in 1905 and 1917 – notably counter-reform after 1881; rural overpopulation and economic stagnation; a crisis of the industrial economy after 1899 and a failure to open up to real representative government. Once total war came along in 1914 the last component in the revolutionary process was in place, but it had begun in 1861.

Professor Christopher Read is based at the University of Warwick.

ACTIVITY

Having read the essay, answer the following questions.

Comprehension

1 Why were both the peasants and the nobility upset by the emancipation?
2 Why did the government strengthen the *Mir*?

Evidence

3 What evidence can you find for:
- the consequences of the emancipation
- its long-term effects?

Interpretation

4 What is Christopher Read's overall judgement about the impact of the emancipation?

WORKING TOGETHER

Work in small groups and split each group into two. As you work through this section one half should write down the strengths/good points about each reform, the other half the weaknesses/limitations. At the end discuss the relative merits of each reform and reach a judgement about how successful it was.

Other reforms

What were the other reforms undertaken by Alexander II and what consequences did they have?

The emancipation edict had removed the gentry's automatic authority over the peasantry and effectively undermined the legal and institutional structure which had existed since the seventeenth century. So it was necessary to bring in new reforms, especially in local government and the justice system, to do the jobs the nobility used to do but also to build a more modern state closer to its Western European counterparts. Liberal enlightened officials were encouraged to take reform further.

The Milyutin brothers

Who were the liberal enlightened officials? Two of the most influential were Nicholas and Dmitri Milyutin, sons of a noble family. Nicholas was the driving force behind the emancipation. Rising from lower ranking posts in the Ministry of the Interior, he gained praise for his plans to reform the municipal government of St Petersburg in 1846. He believed it was his duty to serve the state honestly and efficiently for the public good, unlike most bureaucrats who were more interested in advancement. His reputation as a reformer gained him access to the St Petersburg intelligentsia where he met men with enlightened ideas about reforming Russia in the salon of the Grand Duchess Elena Pavlovna. In 1858 Nicholas became Deputy Minster of the Interior. It was his skill in planning reform which got him appointed to the Editing Commission drawing up the Emancipation Statutes in 1859. He drove the process forward despite the opposition of other officials and groups in society who opposed change. He had the ability to take an overview of this most complicated piece of legislation. But after it became law he was dismissed by Alexander to appease nobles who considered Milyutin too liberal.

His brother, Dmitri, chose the army rather than the civil service and was wounded in active service. While recovering he travelled around Europe and became convinced of the need for reform in Russia. He was also a brilliant scholar who wrote and lectured about the value and importance of military statistics. Like his brother he moved in circles where he associated with future reformers although his views were probably more right wing than those of his brother. As an opponent of serfdom, he freed his own serfs some time before the emancipation legislation. He served as a major general within the War Ministry during the Crimean War. He became the War Minister in November 1861 and spent the next twenty years implementing a series of reforms (see page 22).

Local government reform, 1864

The government introduced a measure of self-government at provincial and district levels. Assemblies (*zemstva*) or councils were to be elected by nobles, town dwellers and peasants. The electoral system favoured the nobility who made up 40 per cent of the members of district *zemstva* and over 70 per cent of provincial councils. This in part was to allow them to keep their control over local areas and compensate them for their loss of authority as a result of the emancipation. They were only introduced into provinces where Russians formed the ruling elites and the majority of the population. This amounted to 19 provinces at the start and had only been extended to 37 out of 70 provinces by 1914. In 1870 a similar system was set up in towns and cities with municipal councils elected by property owners.

The councils had general responsibilities for health, education, the maintenance of roads and bridges and local economic affairs. They were empowered to levy a small tax to pay for these. They were elected for three years and each *zemstva* chose from among their members a governing board. *Zemstva* flourished up to October 1917. They employed teachers, doctors, lawyers, agricultural experts and other professionals who became known as the 'third element'. They played an increasingly important role in local areas.

> *Zemstva (singular, zemstvo)* – Elected district and provincial councils.

Consequences

- The *zemstva* brought improvement to the areas in which they operated, building better roads, health facilities and primary schools, and developing areas like transport, street lighting, drainage and water supply. For instance, the hospitals and roads they built were of lasting benefit.
- The nobles and others running the councils gained political experience in managing their own affairs and many wanted to see this taken through to a national level.
- Members of the professional third element developed self-esteem and began to make demands for social reform and improvements in living conditions. Many became hostile to or frustrated with the state. Geoffrey Hosking says they 'believed themselves to constitute a kind of "alternative establishment", more truly representative of the Russian nation and more genuinely able to serve it than the regime was'.

There were weaknesses and limitations:

- *Zemstva* were only introduced in a limited number of provinces and they were slow to get going, so they did not achieve much early on.
- Restrictions were placed on their powers of taxation and they had trouble raising taxes.
- They were dominated by the nobility. Many nobles did not take their responsibilities seriously and some took advantage of the situation to run affairs in their own interests.
- The results were patchy. While the more enterprising *zemstva* pushed ahead with works, there were also indolent *zemstva*.
- The local Marshalls of the Nobility and governors vetoed some of their decisions and hampered them.
- The peasants did not really participate, put off by the nobility, and they resented paying the *zemstvo* tax which was proportionately higher on their land than on private estates.

The original plan for the *zemstva* had been bold and constructive, designed to establish some participative self-government. But it was whittled down in the interests of the landed nobility. However, good liberal *zemstvo* men like Prince Lvov (we shall meet him later) had a real passion and enthusiasm for improving local conditions. The *zemstva*, as an autonomous source of authority, did cause disquiet in central government where there was apprehension about any bodies, even relatively conservative ones, outside its control and where it was felt that the *zemstva* disturbed the smooth flow of directives from St Petersburg. An uneasy relationship developed between *zemstva* and government over the following years, particularly in the lead up to the 1905 revolution.

Judicial reforms, 1864

By the middle of the nineteenth century Russian courts were notorious for their corruption, delay and inefficiency. The whole judicial system was chaotic, and favoured the rich. It justified reform in its own right but the abolition of serfdom meant that the way justice had been administered at local level (where the serf owner was often the local magistrate) had to change. So the whole legal structure was reviewed, leading to the passing of reforms in 1864, which were then introduced during 1865.

Main problems with the old system

- There were a huge variety of courts between which cases could be transferred, taking a very long time, sometimes years.
- Most judges had had no legal training and many were illiterate. This put enormous power in the hands of the court secretaries, especially as all evidence was written. The court secretaries relied on bribes to maintain their lifestyles.
- The judges received a pile of documents on which they had to adjudicate according to certain rules, for instance, in evidence the word of a noble was taken over a peasant, the word of a man over a woman.
- The defendant never saw the judge so the written evidence, often unreliable, was rarely challenged.
- The police had great power to levy fines and they also were amenable to bribes.

Main features of the reforms

The reforms established a new system of civil and criminal courts based on concepts drawn from Western systems of law, concepts alien to the Russian tradition and to the autocracy. They provided for justice at lower levels and set up courts for dealing with more serious offences. The main changes were:

- The judicial system was simplified with fewer courts. Cases from lower courts could generally only be transferred to one or two other courts. Each province was to have its own court.
- Judges were paid good salaries and could not be removed from office. This made them more independent, especially as they could not be dismissed for delivering verdicts that displeased the government.
- Civil and criminal courts were open to the public and the proceedings were reported.
- Jury trials were introduced for more serious criminal cases, taking courts further out of the control of central government. Evidence and the testimonies of witnesses had to be given orally and could be tested and challenged in open court. There were now prosecutors and defenders who could summon their own witnesses. Moreover, the voting on the verdict by juries was kept secret to protect them from intimidation.

- A system of Justices of the Peace (JPs) was established. These were magistrates elected by the district council. They dealt with small cases involving minor disputes. Appeals against their decisions could go to a higher authority.
- Where offences solely concerned peasants, separate village courts were used. These comprised judges elected and drawn from the peasantry who often were illiterate.

Consequences

- Russians could get a fairer trial than before and there was greater access to justice (especially through JPs). The person accused (defendant) had much more protection since, although preliminary investigations were secret, court proceedings were public. So there was less corruption and fewer attempts by the police or administrators to pervert the course of justice.
- JPs' courts worked quickly, cost nothing to those appearing in them and were perceived as dispensing equitable judgements. These were respected by humble workers and peasants often because they protected the small man against local officials.
- During the 1860s and 1870s an independent and articulate legal profession came into being to fulfill the roles of prosecutors and defenders, trained in the skills of argument and persuasion. Many became accomplished advocates of reform; some went on to become parliamentarians in the *Duma*. Others became revolutionaries.
- The reforms challenged the political authority of the autocracy in a number of ways:
  - Independent courts and judges meant that an independent source of authority existed and the regime could not act in the arbitrary way to which it was accustomed. This made its way into the public consciousness – the idea of the rule of law.
  - The new freedoms for lawyers meant the courtroom could become a space for challenges to the government. The courtroom was the one place in Russia where there was genuine free speech. Since many of the accused were in some way a victim of government action or government officials, defence lawyers would often be critical of the regime in presenting their case. Some defendants, accused of political offences, made speeches from the dock, reported by newspapers.
  - The new juries showed themselves to be independent. Sometimes they would acquit people whom the regime would have liked to see given long sentences. The most famous example of this was the case of Vera Zasulich (see box opposite).

There were a number of serious weaknesses:

- The separate courts for peasants (the vast majority of the population) meant that as a class they were largely outside the mainstream judicial system, emphasising their lower status.
- Some courts remained outside the system including Church courts (which handled divorce cases) and military courts. Government officials could not be tried in the system. Revolutionaries were tried by special courts in the 1870s.
- The bureaucracy did still intervene so trial by jury could not always be guaranteed.
- The reforms had most impact in the large cities, especially St Petersburg and Moscow where the most controversial trials took place.

> *Duma* – Russian parliament after 1905.

> ### The case of Vera Zasulich, 1878
>
> Vera Zasulich shot and wounded the governor of St Petersburg, General Trepov. She admitted this but the jury, who accepted her plea that the act was politically justified, brought in a not guilty verdict. Trepov was well-known to be exceptionally cruel and flogged prisoners, one for refusing to remove his hat in Trepov's presence. The defence counsel brought in political prisoners as witnesses to the flogging, young well-educated men who looked pale and worn after months of imprisonment. Their testimonies moved the jury and public. The public applauded the verdict. The government never again risked an important political trial in the regular courts.

The judicial reforms have been seen by some historians as some of the more successful reforms despite the drawbacks identified above. They backfired on the regime by introducing the notion of the rule of law and an independent judiciary which challenged the authority of the autocracy and created a group of people – lawyers – who were to become active in the reform movement.

Military reforms, 1861–81

The poor showing of the Russian army in the Crimean War provided a strong impetus for military reform. To remain a world power and be able to defend itself, Russia had to modernise its army. In the Russian military mindset of the nineteenth century, Russia had not only to have the largest army in Europe but one that was equal in size to the German and Austrian armies. It was, however, extremely expensive to maintain an army of this size. In the 1860s the army was reckoned to take up one-third of the government's income. One of the reasons why it had remained so large was because the government had been reluctant to return soldier serfs to their villages where they might use their training to promote discontent, so they had kept soldiers in service for 25 years, in effect life. After emancipation, this was not deemed necessary.

Main changes

The reforms were undertaken by Dmitri Milyutin (see page 18) over a twenty-year period, 1861–81.

- Universal conscription was introduced: all social classes were liable for military service at the age of 21. Generally one-quarter would be chosen by lot to serve. This could be avoided if medical evidence was provided or deferred for students to complete their studies.
- The standard length of military service was reduced to fifteen years, six of which would be in active service and nine in the reserve. From 1862 to 1870 the reserve increased from 210,000 to over 550,000.
- The administration of the army was reorganised into fifteen military districts with more autonomy given to district commanders. This made it easier to bring in the reserve in time of war.
- Officer training was radically improved. Military colleges were established, admitting recruits who were non-nobles. Promotion was made more open to other classes to improve the leadership pool. A broader education was provided and education was required for commission. There were specialised officer schools for the artillery and engineers.
- A staff college was established with high standards offering accelerated promotion for graduates.
- Modern rifles and artillery were introduced but this was a slow process and technological progress in weaponry meant some weapons were superseded before they were fully introduced.
- There was a reduction in the number of offences that carried corporal punishment and flogging was abolished.
- Conditions improved for ordinary soldiers, for example, they were housed in barracks.

Consequences

- The reforms were a genuine attempt to break down class privilege and create an army based on merit. The result was a smaller and more professional army which was to some extent less brutal and class-ridden. However, there was still a high proportion of the nobility among officers and when Alexander III became tsar he restricted entry to officer training mainly to the nobility. There was also a tendency to appoint untrained members of the royal family to key military services for which they were unsuited. A fully professional army posed a threat to the autocracy as it was the main means by which they stayed in control.

- There was a significant saving in government expenditure as the standing army was smaller and supported by a trained reserve which could be mobilised.
- The reforms were opposed by the nobility who did not want their offspring to mix with the lower classes. They preferred the old system where their sons went into the army as volunteers and dominated the officer corps. Merchants also objected as they did not want their sons to do compulsory military service. However, some were able to find substitutes to replace their sons.
- The army still relied mainly on peasant conscripts who were uneducated and illiterate. This reduced the effectiveness of their training.

Education reforms, 1863–64, and censorship

Alexander recognised that a modern state required a more educated population. The *zemstva* took over the responsibility of running many schools from the Church and, with the employment of more professional teachers, the quality of teaching rose.

- In the first decade of Alexander's reign the number of pupils roughly doubled. New primary schools were built and were open to all classes. Between 1856 and 1878 the number of primary schools increased from 8,000 to nearly 25,000 with 1 million pupils in attendance.
- Secondary schools were also opened to all classes and numbers doubled in the 1860s. The curriculum was extended to include a wider range of subjects. Schools could focus on the classics (Latin and Greek) or modern subjects such as mathematics, science and languages.
- Higher education was thoroughly overhauled and the constraints were relaxed. Universities regained the right to govern themselves, choose their own professors, design their courses, and admit and discipline students. Women could attend courses but not take degrees. There was a radical change in professors: 50 per cent left their posts from 1854 to 1862. Enlightened, even liberal-thinking, professors were appointed like the famous doctor and educational theorist Nicholai Pirogov. From 1865 to 1899, student numbers grew from around 4,000 to 16,000. Students were drawn from wider social groups including the sons of peasants and lower-ranking townspeople.

Consequences

- The increase in primary schools had a huge impact in later years as a more literate peasant population took on new aspirations (see page 62).
- The regime needed students trained to high standards to build a modern state but it did not want them to question the regime. However, higher education tended to foster an independent spirit and critical mind. Students began to play a more significant part in society.
- Many students relied on state financial help and were poor and undernourished. They formed mutual-aid groups organising communal kitchens and libraries. They reacted against poor teaching, the strict regulations and the heavy-handed action of the authorities and police. They

formed study circles discussing radical ideas and the injustices of the tsarist system. This led to protests, disturbances and arrests. As a result, many of them became radicalised and joined the growing ranks of revolutionaries (see the section on revolutionaries, page 26). Once again reform had resulted in people questioning the political authority of the regime.

Censorship

In the 1860s the hitherto rigid system of censorship was relaxed:

- Newspapers, books and periodicals no longer had to submit to prior censorship (preventive censorship).
- Newspapers could discuss government policy and editors were given more freedom.

However, the Ministry of the Interior could still withdraw any publication deemed as dangerous and fine or close down periodicals.

This more generally relaxed atmosphere led to a huge growth in the number of books and periodicals published. There was a growing literate readership to buy a 'good' story. Bolder editors were prepared to push the boundaries of what was deemed dangerous. Some journals were overtly radical and critical of the regime. The Ministry of the Interior did close some down and punished delinquent editors. Others took more moderate lines but were critical of the government, for instance, when reporting court cases. Some reported social problems like crime, alcoholism and the sufferings of groups like peasants – areas on which the government might not welcome reporting but which they could scarcely prohibit. Public opinion was taking shape and becoming more informed. It was not necessarily anti-government but an autocratic regime does not generally appreciate the free flow of opinion.

KEY DATES: REFORMS

1861 Emancipation of the serfs.

Military reforms begin.

1863 Changes in education begin – primary and secondary education extended, greater freedom for universities.

1864 Local government reforms.

Judicial reforms.

1865 Censorship laws formalising relaxation of censorship.

Reform	Main features
Emancipation of the serfs, 1861	Serfs legally free to marry, vote, leave land and trade.
	Land allocated with freedom – house and plot plus share of strips in village fields.
	Land handed over to village to allocate to peasants.
	Land overvalued.
	Amount of land received usually smaller than previously worked.
	Peasants had to buy land by means of redemption payments.
	Mir given greater power over lives of peasants. Measures to stop them leaving village.
	Nobles got choice of best land and compensated in government bonds.
Local government, 1864	Elected councils (*zemstva*) to run aspects of local government, such as roads, health and schools, in rural areas.
	Electoral system favoured nobles.
	Appointed professionals such as teachers and doctors.
1870	Extended to take in town councils.
Judicial, 1864–65	Simplified court system.
	Independent, salaried judges.
	Courts open to press and public.
	Trial by jury for criminal cases. Evidence and witnesses could be challenged.
	JPs for smaller cases.
	Separate peasant courts.
Military, 1861–81	Universal conscription for all classes over 21.
	Military service reduced to fifteen years, six active and nine in reserve.
	Officer training overhauled – military colleges, open to other classes, better education required.
	Re-organisation of administration – fifteen military districts.
	Modern rifles and artillery.
	Corporal punishment reduced.
Education, early 1860s	*Zemstva* took over responsibility for running many rural schools.
	Many more schools built – primary and secondary.
	Secondary schools could focus on classical or modern subjects.
	Universities given much greater freedom over intake, curriculum and discipline.
After 1866	Ministry of Education took some control of schools away from *zemstva*.
	Restrictions and crackdown in universities.
Censorship, early 1860s	Relaxation – newspapers, books and periodicals did not have to be submitted for prior censorship.
	Newspapers could report government policy and jury trials.

▲ **Figure 2** Summary chart of Alexander II's reforms.

3 Reaction and revolutionaries

In this section we shall look at the way Alexander's reign changed course after 1866, as more reactionary policies were adopted, and the growth of opposition.

Reaction

How did the Tsar's policies change after 1866?

In 1866, a former student called Karakazov, who belonged to one of the new revolutionary groups in Russia (see page 27), narrowly missed the Tsar with a pistol shot. Here was the evidence conservatives needed to show the product of reforms in education and censorship. They pressed Alexander to put a halt to the reforms and reverse them. Alexander was tired of the criticism from all sides. Instead of contentment, his reforms and relaxation had led to disruption and increasing demands he was not prepared to meet. His reforms had given reason and scope for dissident and radical groups to work against the autocracy. Also unsettled by the Polish Revolt of 1863 (see page 47), he decided to put a lid on the malcontents, rein back on some of the earlier measures and bring in more reactionary policies.

Liberal ministers now lost influence in the government and some were sacked. Those in Alexander II's family with liberal leanings, such as his brother Constantine, found it difficult to gain access to the Tsar. In came a wave of conservative appointments. Chief among them was Count Peter Shuvalov who was made head of the 'Third Section'. He brought with him an air of fear and mistrust which permeated the court. He:

- vetted appointments and made sure conservatives gained posts
- tightened up censorship and closed down some periodicals
- brought in tighter controls of students and their organisations
- made use of military courts to try more serious political cases as these were not open to reporting and were likely to reach the verdicts the government wanted
- increased the use of rule by decree.

His ally was the new reactionary Minister of Education, Count Tolstoy. He believed that revolution originated in the schools and universities, and particularly in the sciences.

- His ministry took greater control of primary schools, reducing the role of the 1864 school boards which were often dominated by liberal *zemtsvo* representatives. Now ministry inspectors were responsible for appointing teachers and opening schools and kept an eye on the moral views conveyed by teachers.
- Classical subjects like Latin and Greek were favoured over 'modern' subjects like history, science and modern languages. Tolstoy even had science withdrawn from some schools.
- Entry to universities was restricted: only those with a classical education could go on to university. This favoured nobles who tended not to do the more technical and modern subjects.
- There was a crackdown in universities and disciplinary functions were transferred to the police. Students associated with revolutionary activities or views were expelled.

Nevertheless, we should not see Alexander's reign split into two halves before and after 1866. Some reforms did continue. The local government reforms were extended to towns and cities in 1870 and the military reforms continued. The first women were admitted to Moscow University in 1872. So, although there was clearly a move towards reactionary responses to the changing situation, Alexander was carrying on some measures of reform.

The revolutionaries

How and why did opposition grow to the tsarist regime?

Many radical intellectuals considered that the emancipation had betrayed the peasants and it was this that kick-started the revolutionary movement in Russia. This view of betrayal is expressed in Source C.

Source C *The Bell* by Nicholas Ogarev, (Kolokol), 15 July 1861, quoted in *The Abolition of Serfdom, 1762–1907* by David Moon, (Pearson Education), 2001, p164.

At that time [19 February 1861] it seemed the government stood at the head of the emancipation of Russia; its standing was unusually bright and happy: [but] it lost it all at once, and finally hope in it, faith in it collapsed once and for all ... With grief in the heart and sadness we must acknowledge that ... personal rights for peasants *who have emerged from servile dependence* do not exist, because *they have not emerged* from servile dependence. ... The old serfdom has been replaced by a new [serfdom]. In general, serfdom has not been abolished. *The people have been deceived by the tsar!*

Much of the support for this new movement came from students. As we saw above, the higher education reforms had created growing numbers of students, especially from poorer backgrounds, who joined student circles and mutual aid groups discussing liberal and radical political ideas. They were fed by the flow of books (see Chernyshevsky, page 29) and articles made possible by the relaxation of censorship. Many of the articles were critical of the government and the Tsar. There was a growing intelligentsia who objected to the treatment of the masses and the hierarchical nature of society. A variety of groups appeared, often with vague and ill-defined aims. Some wrote manifestos advocating revolution like the one shown below. Probably the most notable of the early groups of the 1860s was the radical Land and Liberty.

Source D Extract from a student manifesto, *Young Russia*, 1862, in *A Sourcebook for Russian History from Earliest Times to 1917* by G. Vernadsky et al. (eds.), (Yale University Press), 1972.

Society is at present divided into two groups that are hostile to one another because their interests are diametrically opposed. The party that is oppressed by all and humiliated by all is the party of the common people. Over it stands a small group of contented and happy men. They are the landowners ... the merchants ... the government officials – in short all those who possess property either inherited or acquired. At their heart stands the Tsar. They cannot exist without him or he without them. If either falls the other will be destroyed ... There is only one way out of this terrible situation which is destroying contemporary man and that is ... bloody and merciless revolution.

According to Source C, why does Ogarev feel betrayed?

Nihilists

Some young people were determined to challenge conventional attitudes and values. Men let their hair grow long and women had it cut short to blur gender differences. They opposed tradition, authority and what they saw as hypocrisy in society. They were ridiculed as 'nihilists' and portrayed in the conservative press as immoral, indecent, godless, free-loving and subversive. But they sought a better alternative and many turned to revolutionary activity.

Why do you think this manifesto (Source D) places so much importance on the role of the Tsar?

Active women

Women played a very active role in discussing social and political issues and in the revolutionary movement, more so than in many other countries. It was accepted in professional circles that women should be well educated. More secondary schools had been opened to girls and although they could not take degrees, women joined and sometimes monopolised higher education courses that universities had been persuaded to put on. More adventurous women went to foreign universities. A significant number were not prepared to put up with the traditional roles and dependence within the family, which had been customary. They wanted to attend university courses and medical schools and be independent. Their self-emancipation was, for them, part of the socialist ideal. For instance, in St Petersburg in the 1860s a women's circle emerged, interested in sexual equality and education issues and then moved on to more radical issues. Many young women joined the 'going to the people' movement in the 1870s.

Vera Figner

Vera Figner worked in a *zemstvo* hospital and gave medical advice to peasants. She and her sister also set up a school, free of charge, which attracted children and adults to learn basic literacy and arithmetic.

That awareness of being useful was the force which attracted our young people to the villages; only there was it possible to have a pure heart and a peaceful conscience.

(From *Russia and the Russians* by Geoffrey Hosking, (Allen Lane), 2001, p311.)

The more restrictive and punitive policies that followed after 1866 added to the ranks of the disenchanted intelligentsia. A wave of arrests following the attempted assassination, the hunting down of activists together with the crackdown in universities and tightening of censorship, led to the increasing radicalisation of students and young people. Police activity inside universities and the banning of student co-operatives intensified antagonism towards the authorities.

The Populists

In the 1870s a new group of revolutionaries took shape – the Populists or *narodniks*. Inspired by the writings of Peter Lavrov (see page 29), they believed in agrarian socialism based around the peasant commune. They thought the commune would provide the route to the 'good' society without the need to go through capitalism and the evils of industrialisation – its factories, mines and wage slavery and where the individual was a dehumanised cog in a machine. They decided to 'go to the people (*narod*)' and spread their message. This was a brave move because they were giving up their current lives (many of them were well-to-do intellectuals), possibly breaking with their families and going to villages to live out their lives among people who had a very different outlook on the world.

Several thousand young people, dressed up in peasants' and workers' clothes, embarked on this venture. Some learnt trades to take with them like joinery, others went as teachers or medical orderlies. In many villages they found incomprehension and suspicion from peasants and were rejected. However, Geoffrey Hosking maintains that recent evidence shows this was not always the case and that the peasants did share some of their views, such as egalitarianism in landholding, and found that the young people, such as Vera Figner (see text box below), had something to offer them.

Nevertheless, village elders, priests and the local police on the whole were not keen on these strangers and reported them to the authorities. Several hundred *narodniks* were arrested and imprisoned for their good intentions. Two large trials were held in 1877 – the 'Trial of the 50' and the 'Trial of the 193'. Some got long sentences but many got light sentences or were acquitted. The court was impressed by the honesty and idealism of the defendants, a large number of whom came from noble or middle-class families, and did not see them as dangerously subversive, but the government did and those who were acquitted were exiled to Siberia.

The revolutionaries re-group

The 'going to the people' movement had failed. Peaceful persuasion did not seem to be the route to change and revolution. The peasants were too conservative. This, together with the harsh treatment of their colleagues, persuaded the revolutionaries that a different approach was needed. Land and Liberty (*Zemlia I Volia*) was reformed with a strong central organisation and a commitment to secrecy and discipline. Cells were formed in villages and towns aiming to support demonstrations and actions against the autocracy. Some of these were very violent, killing informers or despotic officials and arranging escapes for imprisoned members of their group. This caused a severe reaction from the authorities and, after the Vera Zasulich case (see page 21), political trials were moved to military courts. Eventually this provoked a split in the movement in 1879 into two groups:

- Black Partition led by George Plekhanov (see below) with Vera Zasulich and others who wanted to promote revolution by peaceful agitation.
- The People's Will who were determined to use terrorist violence to achieve their revolutionary aims – destruction of the state and land redistribution. In particular they became focused on killing Alexander II as a way to initiate revolution. On 26 August 1879 they condemned him to death for 'crimes against the people'. Over the next two years they made several unsuccessful assassination attempts until March 1881 when luck favoured them (see page 30).

The development of Russian revolutionary thought

Members of the Russian intelligentsia were attracted to socialism because it was a science-based doctrine. But it took a particular Russian form around the notion of the egalitarian peasant commune and the workers' artel (co-operative association of craftsmen living and working together).

Alexander Herzen believed the commune's attributes of collective responsibility, communal welfare and co-operation at work prepared people for socialism and, like other agrarian socialists, thought that Russia could avoid capitalism altogether. He hoped that this new society would take shape after the serfs were emancipated. But when he saw the results of the emancipation statutes he led the criticism of its terms in the radical newspaper *The Bell* where the phrase 'Land and Liberty' was coined. This became the slogan of the revolutionaries who first made their appearance in Russia in the early 1860s.

In 1862 an influential novel, *What Is to Be Done?* by Nicholas Chernyshevsky was published. It features a circle of political activists led by Rakhametov, who leads an ascetic life, abstaining from sex, eating moderately, body-building to prepare himself for the coming revolution. This image had a powerful appeal to revolutionaries including the young Lenin. It encouraged them to set up groups of their own.

According to Robert Service, Lenin also admired a much more dubious character who appeared on the scene at this time: Nechaev published the *Catechism of the Revolutionary* which declared that a revolutionary should be totally dedicated, hard, ruthless and unmoved by feelings for the sake of prosecuting the revolution. He organised the membership of his group in small cells, unknown to each other, highly disciplined and directed by a central committee. His ideas may have filtered through to Lenin in respect of the dedication of the revolutionary and the organisation of a revolutionary party.

Particularly influential in the Populist movement of the 1870s was Peter Lavrov whose *Historical Letters* (1869) were widely read. He maintained that intellectuals owed their education to the toil of the masses and that they should repay this debt by sharing their learning with the peasants and raising their culture and consciousness so they could bring their socialist potential to fruition. This inspired the *narodniks* going out to the villages to take their message to the people.

A different line was taken by George Plekhanov in the 1880s after the failure of the *narodniks* in the 1870s. He maintained that the future of revolution did not lie with the peasant and the commune. Capitalism had already arrived in force and was evident in the growth of railways, factories, mines and foreign investment, so there was no hope of transforming Russia into a socialist society without undergoing the stage of capitalist development. So revolutionaries should now place their faith in the urban working class and look to Marxism (see page 86) as the key to understanding and transforming Russia.

The assassination of Alexander II

On 1 March 1881 Alexander II was travelling by coach to the Winter Palace in St Petersburg with an escort of Cossacks. On a street corner near the Catherine Canal, a member of The People's Will hurled a bomb. It did not stop the Tsar's iron-clad coach but several of the Cossacks were fatally injured. The Tsar stopped and climbed out to comfort them, at which point a second bomb was thrown, fatally injuring the Tsar. He insisted on being taken to the Winter Palace where he died an hour later. Five members of The People's Will were convicted and sentenced to death. On 3 April, wearing the word 'TSARICIDE' on a placard on their chests, they were led out for public execution before a vast crowd.

A change of course?

Was Alexander II intending to make more liberal concessions?

The last years of Alexander II's reign were clouded by terrorism. Government officials were attacked and killed all over Russia. Attempts were made to blow up the royal train and an explosion under the dining room of the Winter Palace killed ten guards. In 1880 Mikhail Loris-Melikov was given the job as head of a special commission with extraordinary measures to restore order. In the same year, 31,000 people were put under police supervision. The future Alexander III described this period as, 'the most terrible and abominable years that Russia has ever experienced: 1879 and the beginning of 1880. There could scarcely be anything worse than this time!'

Alexander II was unpopular with sections of the public who had shown that they were not keen on unadulterated repression. Despite this, many thousands turned out in February 1880 to cheer the Tsar on the 25th anniversary of his accession. Loris-Melikov, now Minister of the Interior, thought that the regime needed to take steps to strengthen the people's trust in the government and show itself to be more responsive to their needs and interests, so he:

- abolished the 'Third Section' and transferred its functions to the Ministry of the Interior and police, instructing them to take interest only in genuinely dangerous people instead of the thousands under surveillance
- proposed more civil rights of the peasants and help to make it easier for them to acquire their land
- proposed that elected representatives of the *zemstva* and larger towns form part of a consultative body to help in the making of laws. Although limited in scope it seemed a first real step to popular participation in national government.

Alexander gave preliminary approval but it got no further than that because he was assassinated.

KEY DATES: REACTION AND REVOLUTIONARIES

1866 Karakazov's attempted assassination of Alexander II.

1870 Town councils set up.

1873 *Narodnik* 'going to the people' movement begins.

1877 Trial of the 50 and Trial of the 193.

1879 The Black Partition and The People's Will revolutionary groups take shape.

1880 'Third Section' abolished.

Loris-Melikov commission to suggest reform.

1881 Assassination of Alexander II.

Alexander and his reforms

How should we assess Alexander's reforms?

With the possible exceptions of Khruschev and Gorbachev, no Russian ruler brought so much relief to so many of his people as did Alexander II, autocratic and conservative though he was.

(From *Endurance and Endeavour 1812–2001*, fifth edition, by J. N. Westwood, (Oxford University Press), 2003, p65.)

Alexander II aimed to strengthen the tsarist regime by resolving the problems of serfdom, modernising the army and bringing Russia into the modern world. Paradoxically many of the reforms he introduced weakened the regime in the long term by creating independent bodies and groups of people who were to challenge its political authority. Alexander was trying to bring about major changes in Russian society while keeping the autocracy intact and perhaps this was unrealisable. Strangely, it was probably because it was an autocracy that he was able to attempt such far-reaching reforms.

Some historians point to the scale of reforms and the attempt to move Russia forward. The emancipation of the serfs, despite its deficiencies, had ended an evil institution, comparable with slavery in America. The Russian historian, Alexander Chubarov, points out that this was achieved without civil war or massive armed force. T. Emmons has described it as 'probably the greatest single piece of state directed social engineering in modern Europe prior to the twentieth century'.

The judicial reforms replaced a corrupt and archaic system with an independent judiciary and fairer justice system. The military reforms created a more professional army with an improved command structure. The local government reforms introduced the *zemstva* which brought improvements in health, education and other areas and suggested the possibility of more participative government. There was a dramatic increase in the number of schools open to all classes, a great success that had a great impact later on. During Alexander's reign, there was greater freedom of expression and action than under his predecessor or his successor.

But for most historians, like Hugh Seton-Watson, Alexander's reforms did not go far enough. This is most particularly the case with emancipation as we saw in the analysis on pages 16–17. The peasants did not get their freedom in a real sense and felt aggrieved. It was the autocracy's chance to provide economic and social stability as a basis for agricultural and industrial growth. But it failed to take this opportunity. Other reforms also had serious weaknesses or drawbacks. The judicial reforms were radical but there were far too many opt-outs, too many special courts outside the system, ways for the regime to get round the courts and try people secretly; also the peasants were not included in the mainstream justice system. The *zemstva* were a bold move, aiming to provide self-government in which all classes participated. But they were watered down, became the province of the nobility and were not the success they could have been. But the major drawback of the reforms was the Tsar's decision not to have a national representative assembly where reform and change could have been discussed and the public engaged. The Tsar was determined to steer his own ship.

The problem for Alexander and any reforming tsar was how to achieve reform without damaging the interests of the privileged classes who were essential to the regime's continued existence. The Tsar feared a backlash from the nobility.

Many members of the court and bureaucrats opposed the reforms and were only too willing to criticise them when things went awry, for instance, when the relaxation of censorship led to criticism, protests and revolutionary activity. These conservative elements were a thorn in the side of the enlightened reformers. It was hard for Alexander to overcome this resistance, especially as some of his own values and views meant he was inclined to agree with the conservatives.

The regime had gone so far and then stepped backwards. It had not been prepared to change its institutions fundamentally. The autocracy was a personalised system of control that was arbitrary in character. It did not want a rational civil service, elected bodies and the rule of law to challenge it. And neither did Alexander. He was no liberal, he was trying to preserve the autocracy. But once the reforms had failed to produce a new more rational system, all the regime could do was to fall back on the police, emergency powers and repression to stay in control and in the end this was the route to their overthrow (see Source E below). Some historians, including Christopher Read on pages 16–17, point to the emancipation as starting the process that ended in revolution in 1917.

Source E *New Appreciations in History 17* by Maureen Perrie, (The Historical Association), 1989, p33.

The 'Great Reforms' must be ranked among the most successful achievements of the traditional autocratic system in Russia. But they were to prove its last creative act. In the aftermath of the terrorist bomb of 1 March 1881, Alexander's successors employed their arbitrary powers in the interests of repression and reaction rather than reform or progress. The next wave of reforms in Russia, after 1905, came not as an initiative from 'above', but as a series of forced and grudging concessions to a revolution 'from below'.

Source F 'Alexander II's Reforms, Cause and Consequences' by Carl Watts, (*History Review*), December 1998, No.32.

When Alexander II became Tsar in 1855, the Russian state was in desperate need of fundamental reform. The programme of reforms introduced by him was radical in comparison with previous Russian experience, but it did not go far enough. The government's commitment to modernize Russia through a process of Westernisation was moderated by its concern to perpetuate the interests of its ruling social class. This approach alienated the Russian intelligentsia and, in doing so, undermined the stability of the regime, compelling it to rely on repression for preservation. This strategy succeeded for some time, but in the long term it was likely to achieve precisely the opposite of its intended effect.

Source G Leroy-Beaulieu, quoted by W. Mosse in *Alexander II and the Modernisation of Russia*, (English Universities Press), 1970, p105.

The emancipation was followed by numerous reforms, administrative, judicial, military ... yet all these reforms, prepared by different commissions subject to rival or hostile influences were undertaken in isolation ... without coherence and without a definite plan. The task was to build a new Russia; the edifice was constructed upon old foundations without a blue-print, without a general plan, without an architect to co-ordinate the different operations. By introducing here and there particular innovations ... into the ancient structure, Alexander in the end succeeded after immense labour in making the new Russia an incomplete and uncomfortable dwelling where friends and opponents felt almost equally ill at ease.

WORKING TOGETHER

1 What are the main criticisms aimed at Alexander in Sources F and G?

2 How far can you reconcile these with the other comments of Westwood (page 31), Emmons (page 31) and Perrie (page 32) above?

3 Divide a piece of paper into four quarters with question titles as shown below. Each student/ pair of students should take one of the quarters and make a list of points to answer the questions.

Different aspects of the same reform will appear in different quarters. For instance, the *zemstva* had a potential to strengthen the regime by providing more open, efficient and effective local government but they also weakened the regime by creating people critical of it.

- In what ways were the reforms successful?
- In what ways were the reforms unsuccessful?
- How did the reforms strengthen the regime?
- How did the reforms weaken the regime?

Chapter summary

- Tsarist Russia in the mid-nineteenth century was perceived as a backward, underdeveloped agricultural country, with poor communications. Over 90 per cent of the population were peasants.

- It was governed by an autocracy ruled by a tsar at the head of a large, inefficient bureaucracy. It was a repressive regime which made use of the secret police and the army to maintain its control.

- Defeat in the Crimean War highlighted Russia's backwardness and prompted the new tsar, Alexander II, to put in motion far-reaching reforms.

- The most important reform was the emancipation of the serfs. They were freed and given an allocation of land but had to pay for it over 49 years. Peasants and nobles were upset by the terms of the emancipation.

- Other reforms included local government reforms which set up *zemstva*, and judicial reforms which set up a system of independent courts and judges.

- These reforms challenged the political authority of the regime and aided the growth of the 'third element', professionals like doctors, lawyers and teachers, who were to push for reform in the future.

- The military reforms created a smaller, more professional army but one still dominated by the nobility and reliant on ill-educated peasant conscripts.

- Reforms in education saw increasing numbers of schools and pupils, and more independent universities; the relaxation of censorship saw an increase in books and periodicals, many critical of the Tsar and his government.

- This period saw the growth of revolutionary groups angry about the injustices of the tsarist system. In the 1870s, the Populists took their message 'to the people' but were not successful and the revolutionary movement split and took different directions.

- After 1866, Alexander II adopted more reactionary policies and approaches.

▼ Summary diagram: How Alexander II's reforms generated challenges to the political authority of the tsarist regime

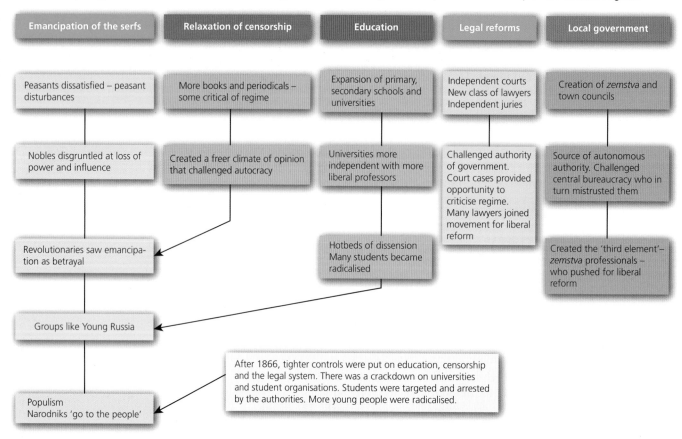

Working on essay technique: focus, structure and deploying detail

As well as learning the facts and understanding the history of Russia in the nineteenth and twentieth century, it is very important to develop skills in answering the types of question that will be set.

Essay focus

Whether you are taking the AS exam or the full A-level exam, Section B presents you with essay titles. Each question is marked out of 25.

AS examination	The full A-level examination
Section B – Answer ONE essay (from a choice of two)	Section B – Answer TWO essays (from a choice of three)

You may come across various question stems, but they all have the same basic requirement. They all require you to analyse and reach a conclusion, based on the evidence you provide.

For example:

- 'Assess the validity (of a quotation)'
- 'To what extent …'
- 'How successful …'
- 'How far …'

The AS titles always give a quotation and then: 'Explain why you agree or disagree with this view'. Almost inevitably, your answer will be a mixture of both. In essence, it is the same task as for the full A-level – just more basic wording.

Each question will reflect, directly or indirectly, one of the breadth issues in your study. The questions will have a fairly broad focus.

> **EXAMPLE**
>
> Look at the following AS-level practice question:
>
> **'Alexander II's reforms were, on the whole, unsuccessful .' Explain why you agree or disagree with this view.** (25 marks)
>
> This type of question requires you to look at Alexander II's reforms and then to decide whether they were successful in some ways and a failure in others, or unsuccessful.

Structuring your answer

A clear structure makes for a much more effective essay. In order to structure the question in the example effectively you need several paragraphs. In each paragraph you will deal with one factor – one of Alexander II's reforms.

You will first have to decide the order of your paragraphs. It may be that you will start with the most important reform, then the second – and so on. Or you may wish to deal with the reforms in chronological order – in the order that Alexander carried them out.

Remember that you also need a short but clear introduction that briefly explains your argument in relation to the question and a conclusion that provides a summary. This is a useful structure to apply to many questions.

Writing a focused introduction

It is vital that you maintain focus on the question from the beginning of your essay. One way to do this is to use the wording of the question to help write your argument. The first two sentences in answer to the practice question, for example, could look like this:

> After 1855 Alexander II introduced a series of reforms to deal with the problems facing Russia that had been highlighted by its defeat in the Crimean War. While his reforms were successful in some ways, in other important respects they were not.

These opening sentences provide a clear focus on the demands of the question, recognising that you have to highlight the reforms of Alexander II and adjudge their success/failure. They provide a spring-board for the clear essay plan suggested above. Remember, you must learn to apply this approach to other questions you may encounter. You are not just learning how to respond to this question.

Focus throughout the essay

Structuring your essay well will help with focus throughout the essay, but you will also need to remember to maintain this throughout the piece. Here are some ideas that will help you to focus your answer.

Use the wording of the question to help write your answer.

> For example, in answer to the practice question on page 35, you could begin your first main paragraph with the most important reform: 'the abolition of serfdom'.
>
> *The problem at the heart of Russia's backwardness was the issue of serfdom and this was the subject of Alexander's most important reform. This was on such an immense scale involving millions of people and the whole social structure of Russia that it was always going to be difficult to manage this successfully.*
>
> The first sentence begins with a clear point that refers to the primary focus of the question (the reform). The second sentence links it to the issue of whether it was successful or not.

Write a paragraph for each of the other reforms. You may wish to number them. This helps to make your structure clear and helps you to maintain focus. Later we will look at prioritising factors in order of importance.

Summary

- Work out the main focus of the question.
- Plan your essay with a series of factors focusing on the question.
- Use the words in the question to formulate your answer.
- Return to the primary focus of the question at the beginning of every paragraph.
- Make sure that your structure is clear to the reader.

ACTIVITY

1 Having now read the advice on how to write a structured and focused essay, plan and write the first sentence to the following A-level practice question:

   'Alexander II deserves the title of "Tsar Liberator".' Assess the validity of this view . (25 marks)

Deploying detail

As well as focus and structure, your essay will be judged on the extent to which it includes relevant and accurate detail. Detailed essays are more likely to do well than essays which are vague and generalised. There are several different kinds of evidence you could use that might be described as detailed. This includes correct dates, views of relevant people, statistics and events. You can also make your essays more detailed by using the correct technical vocabulary. Here you could use words and phrases such as 'emancipation', 'Mir', 'zemstva' and 'enlightened officials' that you have learned while studying this subject.

ACTIVITY

2 Consider the following AS-level practice question:

   'The reforms of Alexander II weakened the tsarist regime.' Explain why you agree or disagree with this view. (25 marks)

- Create your own brief essay plan for this question, making a list of points you will include.
- Using your notes from this chapter, find at least three pieces of detail to support each of these points. It is best to use different types of detailed evidence, for example, not just statistics or technical vocabulary, but also dates and specific people.

Autocracy and modernisation

The chapter looks at the nature of autocracy and how Alexander III sought to preserve the autocracy and the integrity of the Russian Empire. It also looks at how modernisation and industrialisation changed Russia. It deals with the following areas:

- The autocracy, its ideology and political authority
- Alexander III as ruler
- Russification, the treatment of ethnic minorities and Jewish people
- Economic developments 1880–1914, industrial and agricultural growth and change
- Social and cultural change, 1880–1914

This chapter covers the central key questions relating to how the Tsar asserted his political authority and governed Russia, how the economy developed and how this generated significant social and cultural change. It also explores the role played by groups and individuals in these changes.

The chapter focuses on the following question:

What were the consequences of modernisation for the autocracy?

This invites you to consider the process of modernisation and explore how this had consequences for the stability of the regime, particularly in respect of the social changes it brought about.

CHAPTER OVERVIEW

This chapter begins by examining in detail the nature of autocracy and the tsarist state. It then looks at the reign of Alexander III, the epitome of an autocrat. After the assassination of his father he introduced a series of counter-reforms which created a more centralised and authoritarian state. The regime experienced thirteen years of peace and stability. He threw his weight behind a policy of modernisation and industrialisation led by Sergei Witte. This resulted in a transformation of the Russian economy from 1880 to 1914. Industry grew at a tremendous pace. The story in agriculture was more mixed but there was an increase in grain production and improvements in other respects. This period also saw dramatic social changes taking place in Russia as urbanisation grew apace.

1 The nature of autocracy and the tsarist state

This section looks at the ideology which underpinned the Russian autocracy and the structure and weaknesses of the tsarist state.

The ideology of autocracy

What were the ideological underpinnings of tsarism?

Three main principles provided the ideological justification for the tsarist regime: autocracy, orthodoxy and nationality.

Autocracy

Article 1 of the Fundamental Laws in 1832 stated: 'The Emperor of all the Russias is an autocratic and unlimited monarch; God himself ordains that all must bow before his supreme power, not only out of fear but also out of conscience'. No other European monarch had the tsar's freedom of action; all were subject to limitations of some kind. There were no institutions in Russia that acted as a check on the tsar – no form of representative assembly and no proper cabinet government. Nor was he constrained by the rule of law. There were practical reasons why some Russians considered that autocracy was the best system for Russia (see Konstantin Pobedonostsev below).

There was more to autocracy than this. The tsar had a special paternalistic relationship with the people. He was the father and his subjects were the children. His duty was to guide them along the right path and their duty was to submit to his will for their own good. Essential to this relationship was 'trust': the people had to trust in the tsar that he would take the right actions for their benefit even if this meant that he had to discipline them for their unruly behaviour at times.

NOTE-MAKING

Make notes under the three headings below but leave space to add other information about these as you continue your study:
- Autocracy
- Orthodoxy
- Nationality

Konstantin Pobedonostsev, 1827–1907

Pobedonostsev is a key figure during the late nineteenth century because he was tutor to both Alexander III and Nicholas II and played an influential role in their lives. Also in 1880 he was made Chief Procurator of the Holy Synod. This gave him great influence over the Church, education and social matters. He advised the tsar on religious matters and had ministerial status, giving him access to top government bodies. His role epitomised the strong connection between autocracy, orthodoxy and nationality. He was an exponent of the Slavophile view that autocracy was the best form of government for Russia and that any concessions to Western liberalism would be disastrous. This view held that Russia was so large and diverse that it was better that one person should have overall control and that any dilution of this authority would result in chaos. He warned Alexander III: 'if the direction of policy passes to some kind of assembly, it will mean revolution and the end, not only of government, but of Russia itself'. He called representative democracy 'the great lie of our time'.

Pobedonostsev was convinced that firmness was the essential characteristic of good government and he was instrumental in driving the repressive measures which were central to Alexander III's reign. He encouraged Alexander and Nicholas to pursue an aggressive policy of Russification (nationality). He sought to re-educate the people by increasing the number of clergy, churches and church schools, particularly in the outlying parts of the Empire. He was deeply antisemitic and encouraged the fierce pogroms launched against Jewish people during the 1880s and restrictions of their political and economic activities. Pogroms were organised, violent attacks on the homes and businesses of Jewish people.

Orthodoxy

The right of the tsar to rule as an autocrat was supported by the Orthodox Church. In the reign of Alexander II, Orthodox priests, once a year in every church, pronounced a curse on:

those who do not believe that the Orthodox monarchs have been elevated to the throne by God's special grace, and that from the moment they are anointed with the holy oil, are infused by the gifts of the Holy Ghost

> (Quoted in *Endurance and Endeavour 1812–2001*, fifth edition, by J. N. Westwood, (Oxford University Press), 2003, p37).

The tsar was God's representative on earth and was entrusted with the duty to look after and care for the people. This tied in with the notion of him as the 'father' and entitled him to their obedience as loyal subjects, giving their submission to the tsar a religious dimension. Any challenge to the tsar was an insult to God. The Orthodox religion was superior and special – the true faith – the religion of 'Holy Russia'. It was the tsar's job to defend the Orthodox faith and the Church supported the tsar in a most direct way. In 1902 the Holy Synod instructed bishops to get their priests 'to explain to their congregations the falseness, according to the word of God, of the appeals of the evil-minded who urge them to destroy the authorities established by the tsar and to attack the property of others'. The Church made sure that the peasants got the message to support the regime clearly in church but also in the many primary schools that the Orthodox Church ran and the curriculum in schools that they influenced. So Church and State were bound up with each other and the Church acted as a prop for the autocracy. There was a strong relationship between the tsar and the Church's senior official – the Chief Procurator of the Holy Synod – who was appointed by the tsar.

Nationality

Just as the Orthodox faith was regarded as superior, so there was a strong belief that Russians had a distinctive way of life, values, beliefs and customs that were superior to the people around them – Russianism. This was due to their special Orthodox faith but also because Russians had a different outlook and perspective on the world as a result of their history and geography. Russians believed that they had a duty to promote their beliefs, customs and worldview to other peoples, hence the policy of Russification that was imposed on non-Russian minorities in the tsarist empire (see page 47). The intellectuals that stressed this position were the Slavophiles (see page 9).

The tsarist state

What elements comprised the tsarist state and how well did it function?

The structure of the state, which is shown in Figure 1 (below), remained largely the same throughout the period from 1861 to 1905, although Alexander III dispensed with the Council of Minsters in 1882. After 1905 the structure was significantly altered with the introduction of an elected parliament, the Duma, which you can read about in Chapter 3.

Institutional and practical weaknesses

The tsar lay at the centre of the autocracy. There were no cabinet meetings to discuss the issues of the day and no chief minister to co-ordinate the policies and actions of different ministers. The tsar was responsible for co-ordinating policy – individual ministers reported to him. This mechanism helped the tsar maintain his power and keep control of what the government was doing. However, you needed a strong tsar who could assert his authority and who had command of the details of policy. A weak tsar, who was not hands-on, was a liability.

There were other weaknesses in the system:

- Ministers and departments did not work with each other or even necessarily consult each other. This made for inefficient government. For instance, some departments would plan to spend large amounts of money but not clear it with the Ministry of Finance, so there would be problems with the budget or the money might not be available. After the Crimean War there was a shortage of money to pay for reforms.
- Ministries competed with each other for control of policy, resources and the tsar's attention. This was especially true of the two biggest ministries – Finance and the Interior. The Ministry of Finance, with staff drawn from the fields of banking and commerce, wanted changes in society to allow

Council of Ministers

- Chaired by Tsar
- Consisted of officials nominated by Tsar
- Discussed draft legislation to go either to Committee of Ministers for further scrutiny or directly into law by royal assent
  (Abandoned by Alexander III in 1882 but brought back after 1905)

The Imperial Council of State

- Members appointed by Tsar
- Gave advice to Tsar on legal and financial matters

Tsar

- Autocrat in control of policy making and its implementation
- All ministers and government offices reported to Tsar

The Committee of Ministers Established 1861

- Ministers, appointed by Tsar, responsible for administration of particular aspects of government affairs
- Reported directly to Tsar
- Did not formulate policies
- Four particularly important ministers: Minister of Interior (domestic affairs, law and order), Minister of Finance, Minister for War, Procurator of the Holy Synod (religious affairs)

The Senate Acted as supreme court in Russia

- Final court of appeal on major legal matters
- Adjudicator of disagreement between landowners over boundaries
- Dealt with titles of nobles

▲ **Figure 1** Main bodies of Russian government, 1861–90.

enterprise and initiative to flourish. This could create circumstances, for example, urbanisation, which could cause social tension or might give the middle classes more power. The Ministry of the Interior, with staff drawn from the nobility and landowners, resisted changes that might threaten social control or create a more liberal Russia. So these two powerful ministries were often pulling against each other and this created confusion and lack of clarity in policy.

- There was incompetence at the top of the system. Ministers often spent their time trying to divine the 'autocratic will' or trying to implant ideas so that they seemed like the tsar's own. Courtiers and unofficial advisers continued to make policies for ministries.

- There were machinations and manoeuvring at the higher levels of the bureaucracy. Deputies schemed to depose superiors so this inclined superiors to hire mediocrities who would be no threat. This was also true of the tsar's appointment of ministers.

- Sometimes elements in government conspired against other elements for political reasons. For instance, the reforms of Alexander II were obstructed and held up by conservative officials in the government who disapproved of them.

- The operation of the government was often kept secret even from officials who had to carry it out.

Source A An employee of the Finance Ministry in a memorandum of 1856, quoted in *Russia in the Age of Reaction and Reform, 1801–1881* by David Saunders, (Longman), 1992, p209.

Nowhere is there so much centralisation and at the same time so little centralisation as there is in Russia. On the one hand the ministries have arrogated to themselves the virtually exclusive right to decide all matters, but at the same time there is not the slightest link between the separate ministries ... Everyone's perpetual concern to safeguard himself against having to take legal responsibility necessitates a fearful expenditure of effort, paper, ink, and time, slows down the transaction of business, removes from the provincial and district agencies all feelings of independence, and teaches them to act surreptitiously if at all. It goes without saying that all of this stops short at the people, who have been abandoned to the authorities' exploitation.

What weaknesses of the system of government of tsarist Russia does the government official (Source A) point out?

The bureaucracy

Bureaucrats in central government were organised in ranks. Peter the Great in 1722 had set out fourteen ranks on the ladder of state service. Nobles served as a matter of service and duty (if they did not go into the military) and, especially after the abolition of serfdom, as a means to obtain a salary. Non-nobles occupied an increasing number of jobs in the bureaucracy as its functions grew in the nineteenth century, requiring new skills more likely to be found in the ambitious children of clergy, merchants or professionals. It was also a way for commoners to become noble because nobility was conferred when you reached a certain rank.

While those who got to the top could do well, the typical bureaucrat was not well paid and had little authority. Lower level ones were very poorly paid. Bribe-taking was common as it was seen as a legitimate way to supplement one's income. Often bureaucrats were more interested in manoeuvring to get to higher ranks and salaries than working for the public good. They sought the approval of their superiors for advancement and could be indifferent to the concerns of the people, so that those who came into contact with them often regarded them as soulless pen-pushers.

The Russian state was top-heavy. There were relatively few officials in the provinces compared with other European countries. The provincial governors had a vast range of duties and discretion. This was increased by the 'temporary' emergency powers of August 1881 (see page 44), for instance, governors could expel people from their home province, close businesses, search homes and so on, without any appeal. They could be cruel and vicious and some misused their police powers. Many solid citizens resented their arbitrary powers and excessive authority. The degree of organisation varied enormously. Some governors did their job very well, others were hopelessly incompetent and their bureaucracies were riddled with corruption. In the final analysis, government relied on coercion to control the population.

At the most basic level, the villages were the responsibility of the local policeman. Not only did he keep order and deal with crime, but he played a role in tax collection and all sorts of administrative duties that involved close contact with the peasants. There were relatively few of them for the territory involved and they were poorly paid and generally of low quality with little training. But they had substantial power after the emergency measures of 1881 were passed.

Proizvol

One of the main criticisms of the central government and the bureaucracy was its arbitrariness (*proizvol*). This means that there were no clearly defined legal rules of administration to which officials had to adhere. They could abuse their authority and violate rules that did exist. It was almost impossible to get redress for any grievances.

The arbitrary ethos which permeated Russian government made it easier for the state to take whatever methods it felt necessary to maintain control without much fear of its actions being subject to scrutiny

(From *The End of Imperial Russia, 1855–1917* by Peter Waldron, (Palgrave Macmillan), 1997, p12.)

---

2 Alexander III, 1881–94

This section looks at the reaction of Alexander III to his father's reforms and describes the counter-reforms he introduced. It also looks at the position of the national minorities in the Russian Empire and the policy of Russification.

Alexander III came to the throne after the horrific death of his father and the turmoil of the last years of his reign. He reacted to this by adopting an approach of uncompromising authoritarianism and conservatism. He presided over a period of thirteen years of peace and stability, determined to re-establish the political authority his father had lost. Conservative nationalists, who had been disillusioned by Alexander II's reforms and vacillations, were in the ascendancy while Westernised intellectuals were unwelcome.

The reactionary Tsar

What was Alexander III's attitude to his role as tsar and what was his character?

When Alexander III came to the throne, he made it clear that he was going to affirm the principle of autocracy in no uncertain terms. On 29 April 1881, in *The Manifesto on Unshakable Autocracy*, he announced that the tsar would 'rule with faith in the strength and truth of the autocratic power that we have been called upon to affirm and safeguard for the popular good from infringement'. He set about turning the clock back, returning to an ideology which stressed Russian uniqueness based on Orthodoxy and the supposed unity of tsar and people.

NOTE-MAKING

Make notes on:
- Alexander's attitudes to autocracy and Western-style parliamentarianism
- his personality, qualities and attributes.

Alexander, the person

Alexander III was 6ft 4ins tall, broad-shouldered and powerfully built. He gave the impression of immense authority and in this sense fulfilled the role of the autocrat perfectly. He was extremely strong: to amuse his children he unbent horseshoes and tore packs of cards in half. He was bulky and bearded with uncouth manners. He favoured a caftan-style uniform with Russian boots. He admired the Cossacks for their way of life, Orthodoxy and loyalty to the Crown, and Lindsey Hughes says he 'might be described as a Cossack Tsar'. He modelled himself and his reign on Muscovy before Peter the Great, to the extent of holding court balls in seventeenth-century dress.

He had been brought up under the influence of his grandfather and this is evident in his military training. He liked military parades, an orderly life with simple, regular meals. He was limited in intellect but was diligent, honest and sincere. He was also strong-willed, determined and ruthless. As second in line to the throne he was shielded from the limelight until his brother's death in 1865. His brother, who had been his parents' favourite child, had seemed a promising heir. But Alexander had to give up his love affairs for duty. He married his late brother's fiancée, Maria Sophia Fredericke Dagmar, daughter of the King of Denmark. She was known as Maria Fedorovna in the Russian court or 'Minni' to her husband.

Alexander was devoted to his family and spent time playing with his children. He enjoyed horse play and practical jokes. He disapproved of immoral behaviour and imposed sanctions on members of the family who indulged in it, including two of his uncles who set up households with ballerinas.

Source B From *The Romanovs* by Lindsey Hughes, (Bloomsbury), 2008, p190.

Alexander reaffirmed the connection between Church and State. In 1884, he recalled the consecration of the Cathedral of Christ the Redeemer in Moscow after his coronation in May 1883:

'This great event ... showed to the whole astonished world and morally corrupt Europe that Russia is the same holy, Orthodox Russia as she was under the Tsars of Moscow and as, God willing, she will remain forever'.

Alexander rejected his father's reforms as 'ill-advised, tantamount to revolution and pushing Russia on to the wrong road' and considered that they, along with the Western ideas that had inspired them, had contributed to his father's assassination. He rejected parliamentarianism saying he 'would not grant Russia a constitution for anything on earth'.

This stance was evident in his appointment of Pobedonostsev – 'the pace-setter of reaction' – as Chief Procurator of the Holy Synod (see page 38). When Alexander convened his ministers to discuss the Loris-Melikov proposals which had been given preliminary approval by his father, Pobedonostsev denounced them as the first step on the slippery slope to Western-style constitutionalism. Loris-Melikov resigned along with other leading liberals like Dmitri Milyutin to be replaced by conservative ministers like Count Dmitri Tolstoy who was made Minister of the Interior.

> What does Source B tell you about the importance of Orthodoxy to autocratic rule?

Maria Fedorovna

Maria Fedorovna was a popular and successful Grand Duchess and Empress. She was the patron of hospitals, girls' schools, orphanages, the Russian Red Cross Society and much more. She tended soldiers during the war with Turkey in 1877–78. She brought back a glittering and lavish court where her sociability and charm compensated for her husband's uneasiness in high society. He remained faithful to her, in contrast to his father's scandalous affair, and every Easter after 1884 gave her a jewelled and highly decorated egg made by Carl Fabergé.

NOTE-MAKING

Draw a chart noting down the main details of:
- the emergency measures
- the counter-reforms

Counter-reforms

In what ways did Alexander III assert tsarist control and authority?

Alexander and his government sought to roll back or curtail the reforms of Alexander II and deal with opposition and perceived threats to the stability of the regime.

Emergency measures

In 1881 the Statute of State Security was passed, giving the government emergency powers to:

- prohibit gatherings of more than twelve people
- prosecute any individual for political crimes
- introduce emergency police rule where public order was threatened
- set up special courts outside the legal system
- close schools, universities and newspapers.

As a result, the Minister of the Interior, provincial governors and police chiefs could do more or less what they wanted, restricting civil liberties, arresting people without having to go to court and closing educational institutions or newspapers if they considered public order was endangered. Most of these 'temporary' measures remained in force until 1917. They initiated a period of repression under Alexander (see below).

Control

- In 1881 a new secret police – the *Okhrana* – was established. A decree of March 1882 allowed the police to declare any citizen subject to surveillance.
- Tolstoy had decided that he wanted government-appointed officials to have direct control over the peasants and the village communes. Members of the gentry were chosen as Land Captains or commandants to control rural areas. They were very powerful and could overrule district courts, with no appeal against their decisions. They were deeply resented by the peasantry.
- Censorship was tightened even further. Publications which criticised the regime could be suspended and editors banned from publishing anything else.

Education

- In 1884 the University Statute brought in strict controls on the universities, reducing their autonomy and student freedom. University staff were appointed by the Minister of Education.
- University courses for women were closed.
- The Church was given more control over primary education.
- Fees in secondary schools were raised to exclude students from lower ranks. The percentage of children of nobles and officials rose significantly.

Local government

- In 1890 the *Zemstva* Act reduced the independence of the *zemstva*. Control became more centralised and they were put under the Ministry of the Interior. Provincial governors could veto and amend their decisions. Generally, central government interfered with or stifled local initiatives. The system to elect members of the *zemstva* was changed in favour of landowners and peasant representation was reduced. Nevertheless, the *zemstva* continued their programme of improvements, such as building roads and hospitals, and played a key role in alleviating the effects of the famine of 1891–92.

- In 1892 the Municipal Government Act did the same to municipal councils. The number of people eligible to vote in elections was cut drastically, for instance, in Moscow and St Petersburg only 0.7 per cent of the population could vote. This favoured richer property owners.

Legal

- The government wanted to regain some of the power passed to the judicial system under Alexander II. However, it found it difficult to interfere directly in the new legal structures and ignore guarantees of judicial independence. So it reduced the scope of offences subject to the full rigours of the system:
  - Court martials were used to try sensitive cases to avoid publicity.
  - The Minister of Justice could order a trial to be held in private.
  - Crimes against the state could be heard in special courts without a jury.
- Judges lost their security of tenure and many were appointed directly from the Ministry of Justice.
- The Justices of the Peace were abolished, their judicial functions mainly passed over to the Land Captains.

The result of the counter-reforms was a huge increase in the centralisation of power. The central ministries and through them local government officials gained much more overall control.

Repression

Following the assassination of Alexander II in 1881, a nationwide police offensive led to 10,000 arrests and the emergency measures of that year saw a crackdown on anybody connected with terrorist or revolutionary activities. The *Okhrana* took shape as a sinister and effective body. It recruited thousands of informers and agents who penetrated revolutionary groups to uncover terrorist conspiracies and sow confusion. Many masqueraded as cab drivers to listen in to conversations; most post offices had a room where mail was read. As the decade progressed, thousands suspected of being a danger to the state, many innocent, were arrested and sent into exile. Once the censorship laws were tightened it was difficult to express a dissident opinion.

Despite this repressive climate, revolutionary parties continued to spring up representing a range of socialist views, some targeting propaganda at workers rather than peasants, but most were short-lived. The People's Will was greatly weakened in this period and never really recovered. In part this was due to police action – every terrorist act was followed by a wave of arrests – but it was also due to the revulsion felt by the public to its violent tactics and the assassination of the Tsar. Under Alexander III, violence was kept under control but the more plots that were uncovered by *Okhrana*, the more government officials were convinced that terrorists were lurking everywhere. One such plot to assassinate the Tsar in 1887 involved a young man called Alexander Ulyanov. He, along with four others, was hanged. He had a younger brother, Vladimir, later to be known as Lenin.

Other more progressive policies

Alexander III's reign was not one of complete reaction. Alexander threw himself behind policies of modernisation and industrialisation and there were a number of reforms.

Economic development

Alexander supported successive finance minsters – Bunge, Vyshnegradsky and Witte – in laying down the basis for future development and creating the industrial spurt of the 1890s. This included railway building, encouraging

Konspiratsia

A murky world of spies and double agents – *konspiratsia* – operated around the big cities. In 1881 Georgii Sudeiken was given responsibility for maintaining public order in St Petersburg, recruiting agents to gain information about potential attacks. He would arrest a revolutionary, 'soften' them up in solitary confinement, then 'persuade' them to become a police spy. In 1882 he turned a prominent member of The People's Will, Sergei Dagaev, into a police spy. But other revolutionaries became suspicious and made Dagaev confess; thereupon they ordered him to murder Sudeiken. This he did with two accomplices.

foreign investment, tariff protection to protect fledgling industries, building up gold reserves and exporting grain to pay for foreign imports and pay interest on foreign loans (see pages 51–53 for a full explanation).

Bunge introduced a number of measures between 1882 and 1897 (see below) to help peasants and improve the living and working conditions of the growing number of workers. Vyshnegradsky ignored the social aspects and ramped up taxes and tariffs to force the peasants to sell more grain. Grain exports increased, but the peasants suffered. Matters reached a head in 1891–92 when harvest failures in the Volga region caused a massive famine while the government carried on exporting grain (see page 82).

Financial and social measures

- 1883–87 Bunge abolished the poll tax and lowered redemption payments but later Vyshnegradsky increased indirect taxes so that the overall tax burden on the peasants was not much changed.
- 1883 the Peasants' Land Bank was set up to help peasants buy land.
- 1885 the Nobles' Land Bank was established, lending money to nobles at low interest rates to pay off debts or invest in land.
- Some measures were taken to improve the lives of workers but they had limited impact. Laws were passed to restrict child labour, limit working hours for women at night, reduce fines for workers, and to provide compulsory education for younger factory children. A factory inspectorate was established to monitor living and working conditions.

LOOK AGAIN

Think back to your assessment of Alexander II and in particular to the criticisms of his reforms. Do you view him and the reforms differently after your work on Alexander III? Or do you feel the son deserves credit for the peace and security he brought to Russia during his reign?

The national minorities and the policy of Russification

What was government policy towards the nationalities?

Ethnic Russians made up around half of the population of the Russian Empire. The other half represented a huge range of culturally diverse ethnic groups as you can see in Figure 2. Many of these resented Russian control and this led to civil disobedience, riots and disturbances in different parts of the Empire. Particularly disturbing for the autocracy was the Polish Revolt of 1863 which seemed to show the development of national elites could lead to dangerous national liberation movements. As a result the government came up with an ethnic strategy – Russification – which meant inculcating across the whole Empire a sense of belonging to Russia.

Nationality	Millions
Russian	55.6
Ukrainian	22.4
Polish	7.9
White Russian	5.8
Jewish	5.0
Kirgiz	4.0
Tartar	3.4
Finnish	3.1
German	1.8
Latvian	1.4

Nationality	Millions
Bashkir	1.3
Lithuanian	1.2
Armenian	1.2
Romanian/Moldavian	1.1
Estonian	1.0
Murdrinian	1.0
Georgian	0.8
Turkmenian	0.3
Tadzhik	0.3

▲ **Figure 2** The major nationalities by mother tongue, 1897. White Russians are the people who live in the area we now call Belorussia.

Pobedonostsev was determined to see the Orthodox Church at the centre of Russification and directed religious policy to this end. He not only desired that all citizens of the Empire should become Orthodox Christians, he also believed that non-Orthodox subjects must be disloyal. Orthodox churches and cathedrals were built all over the Empire and the clergy was increased to fill them. Even as far afield as central Asia, the Orthodox Church carried out a policy of mainly forced conversion with perhaps 100,000 Muslim Tartars becoming Christians (though many subsequently reverted to Islam). There was a determined attempt to exert control over previously autonomous Churches like the Georgian Orthodox Church, where troops were used to try to pull clergy into line. There was a campaign to supplant the Lutheran Church in the Baltic provinces; landless Orthodox peasants were provided with land to farm and money was poured into Orthodox-controlled schools. It is estimated that 37,000 Lutherans converted to Orthodoxy during Alexander III's reign. In the capitals of Estonia and Latvia, huge onion-domed cathedrals were built, which Geoffrey Hosking likens to 'alien monsters looming over ... medieval architecture'. It is not surprising that this religious dimension of Russification created enormous hostility among the national minorities. The various Churches, which included the Catholic Church in Poland, and religious sects deeply resented government interference in their religious practices.

Nationalities had to adopt the Russian language, culture, customs and religion, thereby losing their own national identity. This process began under Alexander II but was promoted most vigorously by Alexander III and carried on by Nicholas II. In practice it meant that the Russian language was used in schools, law courts and regional government. Also Russian officials were brought in to run regional governments in non-Russian parts of the empire like Poland, Latvia and Finland. Usually it was Russians who got the important jobs in government and state-sponsored industry. What made it worse was that the minorities had to pay large sums to the imperial treasury.

The emphasis on the superiority of the Russian way of life infuriated the national minorities who saw Russification as a fundamental attack on their way of life, their national and cultural heritage, and a monstrously unfair policy that discriminated against them. This was especially true in respect of religion.

The tsarist government underestimated the strength of nationalism and its focus on Russification and the transformation of minority nations only served to inflame it. During the nineteenth century there were a number of uprisings and protests from national groups seeking greater personal freedom and more autonomy (self-government) in their parts of the Empire. These tended to occur in one region at a time and the tsarist government was able to suppress them. It seems strange that the government sought to antagonise and alienate such a large section of its population. It drove many into the ranks of the revolutionaries. In the end Russification weakened the Empire.

The experience of different national groups varied; not all opposed the tsarist regime. We can look at some examples.

The Poles

The Poles were on the edges of the Empire and never wanted to be under tsarist rule. It was a sensitive region. Alexander II's reforms had restored a degree of autonomy but this only raised expectations and the Poles wanted more independence. In 1863 Polish rebels attacked what they saw as a pro-Russian regional government and a year of insurrection followed. This was put down but the regime regarded the Poles as disloyal. Hundreds of Polish noblemen were exiled to Siberia and their estates given over to incoming Russians. Polish serfs were given more generous terms of emancipation than Russian ones in an attempt to secure their loyalty to the Russian state and prevent more disturbances. But at the same time the policy of Russification was intensified, particularly under Alexander III. The Polish language was prohibited in schools and colleges. Russians took the top jobs in government, for instance, Russians replaced Polish executives and engineers on the railway system; even railway announcements were in Russian. The industrial change and social upheaval that affected the whole empire led many Poles into revolutionary groups and they were one of the first national groups to take advantage of the opportunities presented by the 1905 revolution.

The Ukrainians

The nationalist movement was not so strong in Ukraine although Ukrainians suffered a similar treatment to the Poles. There had been a big influx of Russians and they had taken key positions in government. Most of the elites in Ukraine were Russian, Jewish, German or Polish.

Ukraine was very important to Russia as the people made up the second largest ethnic group in the Empire and produced a good deal of its grain. But Ukrainians were more integrated in the Empire, and included the Cossacks who were loyal supporters of the Tsar. There was a developing Ukrainian intelligentsia and Ukrainian cultural societies were being formed in the towns. There was some attempt to develop a literary language but the Tsar, mindful of how this might encourage nationalism, issued a decree prohibiting the publication of books in Ukrainian and the use of Ukrainian in the theatre.

Jewish people

Jewish people, who formed a sizeable ethnic group, around 5 million in the 1880s – were forced to live in an area called the Pale of Settlement on the eastern borders of Poland, Ukraine and White Russia. Here they faced prejudice and persecution with restrictions on their way of life. Most lived in poverty. Under Alexander II, wealthier, educated or skilled Jewish people were allowed to settle in other parts of the Empire but this was stopped after the Polish Revolt in 1863 and Jewish people's civil rights were restricted.

Under Alexander III they faced a wave of antisemitism. Both Alexander III and Pobedonostsev supported pogroms and attacks on them, which they viewed as 'justified' because of the involvement of some Jewish people in the revolutionary groups of the 1870s. Religious hatred also played a part, with Jewish people seen as 'Christ killers' and thus 'legitimate' targets.

Over the thirteen years of Alexander's reign, various rules and bans were imposed on them. Jewish people:

- were not allowed to own property and land in rural areas, even inside the Pale
- could not hold government office, run schools or appeal against a court sentence
- could be deported if they lived outside the Pale, for example, in 1891 Jewish people were expelled from Moscow
- were not allowed to work in the legal, military or medical professions
- had restrictions placed on their entrance to universities and secondary schools
- were denied the vote in *zemstva* and municipal elections
- were forced to sell up businesses, and their rights to trade or sell products, for example, liquor, were restricted.

WORKING TOGETHER

Research

Investigate some of the other national minority groups:
- the Finns
- the Baltic area groups, for example, Estonians and Latvians
- the Caucasus groups, for example, Georgians and Armenians
- Muslims of central Asia, for example, in Turkestan.

You could take a nationality each and report back your findings.

In each case:
- give brief details of their relationship with Russia (e.g. how they came to belong to Russia)
- describe the stage of development (or not) of their national identity
- explain whether they were antagonistic towards the tsarist regime or more integrated.

In the early 1880s there were a series of pogroms carried out in a number of cities. These involved armed groups breaking into Jewish homes, destroying and stealing property, beating men up and raping women, even murder. The local authorities and police turned a blind eye or were involved themselves. Agents from the Ministry of the Interior backed or even planned pogroms along with extremist antisemitic groups. Pogroms were particularly bad after 1905 (see page 90).

All in all it amounted to a pervasive attack on Jewish people's civil rights and their ability to live and work in Russia. This continued throughout the reign of Nicholas II who was deeply antisemitic. As a result, huge numbers of Jewish people emigrated to the USA and western Europe, particularly in the 1880s. But a large number of others, unsurprisingly, joined revolutionary groups. Jewish people were a significant part of the Russian intelligentsia and were attracted by socialism and Marxism. In 1897 Jewish people formed their own 'Bund' or union which played a role in the development of the social democratic movement. Jewish people made up a disproportionate number of the leading members of the Bolshevik Party including Leon Bronstein (Trotsky), Martov, Zinoviev and Kamenev.

The death of Alexander III

Alexander III died suddenly on 1 November 1894 of a kidney complaint; he was 49. His father had shaken the personalised power structure of the autocracy. Alexander III's policies of repression had restored the regime's political authority and given Russia thirteen years of peace. In doing this he had abandoned any attempt to build the institutions of civic society based on the rule of law. He had strengthened traditional elites and antagonised social and ethnic groups throughout the Empire. The educated intelligentsia had become alienated and many fled abroad, some to plan revolution. Those who hoped for more representation in government at local or national level were left frustrated and angry. Alexander had done his son no favours. He had pressed ahead with industrialisation but had not provided any mechanisms to deal with the social pressures and tensions this generated. All the regime could fall back on was repression to maintain order and stability.

KEY DATES: ALEXANDER III, 1881–94

1881 Alexander III becomes tsar.

1881 Statute of State Security – emergency powers introduced.

Okhrana (secret police) established.

1883 Over the course of several years the poll tax was abolished.

1883 Peasants' Land Bank set up.

1884 University Statute – stricter controls on universities.

1885 Nobles' Land Bank set up.

1889 Office of Land Captain established.

1890 *Zemstva* Act.

1892 Municipal Government Act.

1894 Death of Alexander.

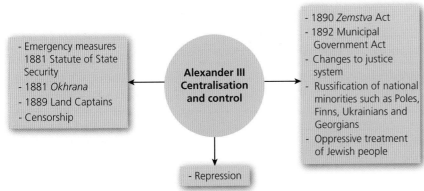

▲ **Figure 3** Centralisation and control under Alexander III

3 Modernisation, 1880–1914

Russia lagged far behind its Western competitors in industrial and technological capacity. It had to industrialise to have any hope of matching countries like the USA, Germany, Britain and France and maintain its world power status. A strong industrial base was needed to provide the military with equipment required for modern warfare, as the Crimean War had shown. Throughout the period 1880 to 1914 the government was highly focused on producing ships, weapons, munitions and related materials. Sergei Witte, Finance Minister 1892–1903, made it clear in his public statements and papers that the dominant motive behind his industrialisation policy was to allow Russia to catch up with the more developed powers, 'particularly in her potential to produce the means of national power, above all armaments'.

Russia was a poor agricultural country where many of the peasants relied on subsistence farming. This dependence on agriculture left it subject to the vagaries of the weather and harvests. It needed to develop its own resources – huge reserves of oil, iron, coal and timber – and build an industrial base to produce manufactured goods, rather than rely on imports. It also needed to take surplus labour off the overcrowded land and generate more wealth.

NOTE-MAKING

Make notes under the following headings:
- Industrial development before 1890
- Witte's personality, abilities, strengths
- Witte's industrial strategy
- Evidence of success
- Criticisms of Witte
- Depression after 1899
- Industrial growth after 1908

Industrialisation

How did industry develop in Russia?

At the beginning of the 1860s industry mainly took the form of:

- state-run factories manufacturing essential goods for the military – uniforms, arms, gunpowder, etc. – using serfs or peasants renting state land
- domestic craft-based industry carried out in the homes of peasants – weaving, spinning, making articles out of wood or bone
- artels – workshops making all sorts of products in metal, leather and other materials for the local domestic market.

The only privately funded industries which were more advanced and on a larger scale were textiles and the sugar industry. The cotton industry was to be found in larger factories in and around St Petersburg, producing 90 per cent of domestic demand. The sugar industry, based in Ukraine, was increasingly mechanised and reduced the reliance on imported sugar.

Alexander II began the process of industrialisation, and under him industry expanded significantly in old and new areas. Much of this was achieved through the use of foreign expertise. The British played an important role in developing large-scale textile factories. In 1868 Alexander invited John Hughes from south Wales to come to Russia to demonstrate what could be achieved by modern methods in iron and steel. This resulted in the establishment of the huge works in the Donbass (part of Ukraine). The Nobel brothers got the oil industry going in the Caucasus. But there was also home-grown industry producing engineering products, particularly for the burgeoning railway industry. Between 1866 and 1881 the number of miles of railway increased from 3,000 to 13,270.

Hughesovka

A case study in foreign involvement in Russian industrialisation

John Hughes had developed his iron-making skills in south Wales where he was born. He had patented inventions in armaments and armour plating and in 1864 had supplied the latter to the Russian naval base at Kronstadt. In 1868, he had been invited by the Russian government to take up a concession, involving land and mineral rights in the Donbass. He set up the New Russia Company Limited with capital of £300,000 from British shareholders. He sailed to Russia in 1870 accompanied by about 100 mostly Welsh ironworkers and miners. There he built a steel works and developed coal and iron ore mines. The settlement was called Yuzovka (Hughesovka). Hughes died in 1889 but his sons took over and the works expanded rapidly in the industrial boom of the 1890s. At the beginning of the twentieth century the population of Yuzovka had reached about 50,000 (one-quarter of whom worked for the New Russia Company) and it was the largest steel works in Russia. Taken over by the Bolsheviks in 1919, it became one of the largest metallurgical centres in the Soviet Union. Its name was changed to Stalino but in 1961 it received its present name, Donetsk.

Witte's industrial strategy

Alexander III threw all his weight behind the industrialisation drive. He may have rejected Western political ideas but he did not reject the economic development necessary for great power status. The drive for industrialisation was a top-down, state-sponsored model to an extent unequalled by any Western country. One reason for this was that Russia did not have a strong entrepreneurial middle class which had the knowledge and expertise to set up and run new industries.

Alexander's early finance minsters laid the groundwork for industrial development. They expanded the railways and encouraged investment. They had brought in progressively higher tariffs through the 1880s to protect the development of Russian industry, for instance by 1891 the duty on raw materials had risen to 30 per cent of their value, allowing the iron industry in southern Russia to develop supplies of coal and iron. But it was the appointment of Sergei Witte, Finance Minister from 1892 to 1903, that proved the real turning point in the story of Russian industrialisation. It was not that his policies were so different from his predecessors', it was the scale and energy that he brought to bear, and his ability to create a climate conducive to industrial development, that gave Russian industry its impetus.

Witte's programme for industrial growth

1 State-sponsored development of heavy industry
2 Foreign loans, investment and expertise
3 High tariffs on foreign industrial goods
4 Strong rouble, adoption of gold standard
5 Raised taxation rates
6 Exports of grain

1 State-sponsored development of heavy industry

Witte launched Russia into an age of heavy industry. He believed that iron, coal and steel industries would form the basis for industrial development as they had done in western European economies. He used the railways as a springboard. Witte had 'a kind of holy passion for railways' and saw them as agents of civilisation and progress. They would link up the vast spaces and the people, farms and factories of the Empire. They would carry the products of the new industry to market and raw materials to factories and industrial plants.

Railway growth (in miles of track)	
1866	3,000
1881	13,270
1891	19,510
1900	33,270
1913	43,850

▲ **Figure 3** Railway growth between 1866 and 1913.

Vodka

The state made a huge amount of money from sales of vodka. In 1894 it was made a state monopoly (duties had been charged on it before) and by 1910 this produced one-quarter of state revenue.

For example, new markets were found in Europe and raw material for cotton textiles were sourced in Asia. Railways would help open up the new oilfields in the Caucasus. More distant areas could be opened up for the supply of food and grain to the cities, encouraging more efficient farming.

Railways also served another purpose: they stimulated the metallurgical, engineering and coal industries. By the end of the 1890s, nearly 60 per cent of all iron and steel was consumed by the railways: four-fifths of locomotives were built in Russia. Witte's most famous project was the Trans-Siberian Railway across Russia which involved 25 factories producing 39 million roubles worth of rails, and other Russian manufacturers producing 1,500 locomotives and 30,000 wagons. There was a railway boom in the 1890s and the extent of railway tracks nearly doubled (see Figure 3).

To achieve this, Witte invested millions of roubles of state money directly into the railways and heavy industry. By 1899, the state bought almost two-thirds of all metallurgical production, controlled 70 per cent of the railways and owned numerous mines and oilfields. Witte also offered loans, subsidies and guarantees of profits to private companies. This was state sponsorship on a massive scale. Witte believed that this was the only way to kick-start industrialisation. Once it had taken off, private businessmen would run and develop industries.

2 Foreign loans, investment and expertise

The state did not have the money in its coffers to pay for this level of state expenditure, so Witte negotiated huge loans, particularly from the French. He also drew in foreign investors to put money into Russian joint-stock companies. By 1900, one-third of the capital in these companies had been invested by foreigners. If you consider industrial enterprises separately, the figure is nearer 45 per cent.

Witte encouraged more foreign companies, engineers and experts (like the Hughes family) from France, Britain, Germany and other European countries to contribute their commercial and technological expertise (16 foreign companies in 1888, 269 in 1900). They were particularly evident in the new industrial areas in the south and in the oil industry. Witte encouraged the growth of private enterprise and, although his critics accused him of creating a dangerous and shameful dependence on foreigners, a new class of go-ahead Russian industrialists, entrepreneurs and businessmen began to emerge, especially in Moscow.

3 High tariffs on foreign industrial goods

Witte continued the policy of high tariffs on foreign imports to protect domestic industries from foreign competition. This meant that companies in Russia bought home-produced iron, steel and other products and less money flowed out of Russia.

4 Strong rouble, adoption of gold standard

A stable currency was essential to attract capital from abroad. Russia had built up its gold reserves and in 1897 adopted the gold standard for the rouble. This meant that exchange rates for the rouble were fixed against other gold-backed currencies, which provided added security for foreign investors.

5 Raised taxation rates

To get revenue for the state Witte raised indirect taxes on everyday items such as kerosene, matches and vodka. This hit the peasants hard and they had to sell more grain to pay their taxes. This allowed Witte to increase grain exports to sell abroad. Workers' wages were kept low so that money went back into industrial development rather than into wage bills.

6 Exports of grain

Grain was an essential element in Witte's strategy. Grain exports were the main means by which Russia could earn more foreign currency to pay the high interest charged on foreign loans and for foreign imports. So the more grain the better.

Did Witte's strategy work?

Witte was squeezing the people very hard but he hoped that industrial growth would take off and create more wealth for everyone before it hurt too much. Up to 1900, his plan seemed to be working. There was a great industrial spurt in the 1890s and the growth rate hit nine per cent. Between 1890 and 1900:

- the production of iron and steel had risen from 9 to 76 million *poods* a year (1 *pood* = 36.11 pounds)
- coal output tripled
- the production of cotton cloth increased by two-thirds.

Russia was now a major world producer of iron, steel and oil. Vast new areas of heavy industry producing iron and coal had opened up in places like the Donbass, and the oil industry in Caucasus had grown rapidly. The industrial areas in St Petersburg and Moscow were buzzing with activity. By 1900 Moscow was the fastest growing city east of New York and one of the ten biggest cities in the world.

But an international recession which started in 1899 put a sudden stop to expansion. Russia entered a deep depression which affected all areas of the economy. The areas that had been growing fast were the areas that were particularly hard hit: in the Donbass region, by 1903, only 23 of the 35 blast furnaces were working and mines were closing. There was also a slump in the oil industry. The railway industry was badly hit and the metal working industry in St Petersburg suffered from falling government orders resulting in the closure of many small firms. Output in basic industries such as iron, oil and coal fell. By 1903 Witte had lost the support of the Tsar and was dismissed. Just as there were signs of recovery emerging in 1903, the Russo-Japanese War and the 1905 revolution held up further industrial development.

Criticisms of Witte's policies

- The interest rates to service foreign debt were very high and a major drain on resources. By 1900, twenty per cent of the budget was used to pay off foreign debt, ten times as much as was spent on education.
- Witte prioritised heavy industry over light industry. This meant that the smaller, sophisticated machine tool and electrical industries that would have reduced the need for imports and helped modernise manufacturing were not developed sufficiently.
- Witte neglected agriculture, which suffered from under-investment.
- He prioritised industrial development over welfare of the population. The very rapid industrialisation meant that working and living conditions for workers in the towns and cities were appalling (see section on social change on page 61). This created social discontent, strikes and general unrest. Witte did little to alleviate these conditions.
- He failed to develop a market in consumer products which would have made life more tolerable for ordinary people. High tariffs on foreign industrial commodities made many goods very expensive for Russians to buy, especially agricultural machinery.

Sergei Witte, 1849–1915

Witte was born in Tiflis in Georgia in 1849 and spent his early years in the Caucasus where he became an expert in railway administration. This led to his appointment in 1889 to the railway department of the Ministry of Finance. His growing reputation saw him soon promoted in 1892 to the post of Minister of Communications and then to Minister of Finance in 1893. It was in this role that he drove the push for industrialisation.

He was the dominant figure of turn-of-the century Russian politics, physically imposing with a massive head and torso on short legs. But he was not popular with the royal court and some high-ranking government officials. He was an outsider, with a background in business, who was married to a Jewish divorcee, and they did not trust or like him. This was in part because he was a difficult personality to deal with, described variously as ill-mannered, tricky, evasive, boastful and quarrelsome.

However, he was also very energetic, highly organised with immense administrative abilities. Intellectually, he towered above the officials and politicians of the time.

Witte was not above the relentless intrigue of Russian government and society. He handed out houses, apartments and bonuses to his minions and allies and gifts to journalists for favourable coverage. He developed a close relationship with the *Okhrana* and his underlings in the Finance Ministry were tasked with overhearing and recording the conversations of rivals. He made the Finance Ministry (with responsibility for communications, commerce and industry) all powerful, with a budget several times that of the Ministry of the Interior and the police.

This attracted jealousy and immense criticism from conservative elements in the government and court circles who did not like the changes he was implementing and thought he was undermining social order. After a decade at the top, the endless attacks and societal critics of his harsh taxation policies contributed to his dismissal in 1903. Nicholas II had lost confidence in him.

Although Witte was a firm supporter of the autocracy, by 1905 he had come to believe that some constitutional reform was necessary as part of the process of modernising Russia. Nicholas brought him back in the midst of the chaos of 1905 to negotiate a successful peace settlement with Japan to end the Russo-Japanese War. Witte was then made Prime Minister, in which role he secured vital loans that kept the regime from bankruptcy. He persuaded Nicholas to sign the October Manifesto granting concessions to the middle classes and establishing a duma or parliament. However, in 1906, when he discovered that Nicholas never intended to honour these concessions, he resigned. For his part, Nicholas never forgave Witte for pushing through constitutional change and Witte was ostracised from the Russian establishment until his death in 1915.

Industrial development, 1908–14

It was only after 1908 that industry began to expand again. Heavy industry was still the driving force. This was in large part due to the government's rearmament programme with huge orders for metallurgical companies to rebuild the Baltic fleet after the losses of the Russo-Japanese War and also to re-stock with weapons generally. P. Gatrell says that 'industrial recovery (1908–13) was a by-product of rearmament'. Industrial production grew steadily at a rate of around six per cent per annum until 1914, although this high rate was largely due to the fact that it started from a low base. Although well behind those of the major Western industrial powers, the achievements were impressive. By 1914, Russia was the world's fourth largest producer of coal, pig iron and steel, and the Baku oilfields were only rivalled by Texas. It was the world's fifth largest industrial power.

Russia had been late to industrialise, but this meant a significant amount of production was carried on in large-scale modern works, employing over 1,000 workers and in some plants tens of thousands, many more than in their counterpart, Germany. The latest most up-to-date technology was being used and technological development was taking place inside Russia. So in this respect Russian industry was quite advanced. The Tsar visited the young aircraft designer Igor Sikorksy, who claimed that Russians would soon overtake their 'foreign teachers'; he had designed the largest aircraft in the world with four engines.

Industrial development was still largely state-led but becoming less so and also less dependent on foreign investment. By 1909–11 domestic investment was three times greater than foreign investment. In the three years leading up to 1913 Russian entrepreneurs were investing in new factories, paper mills, mines and power plants. They had started 774 joint-stock companies, three times as many as were started in Germany in the previous five years. The urban middle classes were involved in stock market speculation. There was a growing internal market and the production of consumer goods rose. Demand was coming from the peasants as the agricultural sector became more successful and prices for farm produce increased. Despite this, as a proportion of total industrial production, the share of consumer goods actually fell from 52 per cent to 45 per cent.

However, there were still structural problems in the Russian economy. The focus on rearmament meant that a coherent plan for developing different sectors of the economy never materialised and so a more balanced economy was not created. For instance, the focus on military requirements meant that industry could not meet the demand for agricultural tools and machinery. The chemical and machine tools industries remained weak, so these goods were still being bought from abroad. Food processing supplied a disproportionate amount – around 50 per cent – of total industrial production and one-third of the entire factory labour force worked in the textile industry. Also, industry was heavily concentrated in areas such as the Dombass and around Moscow and St Petersburg; so it was not spread evenly across Russia.

Russian industry was a peculiar mixture. Although there were large-scale modern works, there were also a huge number of small-scale craft workshops. According to Alec Nove, 67 per cent of industrial workers worked in these small-scale workshops but they only produced 33 per cent of total industrial output. This meant that their productivity was low. Russian industry had taken great strides forward but it was still a work in progress.

	Coal	Pig iron	Oil	Grain
1870	0.68	0.33	0.03	–
1880	3.24	0.42	0.5	–
1890	5.90	0.89	3.9	–
1900	16.10	2.66	10.2	56
1910	26.80	2.99	9.4	74
1913	35.40	4.12	9.1	90
1916	33.80	3.72	9.7	64

▲ **Figure 4** The tsarist economy: annual production (million tons), 1870–1916.

Some historians consider that the economy was stabilising and set to do well if growth rates had continued at the same pace. Alexander Gerschenkron, a Russian-American economist, thought that the signs were so encouraging that, if the First World War had not occurred, Russia was well on the way to developing into a successful modern industrial state. Others, more pessimistic, contend that, despite its growth, Russia was still backward in many respects and falling behind more advanced industrialised countries, especially in terms of production per head of the population. Peter Waldron in Extract B on page 77 says that Russia had a long way to go before it could be said to have successfully modernised.

Comparing Russia with other countries

- Per capita income in Russia in 1913 was one-tenth that of the USA and one-fifth that of Britain.
- Per-capita output was only half that of the Austro-Hungarian Empire.
- Industrial growth was still less rapid than in the USA and Germany so the gap in productive capacity widened.

1913	Russia	USA	UK
Electricity (milliard kWhs)	2.0	25.8	4.7
Coal (million tons)	29.2	517.8	292.0
Oil (million tons)	10.3	34.0	–
Pig iron (million tons)	4.2	31.5	10.4
Steel (million tons)	4.3	31.8	7.8
Cotton textiles (milliard metres)	1.9	5.7	7.4

▲ **Figure 5** Industrial output in Russia, the USA and the UK, 1913.

Country	1894 roubles per capita	1913 roubles per capita	Growth (%)
United Kingdom	273	463	70
France	233	355	52
Italy	104	230	121
Germany	184	292	58
Austria-Hungary	127	227	79
Russia (in Europe)	67	101	50

▲ **Figure 6** National income by country, in 1894 and 1913.

What do Figures 5 and 6 tell you about the economic performance of Russia in comparison with other countries?

Agriculture, 1880–1914

Was there a crisis in agriculture in Russia and was it making progress?

The traditional view of Russian agriculture in the half century after the emancipation was that it failed to make real progress and continued to produce low yields, made worse by a rapidly increasing population which put pressure on the land, leading to the impoverishment of peasants. Recent evidence suggests that the performance of the agricultural economy was much better than previously thought. What emerges is an uneven picture with some areas doing better than others.

Agricultural production was stagnant between the 1860s and 1880. The practice of agriculture changed little in the years immediately following emancipation especially under the influence of the conservative *Mir*. Peasants continued to farm using the strip system and yields remained low. Many peasants had to rent land from estate owners to supplement their own strips and often paid for this with labour on the estate, as did those who fell into debt, owing rent arrears or redemption payments, etc. This was most commonly the case in the traditional centres of agricultural production – the Black Earth region in the central areas and the Volga.

WORKING TOGETHER
Collecting evidence

Work in pairs or groups of four. One person/pair collects evidence to support the claim that agriculture was improving and changing for the better, the other that there was still a crisis in agriculture, with impoverished peasants and limited improvements. You will add to this when you look at Section 4 on the peasants (see page 63).

When you have done this, both sides can present their evidence to support their side of the argument. Make sure you get copies of each other's work.

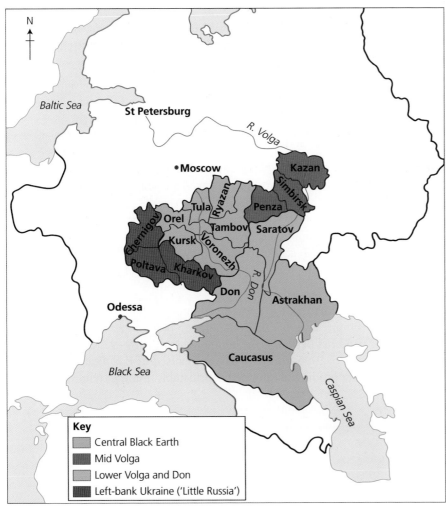

▲ **Figure 7** Map showing the central agricultural regions.

Key
- Central Black Earth
- Mid Volga
- Lower Volga and Don
- Left-bank Ukraine ('Little Russia')

Change and geographical variations

The situation began to change after 1880. Some peasants were taking advantage of the market in land that had opened up as a result of emancipation. Peasants could now buy and sell land – aided by the creation of the Peasants' Land Bank in 1883 – and they could take advantage of the large quantities being put on the market by the nobility. Between 1877 and 1905 the amount of land owned by the peasants grew from 6 million to 21.6 million hectares. By 1905, 27 per cent of landlord land had passed to the peasantry. More than this, the peasants were renting land from the nobility in ever increasing amounts, much more than they bought. By 1913 peasants owned 66 per cent of arable land and rented more. It is now argued that yields were higher on peasant land.

Agricultural production grew rapidly. Grain production grew by 2.1 per cent annually between 1883 and 1914, or by 1.1 million tons per year. This kept it ahead of the substantial increase in population. But this picture of growth conceals great geographical variations in production and it was in the central agricultural region that production was weakest. There are various reasons for this:

- The amount of land received by each peasant household after emancipation was less than previously farmed.
- The communes were conservative and used old-fashioned agricultural methods.
- The huge increase in population (from 50 to 79 million during 1861–97) created pressure on the land. When land was repartitioned, households ended up with smaller, less efficient units.

Stephen Wheatcroft argues that it is here that you can identify the signs of agricultural crisis and low yields. This was a huge area and the most densely populated part of rural Russia and there was considerable poverty.

Outside of this central area there was more prosperity and progress:

- In parts of the Baltic, landowners with access to Western grain markets had established capitalist farms worked by wage-labourers.
- In western Ukraine there were huge sugar-beet farms.
- In the fertile regions of the south, mixed farms were producing grain and other products (see below).
- In western Siberia, with access to markets by way of the Trans-Siberian Railway, peasants were producing cereals, livestock and dairy products, particularly butter.

Historians now consider that there was a real improvement in food supply throughout the Empire and that the consumption of grain per head had increased. For two brief periods – the famine years of 1889–92 and the revolutionary years of 1905–07 – bad harvests caused by bad weather and drought meant that production dropped considerably. But the trend was upward.

New methods and approaches

The commune was not such a barrier to change as has been thought (although it remained conservative in the central region). In more fertile regions pastureland and meadow was used to produce arable crops. Some communities started to use different crop rotations, new varieties of crops, fertilisers, iron instead of wooden ploughs and other new methods. Potatoes became more important and production grew by 43 per cent between 1880 and 1913. Increasing urbanisation and improved transport also affected areas near large cities and towns, such as Odessa. Here peasants were growing fruit and vegetables or supplying dairy products for the market, giving them increased income. There was also a burgeoning co-operative movement in some villages which provided facilities for credit and savings, such as loans to buy livestock and tools.

It was not just peasants who were adopting new approaches to farming. Although many nobles had sold land or were renting to peasants, others started to build more commercial farming operations to supply markets, using agricultural labourers or, as the beginning of the twentieth century progressed, mechanised equipment such as threshing machines. This was particularly the case after prices for grain and other products rose in the late 1890s.

Stolypin's agrarian reforms

The 1891–92 famine (see page 81) prompted the Russian government to look more closely at agriculture and what they perceived to be a lack of progress. Historians now think that most of the reports they were getting were from the poorly performing traditional agricultural areas where peasant poverty was at its worst. The reports painted a picture of the 'dark masses' – drunken, illiterate, violent and rebellious peasants who needed to be educated. The government was also concerned about the dangerous and threatening peasant disturbances of the early twentieth century and particularly of 1905–06 (see page 82).

Peter Stolypin, who became Prime Minister in 1906, believed that peasant prosperity was the key to political stability and thought his land reforms would transform Russia into a stable and prosperous country. He identified the peasant commune with its antiquated farming methods which 'paralysed personal initiative' as the problem. His reforms, carried out from 1906 to 1911, aimed to:

- allow peasants to leave the *Mir* (commune), to consolidate their strips of land into a single unit
- reduce the power of the *Mir*
- redistribute the land of some nobles
- help go-ahead peasants to buy land from less enterprising peasants and create larger, more efficient, farms.

He called it 'a gamble not on the drunken and feeble but on the sober and strong'. Financial assistance was provided by the Peasant Land Bank to help the independent peasant buy land. Also, he thought that making peasants into independent property owners and giving them full civil rights would give them a stake in the country and lead to them becoming supporters of the regime. Over the next few years there was a transfer of land from the poorer peasants to the more enterprising.

It was a slow process disentangling the land from the commune and trying to ensure that each household gained land equivalent to the quality of the strips they would surrender.

The consolidated holdings took two forms:

● the *khutor* – where the owner lived on land with his own house separate from the village
● the *otrub* – where the owner had land in one unit but lived in the village with rights of access to communal pastures and woods.

The response of the peasantry was mixed. Some relished the chance to escape from the restrictions of the *Mir*. Others saw those who left – the 'Stolypin separators' – as traitors to the peasant tradition. By 1914 only about ten per cent of households in European Russia had set up farms separated from the commune land (see Figure 8, opposite). Of those, only a minority lived on farms in the western European sense, with a cottage and fields fenced off from their neighbours. The reform was more successful in the west – in Ukraine and Belorussia – than in other parts of Russia where reform was most needed, especially the densely populated central regions.

The view of Abraham Ascher is that, 'given more time for implementation, the agrarian reforms might have contributed to a more moderate revolution than the one of 1917'. Judith Pallot argues that, 'Stolypin's reforms were "in essence a utopian project", and too narrowly conceived to create a loyal peasantry and modernise peasant farming – there were alternatives which could have done as much if not more to increase peasant farm productivity.' She points out that some go-ahead communes were employing new methods and new crops (see above) while some 'separators', eager to make a quick profit, used poor farming methods that exhausted the soil.

By 1914, Russia had become the largest cereal exporter in the world. Investment in agricultural machinery rose at an annual rate of nine per cent between 1891 and 1913. Potatoes, dairy products and sugar beet were being produced for the market on a large scale. On the other hand, over-concentration on grain production for export contributed to the failure of livestock to keep pace with population increase. While the total number of horses, pigs and sheep increased, the number per capita fell. In 1914, the vast majority of agricultural production, in what was still an overwhelmingly agricultural country, was the responsibility of 20 million peasant households, most of whom were still organised in rural communes, many of which used traditional, old-fashioned methods of farming. The three-field strip system was still in common use as were wooden ploughs and there was a lack of capital and draft animals. Large parts of the agricultural sector of the economy remained unmodernised despite the improvements in overall production.

Year	Independent households
1907	48,271
1908	508,334
1909	579,409
1910	342,245
1911	145,567
1912	122,314
1913	134,554
1914	97,877

▲ **Figure 8** The number of peasant households becoming independent 1907–14 (out of an estimated total of 10–12 million households).

4 Social and cultural change, 1880–1914

Modernisation and industrialisation had a huge impact on Russian society between 1880 and 1914. Major Russian cities were evidence of the social and cultural changes taking place. By 1914 they had electric street lighting, cinemas, theatres, the opera and ballet, new museums, large department stores and a popular press. They also had huge industrial factories, myriad small workshops, dank tenement buildings and cholera. St Petersburg was the most expensive and the most unhealthy city in the world.

Social change, 1880–1914

How was Russia affected by industrialisation and urbanisation?

The pace of economic change was reflected in the social upheaval which Russia underwent in the period 1880–1914. Cities and towns grew rapidly and introduced a new social environment. Urbanisation also had a huge impact on the lives of peasants. Russian society became more complex as the working class and middle class developed and the role of nobles was in a state of flux.

An important factor in this period of rapid social change was the huge increase in population. The total number of inhabitants of the Russian Empire grew from 74 million in 1858 to 128 million in 1897 to 178 million in 1914. Around 80 per cent were peasants. This had a huge impact on the countryside but it was the growth of the cities that was most startling.

Between 1863 and 1914 the population of St Petersburg had quadrupled to 2.2 million (see figure 9). Moscow had more than 1.7 million inhabitants by 1914. And these growing cities were full of peasants working in factories and as street vendors, builders, shop assistants and domestics. In 1890 over two-thirds of the population of St Petersburg had been born outside the city; in Moscow the proportion was even higher.

The workers

The workforce grew rapidly in the 1880s and especially the 1890s. By 1900, the urban workers numbered around 3 million although this was only 2.5 per cent of the total population. Around one-third had fathers who had been industrial workers. The rest, ex-peasants, retained their family and village connections and many returned at harvest time to work on the land. Even in 1907 half of Moscow printers, the aristocracy of the working class, still kept farms in their home villages while 90 per cent sent money back to relatives. So there was constant interaction between town and country.

Source C *The End of Imperial Russia, 1855–1917* by Peter Waldron, (Palgrave Macmillan), 1997, p82.

Semen Kanatchikov, who went to work in Moscow from his village at the age of 18 in 1895, describes how the peasant patternmakers he worked with 'would every payday without fail send part of their money back to the village … On holidays they attended mass and visited their countrymen and their conversations were mainly about grain, land, the harvest and livestock.'

WORKING TOGETHER

Work in pairs or small groups. Divide a page into two and add two headings: 'Change' and 'Continuity'. Look through this section and identify examples to go under each heading. Write two or three sentences to explain each example or provide some evidence (such as figures). These will be very useful when writing about social change, describing how some things changed but others remained the same or similar. At the end, compare your points with other members of the class.

Year	St Petersburg (in millions)	Moscow (in millions)
1881	0.928	0.753
1890	1.033	1.038
1897	1.265	1.174
1900	1.440	1.345
1910	1.905	1.618
1914	2.218	1.763

▲ **Figure 9** Growth in the population of St Petersburg and Moscow.

Other cities and towns

In 1897 only 19 cities had more than 100,000 inhabitants. By 1914 the population of cities like Riga and Kiev had almost doubled. Only 74 towns had access to electricity and 35 to gas. Homes and streets were mainly lit by kerosene when much of the housing was made from wood, increasing the likelihood of fires. Only around 200 had piped water and 38 a sewage system. Insanitary conditions in cities and towns led to outbreaks of cholera and typhus.

What does Source C suggest about the relationship between city and country?

▲ A soup kitchen for unemployed workers, c.1900.

Working and living conditions

Many workers were employed in large factories containing thousands of workers. But most workers were employed in small workshops in towns or small factories. Wherever they worked, working conditions were grim. Long hours, normally over eleven hours a day but often longer, were compounded by a harsh environment where workers were disciplined and fined for the smallest infractions. Accidents, causing death or serious injury, were common and there was a high rate of disease. Wages were generally low apart from a small section of skilled workers. A few factories had model employers.

In the 1890s employment was not stable or secure: in some factories the labour force changed regularly and employers had a hard job to hang onto workers. At the other extreme it could be difficult to get an unskilled job and many fell into dispiriting destitution. This instability contributed to the volatile nature of the cities.

Some factories had dormitory accommodation attached and it was not unknown for workers coming off shift to get into the beds of the workers going on shift when the factories were kept going 24 hours a day. Living conditions were usually dirty and unsanitary whether in the dormitories or in the huge overcrowded tenement buildings in Moscow and St Petersburg. Privacy was a luxury, with men, women and children living alongside each other, separated only by a curtain – cooking, eating, sleeping and having sex. Workers often slept on plank beds in dirty grease-covered bedding. In smaller workshops some slept around their machines. One immigrant worker was lucky enough to share a private room, which stank of 'humanity', with fifteen other men: he slept on a cot which was full of 'bed bugs and fleas'.

The cities had poor sanitation and were generally very unhealthy. As late as 1911 Stolypin talked of the problems of typhus, smallpox and cholera in St Petersburg where one-third of deaths were caused by infectious diseases. Other cities were no better, although Moscow improved its water supply.

The traditional family structure was dislocated by urbanisation. Fewer townspeople were married or married later and had fewer children. Initially when peasant migrants moved to the cities, wages were too low to support a family living in separate accommodation. Women who moved to cities tended to remain single. This pattern changed as men became more established towards the end of the nineteenth century. Some brought wives from their villages to join them and families grew in size.

Workers' support and associations

Peasants from different regions or villages often worked and lived together to ameliorate the dislocation of moving to the city. Informal organisations of workers (*artels*) rented communal apartments and would employ a woman to cook for them. These co-operative ventures generated a sense of community. There were other things for workers to do. Respectable workers were likely to attend the music hall, tea-drinking clubs, dances and lectures on self-help arranged by mutual aid societies. For instance, the Museum of Assistance to Labour organised free lectures and discussions for workers; these 'People's Universities' offered evening classes. Some Marxist groups invited workers along to reading circles, talks and social events. There were more primary schools in the cities and towns and this was changing aspirations. The literacy rate among male urban workers was high; according to the 1897 census 57.8 per cent could read and among more skilled workers, like metal workers, almost three-quarters were literate. They were reading popular broadsheets, cheap thrillers and political leaflets. These workers, particularly skilled workers, had aspirations to better themselves and improve their quality of life.

Trade unions were illegal until after the 1905 revolution, apart from the Zubatov trade unions (see page 79), but became popular once legalised. It was clear what the workers wanted: higher wages, shorter hours, better working and living conditions and educational opportunities. 'Dignity' ranked high alongside these: workers wanted to be spoken to with respect and not treated to continual physical and, in the case of women, sexual, harassment. However, the government was not addressing their demands or aspirations and did little to improve their working lives or the terrible conditions they lived in. This, along with other factors, prompted workers' action in the 1905 revolution.

Did things improve after 1905?

Despite the upheaval of the 1905 revolution (see pages 91–98) and booming industry after 1908, the Russian government had made no real attempt to improve workers' conditions in contrast to the social reforms enacted elsewhere in Europe. In 1912, limited insurance had been introduced for accidents and sickness but this covered only a minority of the workforce. People still worked long hours for low pay, less than one-third the average in western Europe. In some workplaces their hours were actually increased after 1905 and others were put onto more demanding piece work. For old age, occupational disease and unemployment there was little or no support. There were some more enlightened employers doing more than the law required. For instance, some provided schools for the children of their workers. Housing conditions deteriorated because of the dramatic increase in the workforce between 1910 and 1914 and there was an intolerable strain on public services.

By 1914, the industrial workforce had established itself as a distinct section of the population: a majority of workers who began employment in 1906–13 were the children of workers. The level of literacy among workers reached 64 per cent in 1914 compared with less than 40 per cent for the adult population in general. This was a more articulate proletariat, able to read and absorb literature, including the revolutionary kind.

Co-operative movement

A very successful co-operative movement developed after 1905. Producers' co-operatives operated in both town and country, but in the towns and cities there were also purchasing co-operatives, which could buy goods cheaper in bulk. The biggest co-operative retail store was Moscow's *Kooperatsiya* with thousands of members. There was also a savings bank movement. The Moscow Narody Bank was 85 per cent owned by the co-operative movement.

Women workers

At the turn of the century around 25 per cent of the workforce were women. They formed a higher percentage in the textile factories around St Petersburg and Moscow. They had similar demands to the men and took part in strikes.

The peasants

Historians have disagreed about what was happening to the living standards of the peasants in the period from 1880 to 1913. Many now think that living standards were rising during this period but, as we saw in the section on agriculture, there were regional variations.

Changes in the countryside

In areas outside of the central agricultural regions area, especially those nearest to cities or with access to transport, many peasants enjoyed higher living standards. Quite a lot were producing foodstuffs for the market. These peasants were able to pay their taxes and mortgages with money to spare. This might account for the increased peasant consumption of consumer goods that historians have identified over this period, particularly in the lead up to the First World War. There was also a small but growing class of more prosperous peasants. Some of these were buying or renting land, employing labour, had several animals and were farming more efficiently – *kulaks*. Later on, after the Stolypin reforms some of these would have been the *khutors* farming their consolidated plots (though not all *khutors* succeeded). Others were becoming merchants making money out of trading goods or builders and property developers like Lopakhin in Chekhov's *The Cherry Orchard* (see page 69). Some became involved in industrial ventures. There was, of course, a lot of variation in earnings from those who were just a little bit better off to those who were relatively wealthy. But there was a growing divide between the richest and poorest sections of the peasantry.

Rural areas were changing in other ways, particularly in areas closest to cities and large towns. The money economy was penetrating the countryside: urban factories were replacing old handicrafts and new technologies – railways, roads, the telegraph – were moving closer to the peasantry. Hospitals, schools, reading clubs and libraries were appearing. The number of primary schools quadrupled between 1878 and 1911. Well over half the children of school age (eight to eleven) were enrolled in primary schools by 1911. Literacy rose from 21 per cent in 1897 to 40 per cent in 1914. Orlando Figes says that this gave rise to a class of literate young men and women more conscious of their position.

Figes also identifies a split between younger and older peasants. Younger more literate peasants were better able to deal with new agricultural technologies and the money economy, e.g. contracts and loans. They were more likely to be the Stolypin 'separators' and they were more likely to go to work for periods in the cities. They wanted education and social betterment, were more progressive and nearer to city culture. Older peasants represented the more traditional village trying to stop these influences.

Migrants

Another aspect of change in this period was the increase in migration in the rural community. Some peasants had been forced off the land by poverty, misfortune or their own mismanagement. They worked as agricultural labourers doing seasonal work like ploughing and harvesting. In the winter they searched for work in factories, dockyards, construction and a host of other occupations. By the turn of the century estimates put the number of migrant workers at some 9 million. Hundreds of thousands flooded into the cities. They could form a disoriented and volatile group in the unfamiliar social environment of the city but some peasants saw city jobs as a step-up from working on the land and a chance for social betterment.

Siberia

Around the turn of the century peasants from the overcrowded central regions were encouraged to migrate to Siberia along the Trans-Siberian railway where new farms were opening up, producing grain and dairy products for the market. Some were successful but many failed or were misled by speculators. Thousands (75,000 in 1910) returned home or joined the migrant labour force, often angry and resentful.

Poverty and traditional life

In parts of Russia things did not change much, particularly in the overpopulated central agricultural region where living standards remained low. Here most peasants sold a small amount of produce and perhaps some handicrafts to pay their taxes and buy a few household goods. Otherwise their farming produced enough food to keep them alive. A *zemstvo* survey in the 1880s found that in the central province of Tambov two out of three households could not feed themselves without getting into debt. Large numbers of peasants lived hard, often miserable lives and many died of diseases such as diphtheria, typhus and syphilis. Government policy added to their misery: redemption payments (until 1907), and taxes – especially indirect taxes on everyday items like oil, matches and tobacco – drove some peasants into debt and poverty.

▲ Peasants in a village near Nizhny-Novgorod, c.1891.

The traditional way of life remained and the patriarchal nature of the family household survived – the male was the head of the household, women's rights were restricted although they possessed substantial authority with clearly defined tasks. The villages looked much the same with huts along the main street. The elders ruled the village through the commune. However, Sheila Fitzpatrick makes the point that it would be wrong to assume that villages remained unaffected by modernisation because a large number of peasant households sent members off to work in the industrial towns so they would have one foot in the old world and one in the modern.

The commune remained strong, particularly in the central agricultural region where patterns of landholding remained more or less unchanged right up to 1917. This was shown clearly when Stolypin tried to break up the communes between 1906 and 1914. The separators faced violence and intimidation and troops had to be brought in to make sure the reforms went ahead. Many of those who did separate continued to live in the village rather than separate farmhouses. Communal institutions remained strong, embodying the peasants' notions of social justice: the *Mir* was appreciated by many peasants as a 'life jacket'.

Something else had not changed, expressed by the liberal *zemstvo* man Prince Lvov:

Every single peasant believed from the bottom of his soul that one day, sooner or later, the squire's land would belong to him

There was land shortage and hunger in the central regions and on the periphery of the centre. These peasants still believed that the land belonged to the people who worked it. They wanted to get their hands on the great estates and the lands they rented from the gentry.

The nobles

Life also changed dramatically for the nobility in the decades after emancipation. The traditional view is that they were in decline – they had lost land, serfs, their status and control of the peasantry, and although generously compensated, much of this money had been used to pay off debts and mortgages. An increasing number of nobles sold their land: in 1861 they owned 80 per cent of land, in 1905 only 40 per cent – and they sold it mainly to peasants. An old way of life was ending and many nobles were unhappy to see it disappear. They moved to the cities and towns in ever increasing numbers.

However, historians like Seymour Becker maintain that many nobles successfully adapted to their changing circumstances and forged new careers and paths.

- A relatively small number developed their estates, using modern methods and more agricultural machinery such as threshing machines. These nobles achieved high yields and grew cash crops for the market.
- Many, as they had for centuries, made an income from the military or civil service. They maintained their stranglehold on the top jobs – in 1897, 1,000 of the 1,400 highest ranking civil servants were nobles.
- A significant number moved into the growing professions – medical, legal and education. For example, in 1880 one-fifth of university professors came from the nobility.
- Some became investors in land, bonds or shares in the new companies. The Nobles' Land Bank lent them money at low rates of interest.
- Some got involved in business ventures. Relatively few became industrialists but in Moscow in 1882, 700 nobles owned businesses and nearly 2,500 were employed in commerce, transport or industry.

The nobles still played an influential role in local affairs. They dominated the *zemstva* and regained some control over the peasantry when the office of Land Captain was brought in, during 1889.

However, many older nobles struggled to come to terms with the new world. They felt increasingly threatened, particularly after the 1905 revolution. So they set up the All-Russia Union of Landowners to represent their interests. They opposed Stolypin's reforms and reinforced the regime's conservatism. This was a mistake because, in encouraging the Tsar to reject further reform, they probably contributed to the revolution that in the end swept away all their power, influence and position.

The middle classes

Many historians prefer to talk of middling groups rather than middle classes in Russia because they were not like the bourgeoisie in other parts of Europe. Though small in number – around 2 million – the business and professional classes were growing and playing an increasingly important role in society.

Industry, business and commerce

The rise of the native merchant industrialists has been neglected in Russian history. They made an important contribution to the economy of this period. The Tretyakovs, the Marmontovs, the Morozovs and other families, often from humble origins, made money from railways, banking, textiles and other industries. Some became patrons of the arts (see page 70), others ran town councils; after 1905 they branched out into newspaper and magazine ownership. They also contributed to philanthropic works, financing hospitals, almshouses, hospitals and clinics. It was the merchant mayors who ensured that Moscow had an electric tram system by 1895 and took control of the water supply. They had a contradictory mindset. Deeply religious, often Old Believers (see page 6), they remained loyal to the monarchy and traditions but also adopted Western technology and innovations and educated their sons in Western ideas.

The number of home-grown businessmen was increasing during the twentieth century. By 1914 there were some 2,000 innovative and successful entrepreneurs. Before 1905 industrialists, businessmen and bankers tended to stay out of politics because many needed government business and sponsorship. After 1908 a significant number took up positions in the Duma, representing a wide spread of political opinion, some in Liberal as well as the rightist parties (see pages 99–102). Industrialists and commerical groups did get together to express their views on matters relating to their field and tried to influence government, but it was only after 1905 that this took on a national dimension. In 1906 the Association of Industry and Trade was formed and had considerable political influence.

The professions

There were probably around 1 million professionals by 1914.

- The number of doctors grew from 17,000 in 1897 to 28,000 in 1914.
- The number of teachers had almost doubled between 1906 and 1914 to over 20,000.
- There were 5,000 veterinary surgeons and 4,000 qualified agronomists in 1914.

They formed professional associations to exchange ideas and experiences. For example, in 1892, the first All-Russian Teachers' Congress met and in 1881 the Pirogov Medical Society was set up. Many of these professionals worked for the *zemstva*, forming the 'third element' – lawyers, statisticians, civil engineers, managers, doctors, teachers, vets and agronomists. As we saw on page 19 they began to see themselves as more representative of the nation and able to do a better job of running things than the regime. Professionals were pushing

Timofei and Savva Morozov

Timofei was an innovator who brought in foreign specialists to develop his textile machinery. He also invested in banks and railways. He instigated a ruthless system of fines in his plants whereby a worker could expect to pay back ten per cent of his wages in fines. Eventually his ruthlessness led to a strike of 8,000 workers which was broken up by armed force. Timofei's son, Savva, was affected by this and set about improving the workers' conditions, housing and medical services. He involved himself in the arts, befriended Chekhov and Gorky and even contributed to the funds of the Social Democratic Party (see page 84). In 1914 the Morozovs had four establishments employing 14,000 workers.

Agronomist – A professional concerned with applying science and technology to use plants for food, fuel and fibre.

for further political reform and many joined liberal groups. The regime was worried by the proliferation of these professional associations and they were right to be. The Pirogov ninth congress in 1904 ended in chaos, with demands for a parliament and cries of 'down with the monarchy'.

Middle-class women had made progress, mainly after 1900. Female teachers, doctors and architects were working for the *zemstva*. Ideals of female liberation had spread among the educated classes and some, like Alexandra Kollantai, could be found in Marxist groups. In 1905 university co-education was won. Women's organisations started to spring up across Russia and in 1908 the First All-Russian Congress of Women was held in St Petersburg: half of the delegates earned their living. The women's movement campaigned for sexual and educational equality. Women enjoyed literary, artistic and journalistic successes.

Voluntary organisations and associations

The numbers of middle-class voluntary organisations and associations mushroomed. In Moscow by 1912 there were over 600. Some dealt with serious matters, for example, the Imperial Economic Society debated the great issues of industrialisation. But others were involved with leisure and entertainment, for example, new technology like bicycles and motor cars. Importantly these professional, commercial and recreational groups were creating a more diverse and less homogenous society. The state could not control them or the views being expressed in them though it did subject some associations to surveillance and intimidation. The regime was finding it hard to come to terms with these new ideas and values, many which had Western origins, which accompanied modernisation (see Source D).

Source D *Nicholas II, Emperor of all the Russias* by Dominic Lieven (John Murray), 1993, p179.

Most educated and urban Russians were liberal or radical in their political sympathies, and this sector of Russian society was equal in size to the town population of one of the bigger Western European states. Already by 1914 some Russian newspapers had circulations of over 100,000. This was the world of Stravinsky, Diaghilev and Chagall. It was also the world of rapid industrial growth and of tremendous expansion of administrative and professional middle-class jobs. Such a large, well-educated and sophisticated society demanded civil rights, and a political voice. It looked with disdain and even shame on a political regime which still rested in part on eighteenth-century principles of absolute monarchy and even older, medieval aspects of tsarist ideology.

> Why, according to Source D, did the educated middle classes present a threat to the tsarist regime?

Russian culture, 1860–1914

How were changes in Russian society reflected in literature and art?

Literature

The period around the middle of the nineteenth century and into the 1860s, 1870s and 1880s was a golden age for Russian literature; Turgenev, Tolstoy and Dostoyevsky were writing at this time. It is important for historians studying this period to look at their work because they were writing about social and political issues and about the nature of Russian society. Also, people were reading them in increasing numbers. They influenced the educated elite. The public library in St Petersburg had over half a million books in it.

> **NOTE-MAKING**
>
> List the ways, giving specific examples (evidence) of how literature, art and music reflected Russian society and the changes it was undergoing.

Turgenev in his *Sportsman's Sketches* (1852) considers the real sufferings of Russian serfs, presenting them as human beings when nobles in Russian society treated them as objects to be bought and sold. In *Fathers and Sons* (1862) a young man, Arkady, and his friend, Barazov, return from university influenced by 'nihilisim', causing distress in the family. In the end Barazov, the nihilist, meets an early death while Arkady falls in love and goes back to managing his father's estate. Turgenev also deals sympathetically with the young Russian radicals of the 1870s in *Virgin Soil* (1877) where he portrays the idealism and naivety of the young populists (*narodniks*) who 'go to the people' to educate them and encourage them in peaceful revolution towards socialism.

In the 1860s Chernyshevsky more directly provided inspiration for young revolutionaries, arguing that unhappiness in the world had economic causes only remedied by socialist solutions. His novel *What Is to Be Done?* was enormously successful (see page 28).

Not all writers were sympathetic to revolutionaries. Dostoyevsky had been arrested and sentenced to death for his membership of an underground group, but he was reprieved at the last moment and turned to the Orthodox Church for salvation. He rejected revolution in favour of the uniqueness of the Russian 'soul', drawing heavily on his Orthodox beliefs. His novels contain complex characters such as the tortured Raskolnokov in *Crime and Punishment* (1866). In *The Brothers Karamazov* (1880), one brother is a cold intellectual atheist in contrast to another who is versed in the Orthodox religion and studies under a holy man at a nearby monastery. A third brother is a wild Russian character prone to violence and mood changes from kindness to cruelty. In this way Dostoyevsky is exploring 'types' of Russians and it is the religious brother who represents the real Russian soul with love and self-sacrifice.

The most renowned writer of this time was Leo Tolstoy, who had fought in the Crimean War. His experiences contributed to his great novel *War and Peace* (1869) which told of the experiences of five different aristocratic families, wealthy and poor, and explored the nature of war, comradeship, and love of the country and Russia. Tolstoy also wanted to look at the reality of Russian life. In *Anna Karenina*, he writes a scene of a harvest in which he shows the close bond between peasants and the land. In the 1880s and afterwards, he turned more to philosophy and writings about morality. He idealised the peasantry and attacked the wealthy, state repression and Church hypocrisy. In his last novel *Resurrection* (1899) he criticises the injustices of the legal system.

Chekhov's *The Cherry Orchard*

By the time he wrote *The Cherry Orchard* in 1904, the year of his death, Chekhov's reputation was second only to Tolstoy's. The play is a satire of the old-world gentry and the cult of rural Russia. Ranyevskaya's feckless family are forced by debt to sell their prized possession, the cherry orchard, to Lopakhin, a merchant whose grandfather was a serf and whose father was a peasant. This social rise was possible after 1861. Lopakhin plans to clear the land and build *dachas* (country homes) on it for the middle class of Moscow and even tries to persuade the family to develop it themselves. They will not, he buys it and the play ends with the sound of the axe. Lopakhin is the first merchant hero to be represented on the Russian stage and, as Orlando Figes has written, Chekhov, in his last play, 'embraces the cultural forces that emerged in Moscow on the eve of the twentieth century'.

RESEARCH

Research the Silver Age of Russian poetry that took place at the end of the nineteenth and beginning of the twentieth century. Read some of the poems of Anna Akhmatova. Make brief notes on your findings.

Music

Russian classical music in this period drew on Russian folk music and melodies which were an important part of national identity. Musicians like Borodin, Mussorgsky and Rimsky-Korsakov aimed to produce a national Russian music. The conquest of parts of Asia during the nineteenth century also added Eastern elements to mainstream music. Tchaikovsky's music drew on folk traditions but was much more overtly patriotic such as in the '1812 Overture'. It also had more Westernised elements in it which gave him a wide European audience, but did not endear him to all Russian critics. At the beginning of the twentieth century, there was a movement away from these national themes and music reflected some of the greater freedom and tumult after 1905. Igor Stravinsky's 'Firebird' marked a new departure from European music and linked with the changes in art that you can read about below.

Maxim Gorky, 1868–1936

Another hugely important writer of this period was Maxim Gorky (born Alexei Peshkov). An orphan at eight, he had a harsh upbringing of poverty and cruelty which he described in his book *My Childhood* (1913). As a boy and young man he roamed the countryside and towns, working in a host of jobs such as dishwasher, icon painter and baker. He took up with a Populist revolutionary in the late 1870s and was bitterly disillusioned by the way they were rejected by the peasants. Gorky turned to writing and started to write short stories which appeared initially in newspapers and journals. His stories were immensely popular and in 1898 his first collection of short stories was published.

Gorky became one of the country's most read authors and a celebrity, the first writer of quality to emerge from the lower levels of Russian society. His stories were consumed voraciously by workers who could identify with his heroes and themes because they drew on the concerns that filled their everyday lives. He emerged as the champion of the poor and the oppressed. His adopted pseudonym Maxim Gorky (*gorky* means 'bitter' in Russian) tuned in with the workers' spirit of defiance. He started writing about politics and the hardships, humiliations and brutal treatment of workers, peasants and Jewish people. He joined political groups and associated with the emerging Marxist Social Democrats, becoming a personal friend of Lenin. He was very influential in the opposition to the Tsar and later played an important role in and after the 1917 revolution.

The arts

In 1863 thirteen artists rebelled against the Academy of Art and its formal style. They called themselves 'the Wanderers' because they wanted to bring their work to the people in travelling exhibitions. Like the writers discussed above and on page 69, these painters believed that art should be useful to society, that it should be primarily concerned with, and subordinate to, reality. They focused their work on the Russian landscape and Russian history. They did not get involved in the growing revolutionary movement of the 1870s but they did depict social problems in their art. Ilya Repin's painting of the *Volga Bargehaulers* (1873, see opposite) portrays the harshness of a group of 'human pack animals'. A contemporary critic called it, 'a commentary on the latent force of social protest in the Russian people'. Dostoyevsky, though, saw it as an epic portrait of the Russian character, and it was Alexander III's favourite painting.

Moscow merchants and the arts

New opportunities afforded by industrialisation allowed some Moscow merchants to become very wealthy indeed. They became vital patrons of the arts, for example Mamontov founded the Abramtsevo colony, Tretyakov became the main buyer of Russian art – he was to give his huge collection and purpose-built gallery to Moscow in 1892, and Shchukin bought modern Western art. He had 37 Matisses and 51 Picassos, held exhibitions of his collection and encouraged young artists.

▲ *Volga Bargehaulers* by Ilya Repin, 1873.

Abramtsevo artists' colony

Abramtsevo illustrates very well what was happening in Russian culture and society. In 1870 an estate from a declining noble family was bought by Savva Mamontov, a railway tycoon, who founded an artists' colony. Mamontov and his wife, Elizabeth, were influenced by the Populists and believed that art was for the education of the masses. It became the focus for the arts and crafts movement and Mamontov wanted to sell its artefacts in Moscow which was 60 kilometres away. Abramtsevo has been described as the ideal *dacha*. Artists, including Repin, flocked to it. Abramtsevo grew out of the Wanderers and has been called the cradle of the modern movement in Russian art. There was a common determination to create a new Russian culture. Elizabeth Mamontov was deeply religious and involved the whole community – artists, craftsmen and peasant builders – in the building of a small church in the colony between 1881 and 1882. It was deliberately modelled on medieval Russian churches and painting, and Repin executed some of the paintings on the screen bearing the icons. There was a great revival in interest in icons but also in the *lubok* tradition of peasant woodcuts. Alexander III used Abramtsevo artists for the decoration of the church built in the old-Russian style over the site where Alexander II had been assassinated. In later years Chekhov knew Abramtsevo well. One of his closest friends had worked there, and it is said to be a model for *The Cherry Orchard.*

RESEARCH

It is difficult to convey the nature of Russian art in a textbook. You need to see it. So search the internet for some of the artists mentioned here and find out about them. Look at the suprematist paintings of Kasimir Malevich and the futurist paintings of Natalia Goncharova. You won't be disappointed.

The Russian avant-garde

Abramtsevo's influence was diverse. There was a direct link between peasant woodcuts and Larionov, Goncharova and Malevich and the Russian avant-garde at the beginning of the twentieth century. Merchants helped again too. The younger generation of merchant patrons collected modern art and Moscow became the centre of the avant-garde at the beginning of the twentieth century. Merchants helped fund the 'Jack of Diamonds' exhibitions. Larionov and Goncharova were key founders of the group and Malevich showed at the first exhibition. One of the organisers regarded the title 'Jack of Diamonds' as a symbol of young enthusiasm and passion, 'for the Jack implies youth and the suit of diamonds represents seething blood'. They declared war on the realist tradition and shocked the public with their art. By this time Malevich believed in the radical reduction of painting to nothing but shape and colour. His revolutionary contribution was *The Black Square* in 1915. It was first shown as part of a group of abstract paintings in a dramatic display in Moscow in December 1915, and was hung high and across a corner, connecting two walls, just as icons were mounted in homes all across Russia. Characteristically immodest, he said *The Black Square* marked 'the beginning of a new culture', which he called suprematism.

Chapter summary

- The autocracy was underpinned by the principles of autocracy, orthodoxy and nationality. The tsarist state had structural weaknesses.
- Alexander III rolled back the reforms of his father with a series of counter-reforms, establishing tighter control of the legal system, education, local government, censorship and peoples' freedoms.
- He took Russia back to a more repressive, arbitrary, personalised autocracy and did not build the institutions of civic society that would have engaged more sections of the population.
- Alexander supported the policy of Russification as a way of controlling and integrating the different nationalities in the Empire; his regime fostered a racist policy towards Jewish people who were excluded from many areas of Russian society.
- Alexander threw his weight behind the modernisation and industrialisation of Russia. This was led by Sergei Witte, Finance Minister from 1892 to 1903. Witte's industrial strategy was based on: developing heavy industry, especially railways; foreign loans, investment and expertise; high tariffs, increased taxation and grain exports.
- There was a great industrial spurt in the 1890s and, after economic depression in the early part of the twentieth century, industrial growth continued from 1908 to 1914. Russia became one of the leading industrial countries in the world.
- Progress was made in agriculture with a general increase in grain production from 1880 to 1914. The central agricultural regions remained weak. Outside the centre, more go-ahead peasants, landowners and communes were trying new crops and methods and prospering.
- From 1906 to 1911, Peter Stolypin brought in land reforms designed to create more productive, independent peasants who would support the regime, but he met with only limited success.
- Russia was undergoing huge social change resulting from industrialisation, changing ownership of land and the penetration of the money economy into the countryside.
- Russian literature and art flourished in this period, which saw the work of some of the world's greatest writers, musicians and artists.

▼ Summary diagram: Economic and social change, 1880–1914

Economic change	Social change
Agriculture	**Peasants and nobles**
After the 1880s peasants buying and renting land from nobles. Some nobles becoming more commercial farmers.	Nobles selling land. Many moving to cities and towns.
Agricultural production rising. New crops and products produced for market particularly near urban areas, ports or where access to transport.	Class of more prosperous peasants developing: some buying and renting extra land, some as *khutors* after Stolypin reforms; others moving into property and business.
Stolypin's reforms – land consolidation – *obtrubs* and *khutors* – limited success: only 10 per cent of households by 1914.	Some peasants better off – higher consumption of grain and consumer goods. Majority still poor because of population increase, taxes and redemption payments.
Commune not so conservative as supposed. New crops, rotations, methods being introduced in some areas.	Commune remained strong. Basic style of peasant life not altered much for majority. Division between older and younger peasants growing.
Livestock not so successful and did not keep pace with population growth.	Growth of immigrant labour working as agricultural labourers and in winter in towns and cities.
Production in central areas remained weak with smaller landholdings and old-fashioned methods. Poor subsistence farming.	Millions of peasants forced off land by poverty or debt, or seeking social betterment, flooding to cities and towns.
Industry	**Working and middle classes**
Industrial spurt in 1890s. Significant growth in heavy industries and railways. Picked up again after 1908.	Cities and towns growing rapidly. Peasants becoming workers but keeping links to home village.
Industrial strategy based on: heavy industry and railways, foreign loans and investment, high tariffs, strong rouble, taxation and grain exports.	Workers employed in large factories of thousands but majority still working in small workshops outside factory legislation.
Industry driven by military needs and this led to unbalanced economy with certain sectors remaining weak.	Working conditions very poor, wages low and hours long. Living conditions – in barracks or tenements – generally appalling, overcrowding, insanitary. Demands to improve conditions led to labour militancy and strikes.
Significant amount of industry in large-scale plants using modern methods of mass production. At same time, most workers in small workshops, less productive.	Middle classes growing but still small proportion of population. Different groups:
By 1914 Russia is a leading industrial nation – fourth or fifth in the word but significantly behind international competitors in per capita income and output.	● Old merchant class diversifying into banking and commercial ventures ● New class of industrialists and Russian businessmen emerging ● Professionals developing associations.

Working on essay technique: analysis

Analysis is a term that covers a variety of high-level skills including explanation and evaluation. In essence, analysis means breaking down something complex into smaller parts. This means that a clear structure which breaks down a complex question into a series of paragraphs is the first step towards writing an analytical essay.

Explanation

The purpose of explanation is to account for why something happened, or why something is true or false. An explanatory statement requires two parts: a **claim** and a **justification**.

EXAMPLE

Imagine you are answering the following AS-level practice question:

'The Russian economy was modernised successfully between 1892 and 1914.' Explain why you agree or disagree with this view. (25 marks)

In this question you would be looking at the industrial and agricultural sectors of the economy. You might want to argue that much of industry was modernised. Once you have made this point, and supported it with relevant detail, you can then explain how this answers the question.

For example, you could conclude your paragraph like this:

Relationship ——— So we can say that substantial sections of ●——— Claim
Russian industry had been successfully
modernised because they were carried on
in large factories using modern mass
production methods and the most up-to-date
technology.
|
Justification

The first part of this sentence is the claim while the second part – and the second sentence – justifies the claim. 'Because' is a very important word to use when writing an explanation, as it shows the relationship between the claim and the justification.

Evaluation

The purpose of evaluation is to weigh up and reach a judgement. Evaluation, therefore, needs to consider the importance of two or more different factors, weigh them against each other, and then reach a judgement. Evaluation is a good skill to use at the end of an essay because the conclusion should reach a judgement which answers the question.

EXAMPLE

Consider the practice question in the example on page 74.

If you were answering this question you might want to weigh up the extent to which the economy had modernised successfully.

For example, your conclusion might read:

> Clearly Russian industry had taken huge strides forward and was using up-to-date modern methods and technology. Growth had been impressive and it was the world's fifth largest industrial country. However, the majority of industrial workers were employed in small-scale inefficient workshops with low productivity and the industrial sector as a whole was unbalanced and uneven. Moreover, the economy was still heavily skewed towards agriculture and although there were significant advances in agriculture and increased overall production, the majority of agriculture was still organised in the traditional strip system using old-fashioned technology and methods. Therefore the Russian economy was not successfully modernised and compared unfavourably with its chief international competitors.

In this example the evaluation is helped by a series of words (highlighted) that help to weigh up the importance of the factors/arguments. This is just one example, but the same is true of answers to other essay questions. 'However' and 'nonetheless' are useful words as they can help contrast the importance of the different factors/arguments.

ACTIVITY

Again, consider the practice question from the example on page 74.

Using your notes from this chapter, write a paragraph about the extent to which agriculture was modernised. Make sure the paragraph:

- begins with a clear point that clearly focuses on the question
- develops the point with at least three pieces of accurate detail
- concludes with explanation: a claim and a justification.

A-LEVEL PRACTICE QUESTION

'The political authority of the tsarist regime had been weakened by the reforms of Alexander II but was restored by his son, Alexander III.' Assess the validity of this view.   (25 marks)

Use the above question to practise all of the essay techniques that you have learned so far.

Working on interpretation skills

Section A of the exam paper is different from Section B (see page 35). Unlike Section B, it contains extracts from the work of historians. Significantly, this section tests different skills. In essence, Section A tests your ability to analyse different historical interpretations. Therefore, you must focus on the interpretations outlined in the extracts. The advice given in this chapter on interpretations is for both the AS and the A-level exams.

- For the **AS exam**, there are two extracts and you are asked which is the more convincing interpretation (25 marks).
- For the **A-level exam,** there are three extracts and you are asked how convincing the arguments are in relation to a specified topic (30 marks).

An interpretation is a particular view on a topic of history held by a particular author or authors. Interpretations of an event can vary, for example, depending on how much weight an historian gives to a particular factor and whether they largely ignore another factor.

The interpretations that you will be given will be largely from recent or fairly recent historians, and they may, of course, have been influenced by events in the period in which they were writing.

Interpretations and evidence

The extracts given in the exam will contain a mixture of interpretations and evidence. The mark scheme rewards answers that focus on the *interpretations* offered by the extracts much more highly than answers that focus on the *information or evidence* mentioned in the extracts. Therefore, it is important to identify the interpretations.

- *Interpretations* are a specific kind of argument. They tend to make claims such as 'Tsarist Russia could not have survived. It was bound to collapse.'
- *Information or evidence* tends to consist of specific details. For example, 'Industry was growing at a fast rate on the eve of the war.'

Analysis of an interpretation

We start by looking at an individual extract and seeing how we can build up skills. This is the essential starting-point for both the AS and the A-level style of question on interpretations. The AS mark scheme shows a very clear progression of thought processes:

Level 5	Answers will display a good understanding of the interpretations given in the extracts. They will evaluate the extracts thoroughly in order to provide a well-substantiated judgement on which offers the more convincing interpretation. The response demonstrates a very good understanding of context. *21–25 marks*
Level 4	Answers will display a good understanding of the interpretations given in the extracts. There will be sufficient comment to provide a supported conclusion as to which offers the more convincing interpretation. However, not all comments will be well-substantiated, and judgements may be limited. The response demonstrates a good understanding of context. *16–20 marks*
Level 3	The answer will show a reasonable understanding of the interpretations given in the extracts. Comments as to which offers the more convincing interpretation will be partial and/or thinly supported. The response demonstrates an understanding of context. *11–15 marks*
Level 2	The answer will show some partial understanding of the interpretations given in the extracts. There will be some undeveloped comment in relation to the question. The response demonstrates some understanding of context. *6–10 marks*
Level 1	The answer will show a little understanding of the interpretations given in the extracts. There will be only unsupported, vague or generalist comment in relation to the question. The response demonstrates limited understanding of context. *1–5 marks*

Now study extract A on page 77 and the practice question below, which is about the modernisation of the Russian economy.

With reference to the extract [A] and your understanding of the historical context, how convincing do you find the extract in relation to the modernisation of the Russian economy between 1890 and 1914?

To help you answer this type of question you need to assess the interpretation in the extract. Carry out activities 1–5 on page 77 to help you do this.

Extract A

Many historians hold that in economic terms tsarist industrialization was a success; a modern capitalist economy was emerging ... that in 1909–13 the state was giving way to the market as the motive-force for industrial development, and that Russian capital and Russian entrepreneurship were replacing foreign capital ... Certainly in the industrial sector the rate of growth of production and the pace of technical modernisation on the eve of war were on the whole impressive. And in the agricultural sector production had been growing more rapidly than population at least since the 1880s, and by 1914 the majority of peasants belonged to various forms of agricultural credit and marketing cooperatives.

Adapted from *Tsarism to the New Economic Policy,* R. W. Davies (ed.), (Cornell University Press), 1991, p 18.

Extract B

The Tsarist economy was honeycombed with fundamental and structural problems. Although Russia by 1913 was one of the great world economic powers in sheer size, in per capita terms her performance was miserable. The economy remained grossly skewed towards the agrarian sector, despite the spurt of industrialization which had taken place at the end of the nineteenth century. Structurally, Russia possessed the features of an early industrializing country and had yet to make the leap to effectively modernize her economic structures and performance.

From *The End of Imperial Russia 1855–1917* by Peter Waldron, (Palgrave Macmillan), 1997, p 68.

ACTIVITY

1 What is the argument for the interpretation in Extract A? (Is it arguing that the Russian economy had been transformed or not?)

2 What evidence can you find in the extract to support the argument? (What details are mentioned to support the argument?)

3 What do you know (what contextual knowledge do you have) that supports these claims?

4 What contextual knowledge do you have to contradict these claims?

5 Using your judgement, are the arguments in support stronger than the arguments against, or vice versa?

Look back at the mark scheme on page 76, and see how your answers might match up to the levels shown there.

In relation to Extract A's assertions about economic modernisation, you should be able to find arguments both to support and to contradict. Remember, you can apply this approach when responding to other, similar, questions.

6 Consider the AS-level practice question below.

With reference to these two extracts and your understanding of the historical context, which of these two extracts provides the more convincing interpretation of the modernisation of the Russian economy between 1890 and 1914? (25 marks)

Follow the same five steps for Extract B as you did for Extract A, then compare the results of the two and come to a conclusion about which extract provides the most convincing interpretation.

Comparing two interpretations

As part of the building up of skills, we move on to comparing two interpretations. Activity 6 is the format of the AS question, but will also be useful in the process of gaining confidence for A-level students.

The top two levels of the mark scheme (page 76) refer to 'supported conclusion' (Level 4) and 'well-substantiated judgement' (Level 5). For Level 4 'supported conclusion' means finishing your answer with a judgement that is backed up with some accurate evidence drawn from the extract(s) and your knowledge. For Level 5 'well-substantiated judgement' means finishing your answer with a judgement which is very well supported with evidence, and, where relevant, reaches a complex conclusion that reflects a wide variety of evidence.

There is no one correct way to write the answer! However, the principles are clear. In particular, contextual knowledge should be used *only* to back up an argument. None of your knowledge should be free-standing – in the question in Activity 6, for example, there should not be a paragraph saying what you know about the topic, unrelated to the extracts. All your knowledge should be used in context. For each extract in turn:

● Explain the evidence in the extract, backed up with your own contextual knowledge. In this example, explain the evidence for the modernisation of the Russia economy by 1914.

● Explain the points in the extract where you have evidence that contradicts the notion that the Russian economy had been modernised.

Then write a conclusion that reaches a judgement on which is more convincing as an interpretation.

3

The collapse of the Russian Empire, 1894–1917

This chapter covers the reign of Tsar Nicholas II, which ended in the collapse of the Russian Empire. It deals with the following areas:

- Nicholas II as a ruler
- Opposition: ideas and ideologies
- Political developments to 1914, the 1905 revolution, Duma government
- The political, economic and social impact of the First World War
- The collapse of the autocracy

The main focus of this chapter will be on the question:

How far did the Tsar contribute to his own downfall?

In this question you will look at how effectvely the Tsar and his government ran Russia from 1905 to 1917 and the causes of the revolution in February 1917. In particular you will cover the breadth key questions of why opposition developed in Russia and how effective it was, and the importance of ideas and ideology.

CHAPTER OVERVIEW

Nicholas II succeeded his father and carried on his policies. Russia was undergoing rapid social and economic change which threatened the stability of the regime. After 1900 an industrial depression resulted in widespread hardship and discontent. The Russo–Japanese War, which showed the government to be inept, acted as a catalyst for the 1905 revolution – a year of disturbances, strikes, mutinies and political action. The tsarist regime survived 1905 intact, but it had conceded an elected duma, a parliament, which suggested that constitutional change was on the cards. However, the Tsar quickly reasserted the principle of autocracy and the first two dumas fell apart in discord and bitterness. Only when the electoral system was changed to favour the propertied classes did a working relationship emerge. The outstanding politician of this period was Peter Stolypin but his programme of reforms met with limited success. The tsarist regime seemed unable to reform itself and all its inadequacies were exposed when the First World War started in 1914. The strains and stresses caused by the war led to the collapse of the Romanov dynasty in the February revolution of 1917.

1 Nicholas II

Nicholas II came to the throne in 1894 at the age of 26 after his father had died unexpectedly. His bad luck was that he had to guide his country through one of the most difficult periods in its history.

Nicholas as ruler

Did Nicholas II's personality and qualities fit him for his role as tsar?

Nicholas was rather overwhelmed at the prospect of taking over from a strong father whom he admired greatly. He declared himself 'wholly unfit to reign'. Compared with his father's huge bulk he had a slight, somewhat diminutive, figure. Although he was well educated, having studied a range of subjects, it was the army to which he was most attached. He loved military life. He came to see it as his personal domain and appointed grand dukes and members of his family, often not very able, to high positions.

In his personal life, he was a loving family man. His private letters and diary provide evidence of his strong religious convictions and his deep affection for his wife and family. He was generally charming and kind to those around him. But Nicholas was also narrow-minded and prejudiced and had no time for people who did not fit into his idea of a true Russian. He was antisemitic and praised regiments that put down disorders.

Khodynka

Nicholas II's reign got off to an ill-omened start. In May 1896, during the celebrations that accompanied his coronation, 1,400 people were killed and 600 injured in Khodynka Field, perhaps in a crush for free beer and food. When, that evening, Nicholas went to a ball organised by the French ambassador there was public outrage at his apparent lack of concern.

▲ Tsar Nicholas II with his family, circa 1900

He could command respect and loyalty but lacked the training and experience for leadership. His poor leadership skills have been recorded by contemporaries and historians: his inability to make decisions; his unwillingness to engage in politics – even to read government reports; his lack of organisational skills ('Unfit to run a village post office' was the comment of an unknown cabinet minister); his weakness; his obstinacy. He found it difficult to say unpleasant things to ministers to their face and would often write them a note after seeing them in which he criticised their ideas and proposals. According to Abraham Ascher, 'He lacked the personal drive and ambition to instill a sense of purpose and direction in the ministers and bureaucracy'.

He was completely wedded to the principle of autocracy. At the very beginning of his reign he stated: 'Let it be known to all that I shall devote all my strength, for the good of the whole nation, to maintaining the principle of autocracy just as firmly and unflinchingly as it was preserved by my unforgettable father.' Like his father he was influenced by Pobedonostsev and like his father he was anxious to maintain the political authority of the regime.

Source A *A People's Tragedy: The Russian Revolution 1891–1924* by Orlando Figes, (Pimlico), 1997, p23.

Nicholas was the source of all the problems. If there was a vacuum of power at the centre of the ruling system, then he was the empty space. In a sense, Russia gained in him the worst of both worlds: a Tsar determined to rule from the throne yet quite incapable of exercising power. This was 'autocracy without an autocrat.' Perhaps nobody could have fulfilled the role which Nicholas had set himself: the work of government had become much too vast and complex for a single man; autocracy itself was out of date.

Source B *Nicholas II: Emperor of all the Russias* by Dominic Lieven, (John Murray), 1993, pp 261–62.

Nicholas II was not stupid. On the contrary, his problem tended to be that he could understand many points of view and wavered between them. The dangers Russia faced were very great … Nicholas loved his country and served it loyally and to the best of his ability. He had not sought power and he was not by temperament or personality very well equipped to wield it. He was a very kind, sensitive, generous and initially naive man. These traumatic years required something very different and would probably have destroyed any man who sat on the throne.

1 Compare Sources A and B. What are the similarities and differences in their views of Nicholas?

2 Using these sources and the information in the text, how well-fitted do you think Nicholas was for the role of tsar?

The Tsarina

Alexandra was born of a German royal house and was a Protestant. She converted to the Orthodox Church and threw herself into learning Russian customs and traditions. However, she developed a strong dislike for court life and this was reciprocated. The court perceived her as cold and aloof and she was compared unfavourably with her mother-in-law, Maria Fedorovna. Alexandra was always regarded as an outsider – the 'German woman' – and was never much liked by Russians. Nicholas and Alexandra had four daughters – Olga, Tatiana, Maria and Anastasia – and one son, Alexis, who was a haemophiliac. Naturally shy, Alexandra sought to create a private world in their palace Tsarskoe Selo just outside St Petersburg, demanding that the Tsar spend the evenings with the family. Alexandra was strong-willed and obstinate. She believed firmly that the Tsar had been appointed by God to be the autocratic ruler of Russia. She was adamant that he should keep his powers and not share them with the people. Her influence on him was great and not always helpful. At crucial moments she would argue against any move towards constitutional monarchy. Also she insisted that they maintain their relationship with the disreputable character Rasputin (see box, page 81).

Grigory Rasputin

Grigory Yefimovich, a Siberian peasant, gained a reputation as a holy man, or *starets*, and the name Rasputin. In 1905, he came to St Petersburg and became known to the royal family. The Tsar's son, Alexis, suffered from haemophilia and Rasputin seemed to be able to stop the bleeding that resulted from this when doctors could not (perhaps through herbal remedies or hypnosis). The Tsarina took this as a sign from God and her favour gave Rasputin an elevated position at court with direct access to the royal family. High society women flocked to him to ask for healing or to carry petitions to the Tsar to advance their husbands' careers. There were rumours that Rasputin solicited sexual favours for this help and that there were orgies. Whatever the truth, the stories of his debauchery caused reputational and political damage to the Tsar. It caused tension between the Tsar and the Orthodox Church (who disapproved of Rasputin); between the Tsar and the Duma because the Tsar censored reports of Rasputin in the newspapers; and between the Tsar and Stolypin who disparaged the effect Rasputin had on the Tsar's public image. Rasputin was to do much more damage during the First World War (see page 108).

NOTE-MAKING

Split a page into two with the headings below. Then, as you read pages 82–3 and 91–5, catalogue briefly the events and people's actions along with the reaction of the Tsar or government. Do this right up to the end of 1905. It will provide a review of how the government handled matters and met the aspirations of different groups. An example is given here.

Events/actions	Reaction of Tsar or government
Famine, 1891–92	Government incompetent, asks for public help
Zemstva want more autonomy. Liberal zemstvo men demand national assembly	Tsar rejects this as 'senseless dreams'

Nicholas, the early years, 1894–1904

What policies did Nicholas follow and how successful were they?

Just before Nicholas came to the throne Russia had been hit by the catastrophic famine of 1891–92 (see box). The government bureaucracy had been exposed and discredited and civil society had to be mobilised to help. People talked about the efficacy of the autocracy and whether it was time for people to play a greater role in government at different levels. The *zemstva*, with a huge amount of support, pressed their case for more autonomy. More liberal and progressive *zemstvo* men like Prince Lvov demanded the calling of a national assembly. And they presented their ideas to the new young Tsar on his accession. But Nicholas denounced them as 'senseless dreams'.

Nicholas continued with the policies of his father. The emergency powers of 1881 were kept more or less intact and the policy of Russification was pursued vigorously. Witte was Finance Minister and was driving forward at great pace industrialisation and modernisation (see Chapter 2). But this threatened the stability of the regime in a number of ways:

- Millions of peasants pouring into the cities to work in factories created volatility and social tension.
- Many workers were concentrated in large complexes and huge factories. This made it easier to organise strikes.
- A more educated workforce (and Witte favoured the spread of technical education) with a high literacy rate (57.8 per cent in 1897) was able to read political literature and articulate their views.
- The growth of the middle classes created pressure for political change, for more accountable and representative government.

As the 1890s progressed, urban workers became more militant. They resented deeply the working and living conditions they had to endure as well as the way they were treated (see pages 61–63). The textile workers in St Petersburg, where the vast majority of workers were women, mounted massive strikes – 30,000 spinners and weavers – in 1896 and 1897. This marked the arrival of a genuine proletariat able to organise itself. This action forced the government to concede the only significant piece of factory legislation in this period – restricting the working day to eleven and a half hours. More worrying for the government was that Marxist Social Democrats (see page 88) were active in encouraging workers to take strike action. The peak for strikes was reached in 1899 and involved nearly 100,000 workers. The government could only deal with them by police repression, arrests, imprisonment, exile and even execution. A special factory police force was established in 1899 and its units stationed permanently near large industrial works.

The turn of the century also saw serious disturbances involving students. What started as a protest against government restrictions on universities mushroomed into huge demonstrations in 1891 when police beat students with whips, arrested their leaders and drafted some into the army. The middle classes were horrified by the police brutality and many students were radicalised. Thousands joined the Socialist Revolutionaries (see page 85).

As Russia moved into the twentieth century it was in an unstable and volatile condition. There had been another famine in the Central Volga region in 1898–9. And then things got worse. An international recession after 1900 caused a deep depression in Russia (see page 51). It affected all areas of the economy and workers were hit by falling wages and unemployment, resulting in widespread industrial action. Workers returned to their villages to stir up peasant revolt where there was already huge anger about taxes and high rents. Poltava province saw the first wave of peasant violence in 1902 because landlords were withdrawing land needed to feed families or renting it out at more exploitative rates. Peasant revolts ripped through the countryside in 1902 and 1903. There was an air of growing internal disorder. The government had no answer other than repression: prisons were filling up with political prisoners. This led Leo Tolstoy to write the famous open letter, shown in Source C. The regime now faced growing opposition and some people were turning to ideas of revolution.

Source C Extract from a letter sent to the Tsar in 1902 by Leo Tolstoy concerning the state of the nation at the beginning of the century. Quoted in *Nicholas II, The Last of the Tsars* by M. Ferro, (Oxford University Press), 1990, pp 73–74.

One third of Russia is under a regime of reinforced surveillance ... The army of policemen, regular and secret, grows continually. The prisons and places of deportation are filled with persons sentenced for political reasons, not to mention the hundreds of thousands of ordinary prisoners to whom the workers must now be added. The censorship has attained a level of oppressiveness unknown even in the abominable period of the 1840s. Religious persecution has never been so frequent and so cruel, and grows worse every day. Troops with weapons loaded ready to fire on the people have been sent into every city ... And the peasants, all one hundred million of them, are getting poorer every year ... Famine has become a normal phenomenon. Normal likewise is the discontent of all classes of society with the government.

> In what ways, according to Source C, was the tsarist regime oppressive in 1902?

Zubatov trade unions

The only constructive response to the problems in the cities came from Sergei Zubatov, head of the Moscow *Okhrana*. He believed that repressive measures alone could not combat working-class militancy: workers had to be convinced that their lives could be improved within the existing system. He thought this could be achieved by giving them trades unions and self-help organisations, supervised and partially funded by the police. Starting in 1901, Zubatov set up three unions in Moscow, which submitted demands to their employers who were pressured by police representatives into making concessions. The Zubatov movement spread rapidly across the south and west of the Empire. However, many in government and the business community feared the unions would politicise workers and harm the economy. When, in 1903, a strike organised by police unions in Odessa escalated into a general strike, Zubatov was dismissed.

Historians have differing views on Zubatov's programme. Christopher Read regards it as a government own goal, one of the self-inflicted blows that caused the 1905 revolution: 'Wherever they were set up, Zubatov unions became a cover for radicals and blew up in the face of their sponsors'. However, Jeremiah Scheidermann points out that it was the only coherent labour policy coming from government quarters.

2 Ideologies, liberals and radicals

This section will look at the proliferation of political organisations and the intensification of political activity around 1900.

NOTE-MAKING

Make notes on each of the different opposition groups using the following headings:
- Origins
- Ideology/main beliefs
- Methods
- Support

The opposition, 1895–1905

What opposition groups developed and what were their ideologies?

The main opposition groups that developed during this period were the Liberals, Socialist Revolutionaries and Social Democrats. These movements were continuations of the pre-existing stream of opposition to autocracy although they had been quiet and subdued under Alexander III. Now in a rapidly changing world they took on a new lease of life and evolved in different ways.

The Liberals

Although the liberal movement can be traced back to the liberal intelligentsia in the 1850s and 1860s who were active in arguing for the emancipation of the serfs and representative assemblies, it is the *zemstva* that have been identified as 'the seedbeds of liberalism'. These councils had created a class of people who became skilled in local politics. They included liberal-leaning members of the Russian nobility as well as representatives of the middle classes. Many middle-class professionals employed by the *zemstva* – the 'third element' (see page 19) – worked at the interface with peasants and workers and had a real desire to improve social conditions. The inadequacies and inefficiencies of government bureaucracy became very apparent to this 'third element' during the 1891–92 famine and thereafter they wanted to see reforms, an extension of freedoms and civil rights, and more participation in government.

The idea of 'liberalism' prevalent in western Europe took a different form in Russia. What Russian liberals agreed on was that reform rather than violence was the way to change the tsarist system and limit the tsar's powers. Liberalism took on a more organised form at the beginning of the twentieth century. In 1903, the Union of Liberation (see page 91) was formed, demanding economic and political reform (see chart below). The Liberals were the major opposition to tsarism before 1905 and in that year formed two major political parties – the Kadets (constitutional democrats) and the Octobrists (see page 99).

Main beliefs	Civil rights and freedom of the individual, the rule of law, free elections, parliamentary democracy and limitation of the tsar's powers, and self-determination for the national minorities. Some believed that the concept of the *zemstvo* should be extended to regional and perhaps national level.
Methods	Reform rather than violent action, political channels through *zemstva*, articles in newspapers, meetings and reform banquets.
Support	Their main support came from the middle-class intelligentsia: lawyers, doctors, professors, teachers, engineers and other professional groups. They also had support among progressive landowners, industrialists and businessmen.

The Socialist Revolutionaries (SRs)

The Socialist Revolutionary Party grew out of the Populist movement. It was a loose organisation accommodating groups with a wide variety of views – more moderate groups following the same lines as the Black Partition and more extreme terrorists following the tradition of The People's Will (see pages 27–28). These groups merged in 1901–02 into the Socialist Revolutionary Party although it was never well co-ordinated or centrally controlled and did not hold its first congress until 1906. SR extremists assassinated as many as 2,000 government officials between 1901 and 1905, including the Minister of the Interior, Plehve, in 1904.

Main beliefs	SRs placed their central hope for revolution with the peasants who would support a popular rising in which the tsarist government would be overthrown. Land would be taken from landlords and divided up among the peasants. Unlike the Populists, the SRs accepted that the development of capitalism was a fact. The leading exponent of their views was Victor Chernov. He accepted that the growth of capitalism would promote the growth of a proletariat (working class) who would rise against their masters. But he saw no need for the peasants to pass through capitalism; he believed they could move straight to a form of rural socialism based on the peasant commune. He saw the SRs as representing 'all laboring people'.
Methods	Agitation and terrorism, including assassination of government officials.
Support	Peasants provided a large popular base but by 1905 industrial workers formed perhaps 50 per cent of the membership, probably because many workers were recently arrived ex-peasants and many had regular contact with their villages. The SRs often bemoaned their lack of strength in villages because most SR committees were run by students and intellectuals in towns. Nevertheless they were the party the peasants recognised as representing them, especially its pledge to return the land 'to those who worked it'.

Karl Marx, 1818–83

The Marxists

In the 1880s, it seemed to some Russian intellectuals that there was no hope of a revolutionary movement developing among the peasantry. Instead they turned to the latest theories of a German philosopher, Karl Marx. The 'scientific' nature of Marxism appealed to them – it was an optimistic theory which saw progress through the development of industry and the growth of the working class to the ultimate triumph of socialism. Marxist reading circles developed and societies and groups were formed. They believed in action and soon became involved in organising strikes in factories. The working class, not the peasants, were the key to the revolution.

Marx was a German philosopher who spent the last years of his life in London. He wrote the *Communist Manifesto* which encouraged workers to unite to seize power by revolution. He also wrote *Das Kapital* which explained his view of history. His views became known as Marxism and influenced the thinking of socialists throughout Europe in the late nineteenth and twentieth centuries.

Marxism

Marxism was attractive because it seemed to offer a 'scientific' view of history, similar to the evolutionary theories of Charles Darwin. According to Marx, history was evolving in a series of stages towards a perfect state – communism. Each stage was characterised by the struggle between different classes. This was a struggle over who owned the 'means of production' (resources used to produce food, goods and so on) and so controlled society. In each stage, Marx identified a ruling class of 'haves' who owned the means of production and exploited an oppressed class of 'have-nots' who sweated for them for little reward. He saw change as being brought about by a revolutionary class who would develop and contest power with the existing ruling class. Economic change and development (economic forces) would bring this new class to the fore and eventually allow it to overthrow the ruling class in a revolution.

Particularly important at the end of the nineteenth century was the move from capitalism to socialism. Marx put forward the view that all value was created by human labour and that the owners of the means of production – the capitalists (for example, factory owners) – took for themselves the 'surplus value' created by their workers. They invested their ill-gotten surplus value (capital) in labour-saving machinery (technology), growing production and their wealth but also reducing wages and eliminating jobs. As a result, wealth would be concentrated in fewer and fewer hands and the workers would become poorer and poorer. Eventually, Marx argued, the workers would rise up in revolution against the capitalists and then create socialism (a state run by the workers on behalf of the workers) which would lead to communism. Figure 1 on page 87 shows the stages Marx thought society would go through on the way to communism

Marx was a determinist: he thought that there were certain forces (economic forces, such as changes in technology) driving history which would lead to the changes he predicted. However, he did give individuals a role in history. He believed that they could affect the course of events, though not the general pattern:

Men make their own history but do not make it just as they please; they do not make it under circumstances chosen by themselves but under circumstances directly encountered, given or transmitted from the past.

His theory gave middle-class revolutionaries an important role in that they saw what the true nature of history was and could help to bring it about. Marx did not think his theories were the final word and he did not think all countries would go through the pattern described; he thought it applied particularly to countries in western Europe. He expected that experience would lead to changes in his theories; he even had a name for this – *praxis.*

FEUDALISM

Government: Absolute monarchy or autocracy.

Means of production: Land; land ownership gives power.

Social organisation: Aristocracy is the dominant group controlling the mass of the population – peasants or serfs – who work on their estates. Peasants (serfs) are virtually owned by their lords and masters.

Revolutionary change: The revolutionary class is the middle class (merchants, traders, manufacturers). As this group gets wealthier, it begins to break down the rules of feudal society which hinder its development, for example, it wants an economy based on money, and labourers free to work in towns.

 this leads to

The bourgeois–democratic revolution
The growth of trade and industry sees the middle classes becoming larger and more powerful. Eventually, they want to reshape society and government to suit their interests, for example, they want to have a say in how the country is run and do not want landed aristocrats determining national policy. The middle classes take power from the monarch and aristocracy. The bourgeois revolution can be violent, as in France in 1789, or more peaceful and gradual, as in Britain during the eighteenth and nineteenth centuries.

CAPITALISM

Government: Parliamentary democracy with civil rights, elections, freedom of the press, etc., but largely run by the middle classes.

Means of production: Industrial premises, factories, capital goods like machinery, banks owned by capitalists. Land becomes less important as industry and trade create greater share of national wealth.

Social organisation: Middle classes or bourgeoisie are the dominant or ruling class although the aristocracy may still hold on to some positions of power and prestige. The mass of the population move from being peasants to being industrial workers – the proletariat, who are forced to work long hours in poor conditions for little reward.

Revolutionary change: As capitalism grows so does the proletariat, since more workers are needed to work in factories and commercial premises. Great wealth and material goods are produced, but these are not shared out fairly. A small bourgeoisie gets increasingly wealthy while the proletariat remains poor. Gradually, the proletariat develops a class consciousness and realises that it is being oppressed as a class.

 this leads to

socialist revolution

The proletariat moves from class consciousness to a revolutionary consciousness aided by revolutionary leaders (often from the middle classes). They now form the great bulk of the population while the bourgeoisie are a tiny minority. They rise up and seize power, ousting their class enemies – the bourgeoisie. The socialist revolution starts in a highly industrialised country.

SOCIALISM

Government: Workers control the state. At first, government is exercised through the dictatorship of the proletariat, a period of strict control necessary to deal with counter-revolution (old capitalist enemies trying to recover power) and to root out non-socialist attitudes.

Means of production: Factories, machines, etc., as in the capitalist period but not owned by individuals. They are owned collectively by everybody.

Social organisation: Everybody is equal, the class system is brought to an end. Wealth and goods produced by industry are shared out fairly. Everybody has an equal entitlement to good housing and decent standards of living.

 After a while there is a …

transition to communism
The need for government declines because there are no competing classes.

COMMUNISM

Government: There is no state, just people who are interested in managing the day-to-day business of keeping society going.

Social organisation: Everybody is equal. There is an abundance of goods produced by machinery rather than by workers' labour, so everyone has much more leisure time. People work on the principle, 'From each, according to their ability, to each according to their needs' – they take out what they need from a central pool and contribute to society in whatever way they can. (Marx's view of communist society is not very clear.)

MARXISM–LENINISM

Lenin developed Marxist theory. Three of the main changes were:

1. The revolution would be accomplished by a small group of highly professional, dedicated revolutionaries. They were needed to develop the revolutionary consciousness of workers and focus their actions.
2. Lenin believed that the revolution would occur during a period of conflict between capitalist powers. He accepted Trotsky's 'weakest link' theory – revolution would start in an underdeveloped country (just like Russia), where the struggle and conflict between proletariat and bourgeoisie was very great, and then spread to more advanced industrial countries.
3. He did not think that the middle classes in Russia were strong enough to carry through a bourgeois–democratic revolution. He believed that the working class could develop a revolutionary government of its own in alliance with poor peasants who had a history of mass action in Russia – that is, the bourgeois and socialist revolution could be rolled into one.

▲ **Figure 1** The route to communism.

The Social Democrats (SDs)

George Plekhanov was the father of Russian Marxism (see page 29). He had translated Karl Marx's work into Russian and saw it as 'the answer' where Populism had failed. Like most radicals Plekhanov was in exile in Europe, having left Russia in 1880. In 1898, in a house on the outskirts of Minsk, he met with a small group of socialist exiles and formed the Russian Social Democratic Labour Party. In December 1900 the Party published a newspaper to unite revolutionaries around the Marxist programme. It was called *Iskra* (spark) as in 'from a spark a fire will ignite' and Lenin was on the editorial board.

In these early years, there were serious disputes about the direction of the Party. Some wanted to encourage trade unions to improve the conditions of the workers. Others wanted the focus to be on revolutionary tactics and the preparation of the working class for revolution.

At the Second Party Congress in 1903, the SDs split into two factions – the Bolsheviks (Majoritarians) and the Mensheviks (Minoritarians). This was largely caused by the abrasive personality of Vladimir Ulyanov or Lenin (see page 89) who was determined to see his idea of the revolutionary party triumph. During the congress the votes taken on various issues showed the two groups were roughly equal. But in a particular series of votes Lenin's faction came out on top (mainly because some delegates had walked out of the conference) and he jumped on the idea of calling his group the majority party (Bolsheviki) which gave them a stronger image. In fact, until 1917, they always had fewer members than the Mensheviks for reasons that will become apparent below.

Source D Leon Trotsky, *Our Political Tasks*, 1904.

> What warning does Source D contain for Lenin's concept of a revolutionary party?

In the internal politics of the party these methods lead, as we shall yet see, to this: the party organisation is substituted for the party, the central committee is substituted for the party organisation, and finally a 'dictator' is substituted for the central committee.

Main beliefs: Both SD factions accepted the main tenets of Marxism but they were split over the role of the Party.	
Bolsheviks	**Mensheviks**
Lenin believed that a revolutionary party should: • be made up of a small number of highly disciplined professional revolutionaries • operate under centralised leadership • have a system of small cells (made up of three people) so that it would be more difficult for the police to infiltrate.	They believed that the Party should: • be broadly based and take in all those who wished to join • be more democratic, allowing its members to have a say in policy making • encourage trade unions to help the working class improve their conditions.
It was the job of the Party to bring socialist consciousness to the workers and lead them through the revolution. Critics warned that a centralised party like this would lead to dictatorship.	Mensheviks took the Marxist line that there would be a long period of bourgeois democratic government during which the workers would develop a class and revolutionary consciousness until they were ready to take over in a socialist revolution.
Support: Their support came mainly from the working class.	
The Bolsheviks tended to attract younger more militant workers who liked the discipline, firm leadership and simple slogans.	The Mensheviks tended to attract different types of workers and members of the intelligentsia, also a broader range of people – more non-Russians, especially Jewish people and Georgians.

Vladimir Ilyich Lenin, 1870–1924

Vladimir Ilyich Ulyanov, later known as Lenin, was born in Simbirsk in 1870 into a privileged professional family. His father was a chief inspector of schools, his mother the daughter of a doctor and a landowner. The Ulyanovs were a self-made, upwardly mobile family but the involvement of Lenin's elder brother in a plot to assassinate Tsar Alexander III saw the family ostracised and had a big impact on Vladimir. Lenin studied law at Kazan University but was expelled for political activity, although he was allowed to sit his exams. For a short time, he practised as a lawyer.

Lenin became more interested in revolutionary ideas and was drawn to the scientific logic of Marxism. In 1893, he moved to St Petersburg and joined Marxist discussion groups where he met his future wife, Nadezhda Krupskaya. He became involved in propaganda for a strike movement in 1895 and was arrested. He spent the next four years first in prison and then in exile in Siberia, where he married Krupskaya. After his release in 1900, they moved to London where Lenin worked on the Party newspaper, *Iskra*. In 1902, he published his pamphlet *What Is To Be Done?* which contained his radical ideas about the nature of a revolutionary party. He put forward his ideas at the Second Congress of the Social Democratic Party which met in 1903 (first in Brussels and then in London). His abrasive personality helped to cause the split in the party into Bolsheviks and Mensheviks.

The Bolsheviks played a relatively minor role in the 1905 revolution and Lenin returned to St Petersburg only in October. But when the revolution failed, he left for exile abroad once more. The years from 1906 to 1914 were frustrating. There were arguments and splits in the Bolshevik Party and membership collapsed.

Political theorist

Lenin is regarded as an important political theorist. The body of his work, including adaptations of Marxist theory, has been called Marxism–Leninism. But he really saw his writings as plans for action. His principal writings include:

- *What Is To Be Done?* (1902) – here he argued for his idea of a revolutionary party:
  - It was to be highly centralised; a clear line of policy would be laid down by the central committee of the Party.
  - There would be a network of agents who would be 'regular permanent troops'.
  - It would be a small, conspiratorial party made up of professional, dedicated revolutionaries.
  - It would act as the vanguard of the working class who would not attain a revolutionary consciousness without clear guidance from the revolutionary elite.

  Lenin encouraged the individual revolutionary to be hard with himself and others to achieve his aims; there was no room for sentiment.

- *Imperialism: the Highest Stage of Capitalism* (1916) – here he claimed that capitalism was a bankrupt system and would collapse in a series of wars between capitalist countries over resources and territory. This would lead to civil war and class conflict within countries, which would facilitate the socialist revolution. This could start in a relatively undeveloped country – the weakest link in the capitalist chain – and then spread to other industrialised countries. Russia seemed to be this weakest link.

- *The State and Revolution* (1917) – this book discussed what the state would be like after revolution. Existing state structures would be smashed by revolutionaries. The transformation of the economy and society would be relatively easy – the spontaneous will of the people would support revolution and they would play a large part in managing their own affairs in industry and agriculture.

Leon Trotsky, 1879–1940

Lev Bronstein was born in 1879 in Ukraine, the son of a well-to-do Jewish farmer. Dissatisfied with society, particularly its treatment of Jewish people, he was drawn to Marxism in his teens and joined a Marxist discussion group. There, he fell in love with Alexandra Sokolovska. Involved in inciting strikes in 1900, both were arrested, got married in prison and were exiled to Siberia. In 1902, Bronstein escaped dramatically by using a false passport signed with the name of a prison warder – Leon Trotsky.

Arriving in Paris, Trotsky met a young Russian art student, Natalia Sedova, with whom he was to live for the rest of his life. He made the journey to London, where he got on well with Lenin and was given the nickname 'The Pen' because of his writing skills. But at the 1903 Social Democratic conference he would not side with Lenin. He prophesied that Lenin's concept of a revolutionary party would lead inevitably to dictatorship. He remained in the Social Democratic Party somewhere between the Bolsheviks and Mensheviks but not in either camp.

He first made his mark in the 1905 revolution, where his oratorial talents led to his becoming deputy chairman of the St Petersburg Soviet. His subsequent arrest and escape established his credibility in revolutionary circles. His analysis of the situation in Russia moved closer to Lenin's when, with 'Parvus' (Alexander Helphand), he developed the theory of the weakest link concerning the weakness of the Russian bourgeoisie and how revolution might begin. He was in the USA when the revolution broke and, hurrying back, he threw in his lot with the Bolshevik Party.

Vera Zasulich, 1849–1919

Trotsky described Vera Zasulich as an 'exceptional person'. The daughter of an impoverished minor noble, she worked as a clerk and became involved in radical politics. She sympathised with the downtrodden and taught literacy classes for factory workers. In 1869 she was imprisoned for revolutionary activities. After her release she became a member of Land and Liberty (see page 27). Incensed by the cruel treatment of prisoners by the Governor-General of St Petersburg, Trepov, she shot and wounded him in 1878. But the jury found her not guilty (see page 21) and she went into hiding, becoming a hero to the Populists. She later went to Switzerland and joined up with George Plekhanov; she translated Marx's works into Russian which influenced the spread of Marxism in Russia. By this time she had renounced violence as a revolutionary tactic. She was a founder member of the Social Democratic Labour Party in 1898 in Minsk and became a member of the editorial board of *Iskra*, the Party newspaper, along with Lenin and others.

In 1902 she was part of the group of Russian revolutionary exiles living in London. Other revolutionaries were somewhat dismayed by Zasulich's slovenly habits. Trotsky describes her as walking around in crudely made clothes, chain-smoking hand-rolled cigarettes, flicking cigarette butts and ash everywhere. But she was held in great respect by the others, including Lenin. At the 1903 Party conference she sided with the Mensheviks.

After 1905, tired of exile and the underground life of revolutionaries, she retreated to a small cottage and her garden in Russia. She was appalled by the Bolshevik takeover in October 1917 and lived out her days in increasing poverty in the Writers' Home in Petrograd. She died at 69 confiding to her sister, 'Everything that was dear to me for my entire, long life has crumbled and died.'

3 The 1905 revolution

This section will look at the causes, course and consequences of the 1905 revolution, in particular the actions and motivations of different groups.

Challenging the tsarist autocracy

How did the 1905 revolution begin?

At the end of 1903 the situation in Russia was volatile (see pages 82–83) and then war was added to the mix.

The Russo-Japanese War, 1904–05

The war with Japan arose out of Russia's expansionist policy in the Far East. Russia wanted to exploit the area in and around Manchuria, rich in resources and markets and also to control the strategic and ice-free Port Arthur. But Japan, which had already taken control of the Korean peninsula, did not welcome Russian intrusion in an area they had marked out for economic expansion. When Japan proposed a compromise whereby Russia would be ceded predominance in Manchuria if it agreed that Japan could control Korea, the Russians treated the Japanese with disdain. Not long afterwards, Japan launched a surprise attack on Russian ships at Port Arthur on 26 January 1904.

The Russians completely underestimated Japan, which had a better trained army and navy, more effective intelligence and was much closer to the action. The Russians suffered several defeats in early 1904 and had to retreat. Public support for the war quickly turned to dismay. In January 1905, Port Arthur fell to the Japanese and in March, the Russian army was defeated at Mukden. The final humiliation was the naval defeat of the Russian Baltic fleet in May. It had sailed almost half way around the world taking over six months, only to be destroyed in under an hour by the Japanese navy in the Tsushima Straits. These disastrous defeats on land and sea led to Witte being sent off to negotiate the Treaty of Portsmouth under which the Russians withdrew from Manchuria and ceded control of Korea and Port Arthur to Japan.

Abraham Ascher suggests that Russia might have avoided revolution in 1905 if it had not provoked a war with Japan – the catastrophic defeats, he says, justified the opposition claims that the autocratic government was 'irresponsible, incompetent and reckless'. The war acted as a catalyst for meltdown in 1905.

Reaction to the war and its effects

The humiliating defeats at the beginning of 1904 rocked the regime which was looking increasingly incompetent. By July the government was very unpopular and assassination of the much disliked Minister of the Interior, Plehve, in that month was met with public indifference. Opposition groups demanded changes in the way the country was governed. When the liberals decided to hold a national *zemstvo* congress in November, over 5,000 telegrams poured in urging delegates to press for fundamental changes such as an extension of franchise, civil liberties and a national representative body. A series of 'banquets', organised by the Union of Liberation, were really political meetings (not allowed by law) where the liberal intelligentsia discussed matters to do with reforming the political system and extending civil rights. The press reported the meetings in a manner that was increasingly hostile towards the government. The fact that the banquets were allowed to go ahead and the press reports were not censored were indications of the government's weakness and insecurity.

> **Union of Liberation**
>
> This was established in 1903 by Peter Struve, a liberal defector from the Marxist movement. He argued that violent revolution would be disastrous for Russia. He believed that Russia needed a period of political and social evolution as in other European countries during which democracy would be established within a constitutional framework.

Father Gapon

In 1903 Father Gapon was allowed by the police to set up the Assembly of Russian Factory and Mill Workers because he was a loyal monarchist. It seems he genuinely wanted to help workers but his union was infiltrated by ex-Social Democrats. As the situation in St Petersburg deteriorated, Gapon helped to write the petition and organise the march. When the violence erupted he is alleged to have shouted, 'There is no God! There is no Tsar'. He went into hiding and later fled abroad. He returned to St Petersburg but was murdered in March 1906, probably by the *Okhrana* but possibly by SRs.

1 What were the workers asking for in the petition (Source E)?
2 What does the tone of the petition tell you about the attitude of the workers to the tsar?

The economic impact of the war added to the misery of the general population. Trade with the East along the Trans-Siberian railway was disrupted by military priorities. Shortages of raw materials, such as silk, cotton and chemicals, affected industries. This led to factories closing, particularly in St Petersburg, with the resultant loss of jobs. With food prices rising and unemployment increasing, the winter of 1904–05 proved one of growing discontent.

Bloody Sunday

At the beginning of 1905, anti-government feelings were running high in the capital, especially when news came through that the Russians had lost Port Arthur. When four workers were sacked at the giant Putilov engineering works on 7 January, a strike was called which drew in over 100,000 workers. At this stage, it was an economic strike concerned with wages and working hours. However, other large industrial enterprises joined in and suddenly tens of thousands were involved. The situation in the city was becoming tense.

A priest, Father Gapon, organised a petition and a march to the Winter Palace to seek the help of the Tsar. The petition called for an eight-hour day, minimum wages and more dignified treatment. It was not aggressive in tone but later parts did call for the right to form trade unions and an elected parliament.

Source E Extracts from the workers' petition to the Tsar, quoted in *Nicholas II, The Last of the Tsars* by M. Ferro, (Oxford University Press), 1990, pages 81–82.

Sire, We, the workers and inhabitants of St Petersburg ... come to You, Sire to seek justice and protection. We are impoverished; we are oppressed, overburdened with excessive toil, contemptuously treated ... O Sire we have no strength left and our endurance is at an end. We have reached that frightful moment when death is better than the prolongation of our unbearable sufferings ... We ask but little: to reduce the working day to eight hours, to provide a minimum wage of a rouble a day ...

Officials have brought the country to complete ruin and involved it in a shameful war. We working men have no voice in how the enormous amounts raised from us in taxes are spent ... We are seeking here our last salvation. Do not refuse to help Your people.

Up to 150,000 men, women and children – all dressed in their best clothes and carrying icons and pictures of the Tsar – set off on the morning of Sunday 9 January. The march was peaceful and well-disposed towards the Tsar. But as the crowd approached the Winter Palace they were charged by cavalry, and troops opened fire. The casualty figures are unclear but some sources put them at around 130 killed and 300 seriously wounded. The events of Bloody Sunday had a profound effect. They changed the character of the demands of the workers from economic to political. They broke the bond between the Tsar and people. The petitioners had always trusted the 'Little Father' to protect them from corrupt or incompetent officials. But they would never trust him again, as Orlando Figes makes clear:

In the one vital moment the popular myth of a Good Tsar which had sustained the regime through the centuries was suddenly destroyed!

The reaction to Bloody Sunday was dramatic. Strikes and disorder quickly spread to other cities and towns. By the end of January, over 400,000 people were out on strike. Demonstrations and disturbances increased in frequency. On 4 February, the Tsar's own uncle, the Grand Duke Sergei, was assassinated. The shocked regime had lost its nerve and had lost control of the country.

▲ A painting of the Bloody Sunday massacre, Makovsky (1846–1920). What message does the artist wish to convey?

The course of the revolution

What were the most significant events of the 1905 revolution?

There was no shape or order to the outburst of anger that followed Bloody Sunday. Disorder in the form of strikes, demonstrations, riots, vandalism and hooliganism increasingly ruled the cities as the police became largely ineffective. In some places armed gangs and criminals roamed the streets and citizens formed militias or vigilante groups to protect themselves. The action was not all from the left. Right-wing groups came out on the streets in support of the Tsar and attacked anybody whom they deemed unpatriotic.

The leaders of the main socialist parties were nowhere to be seen, as they were mainly in exile in Europe. The workers started to form factory committees to represent themselves, but strikes were spontaneous rather than planned. It was the liberals with the support of students who made the running. In May, a number of professional organisations (such as lawyers, engineers) and trade organisations (such as clerks and book-keepers) came together to form the Union of Unions – a sort of umbrella body – to press the cause of liberal political reform, and notably request a national representative assembly elected by universal suffrage. Political meetings were held in universities thrown open by students. Hundreds of *zemstva* and city councils sent in petitions demanding political change. Added impetus was given to their demands when the Russian Baltic fleet was wiped out at Tsushima (see page 91) in the most humiliating manner in the middle of May. The government was condemned as incompetent and reckless.

Terrorism

During 1905, 3,600 government officials were killed or wounded. This produced fear in the minds of officials and played its part in destabilising the tsarist regime politically and psychologically.

The peasants

The mood of revolt spread to the countryside as the summer arrived. Peasants took advantage of the upheaval. In June and July they began seizing land, grain and animals, burning landlord's houses, cutting timber illegally and refusing to pay rents and taxes. Their general demands were land, the end of redemption payments and a reduction in rents. There was no co-ordinated peasant movement but a whole range of peasant unions and societies appeared. At the end of July, the All-Russian Peasant Union met near Moscow. In a few places peasants set up what were in effect peasant republics, although this meant self-government rather than the overthrow of the monarchy. The army was used to put down peasant uprisings but it was mainly composed of peasants, and mutinies began to spread as whole units refused to carry out orders.

The nationalities

The national minorities took advantage of government disarray in Russia to demand autonomy, democratic government and the end of Russification. The Poles and the Finns demanded outright independence. In many areas, the struggle became very violent, for example, in Caucasus, where officials were attacked. There was a strong nationalist character to demands, for example for local language and culture to be taught in schools. The Tsar dispatched 10,000 troops to Georgia to try to keep it under control. In Poland, there was a virtual state of civil war and the tsarist regime had to keep a force of 300,000 soldiers there. Russian troops shot 93 Poles who took part in demonstrations sparked by Bloody Sunday. This provoked more demonstrations with slogans such as 'Down with Tsarism!' and 'Long Live an Independent Socialist Poland!'. Popular unrest in the Baltic States followed a similar pattern.

The mutiny of the battleship *Potemkin*

With so much of the army being required to deal with the peasants and the nationalities it came as a profound shock when on 14 June the crew of the battleship *Potemkin* mutinied over harsh conditions and being given rotten meat to eat. They seized control of the ship and sailed to Odessa, which was in a state of turmoil with daily demonstrations. The arrival of the ship was warmly received by huge crowds. Troops were ordered to disperse the crowds and opened fire, killing as many as 2,000 citizens. The *Potemkin* escaped, hoping to stir up mutiny on other ships. But, failing to find support, the sailors surrendered the ship in a Romanian port in exchange for safe refuge. This was not only an embarrassment for the government but also a huge wake-up call. The loyalty of the armed forces was paramount. With the growing insurgency in the country, defeats in the war and the possibility of further mutinies in the armed forces, the Tsar realised that he had to end the war with Japan. He called reluctantly on the services of Sergei Witte who negotiated peace in the Treaty of Portsmouth between Russia and Japan on 29 August 1905.

Matters come to a head

In September, labour unrest reached a new level of intensity when a general strike was called. It started with printers (educated and skilled workers) and spread to railway workers who brought the central railway system to a halt. In St Petersburg, Moscow and other cities, industrial and utility workers, shop assistants, actors, bank employees and even staff from government offices – up to 2 million workers – supported the strike. This caused real hardship: food and medical supplies ran short, unburied bodies piled up and there was an explosion of criminality. Middle-class professionals, even some industrialists, supported the strikers and gave money. Barricades went up, manned by a motley mix of workers, students and professionals, initiating clashes with police and Cossacks. The general strike carried on into October.

Particularly significant was the formation of the St Petersburg Soviet on 13 October. Prompted by Mensheviks, the soviet of workers' deputies met to co-ordinate the activities of workers in the general strike. It was made up mainly of representatives elected from factories. It not only directed the general strike, informing workers through its newspaper *Izvestia*, but it also sorted out matters like food supplies. Leon Trotsky, who became deputy chairman, was a driving force, noted for his fiery speeches. The urban workers had emerged as an organised force confronting the autocracy.

The October Manifesto

The Tsar tried to ignore the strike but the country was on the edge of disaster and the Tsar's advisers persuaded him that something had to be done. He turned to Witte, recently returned from successful peace negotiations. Witte told Nicholas that he had to choose between two courses of action – the first was to put down the uprising brutally, the second was to introduce reforms, his favoured option. Nicholas preferred a military dictatorship to constitutional government but his advisers and generals agreed with Witte, and Nicholas was therefore dragged reluctantly to agree to the October Manifesto on 17 October. This conceded:

- civil liberties – freedom of speech (end of the censorship of the press) and conscience, freedom of association and the end of unwarranted arrests
- an elected duma (parliament).

The liberals hailed the October Manifesto as the first step towards constitutional government and for them the main aim of the campaign had been achieved. They now moved to support the Tsar. Witte had achieved what he had set out to do – to isolate the radicals by accommodating the liberals. The St Petersburg Soviet called off the general strike since it was bringing severe hardship to most of those who were involved.

After the granting of the Manifesto there was a brief period of celebration in which political meetings were held in the streets and parks, and new newspapers and publications flourished, testing out the end of censorship. Around this time two important new liberal political parties were formed – the Constitutional Democrats or Kadets and the Octobrists – reflecting two different strands of liberalism (see page 99).

But the peace did not last long. At the end of October there was an explosion of violence. The Tsar's supporters were incensed by the triumphalism of the liberals and socialists. There was fighting between right and left on the streets. Right-wing paramilitary gangs called the Black Hundreds marched around carrying portraits of the Tsar. Tacitly supported by the police, they mounted violent revenge attacks on anybody perceived to be on the left or anti-Tsar. A particularly nasty aspect of this was a concerted attack on Jewish communities, involving the burning of Jewish houses and businesses, rape and looting; over 3,000 Jewish people were murdered in the last two weeks of October 1905.

Soviet – The word *soviet* in Russian simply means 'council'. Factories sent representatives to the council to protect their interests and put across their point of view. In principle any deputy could be recalled at any time if he failed to satisfy his constituents. By the end of November, there were around 80 soviets in a number of cities and in the countryside. They demonstrated the workers' ability to develop an effective form of organisation.

A reluctant tsar

The extent of the Tsar's reluctance to grant constitutional reform is revealed by the story that Grand Duke Nicholas, the Tsar's uncle, pulled out his revolver and threatened theatrically to shoot himself if Nicholas did not agree to the concessions.

The Union of Russian People

During 1905, several monarchist organisations were formed, calling for a complete restoration of the autocracy. Chief among them was the Union of Russian People which had 1,000 branches by the end of 1906. It was instrumental in forming the Black Hundreds. It was anti-liberal, anti-socialist and antisemitic and considered that Russia had been taken over by the intellectuals and the Jewish people. Money was chanelled to it by the Ministry of the Interior; it had police sympathisers and it was favoured by the Orthodox Church. The Tsar wore the Union's badge and wished it 'total success'.

1 What does the Tsar's letter (Source F) tell you about his attitude to the people who wanted change in 1905?

2 Using this source and the other information here, what do you think the Tsar had learnt from the 1905 revolution?

Source F Tsar's letter to his mother, 27 October 1905. Quoted in *A People's Tragedy: The Russian Revolution 1891–1924* by Orlando Figes, (Pimlico), 1997, p127.

My dearest Mama …

I'll begin by saying that the whole situation is better than it was a week ago … In the first few days after the Manifesto the subversive elements raised their heads, but a strong reaction set in quickly and a whole mass of loyal people suddenly made their power felt … The impertinence of the socialists and revolutionaries had angered the people once more; and because nine-tenths of the trouble makers are Jews, the people's whole anger turned against them. That's how the pogroms started.

The tsarist regime regains control

How was order restored?

The new Minister of the Interior, P. N. Durnovo, an uncompromising reactionary, was now determined to re-establish government control, particularly as the St Petersburg Soviet had built up an armed militia of some 6,000 men. On 3 December the leaders of the St Petersburg Soviet and hundreds of its deputies were arrested. This caused an armed uprising in Moscow led by the Social Democrats and barricades were erected. The uprising was crushed, followed by a brutal crackdown with mass arrests, beatings and summary executions. The government now felt confident to take control and moved against any civilians defying authority. The *Okhrana* and the police arrested hundreds of people.

It took longer to restore order in the countryside. A wave of peasant unrest and violence had reached its peak in November, partly because of the deterioration in economic conditions due to the poor harvest. Some of the peasant anger was assuaged when the government promised to cut redemption payments in half in January 1906 (and end them completely by January 1907); it also announced the setting up of the Peasants' Bank to help them buy land. But peasant disturbances continued through most of 1906.

Troops were sent out on punitive expeditions using brutal methods – beatings, rape, flogging and executions – to bring the peasants under control. Between mid-October 1905 and April 1906, as many as 15,000 people were executed and 45,000 deported. The troops worked their way through the Baltic provinces, Ukraine and the Caucasus. In the summer of 1906, field court martials were introduced to deliver fast trials and fast executions (within 24 hours of sentencing). Peasants were hanged in their hundreds. The noose used in the hangings became known as 'Stolypin's necktie', after Peter Stolypin, the new Minister of the Interior (see page 102). This cold-blooded repression had its effect and the resistance to the authorities was everywhere in retreat. The old order was back.

Why was the Tsar able to survive the 1905 revolution?

The Tsar survived the 1905 upheaval for a number of reasons:

- Crucially, the army remained loyal, although there were a number of minor mutinies mainly involving refusal to obey orders. About one-third of infantry units were affected by some kind of disturbance. On 6 December military reforms brought the soldiers back on side. Their pay was increased and their terms of service reduced, for example, from four to three years for infantrymen. They had demanded better food and now, for the first time, they were promised increased meat rations and tea and sugar. Also, they

NOTE-MAKING

Draw a spider diagram to note the reasons why the Tsar survived 1905.

would no longer be required to do forced labour in the civilian economy. The elite army units and the Cossacks had not been touched by mutinies and were rewarded with money and privileges.

- The relatively quick end to the war with Japan and the reasonable peace treaty meant that the Tsar did not lose the support of the military. Also, Nicholas was able to bring back troops from the front to suppress uprisings and disturbances.
- The government used brutal, repressive measures to bring the populace into line and beat them into submission. These methods were effective in re-establishing government control across the Empire.
- The different groups opposing the Tsar – workers, peasants, liberal middle classes, students and national minorities – had different aims and purposes. They were not able to provide a co-ordinated and effective opposition to bring the Tsar down.
- The October Manifesto split the liberals and socialists. The liberals wanted political reform and movement towards a constitutional democracy; the socialists wanted a social revolution. Many liberals felt they had got what they wanted out of the Manifesto and withdrew from further action. This left the socialists isolated and it was much easier for the government to crush them.
- The violence and criminality evident throughout 1905 had put a huge scare into the middle classes. They were frightened by the coarse proletarians on the streets and the intimidating forces that had been unleashed. Houses had been burgled, sons and daughters assaulted, crude behaviour experienced. They wanted it to stop and a return to authority and control. Even Peter Struve, the ex-Marxist, remarked: 'Thank God for the Tsar, who has saved us from the people.'
- The revolutionary parties were not ready for the 1905 revolution and did not play a huge role in events. In fact, the revolutionaries irritated the workers when they squabbled over political ideology. The workers were more concerned with improving their pay and conditions. The Mensheviks did play an important role in the creation of the St Petersburg Soviet and the Bolsheviks were active in radicalising the soviets at the end of 1905 and organising the Moscow uprising in December.
- By the end of 1905, the government was in deep financial trouble. The cost of the war and falling tax revenues were driving the government to the brink of financial collapse. However, Witte secured a huge loan, largely from French bankers, in April 1906. This loan stabilised the economy and gave the government money to pay for its functions for a year. It also paid for the troops who were needed to restore order.

The significance of 1905

The tsarist regime had come through its first real challenge with its institutions intact. It had shown it could survive as long as the army remained loyal. There were mutinies but these were, on the whole, limited in scope and nature. Moreover, the revolutionary parties had played a relatively small part and seemed to present no real threat. Also it appeared that the liberals had no appetite for revolution. Two of the most significant outcomes of 1905 were the Duma and the formation of the liberal political parties. This seemed to offer the liberals and middle classes opportunities in the future to participate in government and they had no wish to see the violence of 1905 repeated.

WORKING TOGETHER

In small groups, write a series of sticky notes. On each one write an outcome from the events of 1905. Include points from the previous section on why the Tsar survived 1905. Each group in turn should submit a note, and stick it on the wall or board, until all the points are exhausted.

Then reflect as a whole class on what the regime should have learned from 1905. Consider how the Tsar and his government should have proceeded if they wanted to survive and to deliver policies to benefit different groups in Russian society.

Ideology and Lenin

From Lenin's standpoint he might well have considered 1905 a dress rehearsal without which 'the revolutions of 1917 would have been impossible'. He drew some important theoretical lessons from 1905, which he was to utilise later on:

- The 'bourgeoisie' and its liberal parties as a political force to combat the autocracy were weak.
- The peasantry had revolutionary potential.
- Nationalist movements in the borderlands could undermine the Empire.

These led him to the key Bolshevik idea that the vanguard of the proletariat, in alliance with the peasantry and nationalities, could seize power without waiting for Russia to go through the 'bourgeois-democratic' revolution and could proceed straight to the socialist revolution.

This all served to reassure the Tsar and his advisers that they were secure and could carry on without making fundamental changes. But this was a false sense of security. They did not appreciate the extent of the disenchantment felt by much of Russian society. Bloody Sunday and the brutal suppression of protest had broken the bond between Tsar and people. The people feared the Tsar but they no longer respected him. The workers were now much more inclined to social revolution, especially as the liberals had deserted them after October. Their protest had not been just about economic demands; it had also been about freedom and the lack of dignity accorded to them in their workplaces and daily lives. In the countryside, landowners noticed that the mood of the peasants had changed and that deference had been replaced by sullen resentment.

The people had experienced political freedoms – the growth of free speech and critical newspapers, the formation of political parties, the soviets and the forthcoming dumas. Liberals, progressive landowners, businessmen and entrepreneurs wanted more freedom of action, civil rights and to escape the heavy hand of the tsarist state. Some areas wanted more self-government or, in the case of the nationalities, independence. These groups would not be happy to see the autocracy go back to carrying on in the same old way.

There has been a tendency for historians to see 1905 as simply part of the build-up to the revolution of 1917, hence Lenin's description of it as a 'dress rehearsal' for the main event. Since it did not change the political or social fabric of the tsarist state, some have said it does not qualify as a revolution. But the historian Abraham Ascher sees it more as an uncompleted revolution. It involved popular protest and a mass movement which opened up new possibilities, including more democratic government through elected dumas and political parties and the expansion of civil rights. The big question now was how the autocracy would respond to these possibilities.

KEY DATES: THE 1905 REVOLUTION

1905

9 January Bloody Sunday.

4 February Assassination of the Grand Duke Sergei.

May Union of Unions formed.

14 June Mutiny of the battleship *Potemkin*.

31 July All-Russian Peasant Union meets.

29 August Treaty of Portsmouth signed – end of war with Japan.

September General strike.

12–18 October Kadet Party formed.

13 October St Petersburg Soviet formed.

17 October October Manifesto.

3 December Leaders of the St Petersburg Soviet arrested.

December Armed uprising in Moscow crushed.

1906 Suppression of peasants and minorities.

4 The constitutional experiment, 1906–14

This section will look at the relationship between the new parliament and the tsarist regime and the role of Peter Stolypin.

The dumas

How far was Nicholas II prepared to work with the dumas?

In the October Manifesto, the Tsar had agreed to the establishment of a duma to represent the people of Russia. This seemed to be a significant step towards constitutional government. However, it was soon clear that Nicholas had no intention of weakening the autocracy. In April 1906, the Tsar issued the Fundamental Laws which stated:

The Sovereign Emperor possesses the initiative in all legislative matters … The Sovereign emperor ratifies the laws. No laws can come into force without his approval.

Moreover, Article 87 of the Laws gave the Tsar the right in 'exceptional circumstances' to pass his own laws without consulting the Duma at all.

The Tsar also announced the creation of a second chamber, the State Council, half of the members of which would be chosen by him. It would have equal power with the Duma and both chambers would have to agree to a legislative proposal before it went to the Tsar for approval. The Tsar retained control of the military and foreign policy as well as the appointment of ministers. All in all, this meant that the Duma had little real power and a limited ability to enact laws.

The liberals were dismayed. This was not what they thought had been agreed in October. This feeling was exacerbated when the system of elections to the Duma was revealed. They had hoped for a universal, equal, secret and direct election. What they got was a complicated system of electoral colleges designed to represent the different social classes. It was profoundly weighted towards the upper classes. For instance, 2,000 landowners were represented by one deputy and 90,000 workers were represented by one deputy. But at least it provided representation for the people across Russia including the nationalities, such as the Poles and Finns.

The dominant political figure in this period was Peter Stolypin who was appointed President of the Council of Ministers in July 1906. He was the most outstanding politician of his time and perhaps the only person who might have steered Russia through this turbulent period. He was a tough conservative and supporter of the autocracy but he also believed that reform was necessary to repair the relationship between tsar and people and bring Russia into the modern age. For a full assessment of him see pages 102–3.

The first two Dumas

Russian society was still in a turbulent state when the first elections to the Duma were held at the beginning of 1906. Nevertheless, people had high expectations of the Duma: it was flooded with petitions, many of them from peasants. The ceremony to open the Duma, held in the Winter Palace, was a tense affair, marked by the division between the Tsar, his family and court decked out in their fine uniforms, dresses and jewellery on one side, and the members of the Duma dressed mainly in the clothing of workers and peasants on the other. One minister confided to his neighbour, 'I even have

The Kadets

Support for the Consitutional Democrats (Kadets) came mainly from the liberal intelligentsia – academics, lawyers, progressive employers, doctors and *zemstvo* men (many of whom were nobles). Their leader was Paul Milyukov, the outstanding professor of history of his day. They wanted a democratically elected assembly, universal suffrage, full civil rights for all citizens, the end of censorship, recognition of trade unions and free education. Despite these avowed aims, they were not a liberal party in the Western sense, calling themselves the 'Party of Popular Freedom'. The left-wing of the party wanted Russia to be turned into a republic while the majority supported the retention of the Tsar as the head of state.

The Trudoviks (labourists)

They were a loose grouping whose main aim was agrarian reform. They consisted mainly of deputies representing the peasants because the SRs had boycotted the elections. Prominent among them later on was Alexander Kerensky.

The national groups

They represented the national minorities, such as the Poles, Finns, the peoples of the Caucasus and central Asia. Most were nationalists seeking to further the interests of their group and more self-government. Some, particularly from the western provinces of the Empire, were Russian nationalists who wanted to preserve the Empire.

the feeling that this man might throw a bomb' and the dowager empress felt threatened, 'so much did they seem to reflect an incomprehensible hatred for all of us'.

Party or group	First Duma	Second Duma	Third Duma	Fourth Duma
SDs Mensheviks	18	47	-	-
SDs Bolsheviks	-	-	19	15
SRs	-	37	-	-
Trudovik	107	104	13	10
Kadets	182	91	54	53
Progressists	27	28	28	41
Octobrists	17	42	154	95
National groups	60	93	26	22
Rightists	8	10	147	154
Others	29	50	-	42
Total	448	518	441	432

▲ **Figure 2** Table to show elected deputies in the Dumas, 1906–14.

The First Duma

In April 1906 the Duma met in its new home, the Tauride Palace. Despite the bias in the electoral system towards the upper classes, it was the Kadets who had won the most seats – over 182 out of 448. The second largest party was the leftist Trudoviks with 107 seats. Other groupings in the Duma were fluid with many deputies not joining any party clearly. The rightists had a much smaller representation (see Figure 2).

There was an air of hostility in the chamber, much of it directed towards the Tsar and his government. The Kadets, annoyed at the limitations imposed by the Tsar, did not hold back. They demanded that the powers of the Duma should be increased and that elections should be universal and secret. They also wanted guarantees of free speech and assembly. There followed two months of bitter disagreement and fierce debates on issues such as civil rights and land ownership. The Tsar, horrified by the hostility and lack of respect, dissolved the Duma which he now considered unworkable. It is reported he said: 'Curse the Duma. It is all Witte's doing.'

Two hundred Kadet deputies took themselves off to Vyborg in Finland where they issued the Vyborg Manifesto urging Russians not to pay their taxes. The government responded by closing down the Kadets' offices and dismissing members of the Party from government service. Many of the rebellious deputies were later arrested and disbarred from re-election. This hurt them in the elections to the second duma.

The Second Duma

Despite the failure of the First Duma to achieve any worthwhile results, peasants and workers still had great hopes for the second Duma and flocked to the polls in huge numbers. Over 70 per cent of eligible workers in St Petersburg voted. It was the left who ran out the winners with over 200 deputies, largely because the revolutionary parties (except the Bolsheviks) had joined the elections for the first time. The Trudoviks were the largest group with 104 deputies; the Kadets, though weakened, had 91. However, the right-wing groupings had also increased their number, with over 60 deputies (many of these were Russian nationalists in the national groups), and the Octobrists now had 42.

The second Duma met in February 1907. It was much more radical than the first and became known as 'The Duma of National Anger'. It was riven by disagreements as right- and left-wing deputies provoked each other. The left made fierce attacks on government ministers and interrupted them when they were speaking in the Duma. After only three months, the Tsar dissolved the Duma using the excuse of the discovery of a plot by Social Democrats to assassinate him.

The Third and Fourth Dumas

After the debacle of the Second Duma, changes were made to the electoral system (known as 'Stolypin's coup', see page 103). The peasants and workers were virtually excluded and non-Russian national groups much reduced. The vote was restricted to the upper and propertied classes. As a result, the Octobrists (154 seats) and Rightists (147 seats) dominated the Third Duma.

The Third Duma

Stolypin was able to work with the Octobrists and those in the centre, and relations between Duma and government were much more co-operative. However, the Third Duma was not subservient; it did not act as a rubber stamp for government policies. It was critical of the government, especially in matters to do with state finances. The right-wing groups tried to put a brake on Stolypin's reforms, in particular his plan to extend the *zemstvo* system to the western part of Russia (see page 103). By 1911 relations were breaking down but at least it showed the Duma could work positively with the government. Government minsters were coming to the Duma to answer questions whereas before they had only explained themselves to the Tsar.

Its main achievements included:

- Stolypin's land reforms, although he faced a lot of opposition
- an education law in 1908, which laid the foundations for universal education, especially compulsory primary schools for eight- to eleven-year-olds
- improvements in the army and navy
- the restoration of the Justices of the Peace, replacing the hated Land Captains
- a progressive national health insurance scheme which would pay sickness benefit to workers.

The Fourth Duma

The Fourth Duma was interrupted by the outbreak of the First World War and met intermittently during the war. Its composition was much the same as that of the Third Duma although the Rightists were stronger and the Octobrists weaker. Its main work involved:

- Continued support and money for the law of 1908, providing for universal education. The number of primary schools had risen significantly up to 1914 and there had been an improvement in literacy rates.
- Reform of the Orthodox Church and the reduction of state control, but Nicholas would make no final decisions on this before war intervened.
- Talks to reduce the huge consumption of vodka because of its impact on public health. No action was taken because the government got so much revenue from it.

It was also critical of the government's handling of increasing social unrest, especially the Lena Goldfields Massacre (see page 104).

The Duma met briefly, but significantly, in 1915 when Nicholas was persuaded to recall it. A 'Progressive Bloc' was formed which offered the Tsar a real chance to work with the people (see page 108). But Nicholas would not countenance it and the Duma was suspended. It met again briefly in 1916 and 1917.

The Rightists

A loose collection of groups on the right with a wide-ranging set of views.

The Octobrists

They took their name from the October Manifesto and thought that constitutional government should go no further than that set out in the Manifesto. However, they did want a new legal order and co-operation between the government and the public. They favoured moderate political reforms. But they also wanted the Tsar to exercise strong government and were nationalists who supported the maintenance of the Russian empire. They were more an association of different groups rather than a defined political party. Their support came from industrialists, landowners and those with commercial interests. This is shown by two of their leading members, Mikhail Rodzianko, a landowner, and Alexander Guchkov, a factory owner.

Progressists

They were mainly businessmen and members of the *zemstva* who wanted to take the programme of reform much further than the Octobrists.

How far was the constitutional experiment working by 1914?

Stolypin was assassinated in September 1911 and, after his death, the constitutional experiment ground to a halt. The new ministers that Nicholas appointed were conservative and unimaginative nonentities who were not likely to cause him any trouble. The power of the prime minister declined and the battles between ministers and conflicting departmental policies returned to its old pattern. There was little chance of a creative relationship with the Duma. Indeed the government abandoned any attempt to present a coherent package of reforms to the Duma. Nicholas and his court cronies were becoming increasingly isolated and depended almost entirely on right-wing support, particularly that of the All-Russian Union of Landowners (or United Nobility).

Nicholas must take a large share of the responsibility for this. He had never really been willing to work with or listen to the Duma. Those close to him were always looking for ways to reduce its power and Nicholas looked for excuses to close down sessions. In Stolypin he had a chance to bring in significant reforms but Nicholas had never backed him in any consistent way and had at the end contrived with his right-wing friends to thwart him. He did not want to change the key institutions of the Russian autocracy or the main legal arrangements. At heart, Nicholas did not believe that democratic government was a good idea; he wanted to preserve the autocracy because he believed it was a better way of running Russia. Not all the blame should be attached to the Tsar, however. The Kadets' demands in the early Dumas were very radical and they were not prepared to compromise or be patient. As a result, the Duma degenerated into quarrels and a bitter struggle between the Tsar and his supporters on the right, and the liberals and other parties on the left. This did not allow for any relationship of trust and co-operation to develop. By 1913, the liberals, a much reduced force, had little hope of getting what they wanted.

Some historians believe that the existence of the Duma showed that political progress was being made. It had done some useful work and there was evidence to show that a working relationship between Duma and government minsters could be established. Further, it provided reason to believe that the regime might slip into some form of constitutional government in the future. Other historians consider that the Duma experiment had failed to bring about any fundamental change to the conduct of government, and the relationship between Tsar and people, and that articulate groups who had participated in the Duma were becoming increasingly disillusioned. The autocracy had fought off any attempt to reform it and the political aspirations of the Russian people had been frustrated. Dominic Lieven, who is generally supportive of the Tsar says: 'Russia's situation in 1914 did not augur well for a peaceful transition to liberalism and democracy. This was partly because the Emperor, who still retained the last word in such matters, could only be pressured into constitutional concessions by the dire and immediate threat of revolution'.

KEY DATES: THE DUMAS

April–June 1906: First Duma

February–June 1907: Second Duma

November 1907–June 1912: Third Duma

November 1912–August 1914: Fourth Duma

LOOK AGAIN

On page 97 the activity asked you to reflect on what had been learned from the 1905 revolution. What do you think now? How well had the Tsar done in the ensuing period up to 1914? Do you think the constitutional experiment could have worked more satisfactorily?

Stolypin

Could Stolypin have saved the Tsar?

Peter Stolypin came to notice as a provincial governor in Saratov where he had forcefully dealt with peasant unrest. He was appointed Minister of the Interior and, soon after, Prime Minister. Stolypin was a strong supporter of the autocracy and opponent of revolution and disorder. He had set up field courts-martial in 1906 to crush peasant uprisings. Under his watch, thousands of peasants were executed by hanging ('Stolypin's neckties') and thousands sent into exile in 'Stolypin carriages' (railway cars). This earned him the enmity of the left who condemned him as a brutal butcher.

However, he was not a diehard supporter of autocracy. Like Witte before him, he believed that reform was essential to solve Russia's problems. He believed that industrial progress alone was not sufficient to take Russia forward and gave his main attention to agriculture. His land reforms (see page 59) had bold aims: to feed the rapidly growing population and create a strong conservative peasantry who would support the regime. If he had succeeded, this would indeed have radically altered Russia's future. But it was always going to take years to work in the face of a deeply conservative peasantry. He did not have that time.

Stolypin was virtually the only prime minister of the constitutional decade to see the Duma as a partner in building a strong Russia. He did not consider that he was limiting the monarch's authority but rather giving it a broader social base. In particular he developed an understanding with the Octobrists which allowed him to push through his reforms. His success suggested the possibility of a working relationship between government and elected assembly.

However, his own actions undermined this relationship. He had, in what was known as 'Stolypin's coup', radically changed the electoral system when the Second Duma proved unworkable. To all intents and purposes he had deprived the workers and peasants of their votes and created a more conservative electorate likely to produce a more amenable Duma. Also, he cynically used Article 87 of the Fundamental Laws which allowed him to pass measures by decree when the Duma was not sitting. In March 1911 he persuaded the Tsar to suspend both houses of the Duma to allow him to force his measure to introduce *zemstva* in the western provinces. This alienated the Duma including the majority of the Octobrists who had hitherto supported him.

Stolypin was assassinated at the theatre in September 1911 but his star was already waning by this time. He had proposed a series of reforms to extend civil rights, reform local government (giving the peasants more influence in *zemstva*) and local justice (abolishing Land Captains) and make changes in education and a reform of emergency powers. The right and those close to the Tsar considered that his dangerous reform policies undermined the principles of autocracy and they worked to block him and get him out of office. When he died, it seems that the Tsar was quite pleased to see the back of him; the Tsar's wife, Alexandra, had always hated Stolypin.

The enmity which confronted Stolypin from all sides demonstrated the difficulty of taking a middle road in Russia. He seemed to understand this himself when he commented to Bernard Pares, a British historian, in 1906, 'I am fighting on two fronts. I am fighting against revolution, but for reform. You may say that such a position is beyond human strength and you may be right.' In the final analysis, apart from his land reforms, he was not able to implement much of his programme of reforms and even then only with the use of emergency powers.

Stolypin remains a controversial figure. He has many admirers who believe that, given the support of the Tsar and the time to implement his reforms, he was the only person who could have saved Russia from revolution and brought about a more peaceful transition into the modern age. According to Richard Pipes, the conservative American historian, 'Stolypin stood head and shoulders above his immediate predecessors and successors in that he combined a vision of the desirable with a sense of the possible; he was a rare blend of statesman and politician.'

Russia on the eve of war

How revolutionary was Russia in 1914?

Some historians argue that the tsarist regime was making progress economically and politically and, given a period of stability, could have developed into a parliamentary democracy and modern industrial state. Others maintain that it was heading for disaster and revolution before the war intervened. Guchkov, the Octobrist leader, told his followers in November 1913 that the government's actions were revolutionising society and the people. 'With every day, people are losing faith in the state and in the possibility of a normal, peaceful resolution of the crisis', the probable outcome of which was 'a sad unavoidable catastrophe'. So, how revolutionary was Russia in 1914?

As we saw in the last chapter, the Russian economy was doing well in the lead up to the war (see pages 55–56). After 1905 the labour movement had retreated due to the repression of trade unions, but there was a revival of militancy from 1912. It started with the Lena Goldfields Massacre in April 1912. Striking workers, protesting about degrading working conditions, low wages and a fourteen-hour working day, clashed with troops and over 200 people were killed and many injured. This opened the floodgates to workers' protests. Workers became increasingly militant and the frequency and scale of strikes increased in the years 1912–14 (see Figure 3). A good deal of these were political as well as economic in character. July 1914 saw a general strike in St Petersburg involving barricades and street fighting.

Some historians have argued that this is evidence that workers were turning to the Bolsheviks and the notion of armed struggle. Support for the Bolsheviks had increased in the larger factories and they had gained control of some of the biggest unions in St Petersburg and Moscow, such as the Metalworkers Union. The Bolshevik paper, *Pravda*, had achieved a national circulation of 40,000 copies per issue, over twice that of its Menshevik rival. Orlando Figes says thousands of strikes under Bolshevik slogans meant that urban Russia arguably found itself on the brink of a potentially more violent revolution than in 1905. However R. B. McKean in his study, *St Petersburg Between the Revolutions: Workers and Revolutionaries June 1907–February 1917* argues that most workers did not work in the larger factories and were not socialists. He says that the strikes were mainly about pay and working conditions and that only a relatively small number were engaged in radical activity.

In other areas of Russian life, there were no indications of imminent revolution in 1914:

- The villages were relatively quiet before 1914 and there had been no major upheavals and disturbances. Several years of good harvests certainly helped. However, Stolypin's reforms had proved divisive and the peasants had not been tied closer to the Tsar as he had hoped. Rural poverty was still very severe in some areas, particularly the populous central districts. The repression of 1906–07 was fresh in people's memories and Orlando Figes says there was a simmering resentment in the countryside.
- In 1914 the army remained loyal. However, Edward Acton points out that the experience of 1905–06 and the subsequent reforms had weakened the reliability of the army as an instrument of control. The mutinies in 1905 and 1906 could not be easily forgotten. Cutting the period of service to three years brought the army into much closer contact with the stresses and strains of civilian society. Also, as the officer corps became more professional, it became more determined not to be used for crushing civilian disturbances.

Year	Total strikes	Strikes regarded as political	Number of strikers
1911	466	24	105,110
1912	2,032	1,300	725,491
1913	2,404	1,034	861,289
1914 (Jan–July)	3,534	2,401	1,448,684

▲ **Figure 3** Number of strikes in Russia in the years 1911–14.

- The liberal opposition was weak and divided and not in a position to cause the regime much trouble. The Octobrists and the Kadets distrusted each other. The Kadets had never really recovered from the early days of the Duma. The Octobrists had lost influence after the Third Duma. Both parties and the liberal middle classes in general feared the masses and so did not want to see revolution.
- Government repression after 1905 had decimated the revolutionary parties.
  - The SRs had been infiltrated by the *Okhrana* and were obsessed with the issue of double agents after the head of their terrorist wing, Envo Azef, had been exposed as an *Okhrana* agent. There were divisions among the leadership, and between the leadership and the rank and file. They were in disarray before 1914.
  - The Mensheviks were doing better. They had taken advantage of the new political freedoms won in 1905 and created a legal labour movement. This had increased their support in the trade unions where they outstripped the Bolsheviks. But they were not contemplating revolutionary action.
  - The Bolsheviks also had been penetrated. Four out of five of the party's St Petersburg committee in 1909 were *Okhrana* agents. Lenin's close confidant, Roman Malinowsky, worked as an *Okhrana* agent and wreaked havoc on the Bolshevik underground between 1910 and 1913. The Bolshevik leadership was either in exile or, like Lenin, isolated abroad. There is evidence as we saw above that workers were becoming radicalised and turning to the Bolsheviks but even as late as January 1917 Lenin said, 'We, the old people, perhaps won't survive until the decisive battles of the forthcoming revolution', so he clearly did not envisage the Bolsheviks leading a revolution in that year.

5 War and revolution

This section will examine the effects of the First World War on Russia and how it contributed to the collapse of the tsarist autocracy.

The impact of the First World War

What impact did the First World War have on Russia?

When war broke out in August 1914, Russia's internal divisions were temporarily forgotten and Nicholas rode a wave of popular support. Paintings of the Tsar were carried in processions and crowds sang the national anthem. The *Times* correspondent wrote:

For perhaps the first time since Napoleon's invasion of Russia, the people and their Tsar were one, and the strength that unity spreads in a nation stirred throughout the Empire.

The German-sounding St Petersburg (Peter's town) was changed to the more Slavonic Russian-sounding Petrograd. But the initial enthusiasm did not last long.

At the Front

The Russians had the largest army and gained some early successes against the Austro-Hungarians. But it was a different story against the Germans. In August 1914, at the battle of Tannenberg, and in September at the Masurian Lakes, the Russians took heavy losses and were driven back. There followed a long retreat and by autumn 1915 they had been forced out of Poland, Lithuania and Latvia. Between May and December of 1915, 1 million Russians were killed and a similar number were taken prisoner. The Russians recovered during the winter of 1915–16 and in the summer of 1916 General Brusilov launched a brilliant

NOTE-MAKING

Make notes on the impact of the war on:
- soldiers and their morale
- the people at home.

The First World War, 1914–18

In the years before 1914, Russia had joined France and Britain in the Triple Entente to safeguard itself against the dual alliance of Europe's central powers – Germany and Austria-Hungary. When the Archduke Franz Ferdinand, heir to the Austro-Hungarian throne, was assassinated in June 1914 these two armed camps were drawn into a war which began in August of that year.

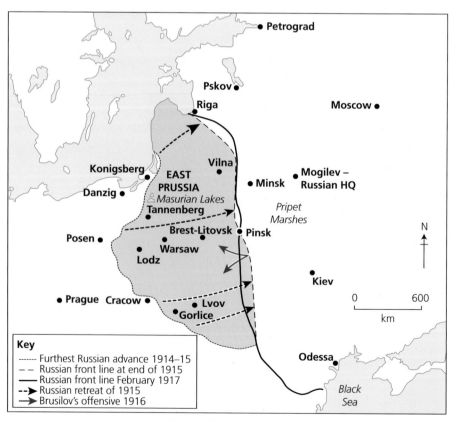

▲ **Figure 4** Map showing Russian battle lines, 1914–17.

offensive, which brought the Austrians to their knees with over half their army killed or captured. But the Germans moved troops to reinforce them and the Russians were pushed back once more.

The real problem for the Russians was at the top: the quality of leadership was poor, with notable exceptions like Brusilov. Many of the top officers had been appointed because of their loyalty to the Tsar. They had no experience of fighting and little military expertise. There was no clear command structure and no war plan was developed. The performance of the War Ministry was dire, compounded by the breakdown of the distribution system: there was a lack of supplies and equipment, especially rifles, ammunition and boots. The shortage of rifles was so bad on some parts of the Front that soldiers had to rely on picking up the rifles of men shot in front of them. Often the war materiels were available but they were not where they were needed.

When Mikhail Rodzianko, the President of the Duma, went on a special fact-finding tour, he received complaints about the lack of basic supplies and found wounded soldiers left in the cold and rain, filth and dirt, pleading to have their wounds dressed. The morale of the soldiers was hard hit by the incompetence of their officers and the lack of regard for their welfare – tens of thousands deserted.

However, the Russian war effort was not the total disaster it has sometimes been portrayed as. The Russian soldiers fought valiantly and had considerable success against the Austrians. Norman Stone has pointed out that by 1916 the Russians were matching the Germans in shell production and there had been a 1,000 per cent growth in the output of artillery and rifles. They had contributed significantly to the Allied victory by mounting attacks on the Eastern Front to relieve pressure on the Western Front. Also, according to Stone, the army was not on the verge of collapse at the beginning of 1917; it was still intact as a fighting force.

The home front

The war put a huge strain on the Russian economy and exposed its structural weaknesses. The railways, which were barely able to cope with freight traffic in peacetime, were now overwhelmed. Moscow, at the centre of the railway system, became a huge bottleneck and the signalling system collapsed. The goods and supplies were available but were not getting to where they were supposed to; instead they ended up in trucks in sidings waiting for engines or lines to be unblocked. Food rotted and factories closed as they were starved of raw materials.

The war had a huge impact on Russians at home:

- It took its toll in a personal way. As the list of casualties (around 8 million) mounted there was hardly a family that had not been affected by a son killed or captured.
- There was severe shortages of food because:
  - the railway system had collapsed
  - food was being sent to the Front as a priority
  - there was a lack of grain coming onto the market. Partly this was because food was being diverted to the military. But also peasants were not selling it because the conversion of factories to military work meant there was little for peasants to buy. Also they could buy less with the money they were paid because of inflation, so many hoarded their grain and food products.
- Inflation hit people very hard; in rough terms, the price of food and fuel quadrupled between 1914 and 1916 while wages only doubled. This meant that people could not afford to pay for basic items.

Inflation

The war was very expensive. The government needed increasing amounts of money to pay for wages, for supplies and to keep business moving. So Russia abandoned the gold standard and started printing more and more notes. The inevitable result of this was inflation as people sought to buy goods that were in short supply.

Petrograd suffered more than other places because it was remote from food-producing areas. By 1916, it was receiving barely one-third of the food and fuel it required. There were endless queues for everything. The shortage of food was a major source of anger, matched only by the ban on vodka sales. Also the influx of refugees from German-occupied areas led to serious overcrowding and a deterioration in living standards. Strikes had broken out in 1915 and they increased in number, frequency and militancy during 1916.

Government incompetence and the role of the Tsar

The bureaucracy, which had never been known for its efficiency, buckled under the demands of total war. Confidence in the government evaporated as its incompetence and inability to organise supplies for the military at the Front and the people in the cities became apparent. Disgusted at the ineptitude of official organs, the *zemstva* and municipalities started forming their own bodies to provide medical care, hospitals and hospital trains for the thousands of wounded soldiers. These bodies eventually united to form one organisation – *Zemgor* – which went on to supply uniforms, boots and tents. Professional groups and businessmen formed War Industries Committees (WICs) to shift factories over to military production. Leading liberals played an important role in these non-governmental organisations that seemed to offer an alternative – and much more effective – form of government. So, even though these organisations were fully supportive of the war, the autocracy regarded them with suspicion and would not co-operate with them. The Tsarina, in particular, saw them as revolutionary bodies undermining the autocracy; and indeed they did act as a focus for criticism of the bureaucracy's failings.

The Tsar was pressurised into reconvening the Duma in July 1915. Progressive elements in the Duma (about two-thirds of the total deputies) formed the 'Progressive Bloc'. They wished to be fully involved in the war effort and wanted to prevent the country slipping into revolution and anarchy, which frightened them as much as anybody else. The Bloc called for a 'ministry of national confidence' in which elected members of the Duma would replace incompetent ministers to form a new government. This offered a real chance for the Tsar to be seen to be working with the people and to offload some of the responsibility for the war. But the Tsar would not countenance it and suspended the Duma, which only met again briefly in 1916 and 1917. The Progressive Bloc became frustrated by his intransigence. In November 1916, Milyukov, the Kadet leader, made a speech listing the government's shortcomings around the question: 'Is this stupidity or treason?' (see Source G). He also declared that the Duma would fight the government 'with all legitimate means until you go'.

Source G Speech by Paul Milyukov to the Duma, November 1916, quoted in *Russia 1914–41*, by John Laver, (Hodder Education), 1991, pp 6–7.

We now see that we can no more legislate with this government than we can lead Russia to victory with it. When the Duma declares again and again that the home front must be organised for a successful war and the government continues to insist that to organise the country means to organise revolution, and consciously chooses chaos and disintegration – is this stupidity or treason? ... We have many reasons for being discontented with this government. But all these reasons boil down to one general one: the incompetence and evil intentions of the present government ... And therefore in the name of the millions of victims and their spilled blood ... we shall fight until we get a responsible government which is in agreement with the general principles of our programme.

Total war – A war which is not restricted to the warfront and where the economy and lives of citizens are bound up in prosecuting the war.

---

1 What does Milyukov mean (Source G) when he says 'and the government continues to insist that to organise the country means to organise revolution, and consciously chooses chaos and disintegration – is this stupidity or treason?'?

2 What answer do you think he expects?

3 What are the reasons they have 'for being discontented with this government'?

The Tsar's actions

In August 1915 the Tsar made a huge mistake: he decided to take direct control of the army and went off to military headquarters in Mogilev, 60km from Petrograd. This had a number of serious consequences for him:

1 He now became personally responsible for the conduct of the war. If things went badly he would be directly to blame; he could not pass off the responsibility to his generals.

2 He was away from Petrograd for long periods of time, leaving the Tsarina and Rasputin in control of the government. 'Lovy,' she wrote to her husband, 'I am here, don't laugh at silly old wifey, but she has "trousers" on unseen.'

Nicholas' absence created chronic instability in the government. There were constant changes of ministers – a game of ministerial leapfrog in which the hand of the Tsarina can be detected. Competent people were dismissed: for instance, the War Minister, Polivanov, who was rebuilding the army and supply system with some success after the disasters of 1915, was discharged. The Tsarina regarded him as a traitor and a 'revolutionist' because of his willingness to work with *Zemgor* and the WICs. Incompetent people were appointed, often because they flattered the Tsarina or because they were recommended by Rasputin. The appointment of Sturmer as Prime Minister in February 1916 caused great disquiet: not only was he incompetent and dishonest but he also had a German name.

The Tsarina and Rasputin became the focus of growing public anger and antagonism towards the regime. She was portrayed as a German spy, deliberately conniving with Rasputin to betray Mother Russia. Pornographic cartoons and letters found their way into the press and implied that she was having an illicit relationship with Rasputin and was under his control. Even the rapidly diminishing supporters of the Tsar could not put up with the degenerate monk and the 'German woman' running the country. In December 1916, a member of the royal family, Prince Yusupov, arranged to murder Rasputin in a last ditch effort to save the autocracy. But the damage had been done: many were now convinced the regime was not worth saving.

It is not surprising that by the end of 1916 support for the Tsar was haemorrhaging fast. The political authority of the Tsar and the regime was disintegrating. All classes in society were disillusioned by the way the government was running the war and since the Tsar embodied the government and had taken direct control of the armed forces it was towards him that the finger of responsibility was pointed. The governing elite was in disarray and even some of the nobility were supporting the Progressive Bloc in the Duma. People were talking about an impending revolution. Guchkov, the Octobrist leader, had actually asked the army generals whether they would support moves to get rid of Nicholas. They indicated they would not intervene to save the Tsar, whom they considered a liability, but they did want to retain the monarchy.

The situation in Petrograd was becoming tense as a police report at the end of 1916 made clear (see Source H on page 110).

Ministerial leapfrog: September 1915 to February 1917

3 Ministers of Foreign Affairs

3 Ministers of Transport

3 Ministers of War

4 Ministers of Agriculture

4 Prime Ministers

5 Ministers of Internal Affairs

The Rasputin effect

The rumours about the Tsarina and Rasputin, which had no foundation in fact, served to mobilise an angry public against the monarchy. This was not lost on the German propagandists who dropped pictures of the Tsar resting against Rasputin's private parts. It was one of the factors contributing to the erosion of support for the Tsar from the top echelons as well as the general public.

WORKING TOGETHER

In separate lists, write the mistakes and failures of the Tsar, Tsarina and the government in the lead up to the February revolution.

When you have done this, compare these with the essay written by Beryl Williams (see page 115) and consider whether it was the Tsar or the war that was most responsible for the revolution in 1917. Draw also on your previous work on Nicholas.

Source H Extracts from a police report in October 1916. Quoted in *End of the Russian Empire* by M. Florinsky, (Collier Books), 1961, pp 165–66.

In the opinion of the spokesman of the labour group of the Central War Industries Committee the industrial proletariat of the capital is on the verge of despair and it believes that the smallest outbreak, due to any pretext, will lead to uncontrollable riots ... the stage for such outbreaks is more than set: the economic position of the masses ... is distressing ... Even if we assume that wages have increased by 100 per cent, the cost of living in the meantime has risen by an average of 300 per cent. The impossibility of obtaining, even for cash, many foodstuffs and articles of prime necessity, the waste of time involved in spending hours waiting in line in front of stores, the increasing death rate due to inadequate diet and insanitary lodgings (cold and dampness as a result of lack of coal and firewood) etc., all these conditions have created a situation that the mass of industrial workers are quite ready to let themselves go to the wildest excesses of a hunger riot.

In addition to economic hardships the 'legal disabilities' of the working class have of late become 'intolerable and unbearable', the denial of the mere right to move freely from one factory to another has reduced labour, in the opinion of the Social Democrats, to the state of mere cattle, good only for the 'slaughter of war'. The prohibition of all labour meetings ... the closing of trade unions ... and so on make the labour masses, led by the more advanced and already revolutionary-minded elements, assume an openly hostile attitude towards the Government.

> What reasons does Source H suggest for growing working-class militancy?

The February revolution

Was the revolution of February 1917 spontaneous?

The winter of 1916–17 was a bitterly cold one and the new year started with strikes and lock-outs. The Tsarina ignored warnings from the secret police and condemned strikers as hooligans. When leading members of the Duma tried to make her aware of how serious matters were, she claimed they were undermining the government. Then, towards the end of February 1917 it was announced that bread was to be rationed. Some women spent almost 24 hours in queues for food. Scuffles over remaining bread stocks turned into riots.

On Thursday 23 February, International Women's Day, the discontent became more focused. What started off as a good-humoured march in the morning took on a different mood in the afternoon. Women, many of them textile workers on strike, took the lead in politicising the march, overturning trams and blocking the streets. The women marched to the Vyborg district of Petrograd, a working-class area with a history of radical action. They persuaded men from the highly politicised Putilov engineering works and other factories to join them. A huge crowd began to make its way towards the centre of the city. They crossed the ice of the frozen River Neva and burst on to Nevsky Prospekt, the main street in Petrograd. The protest started to gather momentum.

Over the next three days, the demonstrations took on a more political nature. Demands for bread were accompanied by demands for an end to the war and an end to the Tsar. Observers reported that there was almost a holiday atmosphere in the city as all classes of people joined in the protests. There was no central organisation of events. No political party was in charge: all the main leaders of the revolutionary parties were abroad or in exile. But socialist cells, particularly Bolsheviks, were active in getting the workers out on the streets. Many factories were shut down and shops and restaurants closed.

The turning points

The weekend of 25–26 February proved the turning point. Demonstrations in the past had been dealt with effectively by troops. The difference this time was that many soldiers refused to take action against the people. When Nicholas realised that things were getting out of hand in Petrograd, he ordered troops to put down the disorders and some regiments opened fire on the crowds, killing demonstrators. This tipped the scales. The crowds became hostile and the soldiers now had to decide which side they were on. One by one, regiments moved over to the side of the people. There was some fighting between the soldiers in different regiments and a number of officers were killed, but this was largely over by 27 February. According to Orlando Figes:

The mutiny of the Petrograd garrison turned the disorders of the last four days into a full-scale revolution.

The Duma takes control

While these events unfolded, the Tsar was still at Mogilev. Rodzianko, the President of the Duma, sent him a telegram explaining how serious things were and suggested that a new government be formed with more power given to elected representatives. Nicholas' answer was to suspend the Duma and send troops to the capital to restore order. But the Duma members remained in the Tauride Palace and held informal meetings while crowds of people outside demanded that they do something.

On Monday 27 February, the Duma formed a special committee made up of representatives of the main political parties. The committee realised that things had gone too far for the Tsar to be involved in any kind of government. The Russian Army High Command had come to the same conclusion and put a stop to the troop movements on Petrograd. Nicholas made a last ditch effort to get back to the capital but his train was stopped outside the city. When the generals told the Tsar they would not support him, he knew the time to go had come. On 2 March he abdicated in favour of his brother Michael; but Michael, realising the extent of anti-monarchical feeling, refused and the Romanov dynasty came to a swift end. The Duma committee set about forming a new government.

The revolution of February 1917 was not a bloodless revolution. Some estimates put the death toll at around 1,500 with several thousands wounded. But it had been accomplished with remarkable self-restraint on the part of the people.

Source I From *The Russian Revolution 1917–21*, by B. Williams, (Blackwell), 1987, pages 8–9.

The fall of the Russian monarchy was accomplished over a ten-day period from 23 February to 4 March 1917. Ten days of popular demonstrations, political manoeuvring and army mutiny developed imperceptibly into a revolution which no one expected, planned or controlled ... Moreover, there was no doubt that the initiators of the revolution were the workers and the reserve troops in the capital ... All the major leaders of the revolutionary movement were in Siberia or abroad when the movement started, and certainly no political party organized the revolution.

Source J *The Russian Revolution, 1917–1921*, by W. H. Chamberlain, (Macmillan), 1935.

The collapse of the Russian autocracy ... was one of the most leaderless, spontaneous, anonymous revolutions of all time.

The role of NCOs and the Petrograd garrison

The NCOs in the army, the non-commissioned officers or sergeants, were crucial in the decision not to open fire on the demonstrators. These men had a more direct relationship with the soldiers than their senior officers and it seems they had decided that they would not fire on the crowds. Also, many of the soldiers in the Petrograd garrison were young reservists who identified more easily with the people on the streets. They were desperate not to be sent to the front line and they shared the dissatisfaction with the way the war was being conducted and its impact on ordinary Russians.

What do Sources I and J suggest about the nature of the February revolution?

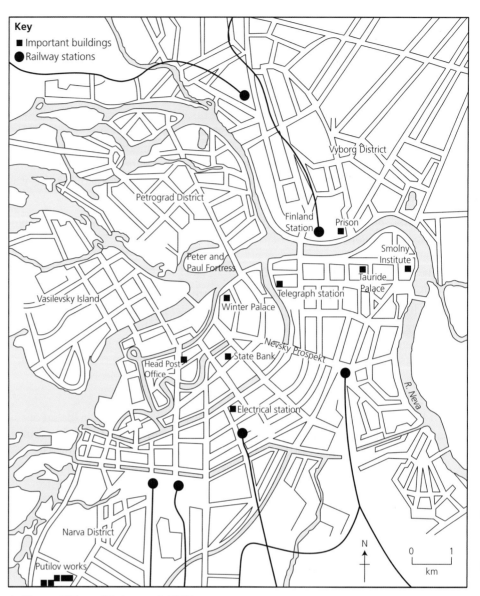

▲ **Figure 5** Map of Petrograd, 1917.

The role of the army

Whereas the army remained loyal to the Tsar in 1905, it went over to the side of the people in 1917. The army of February 1917 was a very different army from the one at the beginning of the war in 1914. Fourteen million men had been mobilised and approximately half of them had been killed, wounded or taken prisoner. A fundamental change had taken place in the officer corps with the promotion of peasant and lower middle-class men who were often liberals or socialists, replacing aristocratic and conservative officers. Also, many of the replacement soldiers were sympathetic to the people on the streets and unwilling to suppress disorders. The generals also played a crucial role when they decided they could not support the Tsar. Probably they hoped for some sort of constitutional monarchy with a new member of the royal family at its head. If they had known what was going to happen later on in the year, they may have acted differently.

Interpretations:

What were the causes of the February revolution?

The causes of the February revolution have been the subject of fierce debate and there are many interpretations partly for political reasons and partly because more archival and other evidence has become available. In all of these, the First World War looms large and it must be remembered that other large empires – the German, Austro-Hungarian and Ottoman – also collapsed at this time. We are going to outline below some major strands of thought but it should be clear that these are generalised positions and the historians within them differ in their own interpretations.

A number of Western historians, such as Robert McKean and Beryl Williams, have argued that:

- The tsarist regime was making progress on the political and economic front before 1914.
- Industrial growth had been dramatic and agriculture was improving with increased production and new crops and methods, although some parts of Russia were still backward.
- The countryside was relatively quiet before 1914 and workers' action was mainly for economic not political reasons.
- There were signs of political progress with government ministers working more with the Dumas, although they would accept that momentum had been lost after Stolypin's death.
- The First World War produced stresses and strains that the tsarist bureaucracy could not cope with and this was the main cause of the February revolution.

The general position is that if the war had not intervened then the tsarist regime would have carried on and developed into a modern industrialised state. Beryl Williams has expressed a variation of this perspective in her essay on page 115.

Other historians, often called revisionists, give more attention to social, economic and institutional factors. They argue that:

- There were underlying weaknesses in the structure of the tsarist regime – its administration, bureaucracy and political institutions.
- The autocratic regime could not cope with the problems resulting from industrialisation and modernisation.
- The majority of peasants lived in poverty, partly caused by the policies of the government, and in certain areas were land hungry and resented the landowners and government officials.
- The demands and aspirations of the workers had not been met.
- Although some in the ruling elite, like Witte and Stolypin, saw the need for reform, the Tsar and his most reactionary supporters were hostile to the political demands and social transformations that reforms entailed and obstinately stuck to an outdated vision of autocracy.
- There was conflict between society becoming more educated, more urban and more complex and a fossilised autocracy that would not concede its political demands for more representation, especially from the growing middle classes.
- The war exposed all these structural and institutional weaknesses, the regime could not cope with the stresses and strains produced by the war, and the February revolution was the result.

Sheila Fitzpatrick argues that Russian society on the eve of the war was so deeply divided and the political and bureaucratic structure so fragile and overstrained that it was vulnerable to any kind of jolt, even without the war.

KEY DATES: WAR AND REVOLUTION

1914

30 July Orders for full Russian mobilisation given

1 August Germany declared war on Russia

1915

July Progressive Bloc formed in Duma

August Nicholas took direct control of army and left Petrograd

1916

1 December Rasputin murdered

1917

23 February International women's day demonstration

25–26 February Turning point, soldiers join the people

27 February Duma special committee formed

2 March Nicholas II abdicated

Historians take all sorts of different positions within these broad arguments. George Keenan who initially thought the autocracy had a good chance of evolving into a constitutional monarchy, but for the war, later changed his mind to maintain that there had not been sufficient political reform to ensure its survival. Christopher Read argues that even those who think that Russia was developing rapidly saw little chance of the autocracy surviving the process. Richard Pipes, a conservative historian and often critical of the revisionists, stresses the weaknesses of the regime in the face of the challenge of modernisation in a deeply divided country. The prevalence and intensity of hatred – ideological, ethnic and social – was such that sooner or later there would again be recourse to violence.

None of these arguments absolve Nicholas II from responsibility for the revolution that unseated him. All agree that his actions before the war (for example, lack of reform, unwillingness to work with *zemstva* and the Dumas, etc.) and mistakes during the war contributed to the collapse of the autocracy.

But the institutional and structural weaknesses of the autocracy cannot be laid solely at his door. They go back much further and, as Dominic Lieven said on page 80, it is doubtful that any tsar would have been able to cope with the problems of modernising Russia within the framework of an autocracy.

Chapter summary

- After 1900, Russia was in a turbulent and unsettled state, made worse by the Russo-Japanese War. The government was seen as incompetent.
- Bloody Sunday initiated a year of strikes, uprisings, mutinies and political action – the 1905 revolution.
- The Tsar was forced to issue the October Manifesto in which he agreed to an elected duma and civil rights. As a result, the liberals and middle classes withdrew from the revolution. The workers were crushed by the authorities and the army suppressed brutally the peasants and national minorities during 1906.
- The tsarist regime survived in 1905 because the army had remained loyal and the opposition lacked unity and common purpose.
- The Tsar undermined the constitutional experiment by announcing the Fundamental Laws which reasserted the principle of autocracy.
- The first two Dumas were riven with disagreements and short-lived. Changes in the electoral system to favour the propertied classes changed the composition of the Duma and some progress in reform was made in the Third and Fourth Dumas.
- Stolypin might have been able to make the constitutional experiment work but he was hated by the right and left and did not receive the support of the Tsar. After his death the regime became increasingly isolated and reliant on right-wing support.
- The First World War had a devastating impact on Russia, with millions killed or wounded, damaging the morale of the soldiers. The Russian economy could not cope with the requirements of total war. The distribution system broke down and there were serious food and fuel shortages in towns and cities.
- The government bureaucracy was incompetent and inefficient, so businessmen and the *zemstva* set up their own organisations to supply the army with the necessary war materials. These offered an alternative form of government.
- The Tsar made fatal mistakes: a) going to the Front and taking personal responsibility for the war; b) leaving in charge the Tsarina and Rasputin who became a focus of antagonism towards the regime.
- By February 1917 support for the Tsar had eroded and the people swept him from power in a spontaneous revolution.

Working on interpretation skills: extended reading

How significant was the First World War in the downfall of tsarism?

Beryl Williams assesses the conditions in Russia which led to revolution.

In 1913 the Romanovs celebrated their dynasty's tercentenary. Huge crowds along the Volga cemented Nicholas II's belief in autocracy, but elsewhere people recalled that the first Romanov had been elected, and there were calls for fuller implementation of the October Manifesto of 1905. Both industry and agriculture grew strongly again after 1909. Russia was becoming a market economy with a developing civil society and a Westernised urban culture. She was the fourth or fifth economic power and catching up with the West, although per capita income remained low. By 1913 the major cities had electric street lighting, cinema, department stores, a popular mass-circulation press and high foreign investment. Primary education and literacy were government priorities. Russia had recovered well from revolution in 1905. 5 10

The Stolypin reforms did not end the commune or create a land of smallholders, but the countryside did change. Ownership was transferred to heads of families and plots were consolidated even if peasants preferred to stay in their villages and keep communal grazing rights. Peasants increasingly bought or rented land and the successful co-operative movement enabled growing for the market and the purchase of town-made goods. Regional variations persisted but peasant incomes were growing. Disputes were now taken to local courts and agronomists taught new production techniques. The countryside was quiet in 1914. 15 20

After 1909 industrial growth was again over six per cent and towns grew rapidly. St Petersburg had the greatest concentration of heavy industry and the revival of a strike movement after 1912 was concentrated in its huge metallurgical factories. Demands were increasingly political, but strikes were short-lived, and it was the young, unskilled workers who were attracted to radicalism. Workers were deeply divided in skills, interests and education and the vast majority were more concerned with obtaining dignified and respectful treatment, better hours and pay and educational opportunities, than in attending revolutionary meetings. Party leaders were in exile or prison and revolutionaries had relatively little influence. 25 30

A growing middle class of merchants, businessmen, artisans and professionals worked with zemstvos. In Moscow merchant philanthropists ran the town council and founded hospitals, schools, worker accommodation, and even theatres. Professional, charitable and mutual-aid societies held congresses and often worked with state officials despite bureaucratic opposition. The State Duma, although with a reduced electorate after 1907, survived with legislative powers, and its work was publicised by a relatively free press. Russia was at the forefront of European culture and despite intellectual talk of a coming apocalypse and 'hooliganism', such fears merely reflected rapid social change. 35 40

Some Ministers were prepared to work with society but Nicholas himself was reluctant to accept the implications of the changes granted in 1905. There was still no cabinet system and in 1913 he was prevented by the State Council from reducing the Duma to a consultative body. Nationality problems were bound to increase in an age of nationalism, but Russia's changes were real and unstoppable and further concessions would probably have come. The army, refunded and professionalised after defeat by Japan, was loyal. Despite its many problems Russia was far from a revolution in 1914.

Ministers believed Russia was strong enough for war, but Durnovo's warning in February 1914 against a war with Germany, Russia's main trading partner, was prophetic. The unexpected length and hardship of the war traumatised Russia, caused immense social disruption and, as in Germany, Austro-Hungary and Turkey, brought down the monarchy. Fifteen million men fought and two million died. Refugees from the German advance flooded the towns. Women went into factories. There was a major revolt in Central Asia. The fronts stretched from the Baltic to the Black Sea. Early defeats lasted through 1915 and weakened the regime, as did public disgust over Rasputin's influence and scurrilous libels about the Tsarina. Increasingly isolated, Nicholas refused to co-operate with patriotic civilian bodies like the Union of Towns and *zemstvos* and the War Industries Committee, or to form a government of national unity. His decision to become Commander in Chief laid responsibility for defeats at his door, and lost him the support of army chiefs.

Ironically by the end of 1916 things were improving, with victories against Austria and Turkey and more aid from the Allies. Industry was now on a war footing and the supply of munitions increased. The army was adequately supplied, but crucially the rear was not. It was the breakdown of the transport system, the failure to feed the towns and the disaffection of reserve troops in the capital which turned, unexpectedly, a bread riot into a revolution.

Beryl Williams, Emeritus Reader in History, University of Sussex.

ACTIVITY

Having read the essay, answer the following questions.

Comprehension

1 What were the main demands of the majority of workers?
2 What specific reasons are given for the February revolution?

Evidence

3 What evidence can you find for:
   - positive changes in industry and agriculture
   - positive changes in society
   - the impact of the war?

Interpretation

4 What is Beryl Williams' overall judgement about the significance of the war?

Working on essay technique: argument, counter-argument and resolution

Essays that develop a good argument are more likely to reach the higher levels. This is because argumentative essays are much more likely to develop sustained analysis. As you know, your essays are judged on the extent to which they analyse. The mark scheme below is for the full A-level. It is virtually the same for AS level. Both stress the need to analyse and evaluate the key features related to the periods studied. It distinguishes between five different levels of analysis (as well as other relevant skills that are the ingredients of good essays).

The key feature of the highest level is sustained analysis: analysis that unites the whole of the essay.

You can set up an argument in your introduction, but you should develop it throughout the essay. One way of doing this is to adopt an argument, counter-argument structure. A counter-argument is an argument that disagrees with the main argument of the essay. Setting up an argument and then challenging it with a counter-argument is one way of weighing up, or evaluating (see page 119) the importance of the different factors that you discuss. Essays of this type will develop an argument in one paragraph and then set out an opposing argument in another paragraph. This approach will be very relevant on certain topics and questions where there are different opinions. We will first look at techniques for developing sustained analysis and argument before looking at the counter-argument technique.

Argument and sustained analysis

Good essays will analyse the keys issues discussed in the essay. They will probably have a clear piece of analysis at the end of each paragraph. This will offer a judgement on the question and is likely to consist or little or no narrative.

Outstanding essays will be analytical throughout. As well as the analysis of each factor discussed above, there will be an overall analysis. This will run throughout the essay and can be achieved through developing a clear, relevant and coherent argument.

High-level arguments

Typically, essays examine a series of factors. A good way of achieving sustained analysis is to consider which factor is most important as in the example on page 118.

Level 5	Answers will display a very good understanding of the full demands of the question. They will be well organised and effectively delivered. The supporting information will be well-selected, specific and precise. It will show a very good understanding of key features, issues and concepts. The answer will be fully analytical with a balanced argument and well-substantiated judgement. _21–25 marks_
Level 4	Answers will display a good understanding of the demands of the question. It will be well-organised and effectively communicated. There will be a range of clear and specific supporting information showing a good understanding of key features and issues, together with some conceptual awareness. The answer will be analytical in style with a range of direct comment relating to the question. The answer will be well balanced with some judgement, which may, however, be only partially substantiated. _16–20 marks_
Level 3	Answers will show an understanding of the question and will supply a range of largely accurate information, which will show an awareness of some of the key issues and features, but may, however, be unspecific or lack precision of detail. The answer will be effectively organised and show adequate communication skills. There will be a good deal of comment in relation to the question and the answer will display some balance, but a number of statements may be inadequately supported and generalist. _11–15 marks_
Level 2	The answer is descriptive or partial, showing some awareness of the question but a failure to grasp its full demands. There will be some attempt to convey material in an organised way, although communication skills may be limited. There will be some appropriate information showing understanding of some key features and/or issues, but the answer may be very limited in scope and/or contain inaccuracy and irrelevance. There will be some, but limited, comment in relation to the question and statements will, for the most part, be unsupported and generalist. _6–10 marks_
Level 1	The question has not been properly understood and the response shows limited organisational and communication skills. The information conveyed is irrelevant or extremely limited. There may be some unsupported, vague or generalist comment. _1–5 marks_

EXAMPLE

Consider the following A-level practice question:

'The political, economic and social progress made by Russia after 1894 ensured that the tsarist regime would have survived if there had not been a war in 1914.' How far do you agree with this view? (25 marks)

Introduction 1 addresses the question but does not develop an argument:

Introduction 1

Clear focus on the question

In the years between 1894 and 1914 Russia had been making progress on a number of fronts. The economy was growing fast and a duma had been established that provided hope of a more representative form of government. However, there were other reasons to suppose that the autocracy had not made sufficient progress to ensure its survival. These include the way the tsar and his ministers treated the duma, the lack of measures to improve the economic and social conditions of the workers and the failure to carry through reforms in the countryside.

Recognises that can't just cover named factor

Wide range of factors

This introduction could be improved by the introduction of an argument. An argument is a type of explanation. It makes a claim about the question and supports it with a reason.

A good way of beginning to develop an argument is to think about the meaning of the words in the question. With the question above, you could think about the words 'how far'.

Here is an example of an introduction that begins an argument:

Introduction 2

The introduction begins with a claim

The Russian autocracy would probably not have survived even if there had not been a war. Progress on the political front had stalled. Industry had structural problems, agriculture was relatively unmodernised and the regime had done little to address the problems of the growing working class or meet the demands of the mass of the peasantry. On the other hand, it can be argued that there was no real indication that a revolution was imminent in 1914. Industry was expanding at a rapid pace, the overall production of grain had risen, the standard of living of many peasants was rising and the countryside was quiet in 1914. Revolutionary parties were weak and disorganised.

Introduction continues with another claim

Includes some factors in support of the claim

This introduction focuses on the question and sets out some of the main factors that the essay will develop. It also sets out an argument that can then be developed throughout each paragraph, and then rounded off with an overall judgement in the conclusion. It also introduces the debate about whether the tsarist regime could have survived and shows that there can be different interpretations.

Counter-argument

As we have seen on page 118, you can set up an argument in your introduction, but you should develop your argument throughout the essay. One way of doing this is to adopt an argument, counter-argument structure. A counter-argument is an argument that disagrees with the main argument of the essay. Setting up an argument and then challenging it with a counter-argument is one way of weighing up, or evaluating the importance of the different factors that you discuss. Essays of this type will develop an argument in one paragraph and then set out an opposing argument in another paragraph.

ACTIVITY

Imagine you are answering the following A-level practice question:

To what extent did the opposition pose a problem for the tsarist autocracy in the period 1894–1917? (25 marks)

Using your notes from this and the previous chapter:

1 Divide your page as follows:

Opposition posed a serious threat	Opposition did not pose a serious threat

2 Consider the following points and place them either in the left- or right-hand column:
   - The Bolsheviks from 1903 to 1914
   - The workers from 1912 to 1916
   - The workers from 1895 to 1905
   - The Socialist Revolutionaries from 1902 to 1914
   - The peasants from 1900 to 1907
   - The 1905 revolution
   - The liberals from 1903 to 1908
   - The Duma from 1906 to 1907
   - The army from 1905 to 1906

3 Now write a short argument that addresses the question of how serious the threat posed by the opposition was. Remember, your argument must contain a statement and a reason.

4 Begin with the side of the argument that you agree with (either the threat was serious or the threat was not serious). Write two sentences that explain this side of the argument.

5 Now write two sentences for the side of the argument that you don't agree with. This is your counter-argument. Remember that it has to consist of a claim and a reason.

6 Use your original argument and counter-argument as the basis for writing two paragraphs in answer to the question.

Remember, you can apply this approach when responding to other similar questions.

Resolution

The best written essays are those which contain sustained analysis. We have seen that one way of achieving this is to write an essay that develops a clear argument and counter-argument (see page 120).

Next you should resolve the tension between the argument and the counter-argument. One way of concluding an essay is to resolve this debate that you have established between the argument and the counter-argument, as in the example on page 120.

EXAMPLE

Imagine you are answering the following A-level practice question:

'The collapse of the Romanov dynasty was the result of the failure of the autocracy to reform itself in the period 1894–1917.' Assess the validity of this view. (25 marks)

A possible way to tackle this question would be to write two clear paragraphs arguing that the revolution of February 1917 was the result of the failure of the Tsar to engage in reforming the autocracy. Then write two paragraphs arguing against this. In an essay of this type you could then resolve the tension by weighing up the argument and counter-argument in the conclusion. In so doing, you can reach a supported overall judgement. For example, a possible conclusion could look like this:

Starts with counter-argument

Limitations of counter-argument

It can be argued that the intolerable strains and stresses of the war caused the collapse of the tsarist empire as it did in other countries like Germany and Austria-Hungary. However, many historians would argue that it was the failure of autocracy, over the previous twenty years, to undertake the reforms required to cope with the problems resulting from industrialisation and modernisation, that really brought about its collapse. The Duma had been a reluctant concession and the Tsar had sidelined it by 1912. Stolypin's attempts to introduce reforms and to broaden support for the regime were blocked by the tsar and conservative interests. The Tsar had lost the support of the workers, peasants and middle classes because of his refusal to concede to their economic and political demands. The autocracy's structural weaknesses, which the Tsar would not address before 1914, meant that it could not cope with the strains of the war and manage the war effort. The war provided the final jolt for a regime that was ready to fall: support for the Tsar haemorrhaged, he lost his political authority and the Romanov dynasty collapsed.

Then has the main claim and justification

Resolves tension

This conclusion evaluates the argument and counter-argument which have been developed in the main body of the essay. It resolves the tension by reaching an overall concluding judgement in relation to the question.

The process of evaluating the argument and the counter-argument is helped by the use of words such as 'however', indicating that the paragraph is weighing up contrasting arguments.

ACTIVITY

Imagine you are answering the following A-level practice question:

'To what extent did the opposition pose a problem for the tsarist autocracy in the period 1894–1914? (25 marks)

Use the ideas on this question on page 119 and look at the work you did on this question in order to complete the following activities.

1 Answer the following questions:
   a) Which is stronger, the argument or the counter-argument? Why is it stronger?
   b) What are the flaws in the weaker argument?
   c) What strengths does the weaker argument have?

2 Having answered these questions write a conclusion that weighs up the argument and the counter-argument in order to reach an overall judgement.

   Use the words 'However', 'Nonetheless', and 'Therefore' to structure the paragraph.

The Bolshevik seizure of power, 1917

4

This chapter looks at the events in 1917 leading up to the second revolution in October when the Bolsheviks seized power. It deals with the following areas:

- Political developments during 1917
- The Bolshevik take-over
- The establishment of the Bolshevik government by December 1917 and opposition to it

The main focus of this chapter is the question:

How were the Bolsheviks able to seize power in October 1917?

This question will consider the weaknesses of the Provisional Government and identify the factors which helped the Bolsheviks take control of Russia in October, especially the role of Lenin. This chapter will cover the key breadth issues of the change in political authority, the development of opposition and the importance of the role of individuals such as Lenin during this period.

CHAPTER OVERVIEW

After the abdication of the Tsar, the Provisional Government was formed to run Russia until elections could be held to choose a Constituent Assembly. But the Petrograd Soviet, formed at the same time, held real power in the capital, creating a situation known as 'dual power'. The Provisional Government faced daunting challenges concerning the war, land distribution, the national minorities and the deteriorating economic situation; it did not deal with these to the satisfaction of the Russian people. The government was reformed and moderate socialist leaders were brought in with Alexander Kerensky as Prime Minister. But they faced opposition from Lenin and the Bolsheviks whose pledges to end the war, increase food supplies and give the land to the peasants, gained popular support. By October the Provisional Government had become very unpopular and Lenin used events to engineer a take-over of power. His new government was fragile and only survived the first few months because of the weakness of the opposition and the measures he put in place to deal with threats and challenges to Bolshevik one-party rule.

121

1 The Provisional Government and the Soviet

This section will look at the relationship between the Provisional Government and the Soviet and consider how effectively the Provisional Government dealt with the main issues it faced.

Dual power

Who was running Russia after the revolution?

The new government created by the members of the Duma was called the Provisional Government because its main job was to run Russia temporarily until elections to a Constituent Assembly could be arranged. Since the old system had been swept away, an assembly was needed to work out how the country should be governed in the future and what form its legal institutions should take. The new Prime Minister for the Provisional Government was Prince G. E. Lvov, a progressive noble, who had successfully run the *Zemstvo* Union, sending materials and medical supplies to the war front. He was popular

Constituent Assembly – An elected parliament whose main job is to write a constitution which sets out a new system of government, including the relationships between the different organs of government, the legal system, and the checks and balances in the system.

The Russian calendar

Tsarist Russia used the Julian calendar while most of Europe had adopted the Gregorian calendar. There was a difference between the two calendars of 13 days. The Bolshevik government adopted the Gregorian calendar on 31 January 1918; the next day was declared to be 14 February.

Some books, including this one, use the old-style calendar (the one used at the time) to date the events of 1917 while others use the Gregorian calendar.

Using the old-style calendar, the dates of the revolutions are 23 February and 25 October. Using the Gregorian calendar, the dates are 8 March and 7 November.

KEY DATES: FEBRUARY–OCTOBER 1917

February

27 Duma committee and Petrograd Soviet formed.

March

1 Order No. 1 issued.

2 Provisional Government formed (Tsar abdicates).

April

3 Lenin returns to Petrograd.

May

2 Milyukov resigns as Minister for War.

5 Coalition government of socialists and Kadets.

June

3 First All-Russian Congress of Soviets begins.

16 Launch of military offensive.

July

3–4 July Days.

5–6 Some leading Bolsheviks arrested in Petrograd. Lenin flees to Finland.

8 Kerensky becomes Prime Minister.

August

26–30 Kornilov affair.

September

9 Bolsheviks gain majority in Petrograd Soviet.

15 Bolshevik Central Committee rejects Lenin's first call for insurrection.

October

7 Lenin returns to Petrograd.

10 Bolshevik Central Committee confirms decision to seize power.

25–26 Bolsheviks seize power.

and a good democrat. The rest of the government consisted of leading liberals, with the Kadets the strongest group. Their leader, Milyukov, was made Foreign Minister. The Provisional Government met on 2 March in the Tauride Palace.

In the same building. at around the same time, another body was taking shape – the Petrograd Soviet. Workers and socialists, mainly Mensheviks, had learnt the lesson of 1905 and quickly came together to build an organisation to protect workers' interests. Factories sent delegates and by 3 March it had 1,300 members. Soldiers also demanded representation and each regiment sent representatives to what was now called the 'Soviet of Workers' and Soldiers' Deputies' although we will refer to it as the Soviet. It soon had over 3,000 members. An executive committee, dominated by Menshevik intellectuals and non-party socialists, was chosen to take key decisions. Its chairman was Chkheidze, a Menshevik.

The most significant first move by either body was the Soviet's Order No. 1 on 1 March (see Source A). This gave the soldiers' committees control of all weapons and stated that soldiers would carry out the orders of the Provisional Government provided the Soviet agreed.

Source A Extracts from Order No. 1, adapted from *A Source Book of Russian History*, Vol. 3, by G. Vernadsky, (Yale University Press), 1972, p882.

The Soviet of Workers' and Soldiers' Deputies has decided:

- In all companies, battalions, squadrons and separate branches of military service of all kinds and on warships, committees should be chosen immediately.

- The orders of ... the State Duma [Provisional Government] shall be carried out only ... [when] they do not contradict the orders and decisions of the Soviet of Workers' and Soldiers' Deputies.

- All kinds of arms, such as rifles and machine guns, must be under the control of the company and battalion committees and must in no case be handed over to officers even at their demand.

- The addressing of officers with titles such as 'Your Excellency', 'Your Honour', etc., is abolished and these are replaced by 'Mr General', 'Mr Colonel' and so on.

Thus a situation called 'dual power' came into being. The Provisional Government was the popularly accepted, although unelected, government but the real power lay with the Soviet. It not only controlled the soldiers in Petrograd and the factories but also the railways, power supplies and telegraph network. The state of affairs was far from ideal for the Provisional Government because it did not have control of the capital and its armed forces. But it had little choice and the two bodies needed to co-operate at this precarious time. Everybody feared anarchy as there was already disorder, looting and violence. The socialist leaders of the Soviet decided to allow the Provisional Government to govern while it kept a close eye on what it was doing. There were three main reasons for this:

- They did not want to provide an excuse for counter-revolution. The Russian High Command had not intervened because the Duma politicians were involved in establishing representative government. But they might have stepped in if they thought a socialist government was about to take power.
- The socialist leaders of the Soviet, mainly intellectuals, had little idea how to run a government. Also they were not sure they could control the masses and were scared that things could get out of hand.

NOTE-MAKING

Make notes on the:
- relationship between the Provisional Government and the Soviet
- significance of Order No. 1
- first measures
- organisations outside the capital.

Alexander Kerensky

One man played an important part in the relationship between the Provisional Government and the Soviet – Alexander Kerensky. He was vice-chairman of the Soviet and Minister of Justice in the Provisional Government. He made sure that the Provisional Government and the Soviet knew what the other was doing.

- The socialist leaders did not think the time was right for workers to take control. In line with classical Marxist theory, they thought they were going through the bourgeois-democratic revolution (see page 87). After this, Russia would have a democratically elected government, run mainly by the middle classes, and industry and capitalism would develop. The proletariat would grow with industrialisation and then, after a period of worker education, the socialist revolution would take place.

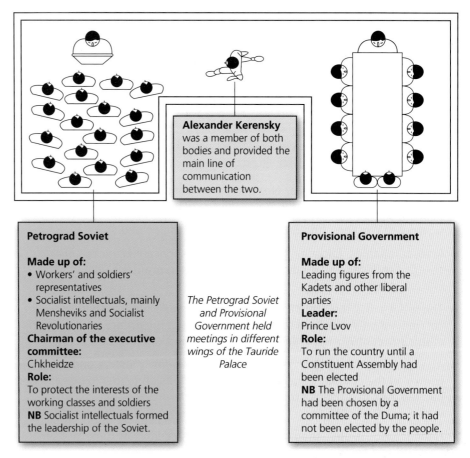

Alexander Kerensky was a member of both bodies and provided the main line of communication between the two.

Petrograd Soviet

Made up of:
- Workers' and soldiers' representatives
- Socialist intellectuals, mainly Mensheviks and Socialist Revolutionaries

Chairman of the executive committee:
Chkheidze

Role:
To protect the interests of the working classes and soldiers

NB Socialist intellectuals formed the leadership of the Soviet.

The Petrograd Soviet and Provisional Government held meetings in different wings of the Tauride Palace

Provisional Government

Made up of:
Leading figures from the Kadets and other liberal parties

Leader:
Prince Lvov

Role:
To run the country until a Constituent Assembly had been elected

NB The Provisional Government had been chosen by a committee of the Duma; it had not been elected by the people.

▲ **Figure 1** The membership and role of the Petrograd Soviet and the Provisional Government.

The honeymoon of the revolution

For the first two months of the revolution, there was little to bring the Provisional Government and the Soviet into conflict. The first measures taken by the Provisional Government met with Soviet and public approval:

- Tsarist ministers and officials were arrested and imprisoned.
- The secret police were disbanded.
- The death penalty was abolished and political and religious prisoners were granted an amnesty.
- Freedom of the press, freedom of speech and religious freedom were guaranteed.
- Elections to the Constituent Assembly were to be by secret ballot and universal suffrage.

In addition, the workers secured an eight-hour working day and the right to form trade unions and strike; and it was agreed that soldiers in the Petrograd garrison would not be sent to the Front. So, people were optimistic about the future. Some of the worst aspects of tsarism were discarded and elections were on the way. Lenin remarked in the summer of 1917 that Russia was the freest country in the world. Indeed, if all of the Provisional Government's plans had been put into practice Russia would have been the most radical liberal democracy in Europe in 1917.

Outside the capital

Support for the new government flooded in from outside the capital where the tsarist administrative system was being dismantled. The signs and symbols of imperial power (coats of arms, statues, portraits of the Romanovs) were torn down and destroyed. The old tsarist governors were dismissed and replaced with commissars. But they were largely ignored. People were setting up their own organisations. These tended to be non-party bodies run by members of the *zemstva*, but their membership rapidly expanded to take in representatives of various workers', soldiers', trade union and other popular committees that mushroomed at the time. However, these bodies were being outstripped by the rapid growth of soviets in the cities and towns. These could be run by non-party socialists, SRs, Mensheviks or by individuals of standing in the community. In many places local control was chaotic.

As news of the revolution spread into the countryside, peasants also started to set up committees and give voice to their opinions and demands. Some villages declared themselves autonomous republics. The Prime Minister, Lvov, who was more radical and populist than other liberals in the Provisional Government, encouraged localities to run their own affairs. The trouble was that a great wave of expectation was building up and the new government was going to find it hard to meet the hopes and aspirations of all of the different groups in Russian society.

> ### The end of monarchy
>
> It is surprising how quickly the tsarist monarchy fell with all its institutions. Nobody really resisted or tried to revive it in the next few years. Trotsky summed it up from his perspective: 'the country had so radically vomited up the monarchy that it could not ever crawl down the people's throat again'.

WORKING TOGETHER

This activity is designed to help you to consider the Bolshevik seizure of power over a broader period of time. Use the chart below to track different groups and bodies through 1917 up until the October Revolution.

Weaknesses /failures of the Provisional Government	Workers	Actions of Lenin and the Bolsheviks	Peasants	Role of the army and soldiers
Note the areas where the Provisional Government was not meeting the demands of different groups and why.	*Note the demands and aspirations of workers, how these were met/not met and their response.*	*Note specific policies and actions which gained support and achieved the take-over.*	*Note what the peasants wanted and their response to developments.*	*Note what the army was doing. Distinguish between the soldiers in Petrograd and the army outside.*

NOTE-MAKING

Divide a page into two columns. Take each of the issues in turn. In the left-hand column write down how the Provisional Government dealt with it and in the right-hand column write down how successful their response was.

The challenges facing the Provisional Government

How successful was the Provisional Government in dealing with the main problems it faced during 1917?

The honeymoon of the revolution did not last long. The divisions between the different parties and factions soon became apparent. The main issues were:

- the war
- the land and the peasants
- the national minorities
- social reform
- the deteriorating economic situation in the cities.

The war

The Kadets wanted to continue the war. They did not want to sue the Germans for peace and suffer the national shame, loss of territory and humiliation this would entail. They were a nationalist party and wanted to retain the Russian Empire intact. Also they did not want to lose the support of their allies – Britain and France. They thought Western support would be needed for the fledgling democracy. In particular, they desperately needed foreign money as the state was nearly bankrupt; financial support was only guaranteed if Russia stayed in the war.

The socialists were divided on the war. The moderate socialists were prepared to support the continuation of the war as they also did not want to see Russia humiliated. Factions in the Mensheviks and SRs wanted a negotiated peace. But they could all agree that it should be a defensive war – that they should only fight to defend Russian territory.

It was this issue that brought the first crisis for the Provisional Government at the end of April. It became apparent that Milyukov, the Minister of War, was committed to an aggressive war in support of the Allies and also hoped to make territorial gains (for example, getting control of Constantinople) if the Germans were defeated. This outraged the socialists in the Soviet and there were anti-war demonstrations in Petrograd. Milyukov was forced to resign.

The Provisional Government was reformed on 5 May. Five socialist leaders joined the new coalition government. The most important of these were the Menshevik leader Tsereteli and the leader of the Socialist Revolutionaries, Chernov. It was hoped that this move would help relations with the Soviet and with the workers and peasants. However, its effect was to distance the moderate socialist leaders from their support base and associate them with the conduct of the war.

The continuation of war was deeply unpopular with many sections of society. It was putting a huge strain on the economy and prevented the Provisional Government from dealing with social reform and other issues at home. Army discipline was breaking down. The peasant soldiers just wanted the war to end and desertions increased as many made their way home in the hope of getting a share of the land that they thought would be redistributed.

July offensive

At the beginning of the summer of 1917, the Provisional Government decided to launch a major offensive against the Germans. The new Minister for War, Alexander Kerensky, threw himself into a propaganda campaign to mobilise the armed forces and the people for a massive attack. Kerensky made patriotic speeches and toured the Fronts. Middle-class civilians volunteered to fight in shock battalions designed to raise the army's morale. However, Kerensky was less successful with the soldiers, who were increasingly unwilling to fight.

The offensive began on 16 June and lasted for about three days. Then it began to fall apart, thousands of soldiers were killed and even more territory was lost. It pushed many soldiers towards the Bolsheviks and led to an armed uprising in Petrograd known as the July Days (see page 133). Moderate socialist leaders in the government lost their credibility with the soldiers and workers.

The land and the peasants

The peasants saw the February revolution and the collapse of central authority as their chance to get the remaining great estates to be redistributed without compensation and they wanted government approval to legitimise this process. But the Provisional Government wanted the Constituent Assembly to resolve the land question. This was partly because it was a huge issue for a temporary government to resolve, but there were other reasons:

- Many of the liberals in the Provisional Government came from the landed and propertied classes and did not wish to see their property simply handed over to the peasants. Moreover, they wanted landowners (often their supporters) to be compensated.
- They were also worried that a land free-for-all would lead to the disintegration of the army as peasant soldiers rushed back to claim their share.

So the peasants began taking the land without government sanction. They also took livestock, tools, timber and anything they could grab from private estates. This began slowly but gathered in pace throughout the summer.

When Chernov, the popular leader of the SRs, was made Minister of Agriculture in May, it seemed that a better relationship might develop between government and peasants. Chernov proposed a scheme whereby peasants would be given the right to use land from private estates (with ownership to be sorted out later), but the liberals in the Provisional Government blocked this. So, during the summer, land seizures increased (237 cases were reported in July). Violence began to increase with attacks on landowners (some out of revenge) and armed robberies becoming more frequent.

The Women's Death Battalion

To try to encourage Russians to fight, a women's battalion was created under the leadership of Maria Bochareva, who had fought in the war and been twice wounded. She hoped to shame male soldiers into fighting. It did not have the intended effect. Some soldiers refused to fight alongside the women and others saw it as an indication of how desperate the army had become.

It was a fundamental weakness of the Provisional Government that it did not appreciate the strength of feeling among the peasants and go some way to meet their demands. The Provisional Government mishandled relations with the peasants in general over this period. Grain was urgently required for the hungry cities; the Provisional Government tried to make the peasants agree to fix grain prices. With inflation rampant, the peasants considered the prices too low and refused to send their grain to the towns and cities. The Provisional Government sent out the army to requisition supplies and suppress disturbances but this served only to make the peasants more hostile.

The national minorities

When the tsarist regime collapsed, the national minorities around the empire either demanded outright independence like the Finns and Poles or wanted more autonomy like the Caucasus. This issue exposed more splits and weakness in the Provisional Government. The Kadets were determined to maintain the integrity of the Empire. They believed that Russia had to keep all the regions together in one centrally governed state if it was to remain a great power. The socialists, on the other hand, believed that non-Russians should run their own affairs and have more self-government.

The Provisional Government was unwilling to see the state break up in the middle of a war and wanted to wait until the Constituent Assembly decided. The matter came to a head over Ukraine. The Ukrainians demanded self-government and the moderate socialists in the government made concessions to them. The liberals, who saw this as the first step towards the break-up of Russia, were outraged and three Kadet ministers resigned on 2 July.

Social reform

The workers had expected social reform after February, with higher wages, better working conditions, shorter hours and more influence in the workplace.

In principle they had achieved some of these aims, but in practice things were moving slowly. Although there were increases in their wages, prices were going up much faster. Strikes increased, taking in a broad range of occupations from kitchen workers to artisans as well as metal workers. Workers now saw themselves as 'citizens' and worthy of respectful treatment by managers, and demanded action on issues such as equal pay for women and the abolition of child labour. There was a new sense of assertiveness, and factory committees, which became the main organ for worker rights, demanded a more active role in the workplace. The workers had become politicised although economic demands were still at the top of their concerns.

The Provisional Government could not handle this labour militancy and was unable to mediate between employers and workers. The employers for their part were angry about the constant strikes and pay demands. They used lock-outs to try to bring the workers to heel. Added to this, factories were closing every day because of the economic situation. In a desperate attempt to save jobs, workers' committees took over some factories completely; but they did not know how to run them and so many closed anyway. Workers were not getting the reform and improved conditions they expected and class antagonism was growing. They turned their anger on the Provisional Government and the moderate socialist leaders in the Soviet.

The deteriorating economic situation

Food shortages, unemployment and high prices had been important factors in bringing about the February revolution. These problems did not go away when the Provisional Government took power. The downward spiral in the economy continued. The railway system, badly dislocated by the war, showed signs of breaking down. Shortages of fuel and raw materials led to factories cutting output or closing – 568 factories in Petrograd closed between February and July with the loss of 100,000 jobs. The scarcity of manufactured goods caused prices to rise rapidly.

Food supply was a major issue. There was a temporary respite in the grain crisis after February, but by the end of the summer the situation was critical because peasants were reluctant to bring their grain to the cities and the harvest of 1917 was poor. In Petrograd, grain prices doubled between February and June and rose again in the autumn. The Provisional Government seemed unable to do anything about the food shortages.

Figure 2 below gives some idea of the rise in the costs of living which was unmatched by wage rises. The workers were becoming incensed, convinced that they were being exploited by speculators. They turned their antagonism on the government, demanding price controls, a halt to speculation and the arrest of profiteers. However, the liberals in the Provisional Government were under pressure from industrialists not to interfere or fix prices and would not act against them. It therefore failed to halt the decline in living standards in the cities.

Cost of food (roubles and kopeks)

	August 1914	August 1917	Percentage increase
Black bread	0.02	0.12	500
Pork	0.23	2.00	770
Cheese	0.40	3.50	754
Butter	0.48	3.20	557
Eggs (dozen)	0.30	1.60	443
Milk	0.07	0.40	471

Cost of other basic commodities (roubles and kopeks)

	August 1914	August 1917	Percentage increase
Cotton cloth	0.15	2.00	1,233
Men's shoes (pair)	12.00	144.00	1,097
Tea	4.50	18.00	1,300
Soap	4.50	40.00	1,780
Gasoline	1.70	11.00	1,547
Candles	8.50	100.00	1,076
Firewood (per load)	10.00	120.00	1,100

▲ **Figure 2** The cost of living before and during the Revolution. From *Ten Days that Shook the World* by J. Reed, (Penguin), 1977, pp 274–75.

2 The October Revolution

This section will look at two key individuals who played major roles in the events taking place in the lead up to the October Revolution. It will consider the main causes of the October Revolution and how the Bolsheviks were able to seize power.

Kerensky and Lenin

Why were Kerensky and Lenin key players in 1917?

There are some remarkable similarities between Alexander Kerensky and Lenin. Both were born in Simbirsk and Kerensky's father was Lenin's headmaster. Both were lawyers.

Alexander Kerensky

Kerensky set up an office in St Petersburg to advise workers. In the 1905 revolution he published a socialist newspaper and was arrested. The four months he served in prison cemented his position in radical socialist circles and in 1912 he was elected to the Duma. He joined the Trudoviki group, leftists associated with the Socialist Revolutionary Party. He was the ideal man in February 1917 to provide the connection between the Provisional Government and the Soviet because he was generally liked in all circles and the workers trusted him. In the early months after February, he was referred to as 'the first love of the revolution'.

A photograph of Kerensky at ▶ his desk in his office in the Winter Palace, 1917.

Source B Orlando Figes describes Kerensky's speech to the Soviet on 2 March 1917, in which he asked for approval of his decision to join the Provisional Government as Minister of Justice. From *A People's Tragedy: The Russian Revolution 1891–1924* by Orlando Figes, (Pimlico), 1997, p337.

'Comrades! Do you trust me?' he asked in a voice charged with theatrical pathos. 'We do, we do!' the delegates shouted. 'I speak, comrades, with all my soul, from the bottom of my heart, and if it is needed to prove this, if you do not trust me, then I am ready to die.' ... He told them that 'his first act' as the Minister of Justice had been to order the immediate release of all political prisoners and the arrangement of a hero's welcome for their return to the capital. The delegates were overcome with emotion and greeted this news with thunderous cheers. Now Kerensky turned to ask them whether they approved of his decision to join the government, offering to resign from the Soviet if the answer should be no. But there were wild cries of 'We do! We do!' and, without a formal vote, his actions were endorsed. It was a brilliant *coup de théâtre*. ... Kerensky was now the only politician with a position in both the government and the Soviet. He was the undisputed leader of the people.

> How does Kerensky engage the members of the Soviet and secure their support (Source B)?

Kerensky became the most influential member of the Provisional Government. As the new War Minister he threw his support behind the war effort (see page 127). Despite the failure of this, Kerensky was a popular choice for Prime Minster in July 1917. He was seen as the 'human bridge' between socialists and liberals, acceptable to the workers and soldiers as well as to the military leaders and the middle classes (bourgeoisie).

Kerensky had great skills as an orator and was famous for his passionate and dramatic speeches. An English nurse, Florence Farmborough, marvelled as people 'kissed him, his uniform, his car and the ground on which he walked'. Kerensky was energetic and tenacious, but he was also temperamental and vain, taking great care of his personal appearance and the image he portrayed. He had a picture of himself at his huge desk printed on tens of thousands of postcards and newsreels made of his public appearances. When he became Prime Minster he seemed to see himself as the man destined to save Russia and adopted a self-important air. He moved into Tsar Alexander III's rooms in the Winter Palace. He was compared to Napoleon and seemed to revel in this role with a bust of the French Emperor on his desk.

The return of Lenin

Stalin and Kamenev were the first leading Bolsheviks to arrive in Petrograd. Kamenev argued for co-operation with the Provisional Government and there was talk that they might re-unite with the Mensheviks. They thought that socialists should work together to take the revolution forward.

Lenin, who was in Switzerland, was eager to get to Petrograd but this involved crossing German territory. However, the Germans were only too pleased to let him through, hoping he would stir up trouble. Lenin arrived at the Finland Station in Petrograd on 3 April and immediately addressed the people waiting for him in a fashion that shocked them all.

Source C Lenin's return to Russia, recalled by N. N. Sukhanov. From *A Short History of the Revolution* by J. Carmichael, (Sphere Books), 1967, pp 80–81.

'Dear Comrades, soldiers and sailors and workers! I am happy to greet in your persons the victorious Russian Revolution, and greet you as the vanguard of the worldwide proletarian army ... long live the worldwide Socialist Revolution!'

... Suddenly, before the eyes of all of us, completely swallowed up by the routine drudgery of the Revolution, there was presented a bright, blinding beacon ... Lenin's voice, heard straight from the train, was a 'voice from outside' ...

I shall never forget that thunderlike speech, which startled and amazed not only me, a heretic who accidentally dropped in, but all the true believers. I am certain that nobody expected anything of the sort.

Lenin's speech at the Finland Station ended the Bolshevik accommodation with the Provisional Government and the other socialists. He called for:

- a worldwide socialist revolution
- an immediate end to the war
- an end to co-operation with the Provisional Government
- the soviets and in particular the Petrograd Soviet to take power
- land to be given to the peasants.

These ideas became known as the 'April Theses'. The Mensheviks condemned them as 'the ravings of a madman', contrary to Marxist theory. Even some members of the Bolshevik Central Committee initially opposed him. But Lenin's personality and power of argument ensured that the April Theses became Bolshevik Party policy. They were turned into slogans: 'Bread, Peace and Land!' and 'All Power to the Soviets!'. These populist slogans were effective propaganda for the masses. Prioritising food supplies ('Bread'), ending the war ('Peace') and putting the workers in control ('Power to the soviets') appealed directly to the soldiers and workers whose expectations and demands were becoming more radical and were moving ahead of the ability of the Provisional Government and the Soviet to satisfy them.

The notion of the immediate re-distribution of land brought the peasants on side. They had no interest in the Bolsheviks but it was the only party that recognised their land seizures as legitimate. In fact, Lenin was stealing the policy of the radical left SRs. This had an added bonus insofar as the left SRs moved to support the Bolsheviks.

The Bolsheviks now provided a radically different alternative to the Provisional Government and the moderate socialists in the Soviet who were increasingly out of touch with workers and soldiers in the streets. The Bolshevik Party became the main focus for the masses dissatisfied with the government's performance.

Lenin's ideological justification for the April Theses

Lenin believed that the bourgeoisie (middle classes) in Russia were too weak to carry through the democratic revolution. The proletariat (the workers), he claimed, had already taken power in the soviets, particularly the Petrograd Soviet, and were the driving force in the revolution. So there was no reason to go through a period of middle-class-dominated parliamentary democracy. However, the proletariat was still relatively small in size and Marxist theory required a population which was overwhelmingly proletarian to carry through the socialist revolution. Lenin maintained that the circumstances in Russia were special insofar as the peasants were a powerful revolutionary force and could be treated as proletarians because they had a consciousness of their class position.

Why does Sukhanov (Source C) find Lenin's speech so startling?

N. N. Sukhanov

Sukhanov was the great diarist of the revolution. He was a Menshevik-Internationalist but his wife was a Bolshevik and he knew the Bolshevik leaders well. They held meetings in his flat including the one in which they decided to seize power.

Lenin's ideas fitted in well with the wider view of world revolution that had been suggested by Trotsky. They believed that a worldwide socialist revolution would start, not in a highly industrialised society, as Marx had suggested, but in a backward country where capitalism was just developing and the conflict between the industrialists and workers was more acute (as a result of low wages, bad conditions, etc.). Trotsky and Lenin thought that 'the weakest link' in the capitalist chain would break first and that once the revolution had begun it would spread to the proletariat in other countries. They considered that Russia was the weakest link and that the war had acted as a catalyst to bring Europe to the brink of a socialist revolution. Lenin was sure that Germany was about to explode into revolution. Both thought that once the revolution started, the proletariat of the advanced capitalist countries would come to the aid of the Russian proletariat and help them to develop the conditions in which socialism could be built.

Red Revolution

How were the Bolsheviks able to seize power?

The July Days

The failed summer offensive in the war had serious consequences for the Provisional Government and the course of events. It had cost the lives of hundreds of thousands of soldiers. The mounting frustration of workers and soldiers erupted at the beginning of July in several days of uncontrolled rioting and general disorder. This became known as the July Days and was the first direct challenge to the Provisional Government.

On 3 July, Sukhanov reported lorries and cars rushing about the city full of 'fierce-faced' civilians and soldiers, and armed groups marching in the streets. On 4 July, 20,000 armed sailors from the Kronstadt naval base arrived in Petrograd. The sailors marched to the Tauride Palace where they demanded that the Soviet take power. Chernov, the Socialist Revolutionary leader, was sent out to calm them down but was seized and bundled into a car. He was rescued by Trotsky but it was touch and go. The atmosphere was very violent and the Provisional Government and the Soviet had lost control of the capital.

Some historians have seen the July Days as an early attempt by the Bolsheviks to take power. Sukhanov reported seeing armed groups led by 'Bolshevik lieutenants'. But the Bolshevik leadership was not ready to seize power and was paralysed by indecision about how to respond. In fact, when the rioting began, Lenin was not in Petrograd. When he returned on 4 July he appealed for restraint. He did not dissociate himself from the demonstrations, but he did not provide coherent leadership.

This lack of leadership proved the undoing of the July rising. Without a clear purpose, the rising lost momentum. Troops loyal to the Soviet arrived and the crowds were dispersed. The Provisional Government also released a letter that appeared to show that Lenin was in the pay of the Germans and had come back to Russia to undermine the Russian war effort. Several leading Bolsheviks, including Trotsky, were arrested; Lenin was forced into hiding in Finland. Bolshevik newspapers were closed. This was a major setback for the Bolshevik cause.

Kerensky and the Provisional Government

The collapse of the summer offensive was a huge blow to the authority of the Provisional Government. As well as lives, a huge amount of territory had been lost. The coalition began to fall apart. The Kadets (liberals) had moved further to the right in favour of law and order, defence of property rights and

The Kronstadt sailors

Kronstadt was a naval base on an island just off the coast near Petrograd. The sailors who lived in the base were, in 1917, extremely radical and supported revolutionary change. Many were Bolsheviks, but anarchists and Socialist Revolutionaries were also very influential. The sailors had their own fiercely independent soviet which was multi-party and chaired by a Socialist Revolutionary. But they had no clear aim when they came to Petrograd.

The Bolshevik Party in July

It seems that in the July Days, lower-ranking Bolshevik Party members were running ahead of their leaders. Membership had soared and it was not the disciplined party, tightly controlled by Lenin, that some have suggested. The party was still quite open: there were fierce debates about policy and ideological disagreement. It was difficult for the Bolshevik leadership to exercise close control of its members. Lenin himself remarked that the rank and file was more radical than the leaders.

KEY DATES: CHANGES IN THE PROVISIONAL GOVERNMENT

1917

March Dominated by liberals (Kadets). One socialist (Kerensky).

May Five socialists join but still dominated by liberals.

2 July Three Kadet ministers resign.

Balance shifts in favour of socialists but liberals still present in significant numbers.

Kerensky becomes Prime Minister.

Kornilov

Kornilov, the son of a Siberian Cossack, had shown some sympathy towards revolutionary change and was popular with his troops. He did not seem to have overt political ambitions and seemed a good choice for the role of Supreme Commander. But Kornilov quickly became the darling of right-wing conservative forces (industrialists, army officers and landowners) who saw in him their main hope for turning the tables on the revolutionaries. It is not clear whether he wanted to set up a military dictatorship or not. He said he wanted the Provisional Government 'cleansed and strengthened' but also that his main aim was to 'Hang the German spies, headed by Lenin ... and disperse the Soviet'.

the integrity of the Russian Empire. They blamed the socialist leaders and the Soviet for the militant strikes in the cities and for conceding self-government in Ukraine. On 2 July, three Kadet ministers resigned from the government. Shortly afterwards, as the July uprising fizzled out, Lvov resigned his post as Prime Minister; he had had enough of politics. He told his secretary, 'I have reached the end of the road and so, I'm afraid, has my sort of liberalism'.

Alexander Kerensky became Prime Minister. He was seen as the only man who could unite the country. The balance in the government had shifted in favour of the socialists but Kerensky was keen to keep liberals in the government to ensure that the middle classes felt they were represented. However, industrialists and businessmen were rapidly losing faith in the government because it could not control the workers and give them the stability they needed to run their businesses; and the landowners were losing faith because the government could not stop the peasants seizing their land and property. Urban workers, peasants and soldiers were demanding more radical action from the government over land reform, the economy and the war, and were becoming increasingly impatient.

By the end of August, the Provisional Government faced serious problems:

- The army was disintegrating: whole regiments were deserting and making their way back home.
- The economic situation in the cities was getting worse. Little grain was getting in from the countryside, and the peasants were being extremely unco-operative. The price of goods and food was rising.
- Control was breaking down in the countryside. Country houses were burned down and landlords killed.
- There was increasing lawlessness in the cities. Robbery and house break-ins were very common; well-dressed people were beaten in the streets.

The Kornilov affair

Kerensky had come to the conclusion that the only course open to him was to restore law and order in the cities and discipline in the army. He desperately needed troops he could count on to carry out his orders and deal with any threat presented by the Bolsheviks. Kerensky appointed a new Supreme Commander of the Russian forces, General Kornilov, and entered into an agreement with him, as he saw it, to bring trustworthy troops to Petrograd. But Kornilov saw it as an opportunity to crush the radical socialists, prevent the worst excesses of the revolution, and restore order and authority in Petrograd. The anxious middle classes saw him as a potential saviour who would protect their property and interests. Kornilov started moving his forces towards Petrograd to establish military control.

Kerensky panicked in the face of Kornilov's move on the capital. He turned to the Soviet for help to defend Petrograd from counter-revolution. The people were terrified by the prospect of a military dictatorship. To them it meant the return of the old order, bloodshed and the loss of the gains of the Revolution. The soldiers in Petrograd were worried they might be forced to go to the Front. In this time of alarm it was the Bolsheviks who came to the city's aid. Bolshevik foot soldiers came out onto the streets alongside soldiers, workers and sailors. They set out preparing to defend the city and were given arms by the Provisional Government. However, Kornilov's troops did not arrive. Railway workers halted the trains carrying them to Petrograd and Bolshevik agents persuaded them to desert their officers. Kornilov was arrested.

The consequences of Kornilov's ill-judged intervention were significant.

1 Kerensky's reputation was irretrievably damaged. Kerensky's wife wrote: 'The prestige of Kerensky and the Provisional Government was completely destroyed by the Kornilov affair; and he was left almost without supporters.'

2 Menshevik and Socialist Revolutionary leaders were discredited because of their association with Kerensky.

3 Soldiers, infuriated by what they thought was an officers' plot, murdered hundreds of officers. Generals could not rely on 'loyal' troops to carry out their orders.

4 Many army officers felt that Kerensky had betrayed Kornilov and were not prepared to fight for him in the coming confrontation with the Bolsheviks.

5 The Bolsheviks rode back on a wave of popular support as the saviours of the city, the true defenders of the Revolution.

Worker radicalisation and Bolshevik popularity

The workers had become highly politicised and radicalised in the months leading up to October. Food was short, wages could not keep pace with rampant inflation and unemployment was rising. Strikes were frequent and militant. Employers, especially those who organised lock-outs, were assaulted and crowds broke into the houses of the middle classes, accusing them of hoarding food. The workers were not prepared to wait for the Provisional Government any longer. As far as they were concerned the government was backing businessmen who were trying to control them (and to some extent this was true) and their expectations and hopes were not being met; in fact their general situation was much worse.

This strong popular movement was moving uncompromisingly for change. But the moderate Mensheviks and SRs in the Soviet (and Provisional Government) did not appreciate this. They had become detached from the mass of the workers. They still believed they could not take the revolution further at this stage and needed to keep the middle classes attached to government and keep the war economy going. This brought them into collision with the popular movement which was looking for the soviets to take the lead and bring about serious social reform as well as improve their economic condition. The only party that did seem to offer them this change was the Bolsheviks. So support flowed to them.

The Kornilov affair boosted support for the Bolshevik Party although it was already growing beforehand. The Bolsheviks were doing well in the cities and were elected in huge numbers onto soviets. On 9 September, the Bolsheviks gained overall control of the Petrograd Soviet and on 25 September Trotsky was elected its President. They also took control of the Moscow Soviet and dominated the executive committees of soviets throughout urban Russia.

What about the peasants?

In September there was an upturn in violence. The peasants were not prepared to wait for the Provisional Government any longer. There was a surge of support for the left wing of the SRs who were collaborating with the Bolsheviks.

What do Figures 3 and 4 suggest about how support for the different parties was changing in the cities? What does the table in Figure 5 suggest?

Accurate figures are unavailable but estimates suggest that membership leaped during the summer:

February	10,000
October	250,000

▲ **Figure 3** Membership of the Bolshevik Party, 1917.

	July	October
Socialist Revolutionaries	375,000 (58%)	54,000 (14%)
Mensheviks	76,000 (12%)	16,000 (4%)
Bolsheviks	75,000 (11%)	198,000 (51%)
Kadets	109,000 (17%)	101,000 (26%)

▲ **Figure 4** Moscow municipal elections, 1917 (figures rounded to nearest thousand).

	Manual workers	Others
March	675	450
April	335	335
September	225	225
October	110	110

▲ **Figure 5** Daily bread rations (grams) per person in Petrograd in 1917.

Zinoviev and Kamenev

Zinoviev and Kamenev were important Bolshevik leaders who had been close to Lenin while he was in exile abroad before 1917. Both men had consistently opposed the idea of the Bolsheviks seizing power on their own, and wanted to work with other socialist groups.

The role of Trotsky

Trotsky had finally joined the Bolsheviks in August, although in spirit he had been with them for longer and was anxious for the Soviet to seize power. He was by far the best orator and could sway crowds. Trotsky's role in the preparations for the October Revolution – persuading Lenin to wait until October setting up and controlling the Military Revolutionary Committee; planning the details of the take-over – has led some to suggest that he was more important than Lenin in the actual seizure of power.

The October Revolution

Lenin had been in hiding in Finland, watching events unfold. He judged that the time was now right for the Bolsheviks to seize power. He thought that a number of factors were working in their favour:

- The Bolsheviks had control of the Soviet.
- Their popularity was at an all-time high and they had done very well in elections to soviets across Russia.
- The liberals and other conservative forces were demoralised after the Kornilov affair.
- The Provisional Government was helpless, extremely unpopular and attracted contempt.

On 12 September, he wrote to the Bolshevik Central Committee urging action. He wrote: 'History will not forgive us if we do not assume power now.' But the other leading Bolsheviks in the Party Central Committee, thinking his plans premature, would not take action. So Lenin came secretly to Petrograd and on 10 October he battered them with argument all night till they agreed. However, Zinoviev and Kamenev still thought that it was too risky to try to seize power and published their views in Gorky's newspaper, *Novaia zhizn*. Lenin never quite forgave them for this. Trotsky urged Lenin to wait until the meeting of the Second Congress of All-Russian Soviets on 26 October.

Kerensky's response to the growing crisis

In the event, Kerensky's actions played into the Bolsheviks' hands. He tried to send the most radical army units out of the capital and there were rumours that he planned to abandon Petrograd to the Germans. This allowed the Bolsheviks to persuade the Soviet to set up a Military Revolutionary Committee (MRC) in case there was another attempted right-wing coup. The MRC, dominated by the Bolsheviks and controlled by Trotsky, now had more direct control over soldiers in the capital and seized great quantities of arms and ammunition.

It was now an open secret that the Bolsheviks intended to seize power. Kerensky, in a last-ditch attempt to recover the situation, tried to close down two Bolshevik newspapers, restrict the power of the MRC and raise the bridges linking the working-class districts to the centre of Petrograd. This was a blunder – it gave the Bolsheviks an excuse for action. They could now say that Kerensky was attacking the Revolution. When Kerensky could not find loyal troops to help him deal with the Bolshevik threat he left Petrograd in a car borrowed from the American embassy.

The Bolsheviks seize control

At the Smolny Institute, the Bolsheviks' headquarters, Trotsky and Sverdlov organised the final stages of the revolution. On the night of 24–25 October, units of the Red Guard (workers armed and trained by Bolsheviks), sailors and garrison soldiers were sent out to seize key points in the city – the bridges, telephone exchange, the main railway stations and the power stations. There was a bit of trouble at the main telegraph office but on the whole any troops on duty just faded away as the Red Guards appeared.

The next day in Petrograd the shops opened as normal, the trams were running and people went about their everyday business. Many of the foreign observers in the embassies expected the Bolshevik move to crumble when people realised what was happening. Meanwhile, the Bolsheviks had decided to move in on the Provisional Government in the Winter Palace. On the night of 25–26 October, Bolshevik soldiers entered the Palace and at 2am arrested what remained of the government.

The storming of the Winter Palace

The storming of the Winter Palace was to become a great Bolshevik myth, defining the heroism of the revolutionaries and the popular nature of the revolution. The Winter Palace was defended by military cadets, soldiers and members of the Women's Battalion. Most of the soldiers, drunk and demoralised, slipped out of the Palace during the afternoon. The Provisional Government sent out messages for help but none arrived. On the evening of 25 October, the cruiser *Aurora* fired a blank shot at 9.40pm to signal the beginning of the attack. The women were allowed to leave unharmed. Bolshevik soldiers filtered into the palace and disarmed the remaining cadets. Eventually, a group discovered the room where the last members of the Provisional Government were assembled and arrested them. This was quite different from the Bolshevik account of events, according to which Red Guards, supported by the masses, had heroically stormed the Palace as portrayed in the painting below.

1 What impression of this event is portrayed by the artist in the painting below?
2 How does this version compare to the description on the left?
3 Why did the Bolsheviks want Russians to believe this version of events?

▲ A painting made in the 1930s by Sokolov-Skalya showing the storming of the Winter Palace.

The same evening the All-Russian Congress of Soviets met. Socialists from other parties denounced the actions of the Bolsheviks. Trotsky replied:

A rising of the masses of the people needs no justification … The masses of the people followed our banner and our insurrection was victorious. And now we are told: renounce your victory, make concessions, make compromises. With whom? … to those who tell us to do this we must say: you are miserable bankrupts, your role is played out; go where you ought to be – into the dustbin of history!

The other main socialist parties stormed from the hall. Only the left-wing Socialist Revolutionaries remained. This was fortunate for the Bolsheviks as it gave them a majority in the congress. Later, Lenin arrived and announced the formation of a Bolshevik government.

While the insurrection in Petrograd was relatively bloodless, this was not the case in Moscow and in some other towns. There were ten days of bloody fighting in Moscow between the Bolsheviks and forces loyal to the Provisional Government before a truce was agreed. Forces under General Krasnov threatened Petrograd but they were turned away by a mixed force of workers, sailors and soldiers. However fragile, the Bolsheviks were in power in Russia.

The All-Russian Congress of Soviets

The first congress, held in June 1917, was dominated by the Mensheviks and Socialist Revolutionaries. Delegates were sent from soviets across Russia. The congress was an important forum and potentially very powerful. The Second All-Russian Congress was called for 25 October. It reflected the Bolshevik success in elections to the soviets but they did not have a majority of delegates. Trotsky engineered the walk out by the other parties. This meant that they were in the majority when Lenin announced the formation of the new government. Trotsky used the congress to claim that they were taking power in the name of the soviets and honouring their pledge of 'All power to the soviets'.

WORKING TOGETHER

You are now going to consider the events of 1917 in a broader context. Review your chart and notes. Then, as a group, reflect on the following:

1 How far had the workers' demands been met since the late 1890s? What had they done to try to improve their situation and with what success? How had events during 1917 changed workers' perceptions and radicalised them?

2 What role had revolutionary parties played between 1900 and 1917? How had Lenin's ideas for the Bolsheviks (since 1903) and his developing ideology allowed the Bolsheviks to be successful when the Mensheviks and SRs were not? How important was Lenin as an individual?

3 How had the role of the armed forces and attitudes of soldiers changed since 1900, between 1914 and February 1917, and from February to October 1917?

4 What role had the liberals played between 1900 and 1917 and why had they failed after February 1917 to achieve success in the Provisional Government?

5 Finally, consider this question:
Could there have been other outcomes in 1917? You might like to read the rest of this chapter before you answer this.

3 The establishment of the Bolshevik state

This section looks at the first few months of Bolshevik rule and examines the steps Lenin took to keep the Bolsheviks in power.

The Bolsheviks in power

How did the Bolsheviks manage to hold onto power in the months leading up to the end of December 1917?

Lenin had taken power in the name of the Soviet. But it soon became clear that it was one party in control when Lenin announced the Council of the People's Commissars, or *Sovnarkom*, as the main instrument of government. The *Sovnarkom* was made up exclusively of Bolsheviks, although some left SRs were invited to join later on. Lenin could have exercised power through the Soviet but did not want to work with other socialists.

Chairman	Lenin
Commissar for Foreign Affairs	Trotsky until February 1918
Commissar for War	Trotsky from February 1918
Commissar for Internal Affairs	Rykov, later Dzerzhinsky
Commissar for Nationalities	Stalin
Commissar for Social Welfare	Alexandra Kollantai
Commissar for Popular Enlightenment (Education and Culture)	Lunacharsky

▲ **Figure 6** Key posts in the *Sovnarkom*.

Lenin had formed a government but its foundations were very shaky. The Menshevik leader Tsereteli thought it would only last a few weeks at best. In the capital, civil servants mounted protest strikes and the State Bank refused to hand over any money. Trotsky was greeted with laughter when he was introduced at the ministry as the new Minister of Foreign Affairs and Alexandra Kollantai had the door of her ministry closed in her face when she tried to get in. It took ten days and armed force to make the bank staff open the vaults. Outside of the capital the Bolsheviks' power was even more limited. Most of the soviets and other local bodies were in the control of the Mensheviks, Socialist Revolutionaries or non-party socialists, and in the countryside the Bolshevik presence was virtually non-existent.

Moreover, there was a great deal of opposition to one-party rule. Hundreds of resolutions and petitions flooded in from factory committees, army units, and Moscow and provincial towns, demanding that there be co-operation between the parties to avoid factional strife and civil war. A petition from the 35th army division made this clear: 'Among the soldiers there are no Bolsheviks, Mensheviks or Socialist Revolutionaries, only Democrats.'

Sovnarkom – Council of the People's Commissars; the top Bolshevik governing body (30–40 members) set up after the October Revolution in 1917. It operated until 1941 but became much less influential after the Politburo was formed in 1919 (7–9 members).

What about the Soviet?

The Soviet became increasingly irrelevant as power moved over to the *Sovnarkom*. The socialist leaders of the Soviet should have been consulted on important policies and decisions, but Lenin had no intention of seeking their approval. The Soviet Executive began to meet less frequently and was effectively moribund although it continued to meet well into the 1930s.

LOOK AGAIN

Think again about the success of the Bolshevik take-over. Does the information here suggest that the workers were supporting the Bolsheviks' rule or something else?

According to Source D, how limited was Bolshevik control?

Yakov Sverdlov, 1885–1919

Another key Bolshevik at this time was Sverdlov, a great organising genius. Born into a working-class Jewish family, he became a Social Democrat in 1905. He was exiled to Siberia with Stalin but they did not get on. He played an important part in organising the October uprising with Trotsky. He was totally loyal to Lenin, who valued Sverdlov's reliability and dependability. After the revolution he was given the job of building up the Party secretariat and establishing a network of Party officials and local secretariats throughout Russia, all reporting to Moscow. In 1922 he would almost certainly have been made General Secretary of the Party – the job which gave Stalin so much power – but he died of flu in 1919.

The railway men's union, backed by the post and telegraph union, threatened to cut off communications if the Bolsheviks did not hold talks with other parties. This forced Lenin to send representatives to talks with other parties about power-sharing, and allow the planned elections to the Constituent Assembly to go ahead at the end of November. Some leading Bolsheviks, including Kamenev and Zinoviev, were in favour of a socialist coalition government. They believed that an isolated Bolshevik Party would have to maintain itself by terror and would not survive the civil war that would inevitably follow. But Lenin made sure that the talks collapsed. He did, however, bring Left Socialist Revolutionaries into the *Sovnarkom* because, with them in his government, he could claim to represent the interests of the peasantry.

Lenin had always intended the Bolsheviks to rule alone. He saw the revolution as a turning point in world history. He had a vision of a utopian world order and was not prepared to see his vision diluted by compromise with other socialists.

Source D From *Russia under the Bolshevik Regime 1912–24* by R. Pipes, (Vintage), 1994, p5.

The Bolsheviks were masters only of central Russia, and even there they ruled only the cities and industrial centres. The borderlands of what had been the Russian Empire, inhabited by peoples of other nationalities and religions, had separated themselves and proclaimed independence … The Bolsheviks, therefore, had literally to conquer by force of arms the separated borderlands as well as the villages in which lived four-fifths of Russia's population. Their own power base was not very secure, resting on at most 200,000 party members and an army then in the process of dissolution.

First measures

In order to survive the first few months, Lenin gave the workers and peasants what they wanted. Edward Acton says: 'No Russian government had ever been more responsive to pressure from below or less able to impose its will upon society.' Power was thrown out to local soviets to manage their own affairs even though they were not, in the main, under central control.

The *Sovnarkom* passed a number of decrees to keep the support of the people. Four particularly important ones were:

- **The decree on peace:** This called for an immediate truce and just peace with 'no annexations, no indemnities'. It aimed to pull Russia out of the war.
- **The decree on land:** This gave peasants the right to take over the estates of the gentry, without compensation, and to decide for themselves the best way to divide it up. Land could no longer be bought, sold or rented; it belonged to the 'entire people'.
- **The decree on workers' control:** Factory committees were given the right to control production and finance in workplaces and to 'supervise' management.
- **The decree on the rights of the people of Russia:** This gave the right of self-determination to the national minorities in the former Russian Empire. This was purely a paper measure since the Bolsheviks did not have control of the areas in which most of these people lived.

October 1917	• Maximum eight-hour day for workers. • Social insurance (old age, unemployment, sickness benefits, etc.) to be introduced. • Opposition press banned. • Decree on peace. • Decree on land.
November 1917	• Right of self-determination granted to all parts of the former Russian Empire. • Abolition of titles and class distinctions. • Workers to control factories. • Abolition of justice system. • Women declared equal to men and able to own property.
December 1917	• *Cheka* set up. • Banks nationalised (put under state control). • Democratisation of army – officers to be elected, army to be controlled by army soviets and soldiers' committees, abolition of ranks, saluting and decorations. • Marriage and divorce became civil matters, no longer linked to the Church. • Church land nationalised.
January 1918	• Creation of Red Army.

▲ **Figure 7** Early decrees issued by the *Sovnarkom*.

Out of control

The Bolsheviks had little control over what was happening in the cities in the days after the Revolution. In Petrograd, thousands of bottles of alcohol were discovered in the Tsar's wine cellars and the crowds drank themselves to oblivion. Despite Bolshevik guards with machine guns to deter them, people only stopped when the alcohol ran out. Drunken mobs of soldiers and sailors roamed the streets. The houses and shops of the well-to-do were plundered and people attacked. A hooligan and criminal element joined in the social revolution which had degenerated into violence and lawlessness. Maxim Gorky, the famous Russian novelist and friend of Lenin, condemned it as a 'pogrom of greed, hatred and violence' rather than revolution. He pleaded with Bolshevik leaders to save buildings and works of art from being destroyed. It was a similar story in many places outside the capital. It took a long time before this lawlessness was brought under control

Dealing with threats and opposition

The Bolsheviks soon took steps to deal with threats from opponents:

- They closed down the opposition press: first the newspapers of the centre and the right, and later the socialist press. The Bolsheviks understood the problems that a hostile press could cause them.
- They turned on opposition political parties. The Kadet Party, which had done quite well in the Constituent Assembly elections, was denounced and outlawed. Leading Kadets were arrested and two were brutally beaten to death by Bolshevik sailors. The Kadets were soon followed into prison by leading right-wing Socialist Revolutionaries and Mensheviks – all this before the end of 1917. The engine of political terror was being cranked up.
- On 7 December, Lenin set up the main instrument of terror – the *Cheka*, or All-Russian Extraordinary Commission for Combating Counter-Revolution and Sabotage. This force of dedicated Bolshevik supporters provided dependable security, bringing units of the Red Guard and military units under its control.

Ideology

In *State and Revolution*, finished just before October, Lenin suggested that the general will of the people would support the revolutionary government. He thought the people would be able to run their own affairs, so there would be less need for bureaucracy. This view seems to be reflected in the decrees giving workers control of the factories and the peasants control of the land.

Lenin also stressed the need for 'the dictatorship of the proletariat', during which remnants of the bourgeois state (civil service, etc.) would be crushed and bourgeois attitudes and values would be squeezed out of society.

- The civil service was thoroughly purged. Junior officials willing to support the Bolsheviks were promoted and Bolshevik officials were brought in. Often third-rate people or corrupt opportunists were put into positions of real power. The bureaucracy that developed was of poor quality but it was obedient.

There was some opposition to the Bolsheviks and there were demonstrations. But the opposition was weak and unco-ordinated. Mensheviks and right-wing Socialist Revolutionaries did not want to get involved in organised violence because they were still acutely aware of the dangers of civil war. Moreover, they still had hopes for the Constituent Assembly and an all-socialist government. They did not really expect the Bolsheviks to survive.

Class warfare

Lenin actively used class warfare as a means of intimidating the middle classes and keeping control. The Bolshevik press identified the *burzhooi* (bourgeois) as the 'enemies of the people'. They were condemned as 'parasites' and 'bloodsuckers'. The state licensed and encouraged the people to plunder the houses of the middle classes, to 'loot the looters'. The legal system was abolished and replaced by revolutionary justice, which was arbitrary and violent in character. Anybody accused of being a *burzhooi* was liable to be arrested, and any well-dressed person found on the streets was at risk of being beaten and robbed.

This played well with workers, soldiers and peasants who supported moves to a more egalitarian society. The abolition of titles and the use of 'comrade' as the new form of address gave power and dignity to the once downtrodden. Workers and soldiers became more cocky and assertive, and rude to their 'social betters'.

> *Burzhooi* (bourgeois) – This term was a form of abuse used against employers, officers, landowners, priests, Jewish people, merchants or anybody seemingly well-to-do. It later became synonymous with people suspected of speculating or hoarding food.

The Constituent Assembly

The Constituent Assembly posed a bigger threat to the Bolsheviks. As we saw, Lenin was forced to allow elections in November, the first free elections in centuries. This gave the Assembly a mandate as the legitimate body to decide the make-up of the future government. When the election results became known, the Bolsheviks found they had won only 175 seats against 410 for the Socialist Revolutionaries and nearly 100 for other parties.

However, Lenin asserted that his Soviet government represented a higher stage of democracy than an elected assembly containing different political parties. He said that the Constituent Assembly smacked of bourgeois parliamentary democracy and declared it redundant. The Assembly was allowed to meet for one day – 5 January 1918 – then the doors were closed and the deputies told to go home. A crowd which demonstrated in favour of the Assembly was fired on by soldiers loyal to the *Sovnarkom*, the first time that soldiers had fired in this way on unarmed demonstrators since February 1917.

	Votes cast (in millions)	Number of seats won	Percentage share of the vote
Socialist Revolutionaries	21.8	410*	53
Bolsheviks	10.0	175	24
Kadets	2.1	17	5
Mensheviks	1.4	18	3
Others	6.3	62	15

*includes 40 Left SRs

▲ **Figure 8** Constituent Assembly elections, November 1917.

Peace

The promise that had brought so many people to the Bolshevik banner was the pledge to end the war. The decree on peace, the first signed by the Bolsheviks on 26 October, was a plea to other nations for an immediate truce and a just peace with 'no annexations, no indemnities'. But the practical resolution proved more difficult. The Russian army was disintegrating as soldiers, who had no desire to die in futile last-minute fighting, wanted to get back home. This represented both good and bad news for the Bolsheviks. The good news was that Russian generals could not use the army against them. The bad news was that the German army was free to walk into Russia and take what it wanted. The Western allies ignored the decree on peace and Lenin now faced a huge problem which was not resolved until March 1918 (see page 159).

Interpretations

Was the October Revolution a popular revolution?

One of the key debates among historians of the October Revolution is whether it was a popular revolution (supported by the workers) or a *coup d'état* (a take-over by a small group of revolutionaries). This has often been an acrimonious debate because it reflects the political views of historians about communism.

Before the collapse of communism in 1991, Soviet historians pursued a clear line that the October Revolution was a popular uprising which was led and carried out by the working class who created the soviets and provided the power base through which the revolution was accomplished; they were supported by the poorer peasants. The Bolshevik Party guided the working classes to success, with Lenin as the inspired leader who directed the Party.

After the Second World War, the West was engaged in a Cold War with the Soviet Union, and the USA funded historical research (Sovietology) to understand the enemy. The predominant view among historians, especially in the USA, was that a small number of revolutionaries seized power in a *coup d'état* and then imposed their ideology on an unwilling population. Lenin is seen as the architect of the revolution at the head of a well-drilled party machine. Historians who take this line include Leonard Schapiro, Robert Conquest, Adam Ulam and Richard Pipes. They believe that the revolution led directly to a totalitarian communist state and so this is sometimes called the 'totalitarian' view. It is also referred to as the 'liberal' view because it was espoused by Western liberal historians who were critical of the Soviet Union in respect of its lack of civil rights and disregard for personal freedom. Historians still take this line today.

In the 1970s, a new generation of historians challenged the 'totalitarian' view. They suspected that the hostile accounts of the October Revolution were part of the Cold War politics of the post-war period. They looked more closely at the role of the Bolshevik Party and workers in the revolution. Historians like Stephen Smith saw a much more active role for the lower ranks of the Bolshevik Party in pushing forward the revolution and suggested Lenin was not so firmly in control and that the Bolsheviks were not so disciplined as had been previously claimed. Sheila Fitzpatrick suggested that it was people – workers, soldiers and peasants – who created the circumstances in which the Bolsheviks could operate. They formed soviets and committees before the Bolsheviks were on the scene. This moves more towards the popular view of the October Revolution. These historians have been called 'revisionists' because they have revised previous views.

Cold War – Post-1945 hostility between the democratic West and the Soviet Union; a war of threats and propaganda, rather than actual conflict in a war between the two sides.

More recently, historians such as Robert Service and Christopher Read have acknowledged that there is room to accept the scholarship of the Cold War historians and of the revisionists. They argue that Lenin was a key figure, saying that without his drive and persistence there probably would not have been an October Revolution. They also say that all the hallmarks of a coup are present in the way that the Bolsheviks seized power. However, they maintain that there was a lot of independent action at local levels in the Party and in the soviets and that the situation greatly facilitated the take-over: the increased radicalism of the workers, soldiers, sailors and peasants cannot be ignored. The extent of their involvement is crucial in assessing whether the events of October 1917 constitute a popular revolution or not. Beryl Williams maintains that workers might support the October Revolution and vote for the Bolsheviks in elections but this does not imply support for one-party rule.

Chapter summary

- The Provisional Government and the Soviet shared power after the abdication of the Tsar while arrangements were made to elect a Constituent Assembly to work out the future system of government for Russia.
- The Provisional Government faced difficult issues concerning the war, land, national minorities, social reform and the economy. It did not deal with these in a way that matched the expectations of the workers, soldiers and peasants.
- Lenin and the Bolsheviks offered a radical alternative programme which included ending the war, giving land to the peasants and power to the soviets, which attracted popular support.
- The Provisional Government was reformed, taking in more moderate socialists but there were splits between liberals and socialists. The Bolsheviks became the focus for opposition to the Provisional Government.
- The frustration of soldiers and workers exploded in the July Days but the Bolshevik leadership was not ready to take advantage of this and the uprising fizzled out.
- Alexander Kerensky was made Prime Minister, but the economic and social situation was deteriorating and order in town and countryside was breaking down.
- Kerensky tried to use General Kornilov to gain control of Petrograd but Kornilov had his own agenda and the affair ended in disaster. This boosted support for the Bolsheviks.
- Lenin persuaded the Bolshevik Party to seize power and, after further inept moves by Kerensky, they did this on 25–26 October, taking advantage of the All-Russian Congress of Soviets.
- The Bolshevik government was on a fragile footing as other socialists, workers and soldiers resisted one-party rule. But Lenin managed to keep the Bolsheviks in power by giving the people what they wanted and establishing the mechanism for control by terror – the *Cheka*.
- Lenin dealt with threats from the opposition by arresting the leaders of other political parties, shutting their newspapers and closing down the Constituent Assembly.

▼ Summary diagram: The weaknesses of the Provisional Government.

Political authority
- Temporary in nature so felt it could not make binding decisions for the long-term future of Russia.
- Shared power with the Soviet, so scope for action was limited.
- Divisions between socialists and liberals led to a lack of clear policies.
- Lacked popular support because its policies and actions antagonised the peasants and radicalised the workers. It:
  - continued the war
  - would not legitimise the peasant take-over of land
  - failed to ensure food supplies to cities because it mishandled relations with peasants
  - refused to give autonomy to national minorities
  - did little about the deterioration of the economy and social reform.
- Could not command support of the Petrograd garrison.

The role of the Kadets
The Kadets moved further to the right and became identified with reactionary military officers, industrialists and landowners. They blocked the government from taking measures that would have gained it popular support. They:
- blocked the land deal and Chernov's suggestions for a compromise
- supported the war and wanted to continue it aggressively
- sided with the employers against the workers over workers' power and working conditions.

Mistakes by Kerensky
- Launched a new offensive against Germany in June.
- Responsible for Kornilov affair, which discredited him and meant officers would not fight for him or the Provisional Government.
- Underestimated the strength of the Bolsheviks.
- By moving against them in October, he played into the Bolsheviks' hands, giving them an excuse to claim they were seizing power in the name of the Soviet.

▼ Summary diagram: Bolshevik strengths and factors in their favour

Bolshevik strengths
- Determined leadership of Lenin, strong sense of purpose.
- Much better organised than other parties.
- Radical policies were in tune with workers' and soldiers' aspirations.
- Brought peasants on side by promising land redistribution.
- Became the focus of opposition to Provisional Government while the leaders of other socialist parties were associated with it.
- Organisation of Trotsky – control of MRC, using All-Russian Congress of Soviets, planning actual take-over.
- Greatest number of active supporters, particularly soldiers and sailors, around Petrograd and Moscow, key places in the revolution.

Other factors favouring Bolsheviks
- The military collapse in September/October meant that the army was not in a position to stop the Bolsheviks.
- While only a small minority of the Petrograd garrison actively supported the Bolsheviks, the majority of soldiers remained neutral and refused to oppose them.
- The economic crisis was acute by October and people were very hungry.
- Radicalised workers who favoured soviet power were prepared to support the party that seemed to offer this.

▼ Summary diagram: How were the Bolsheviks able to stay in power?

Weak opposition
- Opposition unable to co-ordinate action against the government.
- Power of the Soviet had declined, so no serious contender on the left to challenge Bolshevik power.
- Forces on the right had collapsed in the capital – no leaders and few active supporters to challenge government.
- SRs and Mensheviks underestimated Bolsheviks and took no direct action because they thought the Bolshevik government would collapse quickly.
- Socialist parties thought the Constituent Assembly would solve the problem, but Lenin just dismissed it.
- Collapse of army meant that officers and conservative forces could not count on any loyal troops to attack the Bolsheviks.

Countered threats and opposition
- Dealt with pressure to form coalition with other socialists by agreeing to elections and talks until government was on a firmer footing.
- Closed down the opposition press.
- Arrested key figures in other political parties.
- Closed down the Constituent Assembly.
- Set up the *Cheka* to arrest dissidents and troublemakers.
- Used class warfare to deflect antagonism onto the bourgeoisie and keep urban population on side.

Policies
Early decrees and measures were well-received by many sections of the people and ensured initial support or muted opposition.
- Decree on peace – generally popular.
- Decree on land gave peasants what they wanted.
- Decree on workers' control pleased workers.
- Eight-hour day and social insurance pleased workers.
- Measures on equality and abolition of titles well received by some sections of the urban population.

Working on essay technique: evaluation and relative significance

Reaching a supported overall judgement is an important part of writing good essays. One very important way to do this is by evaluating the relative significance of different factors, in the light of valid criteria. 'Relative significance' means how important one factor is compared to another. This section examines how to evaluate and how to establish valid criteria.

The purpose of *evaluation* is to weigh up and reach a judgement. This means that you need to consider the importance of two or more different factors, weigh them against each other, and then reach a judgement. Evaluation is a good skill to use at the end of an essay, because it helps support your overall judgement.

The best essays will make a judgement about which was most important factor based on valid criteria. This is called *relative significance*. It is up to you to come up with valid criteria. Criteria can be very simple – and will depend on the topic and the exact question.

The following criteria are often useful:

- **Duration**: which factor was important for the longest amount of time?
- **Scope**: which factor affected the most people?

- **Effectiveness**: which factor achieved most?
- **Impact**: which factor led to the most fundamental change?

For example, you could compare the factors in terms of their impact or duration (important over a long period of time). In the essay guidance you worked on at the end of Chapter 3 (page 117) you could argue that the most important factor that caused the collapse of the old regime was the war because of its impact on the Russian economy and people – and historians do argue this case. However, you could take the line that the tsarist regime failed because it had not reformed itself or its structures over a long period of time, even stretching back to 1861 – and historians argue this case. Both are important factors in causing the February Revolution which removed the Romanovs but historians make a judgement based on the evidence about which one they consider more important or more significant. You have to do the same in your essays. An example is given on page 148. Read this then carry out the activity below.

ACTIVITY

Use the technique on page 148 to address the following A-level practice question:

'Lenin's greatest contribution to revolution in Russia between 1894 and 1917 was as a revolutionary theorist, rather than as the man who pushed for the Bolsheviks to seize power in October 1917.' Assess the validity of this view. (25 marks)

Think about the following when planning your answer to this question. The same points can be taken into consideration for other questions of this type:

- The question states 'revolution in Russia between 1894 and 1917' so you will need to look at 1905 and February 1917 (not just October 1917) and also the role Lenin and the Bolsheviks played in developing revolutionary consciousness in these years as a whole.

- Identify key aspects of Lenin's revolutionary theories.
- How important were his ideas in making him leader of the Bolshevik Party?
- Decide on the criteria by which you will judge the relative importance of his role as a theorist as opposed to pressing for action in 1917.
- The question states 'contribution to revolution'. Would there have been a second revolution in 1917 (though not necessarily a Bolshevik one) even if Lenin had not been pressing for it?

Now write an argument in one or two sentences that summarise Lenin's contribution to revolution.

Support this by writing additional sentences which are specific to the areas you have chosen. Use words such as 'however', and 'nonetheless' to weigh contrasting points.

EXAMPLE

Consider the following A-level practice question:

'Bolshevik success in the October Revolution was due to the failure of successive governments since 1895 to meet the demands and aspirations of the working classes.' Assess the validity of this view.

(25 marks)

With this type of question you have to weigh up and make a judgement about the factor you consider most important. The factor highlighted is to do with the working classes but there are other factors which could be taken into account, for instance:

- the role of the peasants
- the role of the army
- weaknesses of the Provisional Government and role of Kerensky
- the leadership, policies and actions of the Bolsheviks.

Historians do take different positions on this, so it is a genuine historical debate. You will need to consider criteria such as duration (building up for a long time), scope (affected the most people) and effectiveness (most effective at the time).

For example, your conclusion might read:

Begins with main argument —

The support of the workers was crucial for Bolshevik success. Their grievances had not been addressed under the Tsar or after February 1917 when they expected their conditions to improve and to receive better treatment. As a result they were at the forefront of the popular movement demanding rule by the soviets. *However, this did not necessarily mean Bolshevik one-party rule, it could have been a socialist coalition government.* — Limitations of main argument

Counter-argument contrast, with precise information in support —

The reason why it was the Bolsheviks who were successful was their policies and the leadership of Lenin. They promised the workers soviet power and workers' control in factories. Lenin promised the peasants they could take the land for themselves without compensation. Lenin said he would end the war immediately so soldiers who did not actively support the Bolsheviks remained neutral. This allowed Lenin and Trotsky to organise the seizure of power with little opposition and take power in the name of the soviets. *Therefore, the most important reason for the Bolshevik success was because Lenin put the Bolsheviks at the head of the popular movement for change, offered different groups what they wanted, and was determined to seize power through a carefully organised coup.* — Resolution of the arguments

In this example, the evaluation is helped by explaining that although the long-term demands and aspirations of the working classes were central to Bolshevik take-over, it was the way that Lenin engaged their support and the tacit support of other groups that was the key to Bolshevik success. 'However' and 'therefore' are useful words as they can help contrast the importance of different factors and different views. 'Clearly' and 'nevertheless' are other useful examples.

This conclusion provides an example of what could be high-level work (if supported in the main body of the essay with appropriate details and precise information) because it reaches an overall judgement and supports it through evaluating the relative significance of different factors in the light of valid criteria.

Working on interpretation skills

The advice given here builds on the help given at the end of Chapter 2 (see page 76).

For the AQA A-level exam, Section A gives you three extracts, followed by a single question. The wording of the question will be something like this:

'Using your understanding of the historical context, assess how convincing the arguments in these three extracts are in relation to ...'   (30 marks)

The A-level mark scheme is very similar to the AS one on page 76.

Level 5	Shows a very good understanding of the interpretations put forward in all three extracts and combines this with a strong awareness of the historical context to analyse and evaluate the interpretations given in the extracts. Evaluation of the arguments will be well-supported and convincing. The response demonstrates a very good understanding of context. *25–30 marks*
Level 4	Shows a good understanding of the interpretations given in all three extracts and combines this with knowledge of the historical context to analyse and evaluate the interpretations given in the extracts. The evaluation of the arguments will be mostly well-supported, and convincing, but may have minor limitations of depth and breadth. The response demonstrates a good understanding of context. *19–24 marks*
Level 3	Provides some supported comment on the interpretations given in all three extracts and comments on the strength of these arguments in relation to their historic context. There is some analysis and evaluation but there may be an imbalance in the degree and depth of comments offered on the strength of the arguments. The response demonstrates an understanding of context. *13–18 marks*
Level 2	Provides some accurate comment on the interpretations given in at least two of the extracts, with reference to the historical context. The answer may contain some analysis, but there is little, if any, evaluation. Some of the comments on the strength of the arguments may contain some generalisation, inaccuracy or irrelevance. The response demonstrates some understanding of context. *7–12 marks*
Level 1	Either shows an accurate understanding of the interpretation given in one extract only or addresses two/three extracts, but in a generalist way, showing limited accurate understanding of the arguments they contain, although there may be some general awareness of the historical context. Any comments on the strength of the arguments are likely to be generalist and contain some inaccuracy and/or irrelevance. The response demonstrates limited understanding of context. *1–6 marks*

Notice that there is no reference in the mark scheme to *comparing* the extracts or reaching a judgement about which of the extracts is the most convincing.

There is an A-level practice question on page 150 and guidance on how to answer it on page 151:

Using your understanding of the historical context, assess how convincing the arguments in these three extracts are in explaining the revolution in October 1917 as the result of the social divisions and grievances that had built up in Russia from 1894 to 1917.

Extract A

The Revolution was truly popular and profoundly democratic … Lenin and his comrades were the illegitimate beneficiaries of the autonomous action of the masses. The revolution of 1917 was the product of popular revolt against oppression. It was accomplished 'not by a political party, but by the people themselves'. Time and again the self-proclaimed leaders of the revolution were taken by surprise by the initiative welling up from below – in January 1905, in February, April and July 1917. The masses were not enticed into revolt by superior leaders. Their extreme radicalism was not the product of manipulation or brainwashing by the Bolsheviks … nor was it the fruit of enlightenment brought to them by the Bolsheviks as the Soviet view contends. The goals for which they strove were their own. They responded to only what fulfilled their own aspirations; the rest they rejected. In this sense, not only February but the whole social upheaval of 1917 was 'spontaneous' – unorchestrated, unplanned but consciously willed, deliberately carried through by millions of ordinary people. The peasants sought to solve the 'agrarian question' in their own way and by themselves, while 'the autonomous action of the working class seeking fundamentally to alter the conditions of its own existence' was 'the most fundamental feature' of the period.

A. Berkman's view summarised in *Rethinking the Russian Revolution* by E. Acton, (Bloomsbury Academic), 1990, p 177.

Extract B

In October 1917 the majority of Russia's lower classes had not been converted to socialism, certainly not in the Bolshevik variant. They had, in fact, a very confused understanding of socialist doctrines and goals. But they did understand that the socialists and the soviets stood and spoke for them against leaders, now called bourgeois, who still asked them to be patient and law-abiding and patriotic. That is why the socialist parties garnered 87 percent of the vote in the elections to the Constituent Assembly and that is why the Bolsheviks took power not in their own name but in that of the soviets and as their defenders against the forces of reaction. It is not so much that Russia and her people were moving towards Bolshevism as that the Bolsheviks were moving towards a country convulsed by a powerful worker-peasant revolt. Besides its proximate causes in war and hunger, that revolt had deep roots in the social divisions, enmities, and grievances of the old order, grievances that the Bolsheviks expressed, mobilized and exploited. In that sense the 'Great October Socialist Revolution' is the last chapter in the history of the old regime that fell in February.

From *Russia in the Age of Modernisation and Revolution 1881–1917* by Hans Rogger, (Longman), 1986, p 288.

Extract C

In February 1917, Russia experienced a genuine revolution in that the disorders that brought down the tsarist regime … erupted spontaneously and the Provisional Government that assumed power gained immediate national acceptance. Neither held true of October 1917. The events that led to the overthrow of the Provisional Government were not spontaneous but carefully plotted and staged by a tightly organised conspiracy. It took these conspirators three years of civil war to subdue the majority of the population. October was a classic *coup d'etat*, the capture of government authority by a small band, carried out, in deference to the democratic professions of the age, with a show of mass participation, but with hardly any mass involvement … He [Trotsky] disguised Bolshevik preparations for the coup behind the façade of an unlawfully convened Second congress of Soviets and entrusted to special shock troops the task of seizing the nerve centres of the government. In theory, the power seizure was carried out provisionally and on behalf of the soviets, but, in fact, permanently and for the benefit of the Bolshevik Party.

From *The Concise History of the Russian Revolution* by Richard Pipes, (Harvill Press), 1995, p 113.

Possible answer

First, make sure that you have the focus of the question clear – the October Revolution was the result of the social divisions and grievances that had built up in Russia from 1894 to 1917.

Then you can investigate the three extracts to see how convincing they are.

You need to analyse each of the three extracts in turn. A suggestion is to start with a large page divided into nine blocks.

Extract's main arguments	Knowledge to corroborate	Knowledge to contradict or modify
A		
B		
C		

- In the first column list the main arguments each uses.
- In the second column list what you know that can corroborate the arguments.
- In the third column list what might contradict or modify the arguments. ('Modify' – you might find that you partly agree, but with reservations.)
- You may find, of course, that some of your knowledge is relevant more than once.

Planning your answer – one approach

Decide how you could best set out a detailed plan for your answer. You could, for example:

- Briefly refer to the focus of the question.
- For each extract in turn set out the arguments, and the corroborating and contradictory evidence.
- Do this by treating each argument (or group of arguments) in turn.
- Make comparisons between the extracts if this is helpful. The mark scheme does not explicitly give credit for doing this, but a successful comparison may well show the extent of your understanding of each extract.
- An overall judgement is not required, but it may be helpful to make a brief summary, or just reinforce what has been said already by emphasising which extract was the most convincing.

Remember that in the examination you are allowed an hour for this question. It is the planning stage that is vital in order to write a good answer. You should allow sufficient time to read the extracts and plan an answer. If you start writing too soon, it is likely that you will waste time trying to summarise the *content* of each source. Do this in your planning stage – and then think how you will *use* the content to answer the question.

Then the actual writing!

- Think how you can write an answer, dealing with each extract in turn, but making cross-references or comparisons, if this is helpful, to reinforce a point.
- In addition, make sure your answer:
  - shows very good understanding of the extracts
  - uses knowledge to argue in support or to disagree
  - provides a clear argument which leads to a conclusion about each extract, and which may reach a conclusion about the extracts as a whole.

Extracts that have an argument and counter-argument

Sometimes an extract will give opposing views or qualification of views within a paragraph – an attempt at providing balance. The extract may reach a conclusion on which argument is stronger, or it may leave an open verdict. Look at Extract D.

Extract D

One of the most basic misconceptions of the Russian Revolution is that the Bolsheviks were swept to power on a tide of mass support for the party itself. The October insurrection was a *coup d'état*, actively supported by a small minority of the population (and indeed opposed by several of the Bolshevik leaders themselves). But it took place amidst a social revolution, which was centred on the popular realization of Soviet power as the negation of the state and the direct self-rule of the people ... The political vacuum brought about by this social revolution enabled the Bolsheviks to seize power in the cities and consolidate their dictatorship during the autumn and winter. The slogan 'All Power to the Soviets!' was a useful tool, a banner of popular legitimation covering the nakedness of Lenin's ambition (which was better expressed as All Power to the Party). Later, as the nature of the Bolshevik dictatorship became apparent, the party faced the growing opposition of precisely those groups in society who had rallied behind the soviet slogan.

From *A People's Tragedy: The Russian Revolution 1891–1924*, by O. Figes, (Pimlico), 1997, pp 460–61.

This extract presents:

- an argument suggesting that the Bolsheviks did not have mass support.
- a qualification that there was a social revolution taking place, seeking to overthrow state power which the Bolsheviks used for their own ends.

If this extract were being studied, your plan would highlight the balance within the extract, and would seek to find evidence to support and refute both sides.

This would have to be reflected in your answer in relation to how convincing the arguments are. An extract that includes counter-argument as well as argument *could* be more convincing, but not necessarily so. It will depend on the context – and your own knowledge which you are using in order to reach a judgement.

Key questions: Russia, 1855–1917

The specification on this topic states that it requires the study in breadth of issues of change, continuity, cause and consequence in the period through six key questions. These have been either featured or mentioned at various points in the four chapters you have studied, and are outlined on pages 153–6. The questions set in the examination (both the interpretation question and the essays) will reflect one or more of these key questions. Even though in the examination the questions may focus on developments over approximately 25–30 years, rather than the period as a whole, it is very useful to pause to consider developments across the wider time period you have studied so far, as this will help you to see and analyse change and continuity with a sense of perspective.

KEY QUESTION 1:
How was Russia governed and how did political authority change and develop?

'governed' means looking at how Russia was ruled and controlled, the way the state was organised, the bureaucracy, the role of the secret police and how individual tsars approached their role and conducted affairs of state

'political authority' refers to the acceptance of the legitimate authority of the state or tsar to rule and exercise power

'change and develop' suggests different, evolving, increasing or decreasing

Questions to consider

- Take an overview of the period. Think about:
  - why Alexander II brought in his reforms
  - what the results of his reforms were
  - what policies Alexander III adopted
  - the situation he bequeathed his son
  - how Nicholas II handled modernisation.
- How did the three key principles of autocracy, orthodoxy and nationality form the core of the tsarist regime?
- Was Alexander III more responsible than his father and son for the 1917 revolution because he halted and reversed the reform of Russian institutions?

Working in groups

Considering the period from 1855 to 1917:

1 Discuss the personalised nature of control in the autocracy, the main weaknesses of the tsarist state and the way it related to the people it governed.
2 What were the similarities and differences in the way Russia was governed under Alexander II, Alexander III and Nicholas II?
3 Did the Russian autocracy try to reform itself between 1861 and 1917? With what degree of success?

KEY QUESTION 2:
How did opposition develop and how effective was it?

'opposition' refers to the people or groups that opposed the Tsar and the ruling elite. This includes opposition from the people, for example, peasants and workers, as well as opposition from revolutionary parties and the liberal intelligentsia.

'how effective' – How much did it disrupt the government? How successful was it in achieving its goals?

Questions to consider

- How did the Populist movement emerge and later develop into the Socialist Revolutionary Party? How effective were the Populists and the SRs?
- Compare the Bolsheviks with the Mensheviks: which presented the most credible opposition before 1917?
- Why did the regime face opposition from the peasants after 1861? What form did it take and how did the regime deal with it?
- How and why did opposition from the working class develop from the 1890s to 1917 and why did it prove particularly potent in 1917?

Working in groups

Considering the period from 1855 to 1917:

1 How did the revolutionary groups/parties develop between 1861 and 1917?

2 Discuss the role of the tsarist secret police – the Third Section and the *Okhrana* – and how effective they were in dealing with revolutionaries.

3 Discuss how the liberal opposition developed from its origins in the liberal intelligentsia of the 1850s to the creation of the liberal parties in 1905 and their role in the Duma. How effective was the liberal opposition?

KEY QUESTION 3:
How and with what results did the economy develop and change?

'results' refers to the outcome of these policies and assessing their impact on the economy – growth, food production, etc.

'how', 'develop' and 'change' involve descriptions and analysis of the policies and process of industrialisation and the policies and progress in the agricultural sector of the economy, and the connection between them

Questions to consider

- What were the motives for industrialisation and how did these drive policies between 1880 and 1914? What was Witte's strategy for industrialising Russia?
- What were the results of industrialisation by 1914?
- Was there a crisis in agriculture?
- What policies were applied to agriculture and how successful were they?

Working in groups

Considering the period from 1855 to 1914:

1 Discuss the impact of the emancipation of the serfs and how it had changed peasant lives and the agricultural economy between 1861 and 1905.

2 Discuss what Stolypin was trying to achieve in his agricultural reforms and how successful they were.

3 Compare the economy in the 1860s with that of 1914. How far was it modernised?

KEY QUESTION 4:
What was the extent of social and cultural change?

'social' refers to people, groups, estates, classes in Russian society

'cultural' refers to ways of life and also more specifically the art, literature, music, etc. of the period

Questions to consider

- What was the impact of population growth on urban Russia and the countryside?
- What were the social and economic conditions like for workers in the cities and did they improve in the twentieth century?
- How did Russian literature, art and music develop in the late tsarist period?

Working in groups

Considering the period 1855 to 1914:

1 How had Russian society changed as a result of industrialisation and modernisation?
2 How much did the lives of Russian peasants change during this period?
3 Discuss how Russian literature, art and music reflected changes in Russian society.

KEY QUESTION 5:
How important were ideas and ideology?

How do you measure importance? At the time? In retrospect?

'ideology' means the ideas which support a political theory or system, such as autocracy or Marxism–Leninism

Questions to consider

- How important was religion to the autocracy?
- Think about the 'revolutionary tradition' in Russia. How did revolutionary ideas develop in the late nineteenth and early twentieth centuries?
- Why was Marxism attractive to Russians?

Working in groups

Considering the period from 1855 to 1917:

1 What ideology under-pinned the tsarist regime? How important was it in deciding the policy and practices of the regime?
2 Discuss the similarities and differences between the ideas of the Populists/Socialist Revolutionaries and the Marxist Social Democrats about socialism.
3 Discuss the importance of Lenin's adaptions of Marxism in bringing about the October Revolution in 1917.

KEY QUESTION 6:
How important was the role of individuals and groups and how were they affected by developments?

How do you measure importance? At the time? In retrospect?

Which individuals would you consider?

Which groups might you consider – and why?

'developments' refers to economic, political and social changes

Questions to consider

- Think about the role the nobility played in the autocracy and how nobles constrained the tsars in introducing reforms.
- How successful were Witte and Stolypin in their attempts to modernise and reform tsarist Russia?
- What roles did Lenin and the Bolsheviks play in the October Revolution in 1917?

Working in groups

Considering the period from 1855 to 1917:

1 How important were the personalities and attitudes of the last three tsars in the collapse of the tsarist regime?

2 Discuss the view that Stolypin was the greatest Russian statesman of the early twentieth century and the only person who could have saved tsarism.

3 Discuss whether there would have been a revolution in October 1917 if Lenin had not been present.

Lenin to Stalin, 1917–28

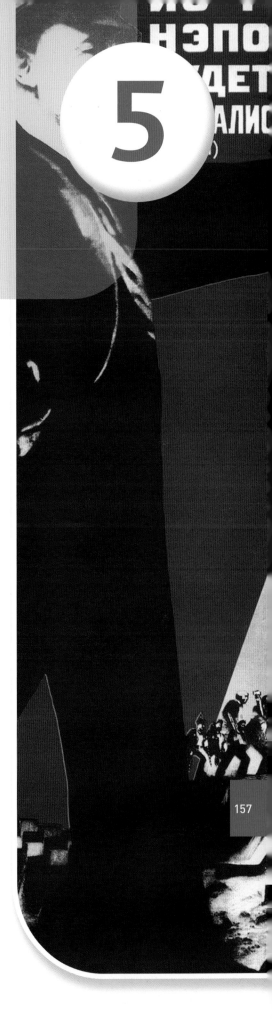

This chapter looks at the nature of Bolshevik rule: how Lenin sought to consolidate and develop it, and how Stalin emerged as leader of the USSR. It examines the changes to the economy, society and culture. It deals with the following areas:

- New leaders and ideologies, Lenin's economic decrees and the consolidation of Bolshevik authority
- Lenin's Russia
- Opposition outside and factions inside the Bolshevik Party
- Stalin's takeover
- The effect of Leninist rule on class, women, young people, religion, propaganda and cultural change

This chapter covers the key questions relating to how the political authority of Lenin and the Bolsheviks changed and developed and their importance. It looks at how opposition developed and was dealt with and how the economy developed and changed. The extent of social and cultural change is examined and the importance of ideas and ideology explored.

The main focus in this chapter will be on the question:

How important was ideology in the development of communist dictatorship, 1917–28?

Within this question you will look at the way in which the Bolsheviks consolidated their political authority between 1917 and 1928 and the role ideology played in this.

CHAPTER OVERVIEW

Ideology mattered to Lenin but hanging on to power mattered even more as he showed in signing the Treaty of Brest-Litovsk in March 1918. This propelled the Bolsheviks into another fight for survival in the ensuing civil war between 1918 and 1921. In this most bitter of conflicts the Bolsheviks were ruthless and employed pitiless class war, something Lenin thought essential at this time. The Bolsheviks won but in 1921 faced a greater challenge. The workers, peasants and Kronstadt sailors, the heroes of the revolution, were in open revolt. To survive, Lenin was forced to abandon War Communism, which fitted with their ideology, for the New Economic Policy (NEP), which did not. Economic concessions were accompanied by political repression and a strengthening of the centralised one-party state.

The foundations of the future communist regime were in place by the time of Lenin's death in 1924. His death left a huge gap in the Party leadership. The struggle over power for the next five years involved ideology as well as personalities. Eventually, it was Stalin who succeeded Lenin. The Bolsheviks wanted to change society and their ideology affected class, women, young people, religion and the arts. The Bolsheviks wanted to harness culture for their own propaganda purposes.

157

1 How did Lenin and the Bolsheviks overcome opposition, 1918–22?

Lenin had spent much of his life up to October 1917 developing Bolshevik ideology. Now he was in power, making real decisions with real consequences. This section will look at the serious challenges the Bolsheviks faced in their first few years in power and in 1921, a real crisis year. This section will consider how the crisis was overcome and power consolidated. It will end with an assessment of Lenin's importance.

Ending the war

How did the Bolsheviks cope with the problems they faced from January to May 1918?

Ideology was supremely important to the Bolsheviks. Lenin had severed relations with his close friend Martov in 1903 over ideology, yet worked happily with Trotsky in 1917 in spite of a decade of argument, because their ideological differences had disappeared. In hiding in Finland in the summer of 1917, Lenin had written *The State and Revolution* (see page 141) – his ideas on how the transition to socialism would be achieved once the Bolsheviks were in power. These optimistic expectations were soon dashed. We have seen in Chapter 4 that the bankers, civil servants and other managers actively obstructed the Bolsheviks. The economy, already in a parlous state, deteriorated rapidly and Lenin countered with a return to labour discipline and one-person management (see below). One of the tasks of the *Cheka* was to deal with 'sabotage' which came to mean disrupting the economy. Lenin had to admit that Russia was not on the threshold of socialism. However, problems did not just come from within, and one of the most pressing was dealing with the war with Germany.

The challenge of ending the war

The Bolsheviks were sure that other countries in Europe would follow the lead set by the decree on peace (page 143) – an immediate truce and a just peace with 'no annexations, no indemnities'. They believed that the war would collapse into a series of civil wars in European countries as the working class fought with the bourgeoisie following the example of the workers' revolution in Russia. They also believed that revolution in Russia could not survive without the support of workers' revolutions in advanced capitalist societies.

But the revolutions in other countries failed to materialise. As the army became incapable of fighting on successfully, Trotsky was dispatched to negotiate a peace settlement with Germany at Brest-Litovsk in December 1917. The terms the Germans proposed were harsh, involving loss of territory and people. Trotsky kept negotiations going as long as he could, hoping that revolution would break out in Germany and Austria. When the Germans grew impatient, he withdrew from the negotiations saying there would be 'neither war nor peace'.

Lenin believed that peace was essential to ensure the survival of the regime. There was no army to fight the Germans and when they began to advance into Ukraine, Lenin feared that they might move on to Petrograd and throw the Bolsheviks out. 'Germany is only pregnant with revolution and we have already given birth to a healthy child. In Russia', he continued, 'we must make sure of throttling the bourgeoisie, and for this we need both hands free.' One of the few in the Party who agreed with Lenin was Stalin.

The Bolsheviks split three ways

When Trotsky returned to Petrograd in January 1918, 63 leading Bolsheviks met. They were divided:

- Thirty-two favoured a revolutionary war.
- Sixteen favoured Trotsky's position of no war but no peace on German terms.
- Fifteen favoured Lenin's policy of peace at any price.

In the Bolshevik Central Committee Lenin still lacked support and the vote was nine to seven to accept Trotsky's policy of 'neither war nor peace'.

However, Bukharin and the Left Communists, sticking to their ideological position, wanted to turn the war into a revolutionary war to encourage a European socialist revolution. So Lenin's pleas for a separate peace with Germany were vigorously opposed.

The Germans resumed their advance. In five days they progressed 150 miles – further than in the previous three years of fighting. Harsher peace terms than originally put forward had to be accepted but only after further debate and Lenin's threat of resignation. Trotsky resigned as Foreign Commissar. On 3 March the Treaty of Brest-Litovsk was signed.

Consequences of the Treaty of Brest-Litovsk

Brest-Litovsk was seen throughout Russia as a 'shameful peace'. No other political party would have acceded to such terms; indeed no leading Bolshevik was prepared to put their name to it. Half the human, industrial and agricultural resources of Nicholas II's empire were lost. This aggravated the severe grain shortages in the cities. The treaty encouraged patriotic Russians to join anti-Bolshevik forces and made civil war, always likely once Lenin refused to share power, almost inevitable. The Left SRs favoured a revolutionary war and resigned from *Sovnarkom* in protest at the treaty.

There had been a short period of intense and quite free debate within the Party. However, after Brest-Litovsk had been ratified at the 7th Party Congress, the Left Communists faded and a potentially disastrous split in the Party was prevented. The Party Congress resolved that a general tightening up was essential. In the historian Mawdsley's view, 'never again would such a major issue be fought out in public, never again would Lenin be so deeply challenged'.

Ideology: Spreading the revolution – Comintern, the war with Poland

Lenin still believed world revolution was needed for the complete victory of socialism to be possible. In March 1919, Comintern (Third Communist International) was set up to guide, co-ordinate and promote the communist parties of the world, but it had little effect. However, in 1920, once the Poles, who had taken advantage of the civil war to take territory from Russia, had been pushed back, Lenin thought there was a chance of spreading revolution by arms. It failed and a disappointed Lenin was forced to rethink the whole question of international revolution.

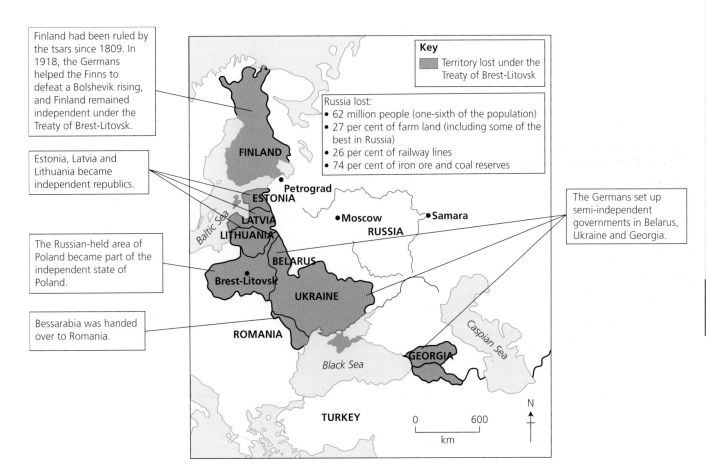

Finland had been ruled by the tsars since 1809. In 1918, the Germans helped the Finns to defeat a Bolshevik rising, and Finland remained independent under the Treaty of Brest-Litovsk.

Estonia, Latvia and Lithuania became independent republics.

The Russian-held area of Poland became part of the independent state of Poland.

Bessarabia was handed over to Romania.

Key
Territory lost under the Treaty of Brest-Litovsk

Russia lost:
- 62 million people (one-sixth of the population)
- 27 per cent of farm land (including some of the best in Russia)
- 26 per cent of railway lines
- 74 per cent of iron ore and coal reserves

The Germans set up semi-independent governments in Belarus, Ukraine and Georgia.

FINLAND

Petrograd

ESTONIA

•Moscow •Samara

Baltic Sea

LATVIA

LITHUANIA RUSSIA

Brest-Litovsk

BELARUS

UKRAINE

ROMANIA

Caspian Sea

Black Sea

GEORGIA

TURKEY

0   600
km

N

▲ **Figure 1** The terms of the Treaty of Brest-Litovsk.

The civil war

Why was there a civil war and what was its impact?

Even before the Bolsheviks seized power Lenin said, 'who does not know that the world history of all revolutions leads not accidentally but inevitably into civil war'. From May 1918 the Bolsheviks were fighting on numerous fronts.

The Reds, the Whites and the Greens

Conflict broke out in May after a revolt by Czech former war prisoners flared up, and from this point anti-Bolshevik White armies strove to overthrow the Reds (the Bolsheviks). There were also the Greens.

- **The Reds** were the Bolsheviks, and as it became clear that White success meant a restoration of the former ruling class and landowners, the Reds gained more support. The peasants hated the landlords more than they hated the Bolsheviks.
- **The Whites** were dominated by senior officers in the Tsarist army but they were divided and unco-ordinated. As well as former tsarists, they included liberals, Socialist Revolutionaries (keen to see the Constituent Assembly running Russia) and other moderate socialists. Probably the only thing that they all had in common was that they were anti-Bolshevik. The Whites were deeply divided and it was not uncommon for White armies to fight each other. Admiral Kolchak overthrew the *Komuch* (see Figure 2, page 161) in November 1918 in a military coup.
- **The Greens** were further evidence that in the civil war the peasants had their own overriding concerns. The Greens were peasant armies, often made up of deserters from the Whites or Reds. Some of these armies fought for the Bolsheviks, some against. Most were more concerned with protecting their own area from the ravages of other marauding armies. Probably the most famous of the Green armies was that of Nestor Makhno, an anarchist, in Ukraine. He was a skilled guerrilla leader who at various times fought the Reds, the Whites and the Germans, but became an ally of the Bolsheviks. The Ukrainians, like many of the peasant armies, were fighting for their independence; another White weakness was their overt Russian nationalism which alienated the national minorities.

Divided and unco-ordinated though they were, three White armies were particularly significant: Denikin's in South Russia, Kolchak's in Siberia and Yudenich's in the north-west. In October 1919 Petrograd and Moscow were threatened. However, once Trotsky had established an effective defence of the main region around those cities, he exploited Red control of the railways to the full and the Whites were beaten back. By the end of the year they were retreating rapidly. This continued through 1920 until Wrangel, who succeeded Deniken in April, the last surviving White general, was defeated in the Crimea in November, finally ending the civil war.

Trotsky's contribution may have been exaggerated by some historians, but in terms of organisation and the ability to inspire his troops he was far superior to anyone on the White side. The Bolsheviks had a clear ideology – they presented the war as a class war and they pursued it ruthlessly. Their propaganda portrayed them as defending the revolution against the Whites. The Whites most serious weakness was their lack of a political programme to appeal to the peasantry.

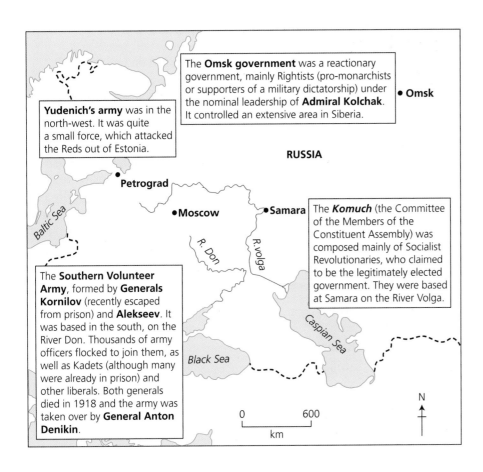

The **Omsk government** was a reactionary government, mainly Rightists (pro-monarchists or supporters of a military dictatorship) under the nominal leadership of **Admiral Kolchak**. It controlled an extensive area in Siberia.

Yudenich's army was in the north-west. It was quite a small force, which attacked the Reds out of Estonia.

RUSSIA

The **Komuch** (the Committee of the Members of the Constituent Assembly) was composed mainly of Socialist Revolutionaries, who claimed to be the legitimately elected government. They were based at Samara on the River Volga.

The **Southern Volunteer Army**, formed by **Generals Kornilov** (recently escaped from prison) and **Alekseev**. It was based in the south, on the River Don. Thousands of army officers flocked to join them, as well as Kadets (although many were already in prison) and other liberals. Both generals died in 1918 and the army was taken over by **General Anton Denikin**.

◀ Figure 2 Main forces of the Whites.

	Why did the Reds win?	Why did the Whites lose?
Geographical factors	• Bolsheviks held the central area, which included Petrograd and Moscow. • Much more heavily populated – Red conscript army outnumbered Whites. • Had industrial resources, armaments factories, Moscow, the rail hub.	• Whites were scattered around the edges of this central area, separated by large distances. • This made communications and co-ordination difficult. • No telephone links.
Unity and organisation	• The Bolsheviks had a single, unified command structure. • Trotsky organised the Red Army into an effective fighting force.	• The Whites were made up of different groups – they could not agree on whether they were fighting for monarchism, republicanism or for the Constituent Assembly.
Leadership	• Lenin used his authority to keep the Reds united, and he backed Trotsky's controversial decision to use ex-tsarist officers. • Trotsky led the Red Army with great charisma. • His special train covered 65,000 miles (105,000 km) from front to front.	• White leaders were, on the whole, second rate. • High level of indiscipline and corruption in the White armies. • Some officers lived in brothels in a haze of cocaine and vodka.
Political factors	• The support of the peasants was crucial since they supplied the main body of soldiers for both sides (though they were just as inclined to desert from Red as from White armies). • Lenin had legitimised their right to the land. • They stood for the revolution.	• The Whites lacked a political programme with any appeal. • If they won, the land would be restored to its former owners. It was the main reason for their failure. • Their refusal to accept national independence movements was disastrous.
Foreign intervention	• Allowed Bolshevik propaganda to present themselves as the defenders of Russian soil against foreign forces.	• Gave the Whites weapons but it was half-hearted and largely ineffective.
Propaganda	• Red propaganda was infinitely superior. The red flag and red star were powerful symbols.	• Whites did not see how valuable propaganda was.

▲ Figure 3 Reasons for the contrasting fortunes of the Reds and the Whites.

War Communism

While Trotsky managed the civil war, Lenin concentrated on building and consolidating the Bolshevik state. He took charge of the day-to-day business of the *Sovnarkom* and the problems he faced were formidable. Chief among these was the rapid deterioration of the economy in the spring of 1918. The shortcomings of handing over control of the land to the peasants and control of the factories to the workers' committees had become apparent. A new approach was needed – it is usually called War Communism. War Communism began with grain requisitioning, but it broadened to include a comprehensive range of state controls over the economy. It was popular with the Party ideologically as the rapid route to socialism.

Grain requisitioning	Labour discipline
In May 1918 a Food-Supplies Dictatorship was set up. Units of Red guards and soldiers forcibly requisitioned food from the peasants who resisted bitterly.	Discipline was brought back to the workplace. There were fines for lateness and absenteeism. Internal passports were introduced to stop people fleeing to the countryside. Piece-work rates were brought back, along with bonuses and a work book that was needed to get rations.
Nationalisation of industry	**Rationing**
The decree on nationalisation in June 1918 brought all industry under state control, administered by the Supreme Council of National Economy (*Vesenkha*). Workers' committees were replaced by single managers reporting to central authorities. These were often the old bourgeois managers now called 'specialists'. By itself it did nothing to increase production.	A class-based system of rationing was introduced. Red Army soldiers and the labour force were given priority. Smaller rations were given to civil servants and professional people such as doctors. The smallest rations, barely enough to live on, were given to the *burzhooi* or middle classes.
Banning of private trade	
All private trade and manufacture were banned. However, industry was simply not producing enough consumer goods, so an enormous black market developed, without which most people could not have survived.	

▲ **Figure 4** The main features of War Communism.

Ideology: Bukharin, Lenin and the transition to communism

War Communism was quickly justified ideologically. These were the heroic years and there was a belief that communism could be achieved rapidly. Bukharin wrote *Economics of the Transition Period* and stated that:

… proletarian compulsion in every form, from firing squads to forced labour, no matter how paradoxical it sounds, is the way to create Communist humanity.

Lenin annotated the chapter on coercion in his copy with great enthusiasm. He filled the margins with superlatives and ended, 'Now this chapter is superb!'

War Communism: ideology or economic necessity?

By May 1918 the country was in a state of economic collapse. Workers' control had made the situation in factories worse. It was a downward spiral:

- An acute shortage of raw materials meant that industrial output, particularly consumer goods, shrank.
- The shortage of goods led to soaring price inflation and the value of the rouble collapsed.
- Peasants would not supply food to the cities if there were no goods for which food could be exchanged and paper money was worthless.
- Food shortages worsened and there were food riots in many cities in early 1918.
- Workers started to flee from the cities in search of food, leaving factories short of workers.

Food prices soared. On average urban workers spent three-quarters of their income on food. The middle classes were in a worse position than the workers. One study in the 1920s found that 42 per cent of prostitutes in Moscow were from bourgeois families. Emma Goldman found young girls 'selling themselves for a loaf of bread or a piece of soap or chocolate'. Members of the nobility fared no better: Countess Witte sold homemade cakes and pies.

A more centralised system of control was necessary to run the economy in order to carry on the war. The Bolsheviks had to make sure the army was supplied:

they needed the factories to produce munitions and other goods and they needed food to feed the workers. But War Communism was not just a reaction to these pressures. For Lenin, it was based on long-term principles. It was an extension of class warfare and no different from the waging of the civil war against external enemies. In fact, the Bolsheviks called it the 'internal front'. Lenin wanted to squeeze out the counter-revolutionary forces whether they came from the left or the right – 'those not being with us are against us'. It was a way of wiping out old bourgeois attitudes and any lingering bourgeois power.

Lenin was supported by other Bolsheviks. They hated the market system and were not unhappy to see it collapse in 1918. They thought centralised control was the way to develop socialism. They had always wanted the nationalisation of industry. Trotsky wanted to see the 'militarisation of labour', in which the discipline and practices of the army would be taken into civilian life to build the new socialist state. At the end of the civil war, he wanted units of soldiers to be drafted into the factories and fields to work under military discipline. War Communism was continued after the civil war was over.

The role of terror

In an increasingly chaotic state, the void was filled by coercion and the *Cheka* became ever more active. Terror was a central part of the Bolsheviks' tactics. While some have argued that it was a response to circumstances, there is no doubt that Lenin believed it was a necessary element of political control.

The Red Terror

An assassination attempt on Lenin on 30 August 1918 launched the *Cheka's* Red Terror, which simply intensified what was already happening. Earlier in August, Lenin sent a letter to Bolshevik leaders in Penza making clear his determination to use terror to intimidate the whole rural population in the fight to obtain food for the towns and the army. It included the following sentence, 'Hang (and make sure the hanging takes place in full view of the people) no fewer than a hundred well-known *kulaks* [better-off peasants], rich men, bloodsuckers'.

From June onwards, Socialist Revolutionaries had been arrested in large numbers, along with anarchists and members of other extreme left groups. Mensheviks and Socialist Revolutionaries were excluded from taking part in soviets. Many Kadets were already in prison, others had fled to the south. One of the most significant victims in this period was the Tsar. Nicholas, along with his family and servants, was shot on 17 July 1918 in Ekaterinburg in the Urals.

Execution, previously the exception, now became the rule. Prisoners in many cities were shot out of hand. Official records put the figure for deaths at the hands of the *Cheka* for the years 1918–20 at nearly 13,000, but estimates put the real figure at 500,000. The *Cheka* fanned the flames of class warfare, as some Bolsheviks talked of wiping out the middle class completely. But the real purpose of the Terror was to terrify all hostile social groups. Its victims included large numbers of workers and peasants as well as princes and priests, prostitutes, judges, merchants, traders, even children (who made up 5 per cent of the population of Moscow prisons in 1920) – all guilty of 'bourgeois provocation' or counter-revolution. The problem was that no one was really sure who the counter-revolutionaries were.

In the cities, *Cheka* arrests had a terrifyingly random character. People were arrested for being near scenes of 'bourgeois provocation' or because they were acquaintances of suspects. In the provinces it was possibly worse, since local *Cheka* bosses controlled their own patch and acted as petty tyrants with no court of appeal. There was little central control. The *Cheka* was particularly

The *Cheka*

The *Cheka* grew rapidly after occupying its new premises in the Lubianka in Moscow at the end of March 1918. By June it had a thousand members and by September most provinces and districts had a *Cheka* branch. By 1921 it had 31,000 'frontline agents' and commissars and a total of 143,000 employees. It worked outside of the law or justice system, reporting directly to Lenin and the Politburo. As one of its founder members put it: 'The *Cheka* is not an investigating committee, a court or a tribunal. It is a fighting organ on the internal front of the civil war ... It does not judge, it strikes.'

The execution of the Tsar and his family

The whole of the Tsar's family and servants were shot in the basement of the house in which they were held. The order came from Lenin and Sverdlov to prevent the rescue of the imperial family by approaching White forces. Their bodies, having been drenched in acid, were thrown into a disused mine shaft and later buried. They were reburied in 1998, in the Peter and Paul Cathedral in Saint Petersburg, where most other Russian monarchs lie.

active in the countryside, helping requisitioning brigades to collect grain from the peasants. Quotas were filled even if this left peasants starving. It was little better than theft and some of the brigades were little more than bandits, taking much more than food. The peasants resisted in a wave of uprisings and attacked the collectors. Bolshevik Party officials were murdered. One *Cheka* man was found with his stomach slit open and stuffed with grain as a lesson to others. The *Cheka* and Red Army units gave no quarter. It would not be unfair to say that the Bolsheviks were at war with the peasants.

To house all these dissident workers, troublesome peasants and bourgeois saboteurs, the Bolsheviks set up concentration and labour camps. The machinery of terror and the police state were created under Lenin, not Stalin. It is almost certain that hundreds of thousands perished, although no accurate figures are available from a time when there was so much dislocation and disorder, and proper records were not kept or were lost.

The multiple challenges of 1921

How did the Bolsheviks overcome the problems they faced?

The problems

Famine, disease and revolt stalked the land. 'Now the Republic hangs by a hair', wrote Bukharin in early 1921. According to *Cheka* sources there were 118 separate risings throughout Soviet Russia in February 1921.

By 1921, the Soviet economy was in ruins. The transport system was on the point of total collapse. Factories could not get the materials they needed and most industrial enterprises had ceased production. Grain production had fallen to disastrously low levels. Famine was rampant in the south and hundreds of thousands died from disease – typhus, cholera, dysentery and the influenza epidemic which raged across northern Europe. In these circumstances, large sections of Russian society were not willing to put up with the continuation of wartime policies.

The main threat to the Communist government came from the peasantry. Now that the civil war was over and there was no possibility of a White victory, the hostility of the peasants to grain requisitioning erupted in a series of revolts which engulfed the countryside. The most serious revolt was the Tambov uprising from August 1920 to June 1921 led by Alexander Antonov. A poor harvest in 1920 had left peasants with almost no reserves of grain. When requisitioning brigades arrived to take what little they had, the peasants reacted violently. This story was repeated in other areas where the Bolsheviks had deliberately set the amount of grain to be procured at unreasonably high levels. The remnants of Green armies, supported by local peasant populations and deserters, proved tough nuts for the Red Army to crack and large areas of the countryside were in open revolt and outside of Moscow's control.

Source A *Lenin* by Beryl Williams, (Longman), 2000, p 135.

For the peasantry, he [Antonov-Ovseenko] admitted, the dictatorship of the proletariat 'directs at them its cutting edge of implacable compulsion' which ignored peasant realities and 'does the countryside no service that is at all perceptible on either the economic or the educational side'. It was a devastating criticism of Bolshevik policies and a recognition that the Party had no firm roots in the villages.

In the cities, the severe winter of 1920–21 brought repeated strikes. On 22 January 1921, the bread ration was cut by one-third in several cities,

---

NOTE-MAKING

Use the headings on pages 164–7 to make notes in two parts:

1 Summarise each problem listed below.
2 Note the action that was taken to deal with it.

- Problems in the economy
- Threat from peasants
- Opposition from workers
- Problems from Kronstadt
- Divisions in the Party

The Bolsheviks and the peasantry

The Bolsheviks weren't peasants and the peasants weren't Bolsheviks. The Bolsheviks wanted to build socialism; peasants with aspirations wanted to farm their own land successfully which might lead to them becoming *kulaks*, or the enemy in Bolshevik eyes. Sent by Lenin to investigate the Tambov rising, Antonov-Ovseenko sent him a long and frank report. He admitted that few *kulaks* existed and that Soviet policies were deeply unpopular. This did not stop Antonov-Ovseenko advocating ruthless action. The Tambov region was swamped by Red troops. Villages were burned and poison gas was used. Tens of thousands of hostages were taken, and thousands more were shot. According to some sources 240,000 may have died in the course of the rebellion.

including Moscow and Petrograd. Food demonstrations had to be broken up by the *Cheka* and special troops because ordinary soldiers refused to fire on the crowds. The situation was not so very different from that of February 1917. Party spokesmen were howled down at workers' meetings and hostile resolutions were passed. Urban workers were particularly angry about the:

- food shortages
- militarised factories – 'worse than a tsarist prison camp' – where workers could be imprisoned or shot if production targets were not reached
- way the state had made their unions no more than instruments to keep the workers under control.

There were calls for 'soviets without communists' and there was a revival in support for other socialist parties. Martial law was imposed in Moscow and Petrograd.

The strikers in Petrograd were supported by the sailors at the nearby Kronstadt naval base who were in close contact with workers. In March 1921, they mutinied in the hope of starting a general revolt against the Bolsheviks. They demanded an end to terror, to dictatorship, to grain requisitioning and to one-party rule.

Within the Party, the Workers' Opposition grew up under Alexander Shlyapnikov and Alexandra Kollontai. They wanted the workers to be given more control of their own affairs and supported complaints about the reintroduction of single managers and the militaristic organisation of the workplace. In particular, they criticised Trotsky's plan to make the trade unions agencies of the state with union officials appointed by the state. The trade union debate caused furious arguments inside the Party at the end of 1920. There were also the Democratic Centralists campaigning for more democracy in the Party.

The significance of the Kronstadt uprising

In 1917 Trotsky called the Kronstadt sailors the 'pride and glory of the Russian revolution'. However, Kronstadt had always had a large number of Socialist Revolutionaries and anarchists and was not always as Bolshevik as has been claimed. Many of the sailors were ex-peasants who had connections with the countryside and supported the peasant revolts. They were determined, too, to assist the strikers in Petrograd. The Kronstadt uprising was roundly condemned by Lenin and Trotsky as a White plot, though in fact the rebels were by and large the same sailors who had fought for the revolution.

Source B Extracts from the manifesto of the Kronstadt revolt of March 1921.

Having heard the report of the representatives of the crews sent by the general meeting of ships' crews to Petrograd to investigate the state of affairs there, we demand:

1 that in view of the fact that the present Soviets do not express the will of the workers and peasants, new elections by secret ballot be held immediately, with free preliminary propaganda for all workers and peasants before the elections;

2 freedom of speech and press for workers and peasants, anarchists and left socialist parties;

5 the liberation of all political prisoners of socialist parties, as well as all workers and peasants, Red Army soldiers and sailors imprisoned in connection with the working-class and peasant movements;

> How far do these demands (Source B) show that the Bolsheviks had betrayed those who had hoped for genuine soviet democracy in October 1917?

7 the ending of the right of Communists to be the only permitted socialist political party;

11 that the peasants be given the right and freedom of action to do as they please with all the land and also the right to have cattle which they themselves must maintain and manage, that is without the use of hired labour.

Lenin called the revolt the 'flash that lit up reality more than anything else'. The revolt was a powerful argument for a change in economic policy. It also lit up another reality: the Kronstadt demands would have been readily accepted by the Bolsheviks before they came to power, now they showed just how far they had fallen short in the eyes of the Kronstadt sailors. The first assault on Kronstadt failed and then Marshal Tukhachevsky was sent in with 50,000 crack troops. The rebels fought tooth and nail to defend their base, and 10,000 were killed. In the following weeks 2,500 were shot by *Cheka* execution squads. Hundreds of others were sent to Solovetsky, the first big labour camp, on the White Sea.

Dealing with the crisis – the NEP

Lenin realised that concessions to the peasants and some measure of economic liberalisation were essential for the regime to survive. It was clear to him that the government could not continue with its policy of War Communism, despite the desire of many Bolsheviks to do so. The NEP (the New Economic Policy) was therefore brought in (see Figure 5). The key element of the NEP was the abolition of grain requisitioning. Once the peasants had given a fixed proportion of their grain to the state (a significantly lower amount than under War Communism) they were able to sell any surpluses on the open market. Small businesses, private trading and the money economy were back. Many Party members considered this policy a betrayal and against Bolshevik ideology. The lifting of the ban on private trade was particularly resented. Lenin had a hard fight to push it through the 10th Party Congress in March 1921. It was a peasant Brest-Litovsk, but would not last for ever. Bukharin backed him: 'We are making economic concessions to avoid political concessions.' What finally persuaded the doubters was the Kronstadt revolt. They realised that splits in the Party could result in their losing power altogether. They were prepared to fall in behind Lenin – as long as the NEP was a 'temporary' measure.

Grain requisitioning abolished	State control of the commanding heights of the economy
Grain requisitioning was replaced by a 'tax in kind'. Peasants had to give a fixed proportion of their grain to the state, but the amount that they had to hand over was much less than the amounts taken by requisitioning. They could sell any surpluses on the open market.	The state kept control of large-scale heavy industries like coal, steel and oil. It also retained control of transport and the banking system. Industry was organised into trusts that had to buy materials and pay their workers from their own budgets. If they failed to manage their budgets efficiently, they could not expect the state to bail them out.
Small businesses reopened	**Ban on private trade removed**
Small-scale businesses under private ownership were allowed to reopen and make a profit. This included businesses like small workshops and factories that made goods such as shoes, nails and clothes. Lenin realised that peasants would not sell their produce unless there were goods that they wanted on sale.	The removal of the ban on private trade meant that food and goods could flow more easily between the countryside and the towns. Privately owned shops were reopened. Rationing was abolished and people had to buy food and goods from their own income. The money economy was back!

▲ **Figure 5** Key features of the New Economic Policy.

Crushing opposition inside and outside the Party

The economic concessions of the NEP were accompanied by a very definite tightening of political control. The Workers' Opposition were defeated and treated with scorn and ridicule by Lenin at the 10th Party Congress. The 'ban on factions' was passed and dealt with splits in the Party and restored discipline. It meant that once Party policy had been agreed by the Central Committee everybody had to accept it and not lobby against it. The penalty for factionalism was expulsion from the Party. It was to be very influential in the power struggle, when any accusation of factionalism could be very damaging.

There had been concern that unhealthy elements had joined the Party; those who were insufficiently communist and even outright hangers on. The solution was a *chistka* (a purging). The first of these was in May 1918 and confined to the expulsion of 'idlers, hooligans, adventurers, drunkards and thieves'. By mid-1919 Party membership was about half the total claimed a year before. During the civil war there was mass recruitment and the Party reached 730,000. In a one-party state there were always going to be careerists joining and periodic cleansings were vital to raise the degree of political dependability. About 220,000 members were purged or left the Party in 1921. Such determination to maintain purity of membership can be traced back to Lenin's wrangles with the Mensheviks in 1903.

Outside the Party we have seen how the Kronstadt and Tambov risings were brutally crushed by the Red Army. As Martin McCauley points out in his essay at the end of Chapter 6 (page 214), 'this marked a new stage in bloodletting'. In Petrograd and Moscow the strikes lost momentum after the arrest of their leaders and the restoration of free trade. The NEP was accompanied by political repression. The Mensheviks and SRs were outlawed. In 1921, 5,000 Mensheviks were arrested for counter-revolutionary activities. There was a show trial of Socialist Revolutionaries; 34 of their leaders were condemned as terrorists and 11 executed.

The *Cheka* was renamed the GPU (Main Political Administration) in 1922 and grew in importance during the NEP. Arbitrary imprisonment and the death penalty continued to be applied after 1922 as an instrument of social policy. Aware of the unpopularity of NEP with Left Communists and the urban workers, the GPU periodically harassed and arrested Nepmen (see page 171) as speculators and class enemies to show that they were keeping capitalistic tendencies under control. The attack on religion (see page 186) was also evidence that there was no ideological backsliding.

Censorship became more systematic. In 1922, dozens of outstanding Russian writers and scholars were deported to convince the intelligentsia not to criticise the government. In the same year, pre-publication censorship was introduced. Books, articles, poems and other writings had to be submitted to the Main Administration for Affairs of Literature and Publishing Houses (*Glavlit*) before they could be published.

How did communist dictatorship develop?

By 1922 a communist dictatorship had emerged. This was always likely given Lenin's refusal to share power and the Bolsheviks' minority status. Two distinct trends were taking place during the civil war:

● The Communist Party began to dominate government.
● The Communist Party itself became more centralised, more bureaucratic and less democratic. Power was concentrated in the hands of a few people at the top.

In 1919, the Politburo was created, forming an inner ruling group of around seven people at the top of the Communist Party. The Politburo soon took precedence over the *Sovnarkom* as the key decision-making body.

Government and Party

In the 1920s the Soviet government and the Communist Party were parallel organisations from the top bodies (*Sovnarkom* for government, Politburo for Party) down though provincial and city organisations to the lowest levels (district soviet for government, local party organisation for Party). Key officials in the government at different levels were members of the Communist Party and only Communist Party members could be elected to soviets.

The *nomenklatura* system

This system was established from 1923 onwards. The Bolshevik leaders wanted to make sure that key personnel in public bodies were drawn from Bolsheviks or pro-Bolshevik workers. So a list of about 5,500 designated Party and governmental posts – the *nomenklatura* – was drawn up. The holders of these posts could only be appointed by the central Party bodies. Overt loyalty counted for more than expertise; people who wanted promotion did what they were told. This tightened the one-party state internally. The people in the *nomenklatura* became an elite.

At district and local level, the local Communist Party organisations took control of soviets across Russia. Party officials ran the soviets and obeyed Party orders above all else. So the soviets were now effectively subordinate to the Party.

From 1919 onwards, the Central Committee of the Party began to appoint its own 'trusted' nominees to key positions in soviets (previously such positions had been filled by people elected by the members of the soviet). This was done to increase the centre's control over local Party apparatus and local government (see the box on *nomenklatura*).

Lenin's achievement and legacy

Did Lenin change the course of history?

One of the key questions in this study is the importance of the role of the individual. Lenin is certainly one who many have claimed changed the course of history. However, before entering this debate we need to look at his final years when, as for much of his career, he was away from the centre of the action.

Lenin's last two years

From mid-1921 Lenin's health declined and he suffered a massive stroke in May 1922. From then until his death in January 1924 his activity was very limited. He clashed with Stalin. Lenin accused Stalin, as Commissar for Nationalities, of Great Russian chauvinism and bullying tactics in his relations with the Georgian Communist Party. Lenin was worried also about the extent

▲ Lenin reading in his office, 1918

of Party bureaucracy and Stalin's increasing power. These concerns and anger at Stalin's abusive treatment of Krupskaya, Lenin's wife, over the telephone were reflected in his testament (see page 180). Another stroke in March 1923 left Lenin without the power of speech and he died before he was able to have Stalin removed as General Secretary. Stalin was a very lucky man.

Lenin's legacy

Lenin remained a revered figure throughout the existence of the Soviet Union; there was no de-Leninisation. His decision not to share power in 1917 was a fateful one. Kamenev, Zinoviev and Rykov were among the Bolsheviks who favoured a socialist coalition. They declared that 'other than that, there is only one path: the preservation of a purely Bolshevik government by means of political terror'. Prophetic words. Power was never shared. It is hard to argue against the view that Stalin's dictatorship was a logical extension of Lenin's authoritarian and centralised regime. Lenin was more ruthless than has sometimes been supposed. He actively encouraged terror to smash his enemies and was a fierce class warrior. Christopher Read has written that Lenin was very different from Stalin, who put 'his own personal malevolent stamp on the Soviet system', but it was Lenin's key principles that were the bedrock of the Soviet system right through to its demise.

Source C *War and Revolution in Russia, 1914–22* by Christopher Read, (Palgrave), 2013, p 174.

If we put them all together – iron discipline; ruthless dictatorship rather than mild, jelly-like or lily-livered proletarian government; **productionism**; a nationwide system of accounting and control of the production and distribution of goods; building Soviet strength for future defence and to enable better assistance to foreign revolutions; one-person management; piecework; bonuses; one-party government; the menace of enemies all around and within; a postponement of world revolution – we end up with something normally thought of as Stalinism.

The role of the individual: Lenin in the revolution

In the interpretation exercise (page 193) a number of claims are made about Lenin's influence in 1917. It is interesting to examine Trotsky's view as he, like Lenin, believed that politics and especially revolutions were about the involvement of the masses. He believed that the masses were the driving force that made Russian revolution possible, although they needed the Bolshevik Party to provide direction. He wrote,

Without a guiding organisation the energy of the mass would dissipate like steam not enclosed in a piston box. But nevertheless what moves things is not the piston or the box but the steam.

However, Trotsky had no doubt about the importance of Lenin's role in April and October 1917 when the Bolshevik Party was divided and unclear on the direction to take. He wrote to Preobrazhensky in 1928,

You know better than I do that had Lenin not managed to come to Petrograd in April 1917, the October Revolution would not have taken place.

Trotsky is even more definite about October:

Had I not been present in Petrograd in 1917 the October Revolution would still have taken place – on the condition that Lenin was present and in command. If neither Lenin nor I had been present in Petrograd, there would have been no October Revolution: the leadership of the Bolshevik Party would have prevented it from occurring – of this I have not the slightest doubt!

The cult of Lenin

- The Lenin cult had begun just after the attempt on his life in 1918 (see page 163). Eulogies appeared in the Bolshevik press giving him Christ-like qualities, as he was unafraid to sacrifice his life for the revolution. Zinoviev made a long address of which 200,000 copies were published. Portraits and posters of him appeared in the streets (none had been produced up to this time) in a deliberate effort to promote his god-like leadership qualities.

- Lenin disliked this kind of adulation and Krupskaya wanted 'no external reverence for his person'. But when Lenin died, Statin insisted that Lenin be embalmed and his tomb turned into a shrine. Lenin's brain was sliced into 30,000 segments and stored so that scientists in the future could discover the secrets of his genius.

- At Lenin's funeral, although Stalin's quasi-religious ode to Lenin is often quoted, Zinoviev's speech was much more powerful and bore directly on the cult of Lenin. It ended, 'When each of us will be faced with making a responsible decision, let us ask ourselves: "What would comrade Lenin have done in my place?"'. In the struggle for power after Lenin's death all the contenders justified their position by reference to Lenin and attacked their opponents by arguing that they diverged from Lenin.

For the Marxist historian Isaac Deutscher (Trotsky's biographer) the idea that without Lenin there would have been no revolution for many years is a startling one. He argues that the revolutionary trend will find or create its leader or leadership from whatever human material is available. The idea of the irreplaceable colossus is 'an optical illusion'. E. H. Carr discusses the role of the great man or woman in history in his book, *What is History?* He is anxious to dispel the idea that great men are jack-in-the-boxes who emerge miraculously from the unknown to interrupt the real continuity of history. For Carr the great man:

is at once a product and an agent of the historical process, at once the representative and the creator of social forces which change the shape of the world and the thoughts of men.

Carr distinguishes between those great men who, like Lenin and Cromwell, helped to mould the forces that carried them to greatness and those who, like Napoleon and Bismarck, rode to greatness on the back of already existing forces.

Did Lenin make a difference?

Answer this question by working in groups of three with each member researching one of the following:

● Lenin's role as founder of the Party and developer of its ideology
● Lenin's intervention at five key points was critical.
● Lenin's role has been exaggerated.

Here is some help to get you started. Page references show where you will find more information in this book and you should use other books too.

Lenin's role as founder of the Party and developer of its ideology

● No one else in the Party had Lenin's prestige and standing. He was able to hold the Party together at difficult times (pages 156–169).
● Examine Lenin's organisational abilities, give examples.
● Give examples of his flexible and pragmatic approach.
● Show how he adapted and developed Marxism and its implications for the Russian Revolution:
  1 His concept of a small, disciplined revolutionary party (see page 84).
  2 His development, along with Trotsky, of the notion that the proletariat could carry through a socialist revolution without going through the 'bourgeois-democratic stage' (see page 93).

Lenin's intervention at five key points was critical.

It can be argued that at each of these five points Lenin was initially in a minority or faced serious opposition but was able to win over the majority. If he had not done so the outcome in each case would have been very different.

1 April Theses 1917 (pages 133–4).
2 Staging the October uprising in 1917 (pages 137–9).
3 The issue of socialist coalition (pages 140–1).
4 Treaty of Brest-Litovsk, March 1918 (pages 159–60).
5 Adopting the NEP, March 1921 (pages 166–7).

In each case explain why Lenin's decision was so important and how the outcome would have been very different if he had not got his way.

Lenin's role has been exaggerated.

● We have seen that Lenin was the absent revolutionary and was in indifferent health from mid–1921.
● Were there times when he followed rather than led the masses?
● Were there occasions when circumstances either helped him enormously or forced decisions on him?
● Was the civil war as important as Lenin's ideas in the development of autocratic rule?

You must provide evidence for your answers.

Discuss your findings and come to a conclusion in your group. All groups should then exchange views in a plenary session.

The Scissors Crisis

Trotsky likened the falling prices for agriculture and the rising prices for manufactured goods to the opening of scissor blades. Trotsky, and what became known as the Left Opposition, wanted to move from the NEP to rapid industrialisation. By the mid-1920s they favoured a permanent Scissors Crisis to squeeze more grain out of the peasants to pay for industrialisation.

2 Economic developments, 1922–28

This section will look at the extent to which the NEP produced economic recovery and how well it was working by the end of 1928.

The impact of the NEP

How far did the NEP produce economic recovery?

By 1922, the results of the NEP were better than anyone expected. There was food in the markets in the cities and brisk trade in other goods. Shops, cafés and restaurants reopened and life began to flow back into the cities. By 1923, cereal production had increased by 23 per cent compared with 1920. In the autumn so much food was flooding into the cities that the prices started to drop while the price of industrial goods rose because they were still in short supply. Trotsky called this the Scissors Crisis. This imbalance was problematic because it made the peasants reluctant to supply food. The crisis was over by April. The government took action to bring industrial prices down and started to take the peasant tax in cash rather than in kind to encourage the peasants to sell their produce. Industrial production did increase too but from a very low base. Recovery was well underway by 1924 with small-scale enterprises responding more quickly than larger-scale industry.

▲ NEP poster. The text reads: 'Out of NEP Russia there will be a socialist Russia (Lenin)'.

One of the chief agents in this revival was the appearance of the private traders, or Nepmen as they came to be called. They scoured the villages, buying up produce – grain, meat, eggs, vegetables – to sell in the markets in the cities. They travelled round the workshops picking up nails, shoes, clothes and hand tools to sell in the markets and to the peasants. Stalls turned into premises and then into much larger shops. By 1923, Nepmen handled as much as three-quarters of the retail trade.

The first three or four years of the NEP were the heyday of the Nepmen. Deals were made, corruption was rife and the rewards were high. Property speculators were back. You could get anything from officials if the bribe was big enough. This was a get-rich-quick society and the Nepmen, a much coarser breed than the old bourgeoisie, displayed their wealth conspicuously. They crowded the restaurants, and then went on to gaming clubs or brothels. Prostitution and crime flourished. The Moscow municipal government got most of its income from taxes on gambling clubs. The Party and its attendant bureaucracy were too small to exert a great deal of control.

How well was the NEP working by the end of 1928?

Experience of, and attitudes, to the NEP varied considerably between countryside and towns and its future was a major issue from 1923 onwards and played its part in the power struggle (pages 180–1).

The NEP and the peasants

The peasants were not producing the quantities of grain the government needed for its industrialisation plans. In 1913, Russia exported 12 million tons of grain; in the best years of the NEP the amount never exceeded 3 million. This was having a devastating effect on foreign trade: in 1926–27 exports were at 33 per cent and imports at 38 per cent of their 1913 levels due to the decline in grain exports. So the Soviet Union could not bring in the technology (machinery, etc.) it needed for industrial expansion.

The grain was simply not reaching the market. There were a number of reasons for this:

- Agriculture was still very backward, relying on traditional methods of farming. For example, in 1927 over 5 million inefficient wooden ploughs were still in use.
- When the land was shared out after the revolution, peasant landholdings had tended to become smaller than before 1917. The large estates and large farms which supplied the cities had disappeared. They had been divided up among the land-hungry peasants. On the majority of these smaller holdings, people ate most of what they produced.
- There was a gap in prices between grain (low) and peasant-desired manufactured goods (high), a return of the Scissors Crisis. Apart from Bukharin and the right, there was an increasing reluctance in the higher reaches of the Party to make concessions to the peasantry again.
- The relationship between the government and the peasants deteriorated towards the end of the 1920s.

The government clamped down on private traders who were paying the peasants around twice the price that the state was paying for grain. So the peasants had to sell at lower prices to the state and had to sell more than before to pay their taxes. This worked initially, but the peasants soon got wise to the government's ploy. Since meat prices were still going up, they started to feed grain to their animals rather than sell it at low prices. Also, they found that there was not much point in having surplus money because there was little they could buy with it, since industrial consumer goods were still in short supply. The peasants started to hold back their grain from the market, hoping for the price to rise.

Was the NEP working for the urban workers?

Urban workers were less satisfied than the peasants. In the first two years of the NEP unemployment rose steeply, particularly in the large state-controlled trusts; they consequently cut their workforce because they had to make a profit. Wages remained generally low and workers found little protection in the market place. It seemed to them that the peasants were doing well at their expense. They also objected to the power of the single managers and bourgeois specialists. Some workers called the NEP the 'New Exploitation of the Proletariat'. By 1928 **real wages** had only just passed their pre-war level. There was an eight-hour working day and other social benefits, but thousands of workers did not have jobs at all. The number of unemployed people increased continuously throughout the 1920s; by the end of 1926 it was over 14 per cent of the employed population, significantly higher than before the war. It was a reminder that the NEP was grounded in the economics of the market. It provided one of the most telling of the Left Opposition's criticisms of official policies.

The workers complained bitterly about the gap between themselves and the better off. They complained about the high prices charged for food by the peasants and market traders, and about the bourgeois specialists and officials who were paid so much more than they were. Women had been particularly hard hit by the NEP. Many had been pushed out of their jobs when the Red Army was demobilised or had been forced to move from skilled to unskilled work. Large numbers of jobless, unsupported women ended up on the streets.

Housing was still a major problem and most workers lived in overcrowded, poor-quality houses and flats. In Smolensk in 1929 many workers with families of six and seven people lived in one room. There was a mounting crime problem in the cities. As a result of the turmoil of the war and civil war, thousands of young people were parentless and rootless, forming gangs which roamed the streets to find their victims. It was hardly the workers' paradise that the revolution had promised.

The grain crisis, 1927–28

The grain procured by the state at the end of 1927 was about three-quarters of what it had been in 1926. Stalin acted decisively. It was his first intervention in the economic sphere and a calculated one. He sent out officials, backed by the police, to seize grain. In January 1928, he himself went to the Urals and Western Siberia on a requisitioning campaign. He got more grain, but the relationship between the peasants and the government was breaking down and there was substantial resistance to Stalin's actions. If the grain crisis was a trigger for action there is little doubt about the direction in which Stalin wanted to go and the role of ideology in this. He told Siberian officials that Soviet agricultural development had come to a dead end and that the only way out was 'the development of large-scale farms of a collective type'. He saw the USSR as a Soviet country and wanted to implant a collective economy in agriculture as well as in industry. Despite resistance to his methods from Bukharin, Rykov and the right, Stalin used them again the following year after the poor harvest in 1928 forced the government to ration bread in the cities. It was the death knell of the NEP.

Real wages – wages in terms of the amount of goods and services that can be bought.

The Urals–Siberian method

Stalin's visit to the Urals, in January 1928, lasted for only three weeks. It is said that this is the only time he visited an agricultural area in his life. During this period, the so-called 'Urals–Siberian method' was developed. This involved grain requisitioning backed up by a series of 'emergency measures' – including the punitive Article 107 of the Criminal Code which allowed for the arrest of any peasants and confiscation of their property if they were suspected of withholding grain.

3 The struggle for power after the death of Lenin

This section will look at the contenders to succeed Lenin, and the role of ideas and ideology in the ensuing power struggle. Then it will examine the different stages in the struggle and interpretations of how Stalin came out on top.

1920s' politics – succeeding Lenin

Why did Stalin emerge as Lenin's successor?

Traditionally the struggle for power following Lenin's death is seen as one between Stalin and Trotsky, in which Stalin defeated his brilliant and charismatic rival by his cunning use of his position as General Secretary of the Party and his ability to outmanoeuvre his rivals. Trotsky was the most formidable of these, and through his writings has been a powerful influence on our perception of the power struggle, but he had effectively been defeated at the beginning of 1924. Stalin's use of his office and his skill in the factional contest were important but are an incomplete explanation of his success.

NOTE-MAKING

Make brief notes on the leadership contenders, identifying their power bases and their strengths and weaknesses as potential leaders.

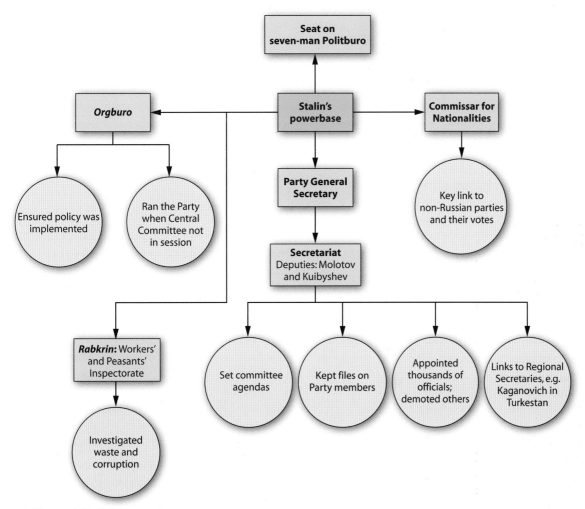

▲ Figure 6 Stalin's power base.

The main contenders to succeed Lenin

Joseph Stalin

Joseph Dzhugashvili was born in Gori in Georgia in 1878. He is one of the few leading revolutionaries who had a genuine working-class/peasant background. His father was a shoemaker who worked mainly in Tiflis, some distance away. Stalin's devout and doting mother brought him up virtually on her own, working hard as a seamstress and laundress to support Joseph.

They were poor and he had a hard upbringing as she beat him for acts of disobedience. However, he did well at school and gained a place at a seminary in Tiflis to train as a priest. But the young Joseph found Marxism rather than God. He was drawn into the underground world of the revolutionaries, writing pamphlets and attending secret meetings. He particularly admired the writings of Lenin. He soon graduated to the full-time role of revolutionary, organising strikes and becoming engaged in a major bank raid to fill the Bolshevik Party coffers.

Between 1902 and 1913, Stalin was arrested frequently and exiled to Siberia, escaping on five occasions. He became hardened, particularly after the death of his first wife in 1907. He later took on the pseudonym Stalin which means 'man of steel'. In 1912, he was invited onto the Central Committee of the Bolshevik Party. He remained in Russia but was arrested and exiled to Siberia for four years in 1913. When the February Revolution broke out in 1917, he was one of the first to arrive on the scene in Petrograd.

He was made editor of *Pravda*, the Party newspaper, and initially, he followed a pro-war line in accordance with the Soviet and other socialists. He changed his line when Lenin arrived and seems to have followed Lenin slavishly thereafter. Stephen Kotkin disputes the 'grey blur' image of Stalin at this time and argues that he was a fully engaged member of the Bolshevik leadership and, 'as the coup neared and then took place, he was observed in the thick of events'.

After the October Revolution, Stalin was made Commissar for Nationalities with an office close to Lenin's and it is likely that at this time he gained Lenin's trust as a devoted Bolshevik operator. The post gave him wide powers of appointment. During the civil war, he was sent to Tsaritsyn (later renamed Stalingrad) to organise food supplies and defend this very important strategic position from the Whites. A former tsarist officer who later defected to the Whites described Stalin as, 'Clever, smart, educated and extremely shifty, the evil genius of Tsaritsyn and its inhabitants … his ability to get things done in whatever circumstances was something to go to school for.' In Tsaritsyn he came into bitter conflict with Trotsky and was removed from his military post for disobedience. He had shown a tendency to disobey orders from the centre, even Lenin's, because he wanted to do things his own way. Lenin, however, set these 'mistakes' aside because he had other work for Stalin.

Good luck helped Stalin in his next advancements. In March 1919, Sverdlov, who had shown himself to be a great organiser, died of Spanish flu. Lenin looked to Stalin. He appointed him head of the *Rabkrin* (the Workers' and Peasants' Inspectorate) with power to inspect all government departments. In May 1919, Lenin put him in charge of the *Orgburo* which controlled aspects of the Party organisation. Stalin was also elected to the new Politburo, which from now on became the main organ of power. In 1922 Stalin was appointed General Secretary, head of the Secretariat, in charge of general organisation – a post created expressly for Stalin. He was the only person to be a member of all three of the Party's leading executive bodies (see Figure 6).

Stalin's appointment to these key positions showed how much trust Lenin placed in him. Other leading Bolsheviks saw these jobs as part of the dull routine of Party bureaucracy and suited to Stalin whom they consistently underrated. They were soon to discover their error.

Leon Trotsky

We looked at Trotsky's early career in Chapter 3 (page 85). Trotsky was the only member of the Communist Party who could rival Lenin in intellect and in his writings on Marxist theory. He was one of the Bolsheviks' best orators. He was particularly popular with the younger, more radical elements in the Party. His contribution in the years 1917–24 had been second, if not equal, to that of Lenin himself. He had planned the October Revolution, persuading Lenin to wait until the end of October. His organisation of the Red Army and his drive and determination had played a significant part in bringing victory in the civil war. His position as Commissar for War gave him a strong base in the army. It meant, though, that Trotsky's rivals saw him as a Bonaparte figure. As good Marxists they had studied the course of revolutions and knew that the French Revolution had led to Napoleon. Trotsky was the obvious candidate in Russia.

Also working against him were his arrogance and aloofness. He seemed dismissive of other leading Bolsheviks, sometimes treating them with disdain and lack of respect. He was short and brusque with people who seemed to be wasting his time and he never went out of his way to endear himself to his colleagues. They felt his uncompromising views might lead to splits in the Party. Many old Bolsheviks regarded Trotsky as an outsider since he had only joined the Bolshevik Party in 1917 and other members were not convinced of his loyalty to the Party. This perception was wrong. He accepted decisions that he did not agree with: famously he argued in May 1924, 'I know that no one can be right against the Party'.

Trotsky had clashed with both Stalin and Zinoviev during the civil war and on various issues afterwards. The historian Ian Thatcher has written that there was a complete breakdown in political and personal relations between Trotsky and the vast majority of the Politburo and the Central Committee in late 1923.

Two other important factors worked against Trotsky in the power struggle. Firstly, he did not like the business of political in-fighting, making deals and alliances. He preferred to work on a level where arguments were hammered out in debate or by the pen, where he was convinced of his natural superiority. This high-minded approach left him vulnerable to less scrupulous colleagues. Secondly, for three years from late 1923 Trotsky suffered attacks of an undiagnosed fever. This sapped his strength and left him less able to deal with the continuous political attacks mounted on him by his enemies. It also meant that he was absent for crucial votes and debates.

Gregorii Zinoviev

Zinoviev was an old Bolshevik, active in the Party as early as 1903. Grigorii (Grisha) Zinoviev and Lev Kamenev were Lenin's closest collaborators before the revolution. Zinoviev returned to Petrograd with Lenin in April 1917 and fled to Finland with him after the July Days. The Mensheviks referred to Zinoviev, before the revolution, as 'Lenin's mad dog'. He was an impressive orator but his speeches were overblown and lacked substance. Zinoviev played an important part in initiating the cult of Lenin after the assassination attempt in 1918. Zinoviev was widely disliked, over-ambitious and flaunted the rewards and trappings of office.

However, Zinoviev, with Kamenev opposed the armed uprising in October and fell out with Lenin about the construction of the new government; he favoured a socialist coalition. As a result, he was not given a major post in the *Sovnarkom* but he was made Party Secretary in Leningrad. This was an important position, allowing him to build up a strong power base. In 1919, he was made Chairman of the Comintern (Communist International founded to co-ordinate and direct the world communist movement) at a time when world revolution was eagerly awaited, and became a full member of the Politburo in 1921.

Lev Kamenev

Kamenev was an active Bolshevik and full-time revolutionary from 1905 and close collaborator with Lenin abroad from 1907 to 1914. His strengths were his literary fluency and personal charm. He built up the Party in the Caucasus and played a part in bringing his nemesis, Stalin, into the Bolshevik camp. Kamenev was a prolific writer and an excellent editor of *Pravda*. He returned to Petrograd in March 1917 and took control of *Pravda* with Stalin. They offered conditional support for the Provisional Government. He opposed Lenin's April Theses briefly on ideological grounds. With Zinoviev, he opposed Lenin in 1917. However, he was made Party Secretary in Moscow, his main power base, and later Commissar for Foreign Trade. This brought him into the Politburo and into a position to challenge for the leadership. His moderation was also seen in the civil war when he sought to reduce the scope of *Cheka* violence. Kamenev was not a natural leader.

Nikolai Bukharin

Bukharin was one of the younger generation of Bolsheviks. Born in 1888, the son of a schoolmaster, he had joined the Bolshevik Party in 1906. He was an important theorist who argued with Lenin about political strategy; his biographer Stephen Cohen points out that no major leader had opposed Lenin more often. It did not, however, affect their personal relations which were very good. He led the left-wing opposition to the signing of the Treaty of Brest-Litovsk and between 1920 and 1921 criticised Trotsky and Lenin in the 'trade-union' controversy. He became editor of *Pravda*, the Party newspaper, in 1918 and remained so until 1929. He remained in Moscow during the civil war and his reputation as a major theoretician in the Party increased. But Lenin added in his testament that 'his theoretical views can only with the greatest doubt be regarded as fully Marxist'.

Bukharin could argue his points fiercely, especially on the NEP of which he became the leading advocate. He believed passionately that the *smychka* – the alliance between the working class and the peasantry which had brought success in 1917 – was essential for the survival of the regime. Consequently he was against Trotsky and the left's pressing for rapid industrialisation in 1923. By now he was moving to the right of the Party. He put forward a moderate peaceful alternative to Stalinism, a socialism with a human face. Lenin did describe him, though, as 'soft wax'.

Bukharin did not become a full member of the Politburo until 1922. He was popular but lacked a strong power base and had not headed any organisation of note other than *Pravda*. Bukharin once described himself as 'the worst organiser in Russia'. He had a following of students but his posts had given him power over words and ideas rather than people and he did not have the skills and political cunning of Stalin.

Alexei Rykov

Alexei Rykov, born in 1881 into a peasant family, became chairman of the *Vesenkha* (Supreme Economic Council) in 1918 and later succeeded Lenin as Chairman of the *Sovnarkom*, having been his deputy from 1921. He was authoritative, outspoken, frank and direct, not always endearing himself to his colleagues. Stephen Kotkin regards Rykov as 'far and away the most important proponent of the NEP' and having a more solid reputation and skill set than Bukharin. Rykov was a talented administrator, more statesmanlike than many of his colleagues, but had a reputation as a drinker.

Source D Extracts from Lenin's words about the contenders in his testament, 25 December 1922.

Comrade Stalin, having become General Secretary, has immeasurable power concentrated in his hands, and I am not sure that he always knows how to use that power with sufficient caution.

Comrade Trotsky, on the other hand ... is distinguished not only by his outstanding ability. He is personally perhaps the most capable man in the present C.C. [Central Committee], but he has displayed excessive self-assurance ... These two qualities of the two outstanding leaders of the present C.C. can inadvertently lead to a split ...

I recall that the October episode with Zinoviev and Kamenev was no accident, but neither can the blame for it be laid on them personally, any more than non-Bolshevism can upon Trotsky.

Bukharin is not only a most valuable and major theorist of the Party; he is also rightly considered the favourite of the whole Party; but his theoretical views can only with the very greatest doubt be regarded as fully Marxist.

Postcript added 4 January 1923

Stalin is too rude, and this fault ... becomes unacceptable in the office of General Secretary. Therefore, I propose to the comrades that a way be found to remove Stalin from that post and replace him with someone else who differs from Stalin in all respects, someone more patient, more loyal, more polite, more considerate.

> What is Lenin saying about the succession (Source D)?

Stephen Kotkin follows the Russian historian Valentin Sakharov in suggesting that Krupskaya, or others in the household, not the stricken Lenin, was the actual author of the testament and its postscript. This does not make it any less important. It was a great blow to Stalin, not just politically but also personally. He survived the political fallout, but Kotkin argues that the testament was to hang over him like 'a sword of Damocles', generating a 'sense of victimhood and self-pity'.

Ideas and ideology in the struggle over power

Ideas and ideology were important. Stephen Cohen has argued that part of the tragedy of the old Bolsheviks was that 'for seven years they fought among themselves over principles, while an intriguer acquired the power to destroy them all'. Stalin was more than just an intriguer. His rivals all produced books explaining Leninism and all looked down on Stalin, who they thought ignorant and ill-educated. Stalin entered the fray too and the formulation of Socialism in One Country was his contribution. It may have been a distortion of Lenin's views but its nationalism and optimism struck a chord.

There were three main issues:

- The future of the NEP
- The growth of the bureaucratic party
- Permanent Revolution vs Socialism in One Country

The NEP and the industrialisation debate

Everybody agreed on the need to industrialise. Industrialisation was the key to creating a large class of proletarian workers to build socialism. Could the NEP provide an effective framework for the industrialisation of the Soviet Union so that it could catch up and overtake the advanced capitalist countries? It was a passionate issue and dominated Party conferences in the mid-1920s. How long should they allow rich traders and peasants effectively to control the new workers' society? When could they push forward to industrialisation?

Attitudes in the Party towards the NEP changed during the 1920s because economic circumstances were changing. In 1924, the NEP was still delivering economic recovery, but after 1925 problems started mounting. A threat of war in 1928 provided an added spur to industrialise more quickly, as did food shortages in the cities after 1927. So, Party members, who had been prepared to go along with the NEP in the mid-1920s, might have adopted a different position in the late 1920s. After 1925 two distinct views had emerged:

- The left wing of the Party, led by Trotsky, joined by Zinoviev and Kamenev in 1926, wanted to end the NEP and go for rapid industrialisation. They argued that the peasants had a stranglehold on the economy. The left wanted to squeeze more grain out of them to pay for industrialisation.
- The right wing, led by Bukharin and backed by Rykov and Tomsky, wanted to keep the NEP going and to encourage the peasants to become richer, so that they would spend more on consumer goods, which would, in turn, lead to the growth of manufacturing industry. They believed that conflict with the peasants might lead to economic collapse and endanger the communist state.

Stalin kept out of the debate and took a position in the centre. Initially he supported the NEP, though he would never have said, 'peasants enrich yourselves'.

Source E 'Peasants enrich yourselves.' From Bukharin's report to a conference of Moscow Party activists, April 1925, in *The Soviet Union: Documentary History Vol. 1, 1917–1940* by E. Acton and T. Stableford, (University of Exeter Press), 2005, p 168.

We are too eager to tread on the toes of the prosperous peasant. But this means that the middle peasant is afraid to improve his farm and lay himself open to heavy administrative pressure; while the poor peasant complains that we are preventing him from selling his labour power to the rich peasant, etc.

... Overall, we need to say to the entire peasantry, to all its different strata: enrich yourselves, accumulate, develop your farms. Only idiots can say that the poor must *always* be with us. We must now implement a policy which will result in the disappearance of poverty.

> Read Source E. Why do you think the phrase 'enrich yourselves' would come back to haunt Bukharin?

The growth of the bureaucratic party

The issues of bureaucracy, democracy and the power of the Secretariat in the Party caused disagreements and arguments in the early 1920s. In 1923, Trotsky raised the issue of bureaucracy which he defined as the mindless and unthinking carrying out of duties laid down by superiors. All Stalin's opponents in the 1920s ended up with the same central grievance: the Party had become 'bureaucratised', and Stalin had killed the tradition of internal party democracy. A bureaucratised party meant the main mass of the party would be excluded from meaningful participation in economic and political decision-making. With the Secretariat appointing local party secretaries on the basis of loyalty to the 'centre' rather than merit, the principle of elections with local party secretaries responsible to their constituency was being lost.

Source F The power of the secretarial hierarchy. From the Declaration of 46 leading Bolsheviks presented to the Politburo, 15 October 1923, in *The Interregnum 1923–24* by E. H. Carr, (Macmillan), 1954, pp 375–76.

We observe the ever increasing, and now scarcely concealed, division of the party between a secretarial hierarchy and the 'quiet folk', between professional party officials recruited from above and the general mass of the party which does not participate in the common life ... Nowadays it is not the party, not its broad masses, who promote and choose members of

> What are the worries expressed here (Source F), and how significant is it that they were present as early as 1923?

the provincial committees and of the Central Committee. On the contrary, the secretarial hierarchy of the party to an ever greater extent recruits the membership of conferences and congresses, which are becoming to an ever greater extent the executive assemblies of this hierarchy.

Trotsky was not one of the signatories of the declaration but those involved were his supporters and their views coincided.

Permanent Revolution vs Socialism in One Country

Trotsky's theory of Permanent Revolution followed the Bolshevik orthodoxy that socialism could not be achieved in Russia without a socialist revolution in the West. This was because the Russian working class was too small and the economy underdeveloped; it needed the support of the working class in the more industrialised countries of Europe. Trotsky felt therefore that the Russians should put energy and money into helping the working class in other countries to stage their own revolutions. They should go on fighting a Permanent Revolution until a world communist revolution had been achieved.

Stalin proposed that, with no sign of the world revolution, the Russians could build a socialist state in the USSR without the help of people from outside. The theory was a complete distortion of Lenin's view but shrewd politics. It had a nationalist and patriotic appeal and it did not dictate a particular economic policy. Stalin's Socialism in One Country was a clever formulation. It allowed Stalin to attack Trotsky for lacking faith in the Russian people and their mission, and to remind the Party of Trotsky's non-Bolshevik past and brand him a Menshevik – a classic term of abuse in the Bolshevik lexicon. Trotsky was to admit, off the record, that the nationalist message played well with rank and file party members.

ACTIVITY

Use Figure 7 to write a summarising paragraph on the different stages of the power struggle within the Party. Note particularly the shifting alliances and how Stalin is able to win key votes – something which makes him a vital ally.

1923 October	Declaration of 46; Left Opposition formed; Central Committee condemns the declaration as 'a factional move'.
1924 January	All against Trotsky. Vote at the Party conference (held before the Party Congress) defeats Trotsky and the Left Opposition.
	Death of Lenin.
	Zinoviev and Kamenev ally with Stalin against Trotsky.
	Decision not to read out Lenin's testament at the 13th Party Congress in May.
	Trotsky's criticisms of the bureaucratic party defeated at the Congress.
	Zinoviev and Kamenev take the lead against Trotsky, and Trotsky reminds the Party of their opposition to seizing power in October 1917.
1925	Stalin now allies with Bukharin, Rykov and Tomsky against Zinoviev and Kamenev.
	When Zinoviev and Kamenev attack Stalin at the 14th Party Congress in December they are defeated by 559 votes to 65 (the Leningrad delegation).
1926 January	Leadership of the Leningrad Party organisation purged.
	Zinoviev and Kamenev join Trotsky to form the 'United Opposition' and make a direct appeal to the Party masses and the workers, trying to organise demonstrations in Moscow. Bukharin takes the lead against them and they are accused of 'factionalism'. All three are expelled from the Politburo by the Central Committee – Zinoviev in July, Trotsky and Kamenev in October.
1928	Urals–Siberian method is used.
1929 April	Stalin turn on Bukharin, Rykov and Tomsky and the 'right deviation' is condemned.
1929 November	Forced collectivisation begins; Central Committee ousts Bukharin from the Politburo for leading the 'right deviation'.
	No one can now challenge Stalin who emerges victorious.

▲ **Figure 7** The different stages of the power struggle.

Different interpretations about why Stalin succeeded

The struggle for power after the death of Lenin is an excellent vehicle for exploring causation in history. There is little agreement on which is the most important factor in the rise of Stalin. In trying to draw up a hierarchy of causes, the different interpretations need examining.

- **The role of the individual:** Stalin seemed safe, competent, unthreatening. Martin McCauley calls Stalin the only politician in the Party with a grasp of game theory. Certainly he was astute and a very effective political infighter whereas his rivals, as we have seen, all had their weaknesses, made mistakes and seriously underestimated Stalin. Trotsky's personality and late Bolshevism certainly worked against him.

- **The importance of ideology:** We have seen the appeal of Socialism in One Country. Stalin believed that by 1928 the NEP had become unworkable and could only be maintained by repeated concessions to the peasants. This would not build socialism. Stalin reverted to Lenin's War Communism strategy as the way to do so.

- **Stalin's control of the Party apparatus:** This allowed him to build up a personal following and remove political rivals and their supporters. It has long been seen as very important in his success. The historian R. V. Daniels in 1960 introduced the idea of the circular flow of power (see Figure 8).

- **Lenin's concept of the Party:** Lenin's concept of an organised, disciplined and centralised Party was always likely to lead to a Stalin figure as Trotsky had warned in 1904 (see Source D on page 88). The ban on factions at the 10th Party Congress in 1921 meant that one by one Stalin's rivals fell victim to the political machine they had helped to construct.

- **The impact of social and cultural factors:** Post-revolutionary circumstances, especially the civil war, reinforced the authoritarian, disciplined structure, with members used to obeying orders. Frustration with the NEP meant that towards the end of the 1920s Stalin could count on the industrial workers' support.

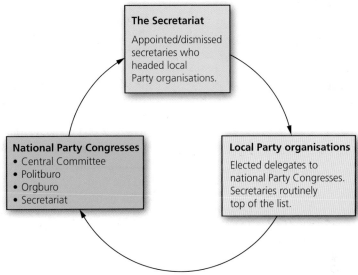

▲ **Figure 8** The circular flow of power.

- **Luck/chance:** Stalin was lucky that Lenin died after a series of strokes and was not able to dismiss him as General Secretary. He was fortunate, too, that Sverdlov, a great organiser, who would have been favourite for that role, died in 1919.

No single factor can explain Stalin's rise satisfactorily, and rather than being mutually exclusive the different factors often overlap. Thus Stalin was a very adept politician who held positions which he could exploit for his own gain. Furthermore by the end of the 1920s his policies had an ideological appeal. Stalin was able to convince the Central Committee and Party Congresses better than anyone else that he was the leader in thought and action that they should follow.

In a well-trodden controversy such as this, new interpretations are more likely to take the form of changes of emphasis or subtle re-evaluations than fundamentally different views. If a historian stresses one particular factor it is because it is top of his or her hierarchy of causes; it does not mean that other factors did not have an influence.

4 Social and cultural developments, 1918–28

In this section the way the Bolsheviks wanted to change society will be examined. They attacked rank and privilege, and a new elite emerged. They challenged deep-rooted social institutions: the family, education and religion. Ideology came to the fore both in the attack on religion and the way artists and film-makers were pressed into service to spread the Bolshevik message.

NOTE-MAKING

Change and continuity

In two columns note what changed and what stayed much the same during this period.

The end of social privilege and the emergence of a new elite

What was the impact of communist rule on society?

The Red Terror had been class based and some Bolsheviks talked of wiping out the middle class completely. Two to three million people had emigrated and the old civil service, military, financial, industrial and professional elites had been swept away. The old ruling classes had been abolished as classes, but many individuals still lived on as state employees. Specialists were needed as civil servants, to run industry and as scientists and engineers. Because of shortages of Party members with the required literacy and numeracy skills, the Party had to look to the bourgeoisie and check on the loyalty of those who were taken on but the 1920s was a decade of specialists. There was a shortage of technically educated people in the Party; only 138 engineers were Party members in 1928. The Party tried to replace them through elite institutions like the Institute of Red Professors. The emphasis in the mid-1920s was on recruiting members of the working class. Rapidly educated proletarians were fast tracked to positions of authority in factories and administration to which their educational achievements and actual skills did not entitle them. Their authority could not be questioned because they had the Party behind them.

In the countryside things were a little different. Although the communists talked about class divisions in the villages and fanning the class war there, the division between town and country was greater than between *kulaks* and middle and poor peasants. The number and wealth of *kulaks* was exaggerated. They might have had two horses, hired labour at busy times and had more produce to sell, but they were not substantially richer than the middle peasants. In some cases former landowners did live alongside their former peasants; in Ukraine 25 per cent of landowners were still farming on peasant-sized plots in the mid-1920s.

Women and the family

The new communist state intended to bring about fundamental changes in the position of women in society. The key to this was economic independence: women should be able to have a job and have some help in looking after a home and family. Kollontai wanted mothers 'to be relieved of the cross of motherhood' by a network of socialist kindergartens. Once freed from the constraints of bourgeois marriage, there would be more equality between the sexes and sexual liberation because people would be freer to choose their partners. Therefore laws were passed immediately to make divorce easier and later, in 1920, to allow abortion on demand.

Alexandra Kollontai, Commissar for Social Welfare, had set the socialist dream for women in motion, but this soon collided with traditional views of relationships between the sexes and the economic realities of life in the Soviet state in the 1920s.

- By the mid-1920s, Soviet Russia had the highest divorce rate in Europe, 25 times higher than in Britain. This situation did not work in women's favour. With easy divorce available, women were abandoned when they became pregnant. One survey from the end of the 1920s indicated that in 70 per cent of cases divorces were initiated by men. Due to the housing shortage, divorced couples often still lived together and domestic violence and rape were common.
- The reality for many Russian children was not a network of socialist kindergartens, but life in gangs that survived by begging, scrounging, stealing and prostitution. Contemporaries estimated that in the 1920s there were between 7 and 9 million orphans, most of whom were under the age of thirteen.
- With the growth of urban unemployment during the NEP, women were forced from skilled to unskilled work – still predominantly in textiles and domestic service, and then from work to unemployment and into prostitution and crime. By 1929 the percentage of women in industrial labour was practically the same as it had been in 1913.
- According to a survey in the 1920s, women in proletarian families worked an eight-hour day outside the home plus an extra five hours in domestic tasks; men did not help with the domestic work.

While there might be talk of equality, traditional views on gender differences remained. Women cared and supported. Men built socialism. The iconography of the new state showed women with children or as peasants. The high-status proletarian was male, a metal worker or a blacksmith. Vera Mukhina's giant statue created for the Soviet pavilion at the 1937 World's Fair in Paris, 'Worker and Kolhoz Woman', shown on page 220, sums this up completely. It was seen as the ideal and symbol of the new Soviet epoch.

Education

Under the NEP, financial pressures meant that the idea of universal schooling had to be abandoned. Many children left school: by 1923, the numbers of schools and pupils were barely half the totals of two years earlier. Schools did not have the proper resources and the teachers were very badly paid (in 1925, a teacher received a fraction of an industrial worker's pay). There was also a lasting legacy of falling standards and failure of authority in many schools. The Bolsheviks wanted to increase the number of Party members, especially those from working-class or peasant backgrounds, who had engineering and technical skills. However, the new Soviet citizen was also to have a knowledge of culture as well as industrial skills. The emphasis on indoctrination remained throughout the 1920s, but a survey in 1927 of schoolchildren aged eleven to fifteen showed that they had become increasingly negative towards communist values as they got older, and nearly 50 per cent still believed in God.

Literacy

Before the revolution, the illiteracy rate was about 65 per cent. The Bolsheviks attached great importance to universal literacy so that all citizens could be both exposed to their propaganda and taught modern industrial skills. In December 1919, the 'liquidation of illiteracy' was decreed for all citizens aged between eight and fifty. Illiterates who refused to learn faced criminal prosecution. Tens of thousands of 'liquidation points' were set up in cities and villages, and between 1920 and 1926 some 5 million people in European Russia went through literacy courses.

Youth organisations

The Bolsheviks did not leave indoctrination to non-communist teachers. They had a mission to capture the hearts and minds of the young. Two youth organisations were set up: the Pioneers for children under fifteen and the *Komsomol* for those from the age of fourteen or fifteen into their twenties. The duty of these organisations was to inculcate communist values and to promote loyalty to the working class. In later years, they were used as instruments of social control and to promote discipline in schools. The Pioneers were much like the Boy Scouts, with activities, trips and camping. The *Komsomol* was much more serious and was used by the Communist Party to take propaganda into the towns and villages, and to attack religious beliefs and bourgeois values. *Komsomol* membership was seen as a preparation for entry into the Communist Party. The *Komsomol* played a very important role in the Cultural Revolution of 1928–31 (see pages 216–17).

The impact of the Bolsheviks on religion

The Bolsheviks were aggressively atheist. In January 1918, they had issued the decree on the separation of Church and State which declared that the Church could not own property, church buildings had to be rented and religious instruction in schools was outlawed. Priests and clerics were declared 'servants of the bourgeoisie'.

At first the war against the Church had mainly taken the form of propaganda, but in 1921 the Union of the Militant Godless was established to challenge the Church more directly. In 1922 the Bolsheviks launched a fierce attack on the Orthodox Church, which was central to the lives of millions of peasants and an integral part of the village community, and enjoying something of a revival at the beginning of the NEP. Orders were sent out to strip churches of their precious items, ostensibly to help famine victims. When clergy and local people tried to protect their churches, there were violent clashes. Lenin, who saw this as the opportunity to smash the Church, overruled a Politburo decision to suspend the action. Lenin's papers include a demand to be informed, on a daily basis, about how many priests had been shot. More than 8,000 people were executed or killed in 1922 in the anti-Church campaign, including the Metropolitan of Petrograd (a very high-ranking churchman), 28 bishops and 1,215 priests. Thousands of priests were also imprisoned.

The *Komsomol* was particularly associated with active hostility to religion. Members were much more of a presence in the villages than the Communist Party in the 1920s. They broke up religious services, played tricks on priests and worshippers and staged parodies of the Orthodox service in the square outside the church. Civil marriage and divorce began to make an appearance in villages although the majority of peasant weddings were still celebrated in church. Men who had served in the army and returned to the village were noted for their indifference to religion, but older women usually remained staunch believers.

Propaganda and culture

How did the Bolsheviks use artists and film-makers, 1918–28?

For Lenin, propaganda, education and cultural development were absolutely central to the building of socialism. Following the October Revolution, the Bolshevik government set up the Commissariat of Popular Enlightenment (Ministry of Education and Culture) headed by Anatoly Lunacharsky. The focus moved away from 'high art' – ballet, opera, fine art and museums – which was regarded as bourgeois and elitist, to 'popular culture' – art directed at the mass audience.

The Bolsheviks were anxious to harness art to the service of the new state. There had been a flowering of creativity in the arts in Russia in the years just before the revolution and this lasted into the 1920s. Innovators in the arts, the avant-garde rejected the art of the past as linked with the bourgeois way of life which was to be destroyed. In the years immediately after the revolution, many of Russia's finest artists took part in the Soviet cultural experiment. The Bolsheviks wanted to keep well-known artists on their side if possible, and many artists, for their part, were encouraged by the ending of tsarist censorship and were excited by the revolution. They wanted to communicate directly with the masses. However, just as the NEP saw a tightening of political control, so in culture there was a move towards greater cultural control.

Agitational art

The avant-garde artists were drawn into producing propaganda for the Bolsheviks. Their designs were reproduced on agitprop trains (mobile propaganda centres), ships and banners, and above all, on posters displayed in the Petrograd ROSTA (Russian Telegraph Agency) windows. More than 1,000 ROSTA posters were created over a two-year period. Lenin wanted to take art into the streets and had a plan for monumental propaganda. He proposed that the streets of the major cities should display posters, slogans and statues to educate the citizens 'in the most basic Marxist principles and slogans'. He personally unveiled the joint statue of Marx and Engels on the first anniversary of the revolution.

Vladimir Mayakovsky, 1893–1930

Mayakovsky was a young poet, playwright and artist of great energy who had joined the Social Democrats at the age of fifteen and was repeatedly jailed as a teenager for subversive activity. He welcomed the revolution wholeheartedly. Mayakovsky worked with the Bolsheviks producing posters and 3,000 captions or slogans on a wide range of topics, from encouraging resistance during the civil war to getting people to drink boiled water during an epidemic. He wrote a number of poems praising Lenin extravagantly including the famous lines, 'Lenin lived! Lenin lives! Lenin will live forever!'.

Mayakovsky was very egotistical: his first play was *Vladimir Mayakovsky* and his first book of poems *'I'*. His autobiography *I Myself* hardly showed him as the collective man. He also wrote the satires *The Bedbug* and *The Bath House*, fierce attacks on the smugness of petty leaders, which exposed communist bureaucracy. Both plays were soon withdrawn. By 1930, he had grown disillusioned with the communists. Always emotionally volatile, unhappy in love and denied a visa to go abroad, he committed suicide in April 1930. In 1935, when Mayakovsky was safely dead, Stalin proclaimed him 'the best and most gifted poet of our Soviet epoch'. Study of his work became compulsory in schools, but his satires were not mentioned and neither was his interest in Futurism nor his suicide.

ART RESEARCH

Research the Constructivist artists Rodchenko, Tatlin and Lissitsky.

These artists wanted to create a new proletarian culture based on the worker and on industrial technology. They concentrated on designing clothes, furniture, offices and everyday objects in an industrial style, using straight lines and geometrical shapes which they thought would liberate people.

- Look at their work – there are plenty of examples on the internet.
- Look at their links with each other and the very influential Malevich, whom you researched in Chapter 2.
- Look at their relationship with the regime. What is the relationship between art and the revolution?

▲ A ROSTA window poster designed by Mayakovsky.

Sergei Eisenstein, 1898–1948

Eisenstein was the best-known Soviet film director of the twentieth century. He worked with the Bolsheviks and for the Moscow Workers' Theatre before moving into the film industry. Two of his best-known films were commissioned by the Central Committee: *Battleship Potemkin* (1925) and *October* (1928). *October* provided the classic heroic images of the revolution, but was far more dramatic than the reality; it suggested that more people were killed and more damage was done to the Winter Palace than was the case in reality.

Another element of mass agitational art was street processions. These built on a rich tradition of public festivals and, in the Orthodox tradition, communist icons were carried across the village or town. May Day and the anniversary of the October Revolution became the great ritual festivals. Probably the best example of mass street theatre was the great re-enactment of the storming of the Winter Palace in November 1920. It involved 10,000 people and included the Winter Palace itself. It was a stage-managed October Revolution as it should have happened, with Lenin directing.

Cinema

Cinema was, in theory, the ideal medium of propaganda: visual, technological, controllable. Lenin was especially keen for it to be used in areas where cinemas 'are novelties, and where therefore our propaganda will be particularly successful'. By the summer of 1918 the agitprop trains were in action and equipped to spread political propaganda through films, plays and other media far and wide. In 1925, however, the Politburo's decision not to intervene in matters of form and style in the arts allowed the Soviet cinema a brief period of great creativity. The most outstanding film-maker of this period was Eisenstein, who was anxious to show the power of the people acting together, as in his famous film of the Bolshevik revolution, *October*. However, Soviet audiences tended to prefer Hollywood comedies to his sophisticated work. Although the number of cinemas grew fast, and 300 million tickets were sold in 1928, the cinemas were almost entirely restricted to the towns.

Chapter summary

- Lenin persuaded the Bolsheviks to sign the unfavourable Treaty of Brest-Litovsk. He knew he had to have peace for his government to survive. The Left SRs resigned from the *Sovnarkom*.

- Lenin saw civil war as inevitable and was prepared to use terror to defeat counter-revolution. The Reds were in a better position geographically, had better organisation, communications and leadership. Crucially, the Whites lacked support from the peasants and national minorities because of their reactionary policies.

- War Communism was adopted in mid-1918. It was popular with the Party ideologically as the route to socialism. The economic situation was desperate and War Communism was meant to meet the needs of the army and the towns. It involved grain requisitioning, which the peasants hated.

- The Bolsheviks were in serious trouble in 1921, facing massive peasant revolts, strikes and opposition from workers, a rising at the Kronstadt naval base, economic distress and famine. Factions inside the Communist Party, like the Workers' Opposition, wanted changes in policy.

- Risings and revolts were brutally crushed, but Lenin made economic concessions, in the form of the NEP, to ensure the survival of the regime. This was accompanied by repressive measures outside the Party, and the ban on factions inside, as the communists asserted their control. By 1924, the Soviet Union was a one-party state.

- The Communist Party was increasingly important at the expense of government institutions. It became more centralised and controlled by a smaller number of people at the top. The Secretariat and Party bureaucracy became particularly powerful.

- At key times Lenin, initially in a minority, persuaded the Party to take action or to change policy. If they had not followed him they would probably not have survived. Lenin's key principles were the bedrock of the Soviet system right through to its demise.

- Stalin, Trotsky, Zinoviev, Kamenev and Bukharin were all contenders in the struggle over power. Issues were as important as the personalities involved and the contenders were anxious to prevent rivals from coming to power and pursuing policies with which they did not agree.

- Stalin was a skillful politician who outmanoeuvred his opponents, and his control of the Party machine was important in his success. Ideology was important too and Party members tended to support Stalin's changes of policy line. Socialism in One Country was optimistic, patriotic and popular.

- In spite of more liberal laws, life for women was very tough. The Bolsheviks saw the role of education, youth movements and the arts as the creation of communists. Their ideology came through, too, in their aggressively atheistic and violent anti-Church campaign.

Ideology	The situation	Result by mid-1918
Lenin determined that the Bolsheviks rule alone.	Opposition from other parties and even some Bolsheviks favours a socialist coalition. Left SRs join the *Sovnarkom* but resign when Treaty of Brest-Litovsk is signed.	Open opposition from other socialist parties. *Komuch* formed.
The early decrees on land and workers' control reflected Lenin's optimism that Russia would move quickly and easily into socialism.	Economic collapse accelerated. Lenin had to admit that they were not on the threshold of socialism.	Centralisation and co-ordination of the economy – War Communism, nationalisation, return of labour discipline and one-person management.
Help would come from the revolution spreading to western Europe.	The Left Communists want to turn the war into a revolutionary war.

As no peace, Germans resume a virtually unopposed advance. | Treaty of Brest-Litovsk signed to save the regime. Important territorial losses.

No sign of the European revolution. |
| Poor and landless peasants would turn against *kulak* oppressors.

Large estates would become collective farms. | Peasant land seizures and distribution recognised, peasants retreat into subsistence agriculture, collective farms largely failed to materialise. | Severe grain shortages in the towns, aggravated by loss of Ukraine. Grain requisitioning begins. |
| Revolution will lead to class war and civil war.

Terror an essential part of the dictatorship of the proletariat stage. | Class war encouraged from the beginning.

Civil war broke out by May 1918. | Red Terror used not just against the old exploiting classes, but against non–Bolshevik socialists, accomplices of the bourgeoisie. |

▼ **Summary diagram 2:** The civil war: mid-1918 to end of 1920

Ideology	The situation	Result at end of 1920
Iron discipline, the dictatorship of the proletariat vital for the road to socialism. Centralised party.	Civil war put a premium on discipline, and a pattern of command in which orders replaced consultation and debate.	The Party became more centralised and hierarchical. Orders were passed from the centre and Party members were expected to carry them out.
Terror an essential part of creating a new society.	Terror to crush counter-revolution.	Estimate of 500,000 *Cheka* executions or deaths in custody.
Lenin saw War Communism as part of class warfare. Many Bolsheviks happy to see the collapse of the market system. They wanted nationalisation of industry and state control. Trotsky wanted militarisation of labour. Great reluctance to abandon War Communism when the civil war ended.	Red Army and towns desperately short of food and supplies.

War Communism introduced:
• grain requisitioning
• nationalisation
• ban on private trade
• rationing
• disappearance of money. | Grain requisitioning deeply resented and drove a wedge between the Party and the peasantry.

Sharp economic decline. Transport disruption. Dramatic decline in population of cities especially Petrograd. Inflation so high money became worthless, workers paid in goods. |
| Spreading the revolution to western Europe. | In 1919 Comintern set up to organise worldwide revolution.

In 1920 Lenin hoped to turn the war with Poland into a revolutionary war. | Polish failure a great disappointment for Lenin. He believed world revolution was needed for the complete victory of socialism to be possible. |

▼ Summary diagram 3: The crisis of 1921

The situation	The response	Ideology
Grain shortage, industrial collapse.	The NEP, end of grain requisitioning, private trade allowed, end of rationing, small businesses allowed.	Clearly went against ideology: NEP dubbed 'a peasant Brest-Litovsk'. Legalisation of private trade a stunning blow.
Peasant uprisings, for example, Tambov.	100,000 troops sent in, whole villages destroyed, estimated 240,000 deaths.	Repression of all opposition. NEP.
Opposition from the workers: strikes and demonstrations.	Dealt with harshly, workers weak with hunger anyway.	Repression of all opposition. NEP.
Kronstadt rising.	Rebels, actually heroes of the revolution, condemned as Whites and ruthlessly crushed.	Popular democracy suppressed. 'The flash that lit up reality' ensures NEP is brought in.
Divisions in the Party: Workers' Opposition, Democratic Centralists.	Ban on factions passed at 10th Party Congress. Workers' Opposition completely condemned.	Leninist premise of the sole, united, disciplined proletarian Party.

▼ Summary diagram 4: The power struggle

Ideology	Role in power struggle
Leninism	All the contenders were at pains to identify themselves with Lenin. Stalin managed to invent for himself the role of Lenin's faithful pupil.
Permanent Revolution vs Socialism in One Country Trotsky's theory of Permanent Revolution followed the Bolshevik orthodoxy that socialism could not be achieved in Russia without a socialist revolution in the West.	Stalin ripped the phrase 'Socialism in One Country' from Lenin's writings. The theory was a complete distortion of Lenin's view, but shrewd politics. It had a nationalist and patriotic appeal. Even Trotsky admitted that Stalin's policy met an emotional need in the rank and file.
The growth of the bureaucratic party This became a central grievance of all the oppositions of the 1920s: the Party had become 'bureaucratised', and Stalin had killed the tradition of internal party democracy.	Stalin's control of the Party bureaucracy made him a useful ally first to Zinoviev and Kamenev and then to Bukharin and the right. He could deliver votes in Party Congresses and in the Central Committee.
The future of the NEP All leading Bolsheviks wanted to industrialise. The issue was how rapidly and whether the NEP could provide an effective framework for the industrialisation of the Soviet Union so that it could catch up and overtake the advanced capitalist countries.	Trotsky and the left, and later Zinoviev and Kamenev, favoured rapid industrialisation. Bukharin, Rykov and Tomsky favoured the continuation of the NEP. Stalin stayed in the centre until January 1928 when, with the left defeated and the grain crisis, he came out strongly in favour of squeezing the peasants and rapid industrialisation.

Working on essay technique

Remember the skills that you built up in Chapters 1–4 on essay writing. The main headings were:

- **Focus and structure:** Be sure what the question is on and plan what the paragraphs should be about.
- **Focused introduction to the essay:** Be sure that the introductory sentence relates directly to the focus of the question and that each paragraph highlights the structure of the answer.
- **How to use detail:** Make sure that you show detailed knowledge – but only as part of an explanation being made in relation to the question. No knowledge should be 'free-standing'.

- **Explanatory analysis:** Think of the wording of an answer in order to strengthen the explanation.
- **Argument and counter-argument:** Think of how arguments can be juxtaposed as part of a balancing act in order to give contrasting views.
- **Resolution:** Think how best to 'resolve' contradictory arguments.
- **Relative significance and evaluation:** Think how best to reach a judgement when trying to assess the relative importance of various factors, and possibly their inter-relationship.

ACTIVITY

Look at the following A-level practice question.

'For the Bolsheviks, ideology was always supremely important.' Assess the validity of this view for the years 1902 to 1928.   (25 marks)

1 At the top of a large sheet of paper, write out the question.
2 Note the dates involved:
   - 1902 is the date of the publication of *What Is To Be Done?*, the founding document of Bolshevism.
   - By the end of 1928 Stalin had won the power struggle.
3 Jot down the main topic areas that you might cover in the answer under the broad headings:
   - Bolshevik ideas before 1917
   - 1917
   - The Bolsheviks in power, 1917–22
   - The power struggle, 1923–28
4 Transform these ideas into a basic plan for an answer. Think of the structure. In outline, what evidence is there that ideology was supremely important? And when did ideology appear to be overridden by the need to survive politically?

5 Now look at the list of essay-writing skills above. See how they can fit into your plan. Some, such as an introduction, will be there automatically. Consider the following:
   - Introduction – is it simple or could it be complex? Does it do more than introduce? Does it highlight the structure of the answer?
   - Where can you add specific details to your plan so that you show a range of knowledge?
   - Does your plan successfully feature analysis and evaluation? Are you sure it will not lead to a narrative or descriptive approach?
   - It does not matter if you come down strongly on one side of the argument, as long as the argument comes through clearly and you show an awareness that there is another side.
   - Can you reach a judgement which 'resolves' any conflicting arguments?
6 Can you add precise details and/or quotations into this structure to provide evidence to support your arguments?
7 Has your answer shown an awareness of different interpretations?
8 Now write your own answer to the essay.

Working on interpretation skills

In earlier chapters of the book you were given the opportunity to develop skills in answering interpretations questions. It is probably a good idea to re-read the advice given earlier in the book at the end of Chapters 2 and 4 (pages 76–7 and 149–52) before you answer the A-level practice question that follows.

Using your understanding of the historical context, assess how convincing the arguments in these three extracts are in relation to Lenin's influence on Russia. (30 marks)

Extract A

The story of the Bolsheviks, the creators of communism, is one of drama and success unparalleled in modern history. From the twenty-odd people who first called themselves by that name in 1903, they grew within fourteen years to a party that seized then governed Russia. Barely more than another generation was to pass before communism would rule over one-third of mankind and aspire to the mastery of the whole world. The history of the Bolsheviks and of the Russian Revolution has to be focused around the life of one man: Lenin. Himself the heir of a long revolutionary tradition, Lenin imparted to Bolshevism and communism not only ideology and tactics but many of his personal characteristics. Yet this founder of a world movement was thoroughly Russian. He and the people he gathered around him cannot be understood except in terms of their contemporary Russia and the native revolutionary tradition which goes back at least to 1825.

Adapted from *Lenin and the Bolsheviks* by Adam B. Ulam, (Secker and Warburg), 1966, p vii.

Extract B

As Lenin the man died, so Lenin the God was born. 'Lenin is dead, Leninism lives', declared Zinoviev at Lenin's funeral. The term 'Leninism' was used for the first time. From this point, the leadership would invoke 'Leninism' to justify its policies – whatever they may be – and condemn its critics as 'anti-Leninist'. Lenin's actual ideas were always evolving and changing. They were often contradictory. Like the Bible, his writings could be used to support many different things, and those who followed him would choose those parts that suited them. Stalin, Khrushchev, Brezhnev, Gorbachev – they were all 'Leninists'. But if there was one unchanging principle – the fundamental basis of the Bolshevik dictatorship for three quarters of a century – it was 'Party unity': the Leninist imperative for every Party member to fuse his personality in the collective and submit to the judgement of the leadership. It was on this absolutist principle that any questioning of the Party line was deemed 'anti-Leninist'.

Adapted from *Revolutionary Russia* by Orlando Figes, (Pelican), 2014, pp 181–82.

Extract C

Lenin did make history. If he had not campaigned for these strategical shifts (April Theses, seizure of power in October, Brest-Litovsk and the NEP) the USSR would never have been established and consolidated. Not everything done by Lenin was carefully conceived. In particular, he had little foresight about what he was doing when he set up the centralised one-party state. One of the great malignancies of the twentieth century was created more by off-the-cuff measures than by grandiose planning. Yet the creation was far from being a complete accident. Lenin, even at his most improvisational, thought and acted in accordance with his long-held basic assumptions. He liked what he had done in his career. He was proud of his doctrines, his party and his revolution. Lenin justified dictatorship and terror. Lenin applauded the political vanguard and the need for firm leadership. Lenin convinced his party that his Marxism was pure and that it embodied the only correct policies.

Adapted from *Lenin* by Robert Service, (Macmillan), 2000, p 10.

6

Stalin's dictatorship, 1928–41

This chapter examines Stalin's dictatorship from the end of 1928 when the First Five-Year Plan began until the German invasion in 1941. It deals with the following areas:

- The Stalinist economy; collectivisation and the Five-Year Plans
- The Great Terror – the purges
- The development of the Stalinist dictatorship
- The effect of Stalinist rule on class, women, young people, religion and national minorities; propaganda and cultural change
- The political, economic and social condition of the Soviet Union by 1941

This chapter will focus on the following question:

What was the effect on Russian society of the Stalin revolution of 1928–41?

This question will look at the way in which Stalin's dictatorship developed between 1928 and 1941, starting with the Great Turn, and the revolutionary impact it had on Russian society.

This chapter will have a strong focus on the concepts of change and continuity. You will be invited throughout the chapter to consider the extent of economic, social, political and cultural change in these years. At the end of it you should also be in a position to assess the degree of continuity from Lenin to Stalin.

CHAPTER OVERVIEW

At the end of the 1920s Stalin made the Great Turn – a radical change in policies designed to transform Russia and establish his credentials as the equal of Lenin. This involved the collectivisation of agriculture and the introduction of Five-Year Plans for industry, setting unrealistically high targets for a centrally planned economy. It was hugely disruptive and carried out at a massive human cost. Forced collectivisation was an offensive against the majority of the population – the peasantry; it brought misery, hardship and famine, and millions fled the countryside for the towns. The plans for industry involved ambitious projects to change Russia into an industrial powerhouse. The new proletariat became part of a workforce, driven by fear, discipline and incentives, moving to and from major projects in what became a quicksand society. Stalin also envisaged a cultural revolution in which a new type of Soviet citizen would be created. To achieve his ends he dominated society by terror, first by purges of the Party and then, in the Great Terror of 1937–38, the wider population. As a result of the purges the Party was totally subservient to Stalin and the use of terror gave him awesome political control. He could kill or arrest anyone he wanted to and yet he could not get people to deliver the economic transformation he desired or create the society he envisaged.

1 The Great Turn in the countryside: collectivisation

Stalin's Great Turn was his plan to bring about an economic, social and cultural transformation of Russia. Change was to be achieved at breakneck pace. Russia's perceived backwardness was going to be overcome in ten years and the country's military security in the face of a possible foreign threat, would be ensured. This change was focused on heavy industry and collectivisation. A siege mentality was combined with the optimistic exhortation that there was no fortress a Bolshevik could not storm. In this section we shall look at why and how collectivisation was enforced and at the enormous changes it brought.

What was a collective farm?

The main type of collective farm was the *kolkhoz* (plural *kolkhozy* and inhabitants of collective farms are sometimes referred to as *kolkhozniks*), where all the land was held in common and run by an elected committee. To form a *kolkhoz*, between 50 and 100 households were put together. All land, tools and livestock had to be pooled. Under the direction of the committee, the peasants farmed the land as one unit. Much larger areas could be farmed more efficiently through the use of tractors and other machinery. These would be supplied by the state through huge machine and tractor stations (MTS). Experts could help peasants to farm in more modern ways using metal ploughs and fertilisers. However, by the *kolkhoz* model statute of 1935 (see page 198) each household was allowed to keep its own private plot of up to one acre.

NOTE-MAKING

Make notes under the following headings as you go through this section.
- Ways in which collectivisation was economically successful for the government
- Ways in which collectivisation was an economic failure
- The amount of change brought about by collectivisation
- Ways in which collectivisation was politically successful for the government
- The human cost of collectivisation

Forced collectivisation

Why and how was collectivisation carried out?

Stalin's experience of implementing the Urals–Siberian method in 1928 and again in 1929 (see page 174) decided him that forced collectivisation and the elimination of the *kulaks* as a class were needed to bring the peasantry under control once and for all. By this time Bukharin and the right had been defeated, and there was a ground swell of opinion among Party activists who were concerned about the amount of power the *kulaks* had over the economy. Stalin hoped that collectivisation would lead to an increase in the state's share of larger harvests at a lower price. It would also make a large pool of surplus rural labour available to industry.

In November 1929 the Central Committee resolved to recruit 25,000 industrial workers (known as the 25,000ers) to go to the countryside alongside Party officials, reinforced by army and police units. They would be given instructions not to come back without organising a collective farm. In the first two months of 1930, roughly half the Soviet peasantry (around 60 million people in 100,000 villages) were herded into collective farms. However, the process was so disruptive that, concerned to ensure the sowing and harvesting of grain took place, Stalin called a halt. In an article in *Pravda* ('Dizzy with success') on 2 March 1930, he hypocritically stated that 'collective farms cannot be set up by force' and accused local officials of excessive zeal. The number of peasant households in collective farms fell from 58 per cent to 24 per cent between March and June. In September, with the harvest in, the collectivisation offensive began again as vigorously as ever and by the end of the 1930s 90 per cent of households were collectivised – 25 million peasant households had been combined into 250,000 *kolkhozy*.

Who were the *kulaks*?

Soviet writers divided the peasants into three classes:

- *kulaks*, or better-off peasants
- middle peasants (those on moderate incomes)
- poor peasants and landless labourers.

An examination of Soviet data shows that the so-called *kulak* might own one or two horses, hire labour at times during the year and produce a small surplus for the market. There was no separate rich peasant stratum. Indeed, once the attack on *kulaks* began, many got rid of some of their animals and other resources so that they would be classed as middle peasants. In practice, a *kulak* was anyone officials decided was one. Often the people they identified were the most enterprising peasants in a village, the better farmers, the ones who had a little machinery and a few animals. So, in getting rid of them, they were destroying the best chance for more successful agriculture.

Gulag – an acronym for the Main Administration of Corrective Labour Camps and Colonies.

The offensive against the *kulaks*

The attack on the *kulaks* was central to the whole collectivisation policy. Stalin called for the liquidation of the *kulaks* as a class on 27 December 1929. Their number was exaggerated and the definition of *kulak* was elastic. Any peasant who opposed collectivisation was dubbed a *kulak* or an ideological *kulak*. The focus on the *kulaks* was deliberate to mask the fact that it was an offensive against the peasantry as a whole. A minority of the poorer peasants supported and at first benefited from *de-kulakisation*. There was no real class division in the villages and no class war to fan. *De-kulakisation* was a way of frightening the peasants into submission.

In a chilling foretaste of what was going to happen in the Great Terror, each region was given a number of *kulaks* to find. They were found whether they existed or not. Quotas were frequently exceeded to demonstrate the vigilance of the GPU (the secret police) or the local Party organisations.

The *kulaks* were divided into three categories:

- counter-revolutionaries who were to be shot or sent to forced-labour settlements
- active opponents of collectivisation who were to be deported to other areas of the Soviet Union, often to Siberia
- those who were expelled from their farms and settled on poor land.

The deported *kulaks*, or rather peasants identified as *kulaks*, played an important part in developing industrial resources in remote places at minimal cost. Inmates of the **gulag** labour camps and punishment brigades built canals, roads or the new industrial centres. Andrea Romano has calculated that in the years 1930–31 about 1.8 million peasants were deported in cattle trucks to Siberia, Kazakhstan and other inhospitable areas, many of them dying there. A further 400,000 households were uprooted but remained in their districts. Some 390,000 people were arrested, most were sent to camps and approximately 21,000 were shot. In May 1933 it was decided to stop the mass deportation of *kulaks*; the disruption of agriculture and the difficulties in organising resettlement were too great. However, this did not mean any let-up of the pressure on *kulaks*. They would be dealt with in a different way, as we shall see in the Great Terror.

As well as its impact on the villages, the campaign had an impact on the towns. Many more families than were deported chose self-*de-kulakisation* and joined the 3 million a year leaving for the towns. This produced overcrowding and strained the rationing system to breaking point.

Peasant opposition

The peasants resisted collectivisation bitterly despite the mass deportations.

- In 1930 there were 13,754 outbreaks of mass unrest.
- The demonstrations, riots and even full-scale uprisings involved over 2.5 million peasants.
- Acts of *kulak* terrorism claimed 3,155 victims among Communist activists and Soviet officials.

In many instances troops had to be brought in. Peasants burned crops, tools and houses rather than hand them over to the state. One of the main forms of resistance was to slaughter animals and eat or sell the meat rather than hand over the beasts to the *kolkhoz*. The dramatic fall in livestock figures, see Figure 1 (page 198) bears this out.

Action by women often proved the most effective form of opposition. There was a wave of 'women's revolts' (*bab'i bunty*) in the North Caucasus in February 1930. Kaganovich, a member of the Politburo, recognised that 'women had played the most advanced role in the reaction against the collective farm'. The women's protests were carefully organised, with specific goals such as stopping grain requisitioning or retrieving collectivised horses. They reckoned, sometimes correctly, that it would be more difficult for troops to take action against all-women protests. The government found their tactics difficult to deal with.

The peasants deeply resented the attack on their traditional ways of life. In 1930 the village commune, the *Mir*, was abolished. Thousands of churches were closed, church bells were melted down and priests persecuted. This was part of the Cultural Revolution (see page 216). Millions just left. Between 1928 and 1941, 20 million peasants made for the towns and industrial areas. Kevin McDermott calls this 'a demographic shift of unprecedented scope that altered the face of the Soviet Union'. The towns were under immense strain and the government brought in internal passports to control the vast movement of people.

Famine

In 1932 and 1933 in Ukraine, a major grain-producing area in the Soviet Union, famine raged. Yet in 1933 state procurements were more than double the level under the NEP and exports continued. To conceal the extent of the crisis people were prevented from fleeing from the famine area. Robert Conquest, one of Stalin's sternest critics writing before the archives were open, stressed that 'the Soviet collectivisation terror took more lives than were lost by all countries on all fronts, in the First World War'. Conquest emphasised Stalin's 'criminal responsibility' for the Ukraininan famine in which 7 million died of starvation and saw it as part of a campaign to smash Ukrainian nationalism. This interpretation is rejected by Wheatcroft and Davies, but they accept that it was a man-made famine caused by ruthless and excessive grain procurements. They have had access to the archives and their figure for deaths is 5.7 million, still 'an enormous figure'.

Hunger meant theft of grain from collective farms soared, most of it by collective farmers themselves. In August 1932, even though he knew there was a famine (he used the word in a letter to Kaganovich and Molotov in June), Stalin himself drafted the 'law of five ears of corn' (see below). *Kolkhozniks* were arrested for 'hairdressing' – the cutting of individual ears of corn in the fields, hence the title commonly given for the law. By the end of 1933 about 1,000 people had been executed – as this figure was only 4 per cent of those convicted, the numbers arrested was clearly huge. Laws like this, and *de-kulakisation*, explain why peasants formed the vast majority of those in Soviet camps throughout the 1930s, and why peasants would remain a substantial part of the prison population until Stalin's death.

Source A From *The Stalin-Kaganovich Correspondence 1931–36*, R. W. Davies, et al. eds., (Yale University Press), 2003, pp 164–65.

the thefts are organised by *kulaks* and other *antisocial* elements who are trying to *undermine our new system* ... make the theft (or stealing) of property in the above-mentioned categories punishable by a *minimum* of ten years' imprisonment, and as a rule, by *death* ... Without these (and similar) Draconian *socialist* measures, it is impossible to uphold and strengthen our *new* system.

We must not delay, it seems to me, the promulgation of such a law.

Stalin's ruthlessness revealed

Stalin took two- to three-month vacations at his *dacha* (country home) on the Black Sea coast. During this time he communicated his political will through confidential letters and coded telegrams to his key henchmen Molotov and Kaganovich. They show that the notorious 'law of five ears of corn' decree of 7 August 1932 to stop theft from collective farms was Stalin's idea (see Source A).

Source A is typical of Stalin's style in these letters. What does it reveal about Stalin and his style, even on vacation?

The *kolkhoz* model statute and private plots

In 1935 a special Party Congress was called to adopt a 'model statute' or charter for collective farms. It remained the basis for *kolkhoz* organisation until well into the 1960s. It laid down rules for the payment of *kolkhozniks* for work on the collective farm and for the relations between the *kolkhozy* and the MTS. It also legalised private plots of up to one acre for each household. Livestock was limited to one cow and calves, one sow and piglets, four sheep, and any number of rabbits and poultry. Livestock was generally pastured on collective land. It has been estimated that these private plots provided 52 per cent of vegetables, 57 per cent of fruit, 70 per cent of meat and 71 per cent of milk as well as butter, honey and wool to Soviet consumers.

Assessing the impact of collectivisation

Did collectivisation bring about a greater change than the October Revolution?

Any assessment of collectivisation reveals a very mixed picture. Economically, it appears to have been a disaster. The fact that grain harvests dropped dramatically in the early 1930s, when grain was most needed, and did not recover to their 1928 level (apart from 1930, which was an exceptional year) until the latter half of the 1930s is a damning indictment. This is an even worse performance when you compare the figures with the last harvest of tsarist Russia in 1913 (80.1 million tons). The Soviet Union also lost a huge proportion of the animal population. Meat production did not reach pre-collectivisation levels until after 1953.

	1928	1929	1930	1931	1932	1933	1934	1935
Grain harvest (million tons)	73.3	71.7	83.5	69.5	69.6	68.4	67.6	75.0
State procurement of grain (million tons)	10.8	16.1	22.1	22.8	18.5	22.6	*	*
Grain exports (million tons)	0.03	0.18	4.76	5.06	1.73	1.69	0.77	1.51
Cattle (million head)	70.5	67.1	52.3	47.9	40.1	38.4	42.4	49.3
Pigs (million head)	26.0	20.4	13.6	14.4	11.6	12.1	17.4	22.6
Sheep and goats (million head)	146.7	147.0	108.8	77.7	52.1	50.2	51.9	61.1

From *An Economic History of the USSR, 1917–91* by A. Nove, (Penguin), 1992, pp 180, 186.

▲ **Figure 1** Agricultural output and state procurement of grain, 1928–35.
*We do not have reliable figures for these years but state procurements continued to rise, so while the average for 1928–32 was 18.06 million tons, for 1933–37 (which included the very good year of 1937) it was 27.5 million tons.

However, although the overall grain harvest declined in the early 1930s, state procurements did not. This was more important to Stalin than making agriculture more productive. The state collected the grain it needed to feed the rapidly growing workforce and to sell abroad to pay for industrial equipment. What is more, dispossessed peasants from the overpopulated countryside fled to the towns, so providing labour for the new factories. Collectivisation had succeeded in its main purpose – to provide the resources for industrialisation.

This view, however, has been challenged by several historians. They believe that valuable resources had to be diverted to agriculture: in 1933 there were less than half the horses there had been in 1928 and there were not enough tractors to replace them. In the vain effort to make good the deficit, tractors alone consumed half the production of quality steel in the USSR in 1932. The memorable lines of choreographed tractors in Eisenstein's film *The Old and the New* were light-years away from the reality on the *kolkhoz*.

For the Party, collectivisation was an essential part of its modernisation drive. The Party did not want a sizeable sector of the economy to be dominated by the private market or to be at the mercy of the peasants who hoarded grain. In this sense, collectivisation was a political success. The Party gained control of the villages and did not have to bargain with the peasants anymore. It had established a system, using local soviets and MTS, of controlling the countryside and making agriculture serve the towns and workers.

As for the impact on the peasants themselves, the death toll and human costs of *de-kulakisation* and the famine were horrendous as we have seen. Millions died and millions fled from or were forced out of the villages. A way of life that had existed for 500 years vanished forever. For those who stayed, collectivisation was 'a second serfdom'. Sheila Fitzpatrick's study of peasant attitudes makes it clear that peasants blamed Stalin for collectivisation and the famine; they saw him as their inveterate enemy, 'they wished him dead, his regime overthrown, and collectivisation undone, even at the cost of war and foreign occupation'.

KEY DATES: COLLECTIVISATION

1928 January Urals–Siberian method adopted.

1929

April Urals–Siberian method used again.

November 25,000ers sent into the villages, the Great Turn underway.

December Stalin announces the policy of 'liquidating the *kulaks* as a class'.

1930

January All-out collectivisation drive begins.

March Stalin's 'Dizzy with success' speech.

September Collectivisation offensive begins again.

1932 August Law of five ears of corn.

1932–34 Famine in principal grain areas.

1935 *Kolkhoz* model statute.

▲ Peasants in Ukraine in 1929 looking at posters encouraging them to join the kolkhoz. The poster reads, 'the farm worker says go to the collectives'.

○
LOOK AGAIN

The state and modernisation

In Russia the state had been the prime sponsor of industrial growth. Witte, Nicholas II's Finance Minister, was the key moderniser in the 1890s and there are clear parallels with Stalin. Like Stalin:

● Witte believed industrial development was crucial for military strength.
● Witte prioritised heavy and large-scale industry at the expense of light industry and the welfare of the peasants.
● Witte's funding came mainly from grain exports.

2 The Great Turn in the towns: industrialisation

The USSR could not have defeated Germany in the Second World War if it had not become one of the world's great industrial powers by 1941. In this section we shall look at the transformation both of industry and of the lives of the people.

The industrialisation of the Soviet Union

How did Stalin set about industrialisation?

We have seen how collectivisation played a vital part in providing resources for industrialisation. Again and again Stalin repeated the urgency of the task. In a speech to industrial managers in February 1931 he stressed that, 'The history of old Russia consisted, among other things, in her being beaten continually for her backwardness'. Stalin listed example after example, which backed up his argument for more effort and sacrifice:

We are fifty or a hundred years behind the advanced countries. We must make good this distance in ten years. Either we do it, or we shall be crushed.

This was the purpose of the Five-Year Plans.

Features of the Five-Year Plans

The plans were dominated by an emphasis on the development of heavy industry. Stalin and the Supreme Economic Council (*Vesenkha*) agreed

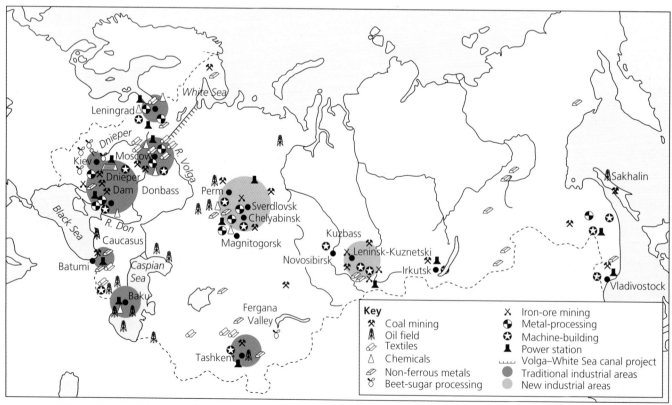

Key

✕ Coal mining	✕ Iron-ore mining
⚓ Oil field	◕ Metal-processing
✍ Textiles	✿ Machine-building
△ Chemicals	⚒ Power station
✍ Non-ferrous metals	⊔⊔⊔ Volga–White Sea canal project
⚵ Beet-sugar processing	⬤ Traditional industrial areas
	⬤ New industrial areas

▲ Figure 2 Major industrial centres in the 1930s.

that the lion's share of investment should go into coal, iron, steel and other heavy industries. These would provide the power, capital equipment and machine tools that could be used to manufacture other products. The Soviet Union would then be less dependent on the West for these goods and could move towards self-sufficiency or 'autarky'. This decision meant that consumer industries producing clothes, shoes and similar products would be downgraded. Soviet citizens were asked to sacrifice their standard of living for longer-term objectives. There were two main reasons behind this:

1 It seemed to the Stalinists that Western industrial revolutions had been underpinned by the initial development in coal, iron and steel.

2 They were driven by the need to develop the sort of industries that could protect the Soviet Union should it be attacked from the West.

Three other features of the plans are worthy of note:

- The setting of production and output targets which industrial enterprises had to achieve was absolutely central. Five-Year Plans set down broad directions and could be changed as they went along. There were also shorter one-year or even quarterly plans which set more specific targets for individual enterprises. The targets were backed by law, so failure to meet targets could be treated as a criminal offence. Bonuses were paid to enterprises that exceeded their plan target.

- Huge new industrial centres were constructed virtually from nothing, for example at Magnitogorsk in the Urals and Kuznetz in western Siberia. Most of these were located east of the Ural mountains, a strategic decision to make them less vulnerable to attack from the West. (See Figure 2, page 200.)

- Spectacular projects were conceived to demonstrate the might of the new Soviet industrial machine. This has been called 'gigantomania'. The Dnieprostroi Dam in eastern Russia was, for two years, the world's largest construction site and it increased Soviet electric power output fivefold when it came on stream. Other projects included the development of Magnitogorsk steel works, the Moscow–Volga canal and the prestigious Moscow metro with its elaborate stations and high vaulted ceilings.

The First Five-Year Plan

As the First Five-Year Plan got underway it was quickly enveloped in 'target mania'. Gosplan (the State Planning Commission) and the *Vesenkha* tried to outbid each other with higher targets. The optimistic original targets were revised upwards almost before the plan was begun. In April 1929, two versions of the plan were produced – a basic and a much higher optimum version. The latter was chosen. This envisaged targets being increased by astonishing amounts, for instance, coal up from 35 to 75 million tons and iron ore from 6 to 19 million tons. To many, these seemed hopelessly unachievable.

This frenetic pace and enthusiasm did not just come from above. The idea that the Soviet Union was at last on the road to socialism, via industrialisation, inspired Party members and urban workers alike. Young people especially were gripped by the feeling that they were creating a new type of society that would be far superior to that of their capitalist neighbours. After the compromises of the NEP, there was a return to the war imagery of the civil war and War Communism. There was talk of a 'socialist offensive', and of 'mobilising forces on all fronts'. Groups of enthusiasts became shock workers who strove to increase productivity and urge each other on with 'socialist competition'. There were 'campaigns' and 'breakthroughs', 'ambushes' by 'class enemies'. People who opposed or criticised the regime's policies thus became guilty of treachery. Bourgeois specialist-baiting and denunciation by workers was positively encouraged from 1928 as part of a 'Cultural Revolution'.

The massive mobilisation of labour played a crucial role as the number of industrial workers in the USSR doubled during the First Five-Year Plan. Collectivisation made a major, if largely unplanned, contribution. Millions poured in from the countryside completely lacking in training or experience of factory life, undernourished and living in extremely poor accommodation and living conditions. It was almost impossible to forge a disciplined and diligent workforce. Specialist-baiting was not conducive to discipline and Stalin called a halt to it in a speech in June 1931. There was a further ideological retreat when Stalin attacked 'petty bourgeois egalitarianism':

Whoever draws up wage scales on the principle of wage equalisation, without taking into account the difference between skilled and unskilled labour, breaks with Marxism, breaks with Leninism.

Higher wages and other incentives were used to encourage workers and this is explored further on page 218, which looks at the growth of inequality.

The authority and status of management was now supported and a decree at the end of 1932 allowed managers to sack unsatisfactory workers and deprive them of ration cards, social benefits and factory housing. However, the managers needed the workers, especially skilled workers, if they were to reach output levels anywhere near their targets. A tough approach would lead to workers literally voting with their feet and moving on in search of better conditions. It was a quicksand society. Labour turnover was astronomically high. At Magnitogorsk alone in the course of 1931 the total number of workers went up considerably but this increase was just a fraction of the number on site at some time during the year. Magnitogorsk was a revolving door (see Figure 3).

Under the First Five-Year Plan industry grew impressively, but there were weaknesses. The chart on page 204 sums these up.

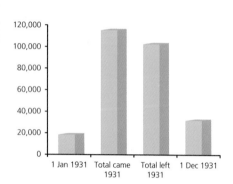

▲ **Figure 3** Workers coming and going at Magnitogorsk, 1931.

The Second Five-Year Plan

The year 1932 was one of crisis but the First Five-Year Plan was presented as a great success by emphasising heavy industry rather than light industry and agriculture, and focusing on quantity rather than quality. The Second Five-Year Plan was more realistic. Total investment was reduced and resources concentrated on completing projects in progress like the big plant at Magnitogorsk and other metal works. Three good years followed from 1934 to 1936. There was a gradual recovery of agriculture, a rapid increase in industrial output and rationing ended in 1935.

At ten o'clock on 30 August 1935, Alexei Stakhanov, a pneumatic-pick operator, began his special shift. After five hours of uninterrupted work he had cut 102 tons of coal, almost sixteen times the norm of 6.5 tons per shift. He was given perfect conditions and, exceptionally, a support team. Afterwards there was a great deal of publicity. Ordzhonikidze, the Commissar for Heavy Industry, had Stakhanov, the 'Soviet Hercules', put on the front cover of *Pravda*. He said, 'In our country, under socialism, heroes of labour must become the most famous'. On 11 September, *Pravda* used the term 'Stakhanovite movement' for the first time and in November Stalin called for Stakhanovism to spread 'widely and deeply' across the entire Soviet Union. Record mania swept the country. The Stakhanovite movement was seen as a way of compelling management to adopt new production methods and increase rates of production. Those reluctant to do so were branded as saboteurs, with the warning 'Such pseudo leaders must be removed immediately'. With pressure from above to meet increased targets and from below from workers wanting to be Stakhanovites, who would have wanted to be a manager in Soviet Russia at that time?

Historians have differing views on the effectiveness of the Stakhanovite movement. Lewis Siegelbaum argues that bonuses and gifts were showered on a favoured few. Ordinary workers, however, responded with violence, sabotage or demands to be classified as Stakhanovites, and the attempt to resurrect the mood of grass roots enthusiasm associated with the First Five-Year Plan broke down due to the purges (pp. 208–213). John Barber, while admitting that the movement fell well short of its objective in raising productivity, feels it may have elevated the status of some workers while simultaneously re-animating the Bolshevik spirit of mass participation and proletarian creativity.

In the second half of 1936 the situation deteriorated: a terrible harvest, shortages, an economic slowdown and dramatic industrial accidents, such as the Kemerovo mine disaster. The imperatives of meeting production targets of the Five-Year Plans led regional Party and economic leaders into self-protective practices that involved a systematic deception of the centre. Desperate to fulfil targets, managers sought to bribe or steal from others to get raw materials; factories turned out substandard or useless products or fiddled the figures. The local Party leadership and even local NKVD often colluded with this because they did not want to be held responsible for unfulfilled targets.

The regime's response to the economic slowdown

The regime explained the slowdown as due to criminal negligence and deliberate sabotage by officials and managers, and indiscipline by rank-and-file workers. Its response was purges of officials and managers and the increasingly tough Labour decrees of 1938 and 1940. Both responses made the problem worse.

Under the Labour decree of 1938 a stricter system of work-record books was introduced. Managers were ordered to refuse employment unless the employee could produce a satisfactory work-book with details of and explanation for his/her previous changes of employer.

The Labour decree of 1940 contained the following terms:

- Working day lengthened from seven to eight hours, and working week lengthened from five out of six to six out of seven days (Sunday was to be the normal day of rest), without additional pay.
- Changing jobs without specific authorisation became a criminal offence, punishable by imprisonment.
- Absenteeism (arriving more than 20 minutes late for work on two occasions) was to be punished by up to six months compulsory labour at 75 per cent normal pay.
- Employers who failed to report cases of the above, or who took on such workers were liable to criminal prosecution.

The Labour decrees were almost universally detested and were a part of the austerity measures brought in to restrict budget expenditure as the large increases in defence expenditure in the Third Five-Year Plan had repercussions throughout the economy. There was a level of popular discontent that dismayed the NKVD.

FIRST FIVE-YEAR PLAN	SECOND FIVE-YEAR PLAN	THIRD FIVE-YEAR PLAN
October 1928 to December 1932 The emphasis was on heavy industries – coal, oil, iron and steel, electricity, cement, metals, timber. This accounted for 80 per cent of total investment; 1,500 enterprises were opened.	**January 1933 to December 1937** Heavy industries still featured strongly but new industries opened up and there was greater emphasis on communications, especially railways to link cities and industrial centres. A total of 4,500 enterprises opened. The plan benefited from some big projects, such as the Dnieprostroi Dam, coming into use.	**January 1938 to June 1941** The third plan ran for only three and a half years because of the USSR's entry into the Second World War. Once again, heavy industry was emphasised as the need for armaments became increasingly urgent.
Successful sectors • Electricity – production trebled. • Coal and iron – output doubled. • Steel production – increased by one-third. • Engineering industry developed and increased output of machine-tools, turbines, etc. • Huge new industrial complexes were built or were in the process of being built. • Huge new tractor works were built in Stalingrad, Kharkov and other places to meet the needs of mechanised agriculture.	**Successful sectors** • Heavy industries benefited from plants which had been set up during the first plan and now came on stream. Electricity production expanded rapidly. • By 1937, the USSR was virtually self-sufficient in machine-making and metalworking. • Transport and communications grew rapidly. • Chemical industries, such as fertiliser production, were growing. • Metallurgy developed – minerals such as copper, zinc and tin were mined for the first time.	**Successful sectors** • Heavy industry continued to grow, for example, machinery and engineering, but the picture was uneven and some areas did poorly. • Defence and armaments grew rapidly as resources were diverted to them.
Weaknesses • There was very little growth, and even a decline, in consumer industries such as house-building, fertilisers, food processing and woollen textiles. • Small workshops were squeezed out, partly because of the drive against Nepmen and partly because of shortages of materials and fuel. • Chemicals targets were not fulfilled. • The lack of skilled workers created major problems. Workers were constantly changing jobs, which created instability.	**Weaknesses** • Consumer goods industries were still lagging, although they were showing signs of recovery. There was growth in footwear and food processing – modern bakeries, ice-cream production and meatpacking plants – but not enough. • Oil production did not make the expected advances.	**Weaknesses** • Steel output grew insignificantly. • Oil production failed to meet targets and led to a fuel crisis. • Consumer industries once again took a back seat. • Many factories ran short of materials.
Comment In reality, many targets were not met. The Great Depression had driven down the price of grain and raw materials, so the USSR could not earn enough from exports to pay for all the machinery it needed. Also, a good deal of investment had to go into agriculture because of the forced collectivisation programme. However, the Soviet economy was kick-started: there was impressive growth in certain sectors of the economy and there were substantial achievements.	**Comment** There was a feeling in the Party that Stalin had overreached himself in the First Five-Year Plan, that targets had been too high. The second plan was more one of consolidation. The years 1934–36 were known as the 'three good years' since the pressure was not so intense, food rationing was ended and families had more disposable income.	**Comment** The third plan ran into difficulties at the beginning of 1938 due to an exceptionally hard winter and the diversion of materials to the military. Gosplan was thrown into chaos when the purges (see page 208) created shortages of qualified personnel, such as important managers, engineers and officials, who linked industries and government.

▲ **Figure 4** The achievements and weaknesses of the Five-Year Plans, 1928–41.

Urbanisation and living standards

One of the most momentous transformations of the twentieth century was the migration of 20 million peasants to the urban centres of the Soviet Union between 1928 and 1941.

This influx worried Party officials who were concerned that their drinking, lack of discipline, religious beliefs and general lack of political consciousness would infect younger workers. These peasants seemed to be the antithesis of the New Soviet Person. Indeed David Hoffman, in his study of peasants in Moscow in these years, argues that they rejected such an identity and never internalised the role of loyal proletarian, nor did they develop an allegiance to the Soviet government.

As the figures show, vast numbers moved into Moscow during the First Five-Year Plan, and while the flow slowed after that there was intense overcrowding. This was true nationally. In new industrial towns like Magnitogorsk it was even worse as the planners were not able to meet the needs of urban dwellers. There, many lived in dormitories and barracks and 25 per cent lived in mud huts they had built themselves. Generally housing remained abysmal; there was intense overcrowding with people living in communal apartments, usually one family to a room. Some had to make their homes in corridors and 'corners' in other people's apartments: those in corridors and hallways usually had beds, but corner-dwellers slept on the floor in a corner of the kitchen or other public space. Except in new industrial cities most communal apartments in the 1930s were converted from old single-family apartments. Not till the Khrushchev period was anything done to improve the terrible overcrowding which characterised the Stalin era.

NOTE-MAKING

Social change: industrialisation

In this chapter we are looking at the impact of Stalin's revolution on Russian society. For the rest of this section, in the second quarter of your piece of paper, make notes on the impact of rapid industrialisation in the same way as you did on the effects of collectivisation.

Urban population	Plan: 32.5 million
	Actual: 38.7 million
	Result: 20 per cent higher than expected
Housing	Plan: 33 per cent increase
	Actual: 16 per cent increase
	Result: 50 per cent shortfall
Moscow population	1929: 2.2 million
	1932: 3.7 million
	1939: 4.1 million
Moscow average living space	1928: 5.9 square metres per head
	1940: 4 square metres per head

▲ **Figure 5** Urban housing statistics in the First Five-Year Plan.

In January 1933 Stalin announced:

We have without doubt achieved a situation in which the material conditions of workers and peasants are improving year by year. The only people who doubt this are the sworn enemies of Soviet power.

This big lie was backed by menace and issued during the famine. If conditions for the peasants were dire, life was not much better in the towns. Rationing which had existed since 1929 would not end until January 1935, real wages declined markedly in the 1930s: Moscow workers' real wages were 52 per cent of their 1928 level in 1932. Nationally the level of 1925 was not regained until the late 1950s. Between 1928 and 1932 the consumption of meat by the Moscow working class fell by 60 per cent and dairy produce by 50 per cent; once again NEP levels of consumption would not be reached during Stalin's lifetime. An increase in the provision of education and health care, and more employment opportunities for women were the only developments to have a positive impact on the standard of living.

Year	Number of women in the industrial workforce
1928	3 million
1936	9 million
1940	13 million

▲ **Figure 6** The number of women in the industrial workforce.

Neopatriarchal – a new form of male domination.

Plebian apparatchiki – working-class communist officials.

How useful is Source B on the scale of change wrought by the First Five-Year Plan?

Women in the workforce

One of the most important sources of new labour was women. Some 10 million women entered the workforce. Women dominated some professions, particularly medicine (though there were only four women head doctors in hospitals) and school teaching. The less well educated, especially tough ex-peasant women, became labourers or factory workers. Generally, women were paid less and found it more difficult to gain advancement than men. Sarah Davies' survey of women workers in Leningrad in 1935 showed that women workers in the city made up 44 per cent of the workforce but were likely to be less well paid, less literate and less involved in political and technical education, and their chances of reaching the top were limited. Of 328 factory directors, only twenty were women and seventeen of these were in textile and sewing factories where well over three-quarters of the workforce were women.

The big increase in the number of women in the workforce saved family incomes from a sharp fall as two incomes were now needed to sustain viable family life. As Geoffrey Hosking has pointed out, women coped with 'the double burden' by limiting the number of children they had. 'In that way the fruits of female emancipation became the building blocks of the Stalinist neopatriarchal social system.'

Shops were characterised by long queues and empty shelves and shopping itself was a survival skill. Sheila Fitzpatrick regards the new distribution system replacing private trade as 'a policy disaster whose dimensions and long-term consequences were exceeded only by those of collectivisation'. It was introduced without any prior planning at a time of general crisis and upheaval; the scale of the malfunctioning and its impact on the everyday life of town-dwellers were remarkable. The conditions of urban life worsened suddenly and drastically with the onset of the First Five-Year Plan and even though the situation improved marginally in the mid-1930s, the distribution of consumer goods remained a problem throughout the lifetime of the Soviet Union.

Source B *Stalin's Russia* 2nd edition by C. Ward, (Arnold), 1999, p 260.

The earthquake of the First Five-Year Plan and its aftershocks refashioned Russian life more fundamentally and affected non-Russian populations more profoundly than did tsarism, the Revolution or the civil war. Peasants left for the towns in swarms. Droves of working men and women traded old lives for new. Thousands rather than hundreds moved upwards across the board. Millions rather than thousands lost their jobs and lives if they fell foul of **plebian apparatchiki** or Stalin's burgeoning state.

LOOK AGAIN

Breadth issue: social change

In Chapters 2 and 3 (pages 63–8 and 81–3), we looked at another time of rapid social change: peasants poured into the cities in the 1890s and working and living conditions were very poor. Tolstoy in Source C (page 83) refers to the degree of surveillance, deportation and famine.

Work in pairs or small groups. Divide a page into two and put two headings: c1890–1905 and 1928–41. Look through this section and pages 63–8 and 81–3 for the 1890s and compare migration, working and living conditions at the different times. At which time do you think conditions were the more difficult? Compare worker reaction at both times to these conditions. What does this tell us about USSR 1928–41 compared with tsarist Russia c1890–1905? At the end compare your points with other members of the class.

A verdict on the Five-Year Plans

The Five-Year Plans did produce real achievement as Figure 4 (page 204) shows. Overall, between 1928 and 1941 industrial output trebled and the annual growth rate was 10 per cent. The total number of industrial enterprises grew from 9,000 in 1928 to 64,000 in 1938. To protect the country from attack from the west a significant part of Soviet industry was relocated in the east in the Urals, Siberia and Central Asia. Defence concerns also drove the 28-fold increase in the production of aircraft and tanks between 1930 and 1940.

These achievements came at the cost of great human suffering and we have noted living conditions and working conditions were often very grim and dangerous. It was a clumsy and wasteful system. Meeting the Plan was everything; quality was sacrificed to quantity. Labour productivity was very low and the use of millions of untrained workers took its toll on them and their machinery. There are accounts of lathes being smashed due to ignorance and of workers measuring things with their fingers because there were no measuring instruments. Most workers had to learn on the job, but there was more attention to training during the Second Five-Year Plan. The development of a massive modern iron and steel plant from nothing at Magnitogorsk was a major achievement, but it provided plenty of examples of inefficiency. Staggeringly large amounts of pig-iron and steel were found to be unusable when the time came to count up output. But even if it was declared defective, it was still sent to metal-starved firms who had little choice but to use it. Blast furnaces and blooming mills lasted a fraction of the time they were supposed to before needing extensive repairs. The American John Scott, an enthusiastic volunteer, noted that the managers at Magnitogorsk spent about half their time trying to wheedle the rivets to fulfil the impossible plans decreed from Moscow, the other half trying to devise ideologically correct excuses for falling short.

Wheedle the rivets – somehow coax out of others, even by cheating, the rivets (bolts for holding together metal plates) needed to try to complete work on the site and reach a target.

Was the continuation of the NEP an alternative to Stalin's policy?

It has been argued that Stalin's policies were so wasteful that almost any alternative would have been better economically. Some economists have made the point that the NEP did provide a viable system of successful industrialisation and would have produced respectable rates of economic growth. But this is to ignore political realities. As Chris Ward writes, this was 'a direction in which the Party never intended to go'. Stalin wanted to build up heavy industry and armaments very fast. Factors like the war scare and ideology, as well as the recurrent grain crises mentioned, meant that by 1929 Stalin was determined to bring grain procurements and the peasants under control so that he could launch the Great Turn. The NEP had always been regarded as an ideological retreat, and young Party activists in particular welcomed a return to the heroic atmosphere of the revolution and the civil war.

KEY DATES: INDUSTRIALISATION

1928–32 First Five-Year Plan.

1931 June Stalin speech denouncing bourgeois specialist-baiting. Wage differentials come in.

1933–37 Second Five-Year Plan.

1935 The Stakhanov record.

1938–41 Third Five-Year Plan.

1938 Labour decree.

1940 Labour decree.

3 The Great Terror

This section will look at Stalin's role and the situation in which he was operating. It will look at the different elements in the Terror and the factors behind them. It will consider how the Terror fits into the Stalin revolution.

Stalin and the different elements of the Great Terror

What was the context in which the Terror took place?

The situation in 1932–33 – the battle against the peasantry, the famine, the suicide of his wife, the revelation of discontent within the Party and the worsening international situation increased Stalin's tendencies to be suspicious and vindictive. It was in 1932 that the most elaborate critique of the whole Stalin era appeared: the Ryutin Platform was a 200-page comprehensive criticism of Stalin's leadership and policies and called for his removal. Ryutin had been a Moscow district secretary and was expelled for his rightist views but the document circulated widely within the Party and Stalin wanted him shot. In the Politburo only Molotov and Kaganovich supported Stalin unreservedly and Stalin was overruled by moderates led by Kirov, and Ryutin was imprisoned. He was shot on Stalin's orders in 1937 and his wife and sons were also killed.

At the 17th Party Congress held in early 1934 there were still undercurrents of disenchantment with Stalin. It was called the Congress of Victors and there was a feeling within the Party that after the successes of the First Five-Year Plan there should be some easing of the pressure – this was not Stalin's view. We cannot be sure exactly what went on in the elections for the new Central Committee, it seems that a significant number of delegates failed to vote for Stalin and that Kirov topped the poll, and that this was covered up. On 1 December Kirov was murdered. Stalin's complicity in the assassination cannot be established, but he certainly took full advantage of it. Zinoviev and Kamenev were blamed and 843 former associates of Zinoviev were arrested at the beginning of 1935. A Party purge was carried out with close involvement of the NKVD for the first time and 250,000 members were expelled. Up to the middle of 1937 the main targets for repression were members of the Party who had in their time participated in the oppositions, or had shown some kind of dissent with Stalin's policies. Until 1937 they were more likely to be imprisoned or sent to the camps than shot.

The worsening international situation after Hitler's rise to power is relevant too. Stalin was acutely aware of the relationship between war and revolution. War had nearly brought down the Tsar in 1905 and did so in 1917. He was going to take no chances; hence his concerns about any fifth column. From 1932 onward fear of social disorder following forced collectivisation, famine and the mass migration of millions of peasants to the towns became a major obsession of Party and police authorities. The largest number of victims of the terror after 1937 were peasants, criminals and people who were dubbed 'anti-Soviet elements'.

NOTE-MAKING

Social change: Great Terror

For this section and in the third quarter of your piece of paper make notes on the impact of the Great Terror on Russian society in the same way as you made notes on the effect of collectivisation and rapid industrialisation.

The impact of Stalin's wife's suicide

Stalin's wife, Nadezda Allilueva, shot herself in November 1932. A contributory factor appears to have been depression caused by the excesses of collectivisation. Some writers suggest he saw her suicide as an act of betrayal and some historians think this increased his paranoia. Kaganovich said he was never the same man again.

Fifth column – a term used to describe enemy sympathisers.

The different elements of the Terror

It is clear that the Terror was a multi-faceted process with the different elements having their own origins and goals but they came together in a dreadful wave of arrests and executions in 1937–38.

'Opposition elements' in the Party and the show trials

Three infamous show trials of 1936–38 were carefully planned by Stalin: they were an effective way to create an atmosphere of intimidation, a sense of danger and the feeling that there were enemies, spies and wreckers around. By the end of the three trials, all the other people mentioned in Lenin's testament had been attacked.

- The first trial in August 1936 involved Zinoviev and Kamenev and fourteen others who had previously been members of the oppositionist groups in the Party. They were accused of being part of a counter-revolutionary bloc, the 'murderers' of Kirov and planning to assassinate the country's leaders in order to seize personal power. They confessed and were executed the next day. These executions were significant because they were the first executions of people who had belonged to the Central Committee. The line had been crossed and many more executions were to follow.
- In January 1937 the main defendants were Karl Radek, a Trotskyite, and Pyatakov, Deputy Commissar for Heavy Industry, both in prominent positions when arrested. It was important to scapegoat economic officials and legitimise criticism of powerful Party members. It highlighted the danger caused by double dealers, a theme the state prosecutor, Vyshinsky, returned to repeatedly. Needless to say they confessed and were found guilty.
- The third trial staged in March 1938 was the most dramatic and involved Bukharin along with twenty others, including Rykov and the former head of the NKVD, Yagoda. It focused on the world conspiracy against the USSR, and provided justification for the mass arrests of 1937. Much more explicitly than in the previous trials, Vyshinsky's final words dwelt on Stalin as the people's defender and hope.

The officer corps

In June 1937, Tukhachevsky, nicknamed the 'Red Napoleon', a hero of the civil war, moderniser of the Red Army and Deputy Commissar of Defence; and seven of the country's senior military commanders were arrested, accused of treachery, brutally tortured (Tukhachevsky's written confession actually had blood stains on it) and shot after a secret trial. Of the 767 members of the High Command, 512 were shot, 29 died in prison, 3 committed suicide and 59 remained in jail. In the army and navy, 10,000 officers were arrested and another 23,000 dismissed, but the number killed was rather modest. We do not know why Stalin decided to decapitate the Red Army. The Nazi intelligence service produced disinformation which may have hoodwinked Soviet intelligence and Stalin into believing they were plotting. The regime acted as if it believed there was a plot. It was a watershed; in the second half of 1937 the policy was to destroy anyone suspected of present or potential disloyalty.

The watcher in the shadows

The British diplomat Sir Fitzroy Maclean was watching proceedings at the third show trial. So was Stalin. Maclean records that a clumsily directed arc-light revealed Stalin's features watching from behind the black glass of a small window high up in the court-room. At the trial Bukharin made a spirited defence of his actions. After he was sentenced, Bukharin made a last plea to Stalin not to be shot, but Stalin orchestrated his death as well as his trial. Bukharin was shot last having been forced to watch the other executions.

The Stalin constitution of 1936

Just as Stalin was about to initiate one of the worst periods of political repression in the history of the USSR, he published the most 'democratic' constitution in the world (passed 5 December 1936). The rights it enshrined included:

- freedom from arbitrary arrest
- freedom of speech and the press
- the right to demonstrate
- respect for privacy of the home and personal correspondence
- employment for all
- universal suffrage for over-eighteens, free elections and secret ballots.

It was a hollow and cynical piece of propaganda since at that very time such rights were being systematically abused. However, the Constitution made it clear that all these rights were subordinate to the interests of the working classes and it was the role of the Communist Party to decide what those interests were. Also, only communists could be put up for elections. So one-party dominance was assured. The Constitution was written by a team headed by Bukharin and Radek, who were both to perish shortly afterwards in the purges.

Mass arrests of loyal party-state bureaucracy

The summer of 1937 saw the start of the denunciation of loyal Stalinists who had been the mainstay of Stalin's majority in the Central Committee. These people, the highest officials below Politburo level, and the thousands of officials associated with and patronised and protected by them – 'their family circles' – were swept away. This was the clan politics to which McCauley refers (page 214). The leadership in every field and every organisation like planning agencies, trade unions, *Komsomol* and education was hit. It set in motion local denunciations too. Stalin's letters to Molotov and Kaganovich are full of attacks on bureaucracy and above all ministries connected with the economy. In a letter to Molotov he coined a barely translatable phrase, typical of his style, when he urged 'inspecting and checking up by punching people in the face'. Under the pressures of the Five-Year Plans, networks of collusion grew up as all tried to survive. The problem was impossibly high targets but Stalin's solution to economic problems was to purge.

- It provided scapegoats for the crises in the economy and the difficulties faced by ordinary people by placing the blame firmly on the Party leadership at republican, regional and district level and on economic managers.
- It swept away the bureaucratic families and clans Stalin distrusted so much.
- The new appointments were younger people, solid proletarian elements who owed their education and appointment to Stalin.

In August 1937 there were show trials of local rural officials unmasked as wreckers. Trials seem to have run into hundreds with Stalin pressing personally for the execution of the convicted. This added to the climate of fear. Officials, professionals and managers in all hierarchies risked being accused of wrecking, sabotage or the abuse of power.

The Great Terror expands: mass operations

Stalin's attack on the political and military elites, the repression of real or imagined oppositionists and the show trials of the old Bolsheviks accounted for a small percentage of the shocking total. The previously secret mass operations account for the bulk of the victims.

NKVD Order 00447

This dreadful document dated 30 July 1937 is at the core in terms of numbers of the Great Terror of 1937–38. It was triggered by the instruction sent by Stalin to Yezhov and the First Secretary of every Republic to instigate a sweep of former *kulaks*, active anti-Soviet elements and criminals. Many former *kulaks* had completed their sentences in special settlements and gulag camps and Stalin feared they would be a threat in time of war. The order divided all these 'anti-Soviet' elements into two categories. People in the first category ('the most active of the above mentioned elements') were to be 'immediately arrested and, after consideration of their case by the *troiki*, shot'. People in the second category were 'subject to arrest and to confinement in camps for a term ranging from eight to ten years'. Quotas of people to be arrested were established for every region and republic. The highest was for Moscow and its region of 35,000 persons of whom 5,000 were to be shot. Estimates of the number of victims of the order vary from 600,000 to 800,000. From the end of August local leaders (like Khrushchev see pages 266–7) made requests to increase the quotas for repression, which were always granted, and the NKVD massively overfulfilled their target. It was social cleansing on a massive scale and its starting point has been seen in forced collectivisation and *de-kulakisation*. While Acton writes that as yet no convincing explanation for this move has been advanced, others argue that it was fear that these 'socially harmful elements, who had all fallen foul of the regime, might provide broadly based support for a "fifth column"'.

Troika (plural, troiki) – a three-man commission set up in all regions and territories to consider the cases of those subjected to 'punitive measures'.

Nicolai Yezhov, 1895–1939

Yezhov had joined the Party in 1917. Stalin brought him into the Central Committee in 1927 and gave him an investigative role before he made him head of the NKVD in September 1936 just after the first show trial. The Great Terror was called the *Yezhovshchina*. Yezhov was only about 1.5m tall and was known as the 'Bloodthirsty Dwarf' or the 'Iron Hedgehog'. One old Communist remarked, 'In the whole of my long life I have never seen a more repellent personality than Yezhov's'. A Soviet account in 1988 in *Komsomolskaya Pravda* talks of Yezhov's 'sadistic inclinations'; that 'women working in the NKVD were frightened of meeting him even in the corridors' and that he lacked 'any trace of conscience or moral principles'.

'National sweeps'

The next largest element, which has only recently been explored by historians, was the mass campaign from August 1937 to uproot and deport national minorities (Poles, Germans, Estonians and others) from the USSR's western borders because of fears that they might form a fifth column and collude with an invader. The 'Polish Operation' resulted in the arrest of around 140,000 people, a staggering 111,000 (approximately 80 per cent) of whom were shot. From February 1938 national operations were the prime function of the NKVD. At least 250,000 were killed and this 'ethnic cleansing' continued during and after the war (see pages 238–9).

How many were killed in the Terror?

We now have NKVD figures for 1937–38: 1.5 million arrested, of whom 1.3 million were sentenced and 681,692 were shot. The most recent analysis suggests under-reporting of executions by some regional NKVDs: figures may have been up to 25 per cent higher and in addition large numbers died in the camps. It looks therefore that based on NKVD data and demographic statistics we reach a figure of between 950,000 and 1.2 million deaths. Not as many as Robert Conquest claimed in the past, but still a truly dreadful assault by Stalin on his own people.

What was Stalin's role in the Terror?

Most historians now identify Stalin as the chief mover, agent and director of the Terror and link it clearly to his personality and his intentions. Even J. Arch Getty, the leading revisionist in this area, now acknowledges in the light of new archival evidence, that Stalin's 'name is all over the horrible documents authorising the terror'.

Repressive policies had been part of Stalin's style from the civil war onwards. The historian Kevin McDermott argues that a major explanation for this, *is Stalin's "class war" mentality, a mindset that accentuated the ever-present spectre of the "enemy from within", be it an expropriated kulak, an anti-social "hooligan", a disgruntled priest, a former White Guardist, or even a disloyal party-state functionary.*

Lenin, as we have seen, was a fierce class warrior and actively encouraged terror to smash his enemies, but Stalin extended and intensified Leninist methods. It is unthinkable that Lenin would have killed his Bolshevik comrades.

Stalin's correspondence shows not just his ruthlessness but also how closely he was involved. He orchestrated both the propaganda campaign in the press and specific points in the prosecution cases in the three major show trials of his old rivals and others. He appointed Yezhov to step up the terror and records show that Yezhov was his most frequent visitor at the Kremlin. Stalin agreed to local requests to increase the quota of victims and he liked to incriminate his top colleagues by making them join him in signing hundreds of death warrants containing thousands of names. He had demanded death penalties at the Shakhty trial, the first big show trial in 1928 (see page 216), and extended this to Party oppositionists after the Ryutin Platform. His willingness to purge whole categories of people was seen when he called for the 'elimination of the *kulaks* as a class'. Only Stalin could start the mass arrests and executions and only he could rein them in as he did in November 1938.

The end of the Terror

Administrative systems were falling apart with key personnel missing and economic growth was severely curtailed. The purges were destabilising Russian society – as Robert Service has put it, 'even the purgers of the purgers of the purgers had been arrested in some places'. Stalin called a halt to the Terror in November 1938 when a joint *Sovnarkom*–Central Committee resolution forbade the carrying out of 'mass operations for arrest and exile'. A week later Yezhov was replaced as head of the NKVD by Beria. There was a review of the arrests and a significant number of people were let out of the gulag. It all served to associate the excesses of the Terror with Yezhov and give the message that now the system had been stabilised. There was no real relaxation in state repression. Yezhov was shot in February 1940.

LOOK AGAIN

Stalin, Malinovsky and the Terror

Simon Sebag Montefiore argues that the *Okhrana* 'were so successful in poisoning revolutionary minds that ... thirty years after the fall of the Tsars, the Bolsheviks were still killing each other in a witch hunt for non-existent traitors'. Stalin's own pre-revolutionary experience is likely to have contributed to his suspicious nature. In 1912 he was betrayed by Roman Malinovsky, a colleague he had trusted but an *Okhrana* agent. Molotov, who in his retirement always justified Stalin's terror said, 'We never forgot the agent-provocateur Malinovsky'.

KEY DATES: THE GREAT TERROR

1932 Ryutin Platform.

1934

January 17th Party Congress.

December Assassination of Kirov.

1936

August First major show trial including Zinoviev and Kamenev.

September Yezhov replaces Yagoda as head of NKVD.

1937

January Second major show trial including Radek and Pyatakov.

June Trial of military leaders.

July NKVD Order 00447.

August National operations begin.

1938

March Third major show trial including Bukharin and Yagoda.

November End of mass arrests/shootings.

December Beria replaces Yezhov as head of NKVD.

Working on interpretation skills: extended reading

Stalin and violence

Martin McCauley considers the shifting use of violence from Leninism to Stalinism.

'Man is violent', the saying goes. Almost all successful revolutions are violent. The Bolsheviks, taking their cue from Marx and the French Revolution, spilled rivers of blood in taking and securing power in Soviet Russia. Lenin, the son of a member of the service nobility, hated his own class and set out to exterminate it. He set up the *Cheka*, the secret police, to liquidate counter-revolutionaries. One did not need to commit a crime to be shot: just belonging to the wrong class was a death sentence. When the Kronstadt sailors rebelled in 1921, they were mown down mercilessly. This marked a new stage in bloodletting. Members of the working class could now be killed. A Red Army was formed to defend the revolution and was used to suppress peasant revolts. In other words, terror was regarded as a natural instrument of rule. Lenin, on his deathbed, concluded that the Terror and the course the revolution had taken had all been a ghastly mistake. But it was too late to change direction. 5

Stalin was heir to this bloodletting tradition. If he could gain control over the secret police, he could use it to build up his own power base. Eventually he did so in the mid-1920s. By 1929 he controlled the Communist Party and the government as well. He did this by building up his own clan or personal group which owed loyalty to him alone. Soviet politics was clan politics. Stalin expected the Soviet Union to be attacked sometime in the future. Hence the Soviet economy was geared for war from the late 1920s onwards. This led to rapid industrialisation and collectivisation of agriculture. The latter was a political, not economic, decision based on the need to feed the burgeoning cities and Red Army. As the peasantry opposed collectivisation, terror had to be deployed to force them into submission. *Kulaks* were often shot and their families sent to the gulag. The rest were herded into collective farms. 15 20 25

The Great Terror is the term applied to the period 1937–38. It consisted of three parts: first, the elimination or deportation of all class enemies; foreigners; and criminals. Second, the murder of leading Bolsheviks who were not members of Stalin's clan; and the liquidation of regional party secretaries and their clans. In the latter case 71 of 73 regional first party secretaries were shot. Third, the top echelons of the military were also killed because Stalin suspected they would not fight to the death in the coming conflict. 30

Stalin murdered millions. Tens of thousands were killed annually during the 1920s but this became millions annually in the 1930s. So was he paranoid or a ruthless Machiavellian wiping out his opponents? New research suggests that the origin of the Terror is to be found in the lobbying of party secretaries for mass executions to rid the country of enemies, priests and the flotsam of society. They raised the spectre of hordes of class enemies in their regions. This was to ensure that their clans remained in place. Stalin responded in 1937 by issuing quotas to be shot or deported. The local bosses lobbied for even greater numbers to be liquidated! When Khrushchev presented a long list to Stalin, he responded: 'There can't be so many!' Khrushchev replied that the actual numbers were even greater. 35 40 45

The Show Trials against leading Bolsheviks such as Bukharin, Zinoviev and Kamenev were political theatre. Confessions were beaten out of them and the message was that no one could be trusted. There were counter-revolutionaries everywhere. Local soviets were encouraged to hold meetings to vent their fury at the betrayal of the revolution by previously venerated Bolshevik grandees. Trotsky escaped the net as he was in exile in Mexico. However Stalin sent one of his agents to put an ice pick through his skull in 1940. The message was clear: Stalin's tentacles extended worldwide.

The Great Terror was turned off like a tap in November 1938. Why? A premonition of a coming war? Declining economic performance? There appear to be no documents so all that is left is guesswork. Fear was not a motivating force during the war of 1941–45. Desire to save the motherland was dominant. Terror reappeared again after 1945 as Stalin sought to cut the victorious military down to size. The elimination of the Leningrad clan and the exiling of thousands of Leningraders in 1948 followed the pattern of the late 1930s. The country was always in a state of emergency under Stalin. Show trials were also held in Eastern Europe after the defection of Yugoslavia from the communist camp in 1948. They chilled the blood and this proved very effective in ensuring loyalty to Moscow. How many did Stalin kill in the Soviet Union and Eastern Europe? About 20 million seems a reasonable estimate.

Another explanation of the use of violence on such a gargantuan scale would be the perceived weakness of the Soviet regime. Miserable living standards led to slack labour discipline. Rapid industrialisation in the 1930s saved the Soviet Union during the war. Would such growth have been possible in a normal environment? Probably not. So one arrives at the unpalatable conclusion that the violence of the 1930s saved the Soviet Union from annihilation during the 1941–45 war.

Martin McCauley is an historian who specialises in the Soviet Union, eastern Europe and China.

50

55

60

65

70

ACTIVITY

Having read the essay, answer the following questions.

Comprehension

1 What does McCauley identify as the purpose of the show trials?
  ● In Russia
  ● In eastern Europe

2 What does McCauley mean by 'clan politics' (line 19)?

Evidence

3 Make a list of the examples of a clan or clans being mentioned in McCauley's essay.

Interpretation

4 Identify the different interpretations of the reasons for the Great Terror mentioned by McCauley.

5 What is McCauley's view of Stalin's role in the Great Terror?

Evaluation

6 Using your own knowledge, write a paragraph explaining how far you agree with McCauley's interpretation of the Great Terror.

4 The political, economic and social condition by 1941

This section begins with the Cultural Revolution, an accompanying element to the Stalin revolution. It came to an end in 1931 and we shall investigate whether it was followed by a 'Great Retreat' looking at society, the arts and literature. We shall examine the state of the Soviet Union by 1941 and assess the nature of Stalin's dictatorship. Finally we shall enter two debates: whether Stalin's Russia was a totalitarian state and how much continuity there was with Lenin's dictatorship.

The Cultural Revolution, 1928–31

What happened to culture and society in these years of turmoil?

Stalin's economic transformation was accompanied by Cultural Revolution, part of his leftist turn. It involved a return to the class struggle of the civil war, with attacks on bourgeois specialists in the industrial workplace and on *kulaks* in the countryside. Its radical programme had an impact on the arts, education and religion. There was an attack on the old intelligentsia and bourgeois cultural values. In schools traditional classroom teaching and discipline were often abandoned in favour of 'socially useful labour' outside school. Non-Marxists working in higher education, in the arts and literature, in schools, in architecture and in town planning were denounced. There was an attempt to find truly 'proletarian' approaches in all these fields.

The emphasis therefore was on educating and promoting workers. Opportunities were offered in technical education to a new cohort of young communists and workers: Khrushchev, Brezhnev and Kosygin, who became key Soviet leaders in the 1950s, 1960s and 1970s, were among the 150,000 workers and communists entering higher education during the First Five-Year Plan. Most trained as engineers and worked briefly before transferring to administrative and political work and becoming the core of the Stalinist elite after the purges and a social basis of support for the regime. They are often referred to as the Brezhnev generation. There was increased social mobility; more than half a million

The Shakhty trial

The Shakhty trial in May 1928 with its attack on 'bourgeois specialists' and engineers has been seen as the start of the Cultural Revolution. The trial of 53 managerial and technical staff accused of counter-revolutionary activities was held at the Shakhty coal mine in the Don Basin. Stalin was closely involved in the proceedings. The staff were forced to confess to sabotage in a show trial staged in Moscow for maximum exposure lasting 41 days. It was attended by 30,000 Soviet inhabitants and filmed for newsreels. Stalin demanded death sentences and five were executed; the rest were given long prison sentences. The aim of this was clear – to show that the non-communist technical elite could not be trusted, to stir up class warfare, intimidate managers and Party officials and prepare the way for rapid industrialisation. The Shakhty trial created shock waves throughout the planning system. Gosplan was purged of pessimists and non-Party members at the end of the 1920s. Statisticians who presented low targets were replaced by those who could paint a more optimistic picture. At the trial, Vyshinsky, who was to be the chief prosecutor in the show trials of the 1930s, was the chief judge.

communist workers moved from manual to white-collar jobs. Sheila Fitzpatrick states that the total number of workers moving into white-collar jobs during the First Five-Year Plan was probably at least 1.5 million.

Creating the New Soviet Person who would embody the morality, values and characteristics that a good Soviet citizen should possess was another of the objectives of the Cultural Revolution. This person would be a willing servant of the state with the right attitudes, far removed from the illiterate, uneducated peasant who exemplified the backwardness which had cursed the USSR in the past. The New Soviet Person was part of new modern industrial society, above all a proletarian with a sense of social responsibility and moral virtue. The *Komsomol* (Young Communists), in particular, enthusiastically took up the challenge and had been itching to move forward towards a more proletarian society with proletarian values. The Cultural Revolution was not simply a manipulation from above; it gained a momentum of its own. The *Komsomol* pushed matters further than the leadership wanted and, having served their purpose, were brought under control. In June 1931, Stalin's speech emphasising the value of the tsarist-educated intelligentsia signalled the end of the Cultural Revolution.

The role of the *Komsomols* in the Cultural Revolution

The *Komsomol* members were aged fourteen to twenty-eight and by 1927 there were 2 million members. It was an exclusive club: many applicants were rejected on grounds of immaturity or insufficiently proletarian social origins. The membership was enthusiastic and leapt at the opportunity to drive the Cultural Revolution. They were to fulfil a number of roles:
- being 'soldiers of production' in the industrial drive; one of the first directors of the Magnitogorsk site described the local *Komsomol* as 'the most reliable and powerful organising force of the construction'
- imposing labour discipline; leading and joining shock brigades
- enforcing collectivisation and collecting state procurements of grain, etc.
- leading the campaign against religion
- keeping an eye on bureaucracy, exposing official abuses, unmasking hidden enemies
- weeding out students whose families had been members of the 'former people', attacking non-Party professors and teachers, with the aim of making the intelligentsia proletarian
- breaking up 'bourgeois' plays by booing, and criticising painters and writers who did not follow the Party line
- reporting on the popular mood.

The attack on religion

Any regime determined to change society fundamentally cannot accept any alternative loyalties. Unsurprisingly the attack on religion was renewed. The suppression of religion in urban areas was relatively straightforward and no churches were allowed in the new cities and towns. However, there was fierce resentment against the *Komsomol* and the League of Militant Godless when they launched a major attack on religion in the villages at the height of the collectivisation drive. It increased peasant opposition even further.

The Cultural Revolution in the arts

Here the Cultural Revolution meant a rejection of the old intelligentsia and was linked with Stalin's attack on the right who were depicted as their protectors. The emphasis was on the proletarian background of artists and some galleries began to label exhibits according to the class origins of the artists. Film-makers including Eisenstein were accused of doing nothing for the workers and peasants. They were told that the principal task of Soviet cinema was to raise the cultural level of the masses. To do this, 'You must either be from the masses yourself or have studied them thoroughly by spending two years living their lives'.

In literature the RAPP (Russian Association of Proletarian Writers) became the dominating force. Socialist construction and class struggle had to be at the heart of literature. Artistic brigades were organised, such as the 'First Writers' Brigade in the Urals', which sang the praises of industrialisation and collectivisation. For some writers it was too much: after witnessing the horrors of collectivisation Boris Pasternak was unable to write at all for a year.

The Great Retreat

There has been a debate about the extent to which the Cultural Revolution was followed by a Great Retreat. There was a return to traditional values in the family, an emphasis on academic standards and discipline at school, and a more conservative style in the arts. However, Stalin was still committed to social transformation and the creation of a New Soviet Person. The Great Retreat naturally opens up some of the contradictions of Stalin's Russia. After the great upheaval of the Cultural Revolution, collectivisation and the First Five-Year Plan, Stalin, the Bolshevik revolutionary, became the enforcer of traditional conservative social and cultural values.

Education and the family

In education, examinations, homework and rote learning were reinstated and later in the 1930s school uniforms reappeared. Similar trends were seen in higher education: old professors recovered their authority and entrance requirements were based on academic criteria. The old intelligentsia returned to favour at the expense of Cultural Revolution activists.

In family life there was criticism of those who took marriage lightly, and children were urged to love and respect their parents, 'even if they are old-fashioned and do not like the *Komsomol*'. The change in emphasis can be seen in the new Family Code of May 1936 in which:

- abortion was outlawed
- divorce was made harder
- child support payments were fixed
- mothers with six children were to receive substantial cash payments.

The birth rate did rise from under 25 per 1,000 in 1935 to almost 31 per 1,000 in 1940. Newspapers reported prosecutions of doctors for performing abortions and some women were imprisoned for having abortions, although the punishment for women in these circumstances was supposed to be public contempt, rather than prosecution.

The return of inequality and privilege

Another contradiction was that Stalin, the egalitarian communist, presided over the emergence of a privileged bureaucratic class and an increase in inequality – indeed this was one of the main reasons why Trotsky accused him of betraying the revolution. The principle of material incentives was firmly established. State officials, military and police officers, other members of the elites, and Stakhanovites were rewarded with better rates of pay, consumer goods and other benefits that only the government could give (private apartments, *dachas*, holidays in sanatoria, access to closed shops, etc.). There were echoes here of the tsarist system where ranks and property were granted to the nobility in exchange for military and civil service. There was an increase in piecework and differentiation in workers' wages – in 1932 the average salary of engineers and technicians stood higher in relation to average workers' than at any time in the Soviet period before and after. In Magnitogorsk there were different menus for different groups of workers. The Party maximum was abolished (it had in theory kept most communists' salaries from rising above the average wages of a skilled worker). It was no longer appropriate for workers to use the familiar form of address to the plant manager.

Russification and the nationalities

There was some reversal too in policies towards the nationalities. Russia was very much the 'first among equals' in the Soviet Union. From 1938 learning Russian became compulsory in Soviet schools and the sole language of the Red Army. Traditional Russian culture came to the fore and heroes of the past like Ivan the Terrible and Peter the Great returned. Russia's mission as a nineteenth-century imperialist power was praised. The emphasis on Russian nationalism was to increase in the Second World War and beyond.

The Great Retreat in the arts: Socialist Realism

A decree of April 1932 abolished all proletarian artistic and literary organisations, like the RAPP, and ordered all artists to come together in a single union. There was a dramatic reversal of the official attitude to the intelligentsia. Avant-garde artists, such as Malevich, were excluded from the mainstream of artistic life. The leading realist artists and sculptors became very successful, guided down the path of Socialist Realism.

The term appears for the first time in 1932. At the newly founded Union of Writers in 1934, Zhdanov proclaimed Socialist Realism to be the 'definitive Soviet artistic method'. 'Soviet literature must be able to show our heroes, must be able to glimpse our tomorrow.' Socialist Realism meant seeing life as it was becoming and ought to be, rather than as it was. Its subjects were men and women, inspired by the ideals of socialism, building the glowing future.

> **LOOK AGAIN**
>
> **Culture: Malevich's response to Socialist Realism**
>
> Fewer paintings could have been further from Socialist Realism than Malevich's *Black Square* (see page 71) of 1915 and when he returned to painting at the end of the 1920s he made some concessions. However, Malevich was Ukrainian and identified with the peasants. Alone among Russian painters he referred to the horrors of forced collectivisation. In his paintings his peasants first lost their faces, then their beards (for the Orthodox Russian, their dignity) and finally their arms (as if in a strait jacket). They are victims, mutilated tailor's dummies. Malevich did produce some conformist paintings like *Portrait of a Record-Setter in Work Productivity*, although the worker looks exhausted rather than exhilarated, but he smuggled in his square in the form of windowless houses, and some works were signed with a little black square. He was arrested, held for two months in 1930 and died of cancer in 1935. Placed on his tomb was a white cube decorated with a black square. His works disappeared from view in Russia until 1988.

◀ *Torso with a Yellow Shirt* by Kazimir Malevich. This picture was painted in about 1932. On the back of it Malevich wrote: 'The composition is made up of the elements of the sensation of emptiness, loneliness and hopelessness of life. 1913, Kuntsevo.' Malevich's meaning is clear but he could not apply a phrase like 'the hopelessness of life' to his own time, hence the pre-revolution date. How is this painting different from the socialist realist images on page 220?

Art

From the beginning of the 1930s, Soviet paintings swarmed with tractors, threshing machines and combine harvesters or else peasants beaming out of scenes with tables groaning with food. It was at the height of the purges that Vera Mukhina's famous *Industrial Worker and Kolkhoz Woman* was sculpted – a massive image of the Soviet people striding into a joyful future. The content of pictures was more tightly controlled. Artists were now given quite detailed guidelines when they were commissioned to produce specific works on a given subject. There were almost no pictures of domestic and family scenes. Golomstock observes, 'To judge from art alone Soviet man passed his entire existence in the factories, on the fields of collective farms, at party meetings and demonstrations, or surrounded by the marble of the Moscow metro!'

▲ *Industrial Worker and Kolkhoz Woman* by Vera Mukhina, 1937. This 78-foot high statue was on top of the Soviet pavilion at the world's fair in Paris in 1937 and was later moved to Moscow where it remains. What is its message?

▲ *Feast on a Collective Farm* by Arkadii Piastov, 1937. Why is this picture a classic example of Socialist Realism?

Music

Socialist Realism extended to music, too. Music was to be joyous and positive. Symphonies should be in a major key. Folk songs and dances and 'songs in praise of the happy life of onward-marching Soviet Man' were the acceptable sounds of music. Shostakovich's new opera *Lady Macbeth of Mtsensk* was attended by Stalin. He did not like it. It was criticised in *Pravda* in an article entitled 'Muddle instead of Music' and banned. Shostakovich never composed another opera.

Literature

By 1932 RAPP was deemed to have served its purpose: it was criticised as being too narrow and was abolished. It was replaced by the Union of Soviet Writers, which included non-proletarian and non-Party writers and had Maxim Gorky (see below), himself a non-Party member, as its first head. The degree of state control, however, was just as strong and Socialist Realism was proclaimed to be the basic principle of literary creation. In this climate, some great writers like Boris Pasternak and the poet Anna Akhmatova practised 'the genre of silence' and gave up serious writing altogether. For Stalin, writers were the 'engineers of human souls', and Socialist Realism was 'the guiding principle': 'Literature should not be a single step away from the practical affairs of socialist construction.' Simple, direct language and cheap mass editions were demanded to make books accessible to a newly literate readership. There was nothing subtle about the titles: *Cement*, *The Driving Axle*, *How the Steel was Tempered*, and *The Great Conveyor Belt*.

KEY DATES: THE CULTURAL REVOLUTION AND THE GREAT RETREAT

1928 Shakhty show trial.
Cultural Revolution begins, coincides with the industrialisation drive.

1931 Stalin makes a speech emphasising the value of the tsarist-educated intelligentsia. Signals end of Cultural Revolution.

1932 RAPP is abolished.

1933 Zhdanov outlines the doctrine of Socialist Realism.

1934 Union of Soviet Writers formed.

1936 Stalin criticises Shostakovich's opera *Lady Macbeth of Mtsensk*.
Family Code

1937–38 Purges hits the arts: around 1,500 writers are killed.

1938 Russian made sole language in the Red Army.

Three writers

Anna Akhmatova (1888–1966) is considered to be one of the greatest poets in Russian history. Much of her work was banned in the 1920s for being bourgeois and individualistic. She was harassed by the regime nearly all the rest of her life and her family and friends were victims of the purges. Pasternak was a friend. She was determined to record the nightmare of Stalinism.

Boris Pasternak (1890–1960) published his first collection of poems, which were influenced by the avant-garde, in 1913. By 1917 he was established as a leading lyrical poet. Although he initially welcomed the Revolution, he soon became disillusioned by the excesses of the Bolsheviks. He was criticised as 'bourgeois' for writing about the individual, love and nature. He would not compromise with Socialist Realism in the 1930s and earned his living as a translator of classics, including Georgian works that Stalin liked. There is a story that Stalin crossed his name off an arrest list in the purges, saying, 'Don't touch this cloud dweller'.

Maxim Gorky (1868–1936) Gorky left Russia in 1921. He had become increasingly disillusioned, writing in 1918, 'It is clear Russia is heading for a new and even more savage autocracy'. Stalin was desperately anxious for Gorky to return so that he could demonstrate that the most celebrated living Russian author was an admirer of the system. Gorky returned permanently in 1931. He was made the first president of the Union of Soviet Writers and flattered on a grand scale – the main street of Moscow was renamed after him, as was his birthplace, Nizhny Novgorod – but he was never to be allowed to leave the Soviet Union again. By the end of his life, he regarded himself as under house arrest. Gorky died rather conveniently for Stalin, two months before the first show trial which he was bound to have criticised openly. At his show trial in 1938, Yagoda, who was head of the NKVD in 1936, confessed to having ordered Gorky's death.

The scale of the Great Retreat challenged

Historians like David Hoffmann and Ewan Mawdsley challenge the idea of a retreat from socialism towards pre-revolutionary ways. They argue that the creation of the new working class and the new intelligentsia meant that:

- There was no retreat on private ownership of land and the means of production, or on hiring labour.
- The rest of the world saw communist Russia as still distinctly anti-capitalist.
- Stalinist culture may have embraced many of the traditions of nineteenth-century Russian realism but the content was 'modern': it was promoted to achieve objectives which the regime chose to stress – economic activity, the socialist utopia, national defence and adulation of the leader. It reflected a changing and advancing rather than a retreating society.

In spite of the Great Retreat in 1941 the new governing elite in practically every field was very differently composed from that of 1928. Further, the attempt to instil socialist values was very different from the social conservatism of tsarism.

The growth of Stalin's power by 1941

What was the basis of Stalin's dictatorship?

It is worth examining the basis of Stalin's dictatorship. There is some overlap between the different factors but it is important to look at his system.

1 A personal dictatorship

Stalin had great determination; as Kotkin has written with reference to Stalin, 'History is made by those who never give up'. In Stalin's system he was supreme. His word was law and no one challenged his authority after 1938. He didn't decide all issues, but he could decide anything he wanted to decide and he was a much more hands-on dictator than Hitler. The whole system was moulded to his will and it was arbitrary and unpredictable.

2 Terror and force

Terror and force were central to his method of rule. The Great Terror had cemented Stalin's control of the Party. The show trials made it clear inside and outside the Party that opposition now could mean death. The NKVD may have been feared by everyone but they operated in dread of Stalin. They were at his beck and call and their network of informants was everywhere. The writer Isaac Babel is alleged to have remarked, 'Today a man only talks freely with his wife – at night with the blankets pulled over his head'. Citizens were encouraged to denounce each other. The numbers in the gulags grew. Internal passports, residence permits and visas were used to control the movement of the population.

3 Ideology

Stalin's commitment to ideology is now seen as important by historians, particularly in the power struggle and the Great Turn. The latter was a socio-economic revolution, a massive upheaval in millions of people's lives in an attempt to build socialism. Stalin was a committed Marxist revolutionary and Stalinism was underpinned by Marxism–Leninism. Kaganovich, described by Molotov as a 200 per cent Stalinist, described the Party as 'an army of revolutionary warriors'. It was Stalin's model of socialism that society would be coerced into following.

4 No political institutions which could offer opposition to Stalin

The purges have been called Stalin's victory over the Party. Old Bolsheviks and anyone who might have offered any resistance to his dominance had been removed. Christopher Read sums up the transformation:

LOOK AGAIN

Political authority

At the end of this chapter, on page 226, we shall be looking at the extent of the continuity between Lenin and Stalin. It is useful to compare the political authority of Stalin, not only with Lenin but also with Khrushchev, and there will be a chance to do this in Chapter 8, pages 279–81.

Source C *The Making and Breaking of the Soviet System* by Christopher Read, (Palgrave), 2001, p 108.

The party had been smashed and turned into a body of social, cultural and economic managers looking to the centre instead of a politically active and faction-ridden organisation of convinced revolutionaries. The party's job was to implement, not to originate policies.

This can be seen in the withering away of the Politburo. On average the Politburo met almost once a week: 43 times in 1932. But in 1938 it met only four times. The frequency of meetings of the Central Committee declined sharply too. The Party Congresses grew further and further apart: 1930, 1934, 1939 and 1952. There was no institutional check on Stalin. Tukhachevsky and the military leadership, and successive heads of the NKVD had been shot, Tomsky had committed suicide; the army, secret police and trade unions were under Stalin's control.

Read Source C. How important were the purges in increasing Stalin's power over the party?

5 **A new governing elite with a vested interest in the system**
The Cultural Revolution and the Great Terror had opened up positions for a new elite of Party and state officials, intellectuals and managers. These people promoted in the 1930s owed nearly everything to Stalin. They have been called a 'ruling class without tenure', under constant threat of demotion, expulsion from the Party, arrest and even death. However they had a vested interest in the continuation of the system. We have seen with the growth of inequality how they were also kept loyal by material rewards and privileges, all the more attractive in this grim decade.

6 **Propaganda and censorship**
Propaganda has been seen as at the heart of the Stalinist system. It was everywhere, pervading all areas of life, including education, youth movements, newspapers, cinema and literature. It was backed up by strict censorship which prevented any competing definition of reality. Its themes were:
● the joys of life in the USSR
● its many achievements
● the horrors of the capitalist West
● the guilt of the enemies of the people and the need to be on guard against wreckers and saboteurs
● the glowing genius of Stalin.
Stalin's statement of 1935, 'Life has become better, life has become merrier', was the refrain which characterised the propaganda of 1936–37. It was important to contrast the good and heroic with the evil traitors. In 1937–38 there were more pictures of young heroes on the front page of *Pravda* than pictures of Stalin. A pioneering flight over the Arctic was greeted with a triumphal parade in Moscow on 15 August 1936, four days before the first show trial started. Similar feats from polar explorers, aviators, sportsmen and others were publicised just before the other show trials. However, in these turbulent years it was possible to persuade at least some of the people that sabotage was going on – nearly everyone had experienced machinery breaking down and there was some popular approval for punishment of the 'wrongdoers'.

7 **The cult of personality**
The cult performed four main functions:
● to underpin Stalin's image as the Lenin of today
● to bind the Party and people to Stalin and by extension to the state
● to identify the achievements of the regime with himself
● to project a father-like persona – ever caring for his children, the Soviet people.

The cult really got going around 1933–34. Praise was heaped on Stalin personally and his link with Lenin and his role in the achievements of the First Five-Year Plan were emphasised. From 1935 onwards, he was portrayed as the *vozhd* (the leader), a genius with great wisdom and even prophetic powers. The disruption and disorientation brought about by the First Five-Year Plan and the Terror meant that this was a bewildering and confusing time. Former heroes were revealed as traitors; wreckers and saboteurs were everywhere. The image of Stalin reassured the people that they had a strong leader to take them through these difficult and momentous times.

Paintings and posters stressed Stalin's humanity and his active participation in the lives of ordinary people. He is seen marching alongside workers or in the fields with the peasants, or inspecting great projects. Stalin's relationship with children was emphasised: no nursery was without a 'Thank you, Stalin, for my happy childhood' painting. As the cult developed, operas and films glorified his role in the revolution or as the chief hero of the civil war. The *History of the All-Union Communist Party* was published in 1938. History was reinterpreted in Stalin's favour and as war loomed, his image became more that of an all-powerful leader.

8 The USSR mobilised economically behind Stalin

The Five-Year Plan became the centrepiece of Soviet life. With collectivisation and the removal of the Nepmen and small businesses, almost everyone was an employee of the state. Every institution had its plan and targets, even corner shops and kiosks. There was a thorough clear-out of economic managers too: 47 per cent of those on government bodies in charge of the economy at the beginning of 1939 (14,585 people) had been appointed in the previous two years. The creation of an urbanised, industrialised and technological society wholly directed by the state was, for Stalin, creating socialism.

9 Russian tradition

This point links with the cult of personality. Stalin himself said, 'the people need a Tsar, someone to revere and in whose name to live and labour'. The historian John Gooding writes about how Stalin put this into practice.

Source D *Socialism in Russia – Lenin and his Legacy, 1890–1991* by J. Gooding, (Palgrave) 2002, p 136.

... the regime under Stalin took the unBolshevik but deeply Russian course of restoring the charismatic element. So successfully did Stalin do this that by the late 1930s much of the population had become abjectly dependent upon him. Lenin's aim of genuine mass support and a real bonding between people and rulers was thus achieved by means that had nothing to do with socialism or the Bolsheviks' original intentions.

Stalin saw himself as being in the same tradition as Peter the Great and Ivan the Terrible, taking the Soviet Union towards socialism and making it into a great industrial power, respected in the world. He praised Peter in 1928, on the eve of the Great Turn, as a moderniser and remarked that Ivan's fault lay in not annihilating enough of his enemies. The appeal to Russian nationalism grew stronger during the Second World War.

Was Stalin's Soviet Union a totalitarian state?

Martin McCauley wonders whether it is possible for a totalitarian state to exist, but thinks that 'Stalin came nearer to creating the model totalitarian state than anyone before or since' (page 259, Extract A). There can be no doubt that Stalin aspired to be a totalitarian ruler but his control was far from perfect. Control over people came nearest to perfection in relation to two groups: those at the very bottom and those at the very top. This is Robert Service's view. Those

Read Source D. Had Stalin become a Red Tsar by the end of the 1930s?

LOOK AGAIN

The role of the individual

When discussing the importance of Lenin, the views of E. H. Carr were mentioned. Stephen Kotkin refers to him too with reference to Stalin.

Source E *Stalin Vol 1 Paradoxes of Power 1878–1928* by Stephen Kotkin, (Allen Lane), 2014, p 739.

If Stalin had died, the likelihood of *forced* wholesale collectivisation – the only kind – would have been near zero, and the likelihood that the Soviet regime would have been transformed into something else or fallen apart would have been high. 'More than almost any other great man in history', wrote the historian E. H. Carr, 'Stalin illustrates the thesis that circumstances make the man, not the man the circumstances'. Utterly, eternally wrong. Stalin made history, rearranging the entire socioeconomic landscape of one sixth of the earth.

in the gulag had no rights and were completely at the mercy of their guards;
Politburo members were just as dependent on Stalin.

The Stalinist state was full of contradictions and inefficiencies. For all his
totalitarian aspirations Stalin was all too aware that he was dependent on the
Party elites and regional subordinates to get his policies put into action. They
in turn had to interact with society as a whole. Outwardly there was obedience
to orders but under the surface there was often considerable disorderliness.
The Soviet people were not just passive agents subject to the instructions,
mobilisation and manipulations of the people at the top. They had developed
a way of coping with the Stalinist state. Sometimes this involved taking
up Communist Party ideas and values, and interpreting them in their own
interests; sometimes it involved resistance and avoidance. Some, of course,
took up the Soviet way of thinking and tried to eradicate anti-Soviet elements
in their life. There was a gulf between the centre and the periphery and in
regions far away from Moscow, McCauley's 'clan politics' (see page 214) could
be a powerful influence. One reason for the purges was to try to gain control of
outlying regions and make them carry out central policies more effectively.

The peasants found all sorts of ways of subverting the running of the *kolkhozy*,
turning matters to their advantage despite the draconian laws designed to
punish them if they stepped out of line. Non-co-operation, lack of effort or
insubordination all contributed to poor performance and this often led to
managers being replaced because they failed to reach targets. Party or local
officials were caught by contradictions in policy, for example, they were supposed
to identify and remove *kulaks* but these were the very people who were most
productive and most useful in fulfilling targets. Even a Politburo commission
referred to the whole *de-kulakisation* programme as a 'dreadful mess'.

As Christopher Read has written, 'In many ways Soviet Russia remained a fluid
and mobile society filtering through the fingers of those trying to control it'.
Police and Party authorities became obsessed by fear of social disorder from
the uncontrolled migration of millions of peasants into towns and cities. Here
socially marginal elements and petty criminals roamed the outskirts. NKVD
Order 00447 of July 1937 was designed to eliminate the 'socially harmful
elements'. What Pasternak called the unprecedented cruelty of Yezhov's time
was in part an attempt to control the 'quicksand society'.

The political, economic and social condition of the Soviet Union by 1941: a summary

Terror was central to Stalin's regime and, although most of its features were
inherited from Lenin, it was very much his regime. After the Great Terror it was
hard to see how he could be removed; the Party had become a submissive tool.
The war and victory were going to make him impregnable.

Stalin's economic policy, especially forced collectivisation, had been hugely
wasteful of lives and resources but there had been economic transformation.
By 1941 the USSR was becoming an industrialised and urbanised society. The
successes were in heavy industry, which was to prove crucial in the war, and
large building projects. The big failures were in agriculture and the production
and, even more, the distribution, of consumer goods.

Most of the population suffered but survived. Millions died. There were big
losers among those who survived too: the peasants and the inhabitants of the
gulags. In society there were some big winners: the Brezhnev generation and
the *nomenklatura*, of which they became part, and which numbered about
600,000 of a population of 150 million at the end of the 1930s. These people

had often been promoted because of the purges. Shock workers and Stakhanovites, too, gained considerably.

How did the people see the regime? The historian John Barber estimated that one-fifth of all workers enthusiastically supported the regime and its politics, while another minority opposed it, although not overtly. This left the great mass of workers, who were neither supporters nor opponents but nonetheless more or less 'accepted' the regime for its social welfare policies. NKVD soundings of popular opinion in the 1930s indicate that the regime was relatively, though not desperately, unpopular in Russian towns but we know just how much it was hated in the villages. If a generalisation is to be made there is much to be said for Service's conclusion:

All in all little political acquiesce would have been obtained if people had not been afraid of the NKVD: silent disgruntlement was the norm.

Interpretations

What was the extent of the continuity between the rule of Lenin and Stalin?
There is an important debate about the extent to which Stalinism was a natural continuation of the ideas, policies and institutions of Lenin's regime. There were bound to be some differences and few would doubt the influence of Stalin's malign and vindictive personality. Furthermore, Lenin's political authority, as the founder of Bolshevism and the man behind the revolution, was unique; the need to be seen as 'the Lenin of today' has been identified by some as a psychological driver for Stalin's revolution.

The position you take on the degree of continuity between Lenin and Stalin largely hinges on the view you take of Lenin. The prevailing orthodoxy during the 1950s and 1960s in the work of Leonard Schapiro and Adam Ulam was that Lenin and a small group of Bolsheviks seized power and imposed their will on an unwilling populace. To stay in power, they applied a regime of terror within the framework of a highly centralised state. Lenin and Stalin were virtually the same: Stalin carried on what Lenin started and Stalinism was simply the fully developed version of Lenin's repressive creed of revolution. This view was attacked in the 1970s and 1980s. Stephen Cohen, for example, while acknowledging that the Bolshevism of 1921–28 contained the 'seeds' of Stalinism, argued that circumstances played their part – the civil war, terrible economic conditions and the failure of world revolution to materialise – and forced Lenin to develop a highly centralised state after the revolution. In this view, Lenin, if he had lived, would have allowed a more enlightened state to develop, would have encouraged more democracy in the Party, would not have supported forced collectivisation or the purges of the 1930s and would have abhorred the cult of personality.

The opening of the archives has challenged the latter view. As Chapter 5 made clear, Lenin was more ruthless than has sometimes been supposed. He actively encouraged terror to smash his enemies and was a fierce class warrior. We can see this in his attitudes towards the peasants and the Church (see pages 163 and 186). He moulded the state out of chaos after the First World War and it was a one-party authoritarian state. This has pushed the prevailing view closer to the continuity side of the argument. For example, in his book on Stalin, Stephen Kotkin thinks continuity is self-evident and wants us to see that much of what is thought of as the worst of Stalin's rule is present or latent in Lenin's. This though, as Source E indicates, does not mean that Stalin did not have a decisive influence.

WORKING TOGETHER

Work in two large groups: one group does Activity one, the other Activity two.

Sub-divide each group into small groups that will compare and discuss their results. At the end, the whole class will come together to discuss the question of continuity between Lenin and Stalin.

Activity one

● Read the introductory paragraphs, the short extract from Kotkin (Source E, page 226) and the historians below writing about the continuity between Lenin and Stalin (Sources F–H).

● The line below represents the two extremes in the debate. Decide where on the line the views of each historian should be placed. Some will be at the ends of the line; others will go part-way along the line, closer to one end than the other. Mark the source letters in the relevant position on your own copy of the line.

| Continuity between Leninism and Stalinism | ——————— | Clear break between Leninism and Stalinism |

Activity two

All groups

In small groups discuss continuity between Lenin and Stalin using the following headings:

● The centralised, bureaucratic, one-party state
● Party democracy and control
● Use of terror, purges and class struggle
● Mass mobilisation including the cult of personality
● Economic policies generally and attitude to the peasants in particular
● Censorship and the arts, nationalities and the Church.

Activity three

Read the three sources below and, treating them as a practice interpretation exercise, in small groups draft an answer to the following A-level practice question:

Using your understanding of the historical context, assess how convincing the arguments in these three extracts are in relation to continuity between Lenin and Stalin.

Source F *Three Whys of the Russian Revolution* by R. Pipes, (Pimlico), 1998, pp 83–84.

I believe that Stalin sincerely regarded himself as a disciple of Lenin, a man destined to carry out his agenda to a successful conclusion. With one exception, the killing of fellow Communists – a crime Lenin did not commit – he faithfully implemented Lenin's domestic and foreign programmes. He prevented the party from being riven by factionalism; he liquidated the 'noxious' intelligentsia; he collectivised agriculture, as Lenin had desired; he subjected the Russian economy to a single plan; he industrialised Russia; he built a powerful Red Army ... and he helped unleash the Second World War, which had been one of Lenin's objectives as well.

Source G 'Lenin: Individual and Politics in the October Revolution' by R. Service, *Modern History Review*, September 1990.

Lenin was not the Devil incarnate. He genuinely adhered to at least some ideals which even non-socialists can see as having been designed to benefit the mass of humanity. Lenin wanted to bring about not a permanent dictatorship, but a dictatorship of the proletariat which would eventually eradicate all distinctions of social and material conditions and would rely decreasingly upon authoritarian methods. Ultimately Lenin wanted to abolish not only the secret police and the army but the whole state as such. If Lenin was therefore to be miraculously brought back to life from under the glass case in his mausoleum, he would be appalled at the use made of his doctrines by Stalin. Lenin was no political saint. Without him Stalin could not have imposed Stalinism. Institutionally and ideologically, Lenin laid the foundations for a Stalin. But the passage from Leninism to the worse horrors of Stalinism was not smooth and inevitable.

Source H *Stalinism* by G. Gill, (Palgrave Macmillan), 1990, pp 62–63.

What is important is that these events were not a natural flow-on of earlier developments; they were sharp breaks resulting from conscious decisions by leading political actors. This means that those arguments that see Stalinism as the inevitable product of the 1917 revolution or of Leninism/Bolshevism are mistaken. Both the revolution and the corpus of theory [body or collection of writings] which the Bolsheviks carried with them had elements which were consistent with the Soviet phenomenon (just as they had elements which were totally inconsistent with it). However, it needed the direct intervention on the part of the political actors in introducing the revolution from above and the terror to realise the Stalinist phenomenon in Soviet society.

Chapter summary

- Stalin used forced collectivisation and *de-kulakisation* to mask an offensive against the peasantry as a whole and to increase state procurements of grain. It involved arrests, shootings and deportation and was met with resistance.

- State procurements increased but grain production fell. The peasants had slaughtered their animals in protest and there was a terrible famine in Ukraine in which 5.7 million died. Vast numbers of peasants fled to the towns.

- The Five-Year Plans were overambitious. They focused on heavy industry and huge schemes were undertaken. Meeting unrealistic targets meant everything so there was falsification, corruption, waste and chaos as well as great effort and achievement. The Second Five-Year Plan was more realistic.

- Millions of untrained peasants flocked to the towns and industrial sites, and the resulting chaos led to severe labour laws to try to control this quicksand society. These laws were often ignored as managers needed workers, especially skilled workers, to meet their targets. Housing was a real problem but workers enjoyed three good years, 1934–36.

- The Great Terror of 1937–38 was a complex phenomenon but Stalin was central to it. As well as hitting the Party and the military, there was the 'social cleansing' of NKVD Order 00447 and national sweeps which accounted for the majority of victims.

- The Terror left the Party cowed and servile; those in office now owed everything to Stalin. The chaos caused by collectivisation and industrialisation, the fear of a fifth column and over-zealous officials had all contributed to the number of victims.

- Stalin's power had increased greatly; there is no example of his being thwarted after the Terror. The cult of personality built him up into an almost god-like figure, an important element in troubled times.

- The Cultural Revolution 1928–31, coincided with the Great Turn and saw a return to class struggle. It was followed by more conservative policies on family values, divorce, abortion, education and the arts. It has been called the Great Retreat. Socialist Realism was the guiding principle for all artists as control tightened.

- Stalin's dictatorship aspired to be totalitarian. He had awesome political control. Everyone was now an employee of the state, but Stalin was incredibly frustrated hence the tough labour legislation. He could kill or arrest anyone but he could not get people to deliver the economic transformation.

- Historians debate whether there is a clear break between Lenin and Stalin or a clear line of continuity between the two. With the opening of the archives, the balance favours continuity.

▼ **Summary diagram: The Stalin revolution**

Year	Collectivisation	Industrialisation	Terror	Other developments
1928	**January** Urals–Siberian Method adopted	First Five-Year Plan begins	Shakhty trial	Cultural Revolution begins
1929	**April** Urals–Siberian method used again **November** 25,000ers sent into the villages, the Great Turn underway **December** Stalin announces the policy of 'liquidating the *kulak*s as a class'	Building of Magnitogorsk begins	**December** Stalin announces the policy of 'liquidating the *kulak*s as a class'	
1930	**January** All-out collectivisation drive begins **March** Stalin's 'Dizzy with success' speech **July** Collectivisation offensive begins again			
1931				End of Cultural Revolution
1932	**August** Law of five ears of corn Famine in principal grain areas	First Five-Year Plan completed Dnieper dam starts to produce electricity Construction starts on Moscow Metro	Ryutin Platform	RAPP abolished
1933	Famine in principal grain areas There were less than half the horses there had been in 1928	Second Five-Year Plan started. Emphasis on cutting waste, realism and raising quality		Zhdanov outlines the doctrine of Socialist Realism
1934	Famine in principal grain areas		**January** 17th Party Congress **December** Assassination of Kirov	Union of Soviet Writers formed
1935	*Kolkhoz* model statute	Stakhanov's record shift Moscow Metro opens		
1936			**August** First major show trial including Zinoviev and Kamenev **September** Yezhov replaces Yagoda as head of NKVD	Family Code Stalin Constitution
1937	Good harvest	Second Five-Year Plan finished	**January** Second major show trial **June** Trial of military leaders **July** NKVD Order 00447 **August** National operations begin	
1938		Third Five-Year Plan begun	**March** Third major show trial **November** End of mass arrests **December** Beria replaces Yezhov as head of NKVD	
1939				18th Party Congress
1940			Assassination of Trotsky in Mexico	
1941		Third Five-Year Plan cut short by war		**June** German invasion of USSR

Working on essay technique

Think back to the advice from Chapters 1–4 and the summary provided at the end of Chapter 5 (see page 190).

Consider this A-level practice question:

'Stalin's Revolution had a more profound effect on Russian society than the Bolshevik Revolution.' Assess the validity of this view.

This is a complex question, which can be approached in different ways. One way, for example, would be to answer the following questions:

1 Is the word 'revolution' helpful or an exaggeration when applied to what happened in Stalin's Russia between 1928 and 1941?
2 What were the different components? What were its aims? (Do not forget the Cultural Revolution.)
3 Class and class war were important in both 'revolutions':
   ● Did a new class take power?
   ● Did a new socio-economic system come into being?
   ● How 'profound' was the change?

This essay title encompasses a wide area, both in breadth and chronologically over nearly a quarter of a century. The essay must be analytical not descriptive. Essays with a strong social history element can become very general so precise examples and evidence are important to clinch marks.

In particular, this essay allows for complexity because social change is not always as easy to measure as political change.

● The Bolshevik Revolution has been seen as central to the history of the twentieth century let alone the history of Russia, but was its effect on society as great as Stalin's?
● It is crucial to assess the impact of the two revolutions on the peasantry which made up the majority of the population.

This complexity can be reflected in your introduction and/or your conclusion.

The subject also gives you the opportunity to show awareness of different historians not always agreeing. In this question this might be because of:

● different views of the role of the individual, particularly Stalin
● different views on how far Lenin was crucial in shaping the Soviet Union.

The Great Patriotic War and High Stalinism, 1941–53

This chapter covers the Second World War and its aftermath, ending in the death of Stalin. The Great Patriotic War, as it was known in Russia, was the supreme test of the regime and Stalin emerged as the triumphant Generalissimo. At the end of the chapter there is an assessment of his legacy. The chapter deals with a number of areas:

- The political, economic and social impact of the war
- The effect on Stalin, the government and 'the people'
- High Stalinism (the name given to the years that followed the war): the revival of terror; the destruction of the 'supposed' opposition and the cult of personality
- The power vacuum on Stalin's death

This chapter covers the central key questions relating to how Stalin asserted his political authority and governed Russia, how the economy developed and how this generated significant social and cultural change. It also explores the role played by groups and individuals in these changes.

The main focus in this chapter will be on the question:

To what extent did the war and its aftermath affect Stalin's position and the way the Soviet Union was governed?

Within this question you will look at the effects of this terrible war on the Russian people and the economy, and the impact on Stalin and the way he ruled.

CHAPTER OVERVIEW

When the Germans invaded the USSR in June 1941 they swept away the Russian forces which were ill prepared for such a devastating attack. The horrors inflicted by the German war of annihilation contributed to an upsurge of patriotism and a civilian war effort which rivalled that of the Red Army. The Soviet Union made a massive contribution to the defeat of Hitler. Stalin's role in all this is central and controversial, but he emerged from the war immeasurably strengthened. Russia had suffered unimaginable loss of life and material damage and Soviet citizens hoped for a more relaxed and humane society. They were to be disappointed. Instead they got High Stalinism. The command economy was very firmly in place with all the emphasis on defence and heavy industry. There was increased repression and the numbers in the gulags swelled. Russian nationalism was combined with a drive for ideological and cultural purity to bring the intelligentsia into line. Stalin remained supreme leader of the one-party state and manipulated the main contenders for the leadership to make sure he stayed in power and achieved the outcomes he wanted.

NOTE-MAKING

Draw two spider diagrams to make notes on the case for and the case against Stalin as war leader. This will be developed in the Working Together activity at the end of this section (page 242) examining why the Soviet Union won the Great Patriotic War.

Nazi–Soviet Pact

On 23 August 1939 the USSR had signed a ten-year non-aggression pact with Germany. The Russians had been worried about the prospect of facing Nazi Germany alone and were not convinced they would be able to form a solid defensive alliance with Britain and France. In return for its neutrality (which freed Germany from a possible war on two fronts) the Soviet Union, in secret clauses, gained the right to occupy eastern Poland, the Baltic States and part of Rumania in the event of war. Soviet security was always Stalin's main concern and this pact was the only way to be sure of avoiding a war in the west, especially since the USSR was not prepared for a major conflict. It also cleared the way for Hitler to invade Poland.

1 The Great Patriotic War

This section will look first at the war and Stalin's role as war leader. Then it will consider the political, economic and social impact of the war.

Stalin's contribution as war leader

Were the Soviet people able to withstand the German invasion *because* of Stalin or *in spite* of him?

On 22 June 1941, the most powerful German army ever assembled in Europe launched Operation Barbarossa and took the Russians completely by surprise.

The war from disaster to triumph

The German attack could not have come at a worse time. The Red Army and Air Force were in transition, changing their organisation, leadership, troop dispositions and defensive plans. Following the Nazi–Soviet Pact, old defensive lines had been abandoned as the USSR occupied its new territories. But the new lines were not ready. The result was disaster.

Disaster

Most of the Soviet aircraft were destroyed on the ground on the first day. There was chaos as the Germans swept eastwards. By December, the Red Army had lost 6 million, either killed in action or taken prisoner. Some of the most industrially developed and fertile land in the USSR, containing two-fifths of the total population, was overrun. The Germans sent three separate armies into Russia. One moved against Leningrad (see Figure 1, page 233) and in September 1941 laid siege to the city, a siege destined to last 900 days. Hitler wanted to preserve his northern troops for the battle for Moscow, a more important objective as the capital and the hub of the entire railway system. The German army advanced swiftly on Moscow and by the middle of October there was panic in the city. Documents, artistic treasures and Lenin's body had been evacuated, and government offices were relocated to Kuibyshev (see Figure 1). Stalin, however, refused to leave the city and a Soviet counter-offensive near Moscow pushed the Germans back 150–200 kilometres in December, the Germans' first major setback. This meant that they could not knock out the USSR in one campaign before the winter set in. The German forces were poorly prepared for the cold, but Hitler ordered them to stand firm.

In the spring and summer of 1942 the Germans continued to advance in the south. The raw new Soviet formations were no match for the *Wehrmacht* (the German army) and the fall of Rostov, with little resistance, marked the Russian army's lowest point. Stalin issued Order 227: 'Not a step back' (see page 235). Hitler was so confident that he divided his forces in the south between conquering the Caucasus, to gain economic resources especially oil, and taking Stalingrad, which was important because of its strategic position.

Triumph

Both sides came to see the struggle for Stalingrad as decisive. From September to November a few thousand courageous Soviet men and women held up the Germans in spite of 75 per cent falling as casualties. This gave time for General Zhukov to set up an encircling counter-offensive. The German 6th army were trapped in a huge pocket. This was reduced gradually and the German surrender came on 31 January 1943. The resilience and dogged resistance of the ordinary Russian soldier delivered victory, although Hitler made strategic mistakes. By this

Key
- - - - 1941 frontier
——— 1939 frontier
——— Furthest German advance 1941/42
▨ Operation Bagration
☐ Operation Babarossa launched with over 3.5 million soldiers in 3 separate armies

Arctic convoys bring aid from Britain and USA

Arctic circle

Pacific route from US west coast to Siberian ports, then aid brought overland

Government offices evacuated here

US aid coming up from the Persian Gulf

Petsamo
Murmansk
White Sea
Archangel
Gulf of Bothnia
FINLAND
L Onega
L Onega
Ural Mountains
SWEDEN
Helsinki
Vyborg
Kazan
ESTONIA
Leningrad
Kronstadt
LATVIA
Riga
1941
Magnitogorsk
LITHUANIA
Moscow
Kaliningrad (Konigsberg)
Minsk
Smolensk
Kuibyshev (Samara)
Warsaw
POLAND
R. Volga
Orel
Kursk
Voronezh
Kiev
Kharkov
R. Dnieper
R. Don
BESSARABIA
1942
Stalingrad
Odessa
Rostov
Gurev
ROMANIA
Astrkhan
CRIMEA
Kerch
Sevastopol
Yalta
Caspian Sea
BULGARIA
Black Sea
Caucasus Mountains
Batum
Tblisi
Baku
Constantinople
Dardanelles
TURKEY

0   300
km

N

▲ **Figure 1** The Eastern Front, June 1941–September 1944.

KEY DATES: TIMELINE OF THE GREAT PATRIOTIC WAR

PHASE ONE: June–December 1941, German advance

22 June Operation Barbarossa: Germany invades the USSR.

19 September Fall of Kiev with huge losses including 655,000 prisoners.

26 September Siege of Leningrad begins. In the starvation winter of 1941 about 800,000 die.

16 October Height of the 'Moscow panic'.

6 December Soviet counter-offensive begins near Moscow.

PHASE TWO: January 1942–January 1943, Stalemate until the decisive victory

1942

8 May German offensive resumes in the south.

28 July Stalin's Order 227: 'Not a step back' issued after the fall of Rostov. The low point of the war.

13 September Launch of German offensive to take Stalingrad.

31 January 1943 Paulus surrenders at Stalingrad. In the whole operation 800,000 German troops are lost.

PHASE THREE: February 1943–August 1944, Germans chased out of Soviet territory

12–15 July 1943 Battle of Kursk.

1944

27 January Leningrad blockade lifted; end of the 900 days siege.

22 June–29 August Operation Bagration.

PHASE FOUR: August 1944–May 1945, The drive to Berlin

2 May 1945 Berlin surrenders.

time a third-generation Red Army was emerging; the first, the pre-war army, had been destroyed in 1941 and the summer battles of 1942 had largely destroyed the second, the hastily produced replacements. Lessons were learned from these disasters; at all levels, command and control were becoming more effective and techniques were developed for conducting mechanised warfare on a grand scale.

In July 1943, at Kursk, in the largest and fiercest set-piece battle in history, involving a huge number of tanks, the Germans were repulsed and the last chance of German victory in the east was snuffed out. In 1944, Operation Bagration (named by Stalin after a Georgian commander in the Napoleonic wars) was launched. Andrew Roberts described it 'as decisive as anything in the history of warfare, and [it] utterly dwarfed the contemporaneous Operation Overlord campaign'. In 68 days the 1.2 million strong German Army Group Centre was destroyed and the Germans were driven from Soviet territory, suffering four times the number of casualties that were being sustained in the west.

Having borne the brunt of the war, Stalin and the Soviet commanders were determined to reach Berlin first. They did so but the Russians suffered 300,000 casualties, including 78,000 dead, and lost 2,000 tanks in three weeks.

The Red Army

The Red Army's ability to mobilise a seemingly endless array of armies and divisions was crucial. As early as August 1941 the German General Heinrici, in letters to his wife, expressed his amazement at the Russians' 'astonishing strength to resist' and their 'astounding toughness'. 'Their units are all half-destroyed, but they just fill them with new people and they attack again.' David Glantz, the leading western historian of the Red Army, has analysed why Red Army soldiers fought so hard.

Although naked fear of the enemy and their own officers and commissars, pervasive and constant propaganda and political agitation, threats of severe disciplinary measures and outright intimidation motivated Red Army soldiers to fight, they also fought and endured because they were patriotic.

This patriotism had a number of different sources – traditional Russian nationalism, some sort of loyalty to the Soviet state or sheer hatred of the German invaders – but it provided a powerful bond and motivating force within the Red Army.

Different views of Stalin as war leader

There is a great deal of debate among historians about Stalin's contribution to victory, not that he and his propagandists had any doubt.

Stalin as a poor wartime leader

Stalin's critics have argued that the Germans got as far as Stalingrad because of his policies. What is the evidence for this view?

- The vast purge of high-ranking Red Army officers, beginning with Marshal Tukhachevsky, the leading military thinker in the Soviet Union, which Stalin launched in 1937 had a traumatic effect. Morale was shattered, initiative and independence of action were stifled. Foreign governments – potential allies as well as the Germans – assumed that the Red Army was a broken shell. This was reinforced by its poor performance in the war against Finland in 1940.

- Determined not to alienate Hitler, Stalin met requirements for deliveries of raw materials under the Nazi–Soviet Pact in full, and ignored 80 warnings in eight months and reports of German troop build-up. As a result the country was unprepared for the German attack with disastrous consequences. By

December, the Red Army had lost 6 million men, either killed in action or taken prisoner. Six days after the German invasion Stalin admitted to a small group of his closest associates: 'Lenin left us a great legacy, but we, his heirs, have messed it up' (the Russian used by Stalin was much stronger and coarser). It was as close as he came to accepting responsibility.

- Nor did Stalin's errors stop there. Stalin's inflexible, stand-fast mentality in 1941–42 prevented tactical withdrawals which would have avoided the catastrophic losses sustained when Kiev was encircled. The over-ambitious counter-offensives of the first half of 1942 led to further big losses of men and territory.
- There is no evidence to suggest that Stalin suffered even the slightest remorse about sending millions to their deaths in battle.

Stalin as a strong wartime leader

The historian John Barber in his essay on 'The Image of Stalin in Soviet Propaganda' points out that from the start of the war Stalin was identified with the motherland (*rodina*).

Perhaps what Stalin represented for ordinary people more than anything else during the war was hope – hope of victory, hope of survival, hope against hope that those in power cared about the millions they ruled.

- Stalin was a rallying force and showed the leadership qualities expected in desperate times. He did not leave Moscow when government offices were evacuated in 1941 (see page 232). Stalin has not been thought of as a great orator and only addressed the Soviet people nine times during the war, but his speeches in 1941 can be compared to those of Churchill in 1940–41 in their effect. Both leaders inspired their armed forces and civilians to fight on. 'Comrades! Citizens! Brothers and Sisters! Fighters of our Army and Fleet! I address you, my friends!' So began Stalin's speech to the Russian people on 3 July 1941, his first since the invasion. He had never addressed the Russian people in such terms before. 'All those years we had suffered from a lack of friendship and the words "my friends" moved us to tears', Konstantin Simonov recalled. Stalin spoke of a 'patriotic war of all the people'.
- As well as speeches there were the ruthless orders. These included Order 270, issued after the surrender of 100,000 encircled men at Uman in northwest Ukraine, and Order 227, issued after Rostov had fallen with barely a fight and when army discipline had begun to break down. Orders 270 and 227 were distributed to all fighting units in the army but not made public. In 227 instructions were issued concerning the establishment of detachments behind front-line forces that would shoot deserters, panickers and unauthorised retreaters. At the Battle of Stalingrad an estimated 13,500 Soviet troops were shot in this way in the space of a few weeks.

Source A Order 270: 16 August 1941.

Commanders and commissars who leave the front or surrender will be considered deserters and their families liable to arrest. The families of Red Army men surrendering to captivity will be deprived of state entitlements and assistance.

Source B Order 227: 28 July 1942.

Not a step back! This must now be our chief slogan. It is necessary to defend to the last drop of blood every position, every metre of Soviet territory, to cling on to every shred of Soviet earth and defend it to the utmost.

(These orders are quoted in full in *Victory at Stalingrad* by G. Roberts, (Longman), 2002, pp 197–210.)

Stalin's behaviour at the beginning of the war

It is a myth that Stalin was pole-axed by the German invasion and was incapable of action. He worked very hard for a week. He then retreated, exhausted and depressed to his *dacha* (holiday home). A day and a half later Molotov and the others who were to form the State Defence Committee went out to see Stalin, to propose the setting up of such a committee and to ask him to lead it. This revived Stalin, he agreed and returned to the Kremlin the next day, July 1.

WORKING TOGETHER

Work together in a small group.
1 Read Sources A and B. With which of the following statements do you agree most?
  a The sources demonstrate Stalin's determination to stop further retreats.
  b Stalin was psychologically preparing the troops to make a final stand at Stalingrad and elsewhere and bolstering those inclined towards heroism.
  c It was the only way of maintaining order under fire among hurriedly and partially trained troops.
  d These orders show Stalin's ruthlessness and disregard for human life.
2 Discuss your decisions and come to a group view.

Source C An ordinary soldier's account of his reaction to Order 227. (Cited in *The Soviet Home Front: A Social and Economic History of the USSR in World War II* by J. Barber and M. Harrison, (Longman), 1991, p 72.)

All my life I will remember what Stalin's order meant ... Not the letter, but the spirit and content of the order definitely made possible the moral, psychological and spiritual break-through in the hearts and minds of all to whom it was read ... The chief thing was that they had the courage to tell people the whole and bitter truth about the abyss to whose edge we had slid.

> Does this reaction (Source C) show that order 227 worked?

The setbacks of 1942 had a sobering effect on Stalin. After this, historian Geoffrey Roberts writes, 'He listened more to the advice of his High Command, the advice got better and he got better at taking it'. Stalin came to rely increasingly on three very able men: Vasilevsky, appointed Chief of the General Staff; Antonov (his deputy) and Zhukov, the hero of Leningrad and Moscow, whom he appointed as his Deputy Supreme Commander of the Soviet Armed Forces. Zhukov and Vasilevsky planned the encircling counter-offensive which was the key to Russian success at Stalingrad.

Victory helped transform relations between Stalin and his generals. In 1943 Stalin accepted Zhukov's rejection of his plans for a 'pre-emptive offensive' in favour of the latter's defence in depth at Kursk. Operation Bagration was carefully prepared by Zhukov and Vasilevsky. In his ability to learn and to trust his High Command in many operational matters, Stalin comes out well in comparison with Hitler who listened to his senior generals less and less.

The political impact of the war

How was the Soviet Union governed during the war?

Although Stalin did not respond publicly to the outbreak of war until 3 July, he was very active in meetings and organisational work. He headed up the powerful State Committee for Defence (GKO) although the initiative for its establishment seems to have come from Molotov.

The GKO and *Stavka*

The GKO was given power over all existing Party and state bodies. Its brief was to supervise the military, political and economic life of the country. Its orders were binding on all institutions and all individuals. Formally at least, centralised control was brought to its peak.

But the GKO could not organise everything in the chaos and confusion of the early months of the war. Local authorities and managers were given wider discretion and autonomy in things like organising rationing or securing labour. The war effort depended a great deal on the people and their voluntary commitment. The war economy played a vital role in Soviet recovery and victory and the GKO deserves credit for this. According to some calculations the USSR was able to devote 50 per cent of its GDP to the war whereas other countries were held at a maximum of about 20 per cent.

The other key body was the Military Supreme Command or *Stavka*. It was responsible for all land, sea and air operations. Its composition was shaped by Stalin, who insisted that leading politicians should belong to it. He did not become Commander-in-Chief until 10 July and Chairman of *Stavka* until 8 August, probably not wanting to be too associated in the public mind with the catastrophe at the front. However, his supremacy was not in doubt. *Stavka* and the GKO were kept separate and it was Stalin who brought them together.

Stalin	Chair
Molotov	Deputy Chair
	Tanks
Malenkov	Aircraft
Beria	Security Police Chief
	Armaments and munitions
Voroshilov	Armed forces representative
Voznesensky	Head of the State Planning Apparatus
Mikoyan	Food supplies
Kaganovich	Food supplies

▲ **Figure 2** State Defence Committee (GKO) membership and responsibilities.

Historian Graeme Gill states that they were the main institutional foci of central political life, but neither body was in a position to impose any significant restraints on Stalin, and in practice, much decision-making occurred informally in Stalin's office. The security apparatus was still active and remained under the control of one of Stalin's closest supporters, Beria (see page 246).

The role of propaganda

The aim of any wartime government is to maintain morale, to persuade the people to make the effort and sacrifice required to achieve victory, and to build confidence in the government's – and especially its leader's – ability to defeat the enemy. There was little chance that the Soviet government would neglect the last point. The early disasters did not lead to any suspension of the Stalin cult.

Source D *Pravda,* 20 July 1941.

At a menacing time, when over our motherland hung grave danger, all the thoughts of the Soviet people turned to the glorious Bolshevik Party, to the father and friend of all toilers – comrade Stalin. 'For the Motherland, for Stalin!' With this fighting cry, soldiers, commanders and political workers of the Red Army accomplished marvels of bravery, destroying fascists ... Comrade Stalin's name is a symbol of great victories, a symbol of the unity of the Soviet people.

Stalin took control of the military command on 20 July. This image of Stalin, in Source D, supplied to the public – of a leader who was brave, all-seeing, steadfast – was a necessary one. It may have been distant from reality, but the contrast between his intervention in the war effort and that of the Tsar, who too had gambled all his power on his ability to save the country from catastrophe, is illuminating. Stalin played an important part; Nicholas remained superfluous to the war effort.

Ilya Ehrenburg, an important writer and wartime propagandist, wrote that the soldiers fervently believed in him: 'On the walls I saw his photograph cut out of newspapers.' The Moscow crisis in 1941 produced Stalin's finest hour. He stayed put and addressed the eve of the anniversary of the Revolution rally in November and the parade in the Red Square. On a film recorded in the Kremlin, Stalin made a passionate appeal to the troops (Source E).

Source E Stalin, 7 November 1941, to the armed forces in Red Square (authors' explanations in brackets).

The whole world is looking to you as the force capable of destroying the plundering hordes of the German invaders. The enslaved peoples of Europe ... look to you as their liberators. A great liberation mission has fallen to your lot. Be worthy of this mission! The war you are waging is a war of liberation, a just war. In this war, may you draw inspiration from the valiant example of our great ancestors – Alexander Nevsky, [who defeated German knights in 1242], Dimitry Donskoy [who beat the Tartars in 1380], Kuzma Minin and Dimitry Pozharsky [who drove the Poles out of Moscow to end the Time of Troubles in 1612], Alexander Suvorov and Mikhail Kutuzov [heroic generals during the Napoleonic wars]. May the victorious banner of Lenin be your lodestar.

Another reason for this style of appeal was that the German front line was now on Russian soil and the composition of the Red Army was now overwhelmingly Russian. The apex of Stalin's career came with the victory parade in the Red Square when the captured German standards were laid out in front of Stalin. He was being recognised, as Robert Service puts it, as 'the father of the peoples of the USSR'.

Read Sources D and E.
1 What is Stalin appealing to in Source E?
2 Are there any implications here about how he sees himself?
3 Compare Sources D and E. How do they differ in the way the appeal is made?

▲ Khmelko's *The Triumph of the Victorious Motherland*, 1949. This scene in Red Square with Stalin in triumph on high and the captured German standards laid out in front of Lenin's tomb looks like a victory celebration at the height of the Roman Empire.

The cult of the personality was at its height. Relentlessly, the message was that victory had been achieved through popular support for, and unity behind, the leadership of Stalin. He was the all-powerful leader – the *Vozhd* – and accorded the title 'Generalissimo'. He appeared to be impregnable.

Repression

While propaganda always played its part in the Stalinist government so did repression. The measures below were all in line with the way Stalin dealt with huge categories of Soviet citizens in the Terror before the war and his determination to take pre-emptive steps to eliminate any 'fifth column' activity.

Nationalities

The Soviet takeover of any territory involved mass arrest, deportations and executions.

- In territory taken as a result of the Nazi–Soviet Pact, 1939–40, 1.5 million people were uprooted and deported to the gulag and exile villages in Kazakhstan and Siberia because they were considered potentially hostile. In April 1940 more than 20,000 officers, police and members of the Polish elite were shot and buried in mass pits at Katyn and elsewhere. Stalin was determined to hold on to the territory and eliminated any potential opposition in advance.
- The Volga Germans were deported in 1941 – although there were no grounds for regarding them as Nazi spies. Settled for centuries and thoroughly Russified in their allegiance, the 600,000 people even included the families of men serving in the Red Army.
- As the Red Army pushed westwards, in 1943 and 1944, exaggerated reports that some members of the population had collaborated with the Germans infuriated Stalin and were used as a pretext to punish entire nations. Only the Chechen–Ligush began an anti-Soviet rebellion as the Germans approached.

- Two million members of ethnic minorities – Crimean Tartars, Chechens and other Transcaucasian populations – were deported to the Soviet interior (see Figure 3). This was ethnic cleansing – Stalin wanted to be rid of troublesome, deeply anti-Soviet people. Their homelands were wiped off the map.
- When Estonia, Latvia and Lithuania were re-annexed in 1944 drastic measures were taken to entrench Soviet power; their elites were arrested and either shot or sent to the camps.

A quarter of the deported nationalities died in transit or in the first five years in special settlements.

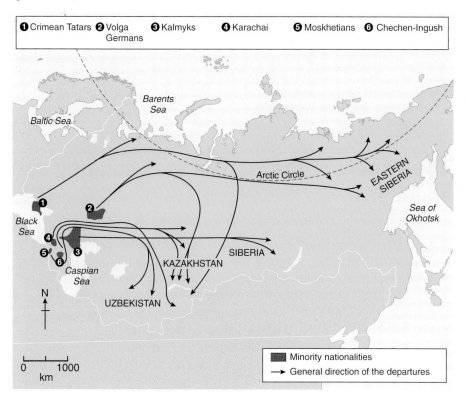

① Crimean Tatars **② Volga Germans** **③ Kalmyks** **④ Karachai** **⑤ Moskhetians** **⑥ Chechen-Ingush**

▲ **Figure 3** Stalin's deportation of nationalities, 1941–45.

The role of the NKVD

The NKVD increased in size during the war. Among its responsibilities were counteracting panic, and monitoring Party and *Komsomol* efforts to maintain morale. A special department was set up to lead the struggle against spies and traitors in the Red Army, and had the authority to execute deserters on the spot. Orders 270 and 227 were distributed to all fighting units in the army. They highlight the dilemma of the Red Army soldier: he was a deserter if he surrendered and a traitor if he retreated. Any officer caught infringing the order would be shot on the spot or sent to the punishment companies. Any soldiers guilty of cowardice or wavering faced the same fate. The punishment companies were overseen by the NKVD and more than 430,000 men served in them, their numbers swollen by gulag inmates and criminals. They were sent through minefields and on other almost suicidal missions. Blocking detachments were placed behind unsteady units 'to shoot on the spot panic-mongers and cowards'. Blocking detachments were abolished in October 1942, but the NKVD continued to carry out the same role.

The return of those stranded in German-occupied Europe

Over 5 million Soviet citizens had been stranded in German-occupied Europe. Some were prisoners of war (POWs), some had been taken to forced labour camps in Germany and Austria, a few had collaborated with the Germans and retreated with them, and up to 150,000 Soviet soldiers had either fought or been forced to fight the Red Army. While the last category might have expected to be treated as traitors, in practice the rest did not fare much better. Stalin believed in Order 270, which had declared POWs deserters. About half were condemned to the gulag, even though many had already suffered horribly in German concentration camps. He wanted all Soviet citizens who had been 'contaminated' by contact with the outside world returned, and Churchill and Roosevelt agreed to do so at Yalta. Some were returned from as far away as the west coast of America; some, like the 32,000 Cossacks, men, women and children, were forced onto trucks and returned to the USSR. Some of the latter committed suicide rather than suffer deportation.

Around 3 million men and women were sentenced to terms in the camps. Only about one-fifth of those who came back were allowed to return home and they were mainly old men, women and children. All those released had the words 'socially dangerous' put on their records and bore the stigma of collaboration or cowardice for years.

The impact of the war on the economy and society

How was the Soviet economy and society mobilised for war?

Stalin, unlike Hitler, realised that victory in 'a war of annihilation' required complete and ruthless mobilisation of the country's entire resources. The Russians set up an evacuation committee two days after the German attack to relocate the machines, equipment and manpower vital for the war effort to the east.

The mobilisation of industry

Up to 1.5 million railway wagon-loads of plant and machinery and hundreds of thousands of workers – between 8 and 10 per cent of the USSR's productive capacity – were moved. In addition, 3,500 new factories were created, most of them dedicated to armaments, and manufacturing industry was converted to war production. In 1942–43 Soviet factories were producing aircraft, tanks, guns and shells faster than German factories, in spite of the terrible losses wrought by Operation Barbarossa, which by November 1941 had halved industrial production.

With an acute shortage of skilled labour, mass production methods and simplification were essential. The famous T-34 tank underwent just one major wartime modification and the hours required to produce it were more than halved. Herculean though these efforts were – and the T-34 and KV tanks eventually outperformed as well as outnumbered the best German Panzer tanks – the Stalinist economic system did not suddenly become a watchword for quality. Some aircraft had a reputation as death traps and in a BBC documentary a veteran of the battle of Kursk said his team of sappers (soldiers with engineering duties) preferred to locate, dig up and re-lay German mines on the battlefield rather than handle Soviet-made mines, which they feared would explode at any moment.

The people and agriculture

This economic achievement depended on the Russian people who had already suffered so much under Stalin. They were extraordinarily resilient. They were severely overworked, under-nourished, very cold and poorly housed. Living standards fell on average by two-fifths. In one relocated tank factory, 8,000 female workers lived in holes in the ground. Life was incredibly hard for the peasants. The countryside had been so stripped of men, horses and machinery that by the end of the war, four out of five collective farmers were women, and carts and ploughs were increasingly pulled by human beings. The state procurement of food from collective farms was probably even more ruthless than during the Civil War. Malnutrition was general and pervasive. Under the rationing system only combat soldiers and manual workers in the most difficult and hazardous occupations were guaranteed sufficient food to maintain health.

The contribution of Lend-Lease

The concentration on war production had become so great that the economic historian Mark Harrison argues that without Allied help in the form of Lend-Lease, predominantly from the USA, the authorities would have been compelled to withdraw major resources from fighting in 1943 to avoid economic collapse. Imported trucks, jeeps and railway resources gave the Red Army vital mobility without which, Khrushchev admitted 'our losses would have been colossal' and that, 'without spam we wouldn't have been able to feed our army'. In 1943 and 1944 Lend-Lease made up 10 per cent of the GDP of the USSR. Even Stalin acknowledged to his close associates that it was 'the coalition of the USSR, Great Britain and the USA against the German-fascist imperialists' that made the defeat of Hitler inevitable.

The resilience of the Russian people

The war was won by the Soviet people and their patriotism, resilience and endurance. The historian Edward Acton has argued that the horrors of Nazi occupation provoked a massive determination to resist and that without it, 'the Soviet regime's capacity to galvanise and mobilise would have come to naught'. The war brought people and regime together.

Source F The American Hedrick Smith recalls a Jewish scientist shocking his friends in conversation in the early 1970s with his description of the war. From *The Russians* by H. Smith, (Sphere), 1976, p 369.

... the best time of our lives ... because at that time we all felt closer to our government than at any other time in our lives. It was not their country then, but our country. It was not they who wanted this or that to be done, but we who wanted to do it. It was not their war, but our war. It was our country we were defending, our war effort.

The massive contribution of women

Soviet women made a huge contribution to the war effort. One million women served in the armed forces. Women were particularly good snipers. The Central Women's School for Sniper Training turned out 1,061 snipers and 407 instructors; its 'graduates' killed 12,000 German soldiers. The feared 'night witches' (night bombers) flew 23,672 sorties in flimsy biplanes and 23 received the Hero of the Soviet Union award. But the women most valued by fellow male soldiers were the medics and signallers. At the front, 100 per cent of the nurses and over 40 per cent of doctors and field surgeons were women, and they, and radio operators, suffered heavy casualties.

However, the perseverance and determination of women in occupied zones and behind the front lines in the factories and the farms contributed just as much, if not more, to their country's survival and ultimate triumph. In industry, women had made up 41 per cent of the workforce before the war and between 51 and 53 per cent during the years 1942–45. In light industry 80–90 per cent of the workforce were women but even in heavy industry the proportion grew sharply.

Lend-Lease – this was US aid in the first place to Britain in March 1941, but extended later to the USSR. It began before the USA had joined the war and enabled the recipients to obtain war supplies for which they could not pay, under the fiction that these supplies would be returned or paid for after the war.

Spam – tinned meat product made mainly from ham.

1 What does Source F tell us about Soviet citizens' attitude to the government during:
   a the war
   b peacetime?
2 How useful is this source to a historian studying the attitudes of the Soviet people?

WORKING TOGETHER

Where do you place Stalin's contribution in the hierarchy of reasons why the Soviet Union won the Great Patriotic War?

One of the key questions is on the role of individuals and groups so there is value in working out the importance of Stalin's contribution. Go through this section and, in small groups, list the reasons why the Soviets won, looking at factors like: the war economy, propaganda, Hitler's mistakes, etc., and decide where you place Stalin's contribution in the hierarchy of causes.

Present your hierarchy of causes and the reasons behind your judgements in order of priority. Compare the priority order given by each group. Can you reach a consensus opinion as a class about your rank ordering of reasons?

In the countryside the proportion of female labour employed in agriculture rose from 40 per cent in 1940 to over 80 per cent by the end of the war, all working predominantly by hand. Urban sieges, rural deprivation, mass evacuation and mass deportation all played havoc with the well-being of millions of families and so hit women very hard.

The price of the war

Soviet losses during the war totalled about 27 million. The victims of Leningrad alone exceeded the total of British and American wartime deaths. Comparing the losses with other countries (including both soldiers and civilians), for every Briton or American who died, the Japanese lost 7 people, the Germans 20 and the Soviets 85. Approximately 70 per cent of Soviet deaths were of men and the majority of these were from the younger generation, the most fit and capable. In terms of overall population in 1946, women outnumbered men by 96.2 million to 74.4 million. There was a rupturing of life at every level. Of a population of about 200 million when the Germans invaded, some 80 million were subjected to German occupation, 25 million were evacuated from their homes to the east, and 29 million served in the armed forces.

Economic devastation was equally great. Areas which had been under German occupation, and this included the best agricultural land in the Soviet Union, were in a desperate state. These areas had suffered three times: the retreating Red Army used scorched-earth tactics, then during the occupation the Germans took everything they could, and finally systematically destroyed everything they could as they in turn withdrew. Towns and villages in the western part of the Soviet Union had been virtually obliterated. Hospitals, radio stations, schools and libraries were targeted where entire townships had not been burnt down. The transport network in the occupied areas needed to be totally rebuilt. The countryside had been stripped of men, horses and machinery.

Dead of which were: • military personnel • civilians	27 million 8.7 million (over 30% of those called up) c18 million
Homeless	25 million
Officially recognised 'invalids' with physical and mental handicaps	2 million
Towns destroyed	1,700
Villages destroyed	70,000
Industrial enterprises destroyed	31,000
Kilometres of railway track destroyed	65,000
Agricultural output lost	40%

▲ Figure 4 Devastation caused by the war.

Little or no official attention was paid to citizens' emotional or psychological recovery, or to burgeoning peacetime problems of alcoholism, adultery and domestic violence – unsurprising afflictions for a country where families had been separated for years, where returning veterans had witnessed near-unimaginable atrocity, and where women far outnumbered men. A general feeling of exhaustion afflicted the population as a whole, and after the first flush of enthusiasm with victory this exhaustion would have its impact on post-war reconstruction.

2 High Stalinism

This section will examine the main features of Stalin's grim post-war rule, often referred to as High Stalinism. It will conclude by looking at the legacy of problems he left his successors.

Post-war reconstruction

On what was reconstruction focused?

There were widespread hopes that the war had transformed relations between the regime and the people, that rigid labour legislation would be relaxed, rationing abolished and the expansion of private plots and peasant markets would continue. Writers, as we shall see on page 249, were optimistic too. In February 1946 in his Bolshoi Theatre speech, his first major speech of the post-war era (see box), Stalin dashed these hopes. He announced that in view of the imperialist danger that continued to threaten Russia, the country would have to endure at least three or four more Five-Year plans.

Industry

The centrally planned economy was back in full force. The plan was a repeat of early versions: 85 per cent of investment was devoted to heavy industry and capital goods (which included armaments). This skewed balance was at its most extreme during Stalin's last years. There was a rhetorical commitment, as in the past, to devoting 'special attention' to improving living standards and the output of consumer goods, but it remained just that – rhetoric. The target was to exceed pre-war industrial levels. To achieve this, the population was mobilised – everybody was to be involved in reconstruction work. In Leningrad, for instance, workers had to contribute 30 hours a month on top of their eight-hour working day; citizens not working had to put in 60 hours and students 10 hours. Other cities probably had similar schemes. Extra labour was provided by prisoners of war (around 2 million) and the inmates of labour camps (around 2.5 million), the population of which had grown very rapidly after the war. These individuals were exploited mercilessly as slave labour on the most unpleasant work, particularly working in the inhospitable north cutting timber, and mining for gold and, importantly, uranium for the new atom bomb, where few survived.

The results were remarkable and undoubtedly owed much to the efforts of the Russian people who were prepared to endure privation, food rationing and long hours for low pay. There was huge growth in heavy industry. Factories and steel works were rebuilt and mines re-opened at astonishing rates. The great Dnieper dam was back in operation and generating electricity by 1947. The same old problems resurfaced – bottlenecks and shortages of raw materials and component parts – but the end product was impressive. Production of coal and steel passed pre-war figures and, according to Alec Nove, industrial production in general passed pre-1940 levels, although the statistics emanating from Soviet sources have to be treated with caution.

NOTE-MAKING

To assess how successful Stalin's policies were in reconstructing Russia after the war, copy and complete this table:

	Industry	Agriculture
Loss/ damage: problems after war		
Main policies		
Positive results		
Negative results		

Stalin's Bolshoi Theatre speech, February 1946

Stalin wrote the speech himself, editing it several times. He prescribed audience reactions: 'furious applause', 'applause and standing ovation', and so on after key paragraphs. Stalin's aim was to convert the USSR into a superpower in a decade. Increasing the level of industry threefold in comparison with the pre-war level was the *only* condition that would ensure Soviet security 'against any eventualities'. In reality there had never been a chance that Stalin would relax the pressure on the Soviet people. To the historian Robert Service, 'his assumptions about policy had hardened like stalactites'. Stalin thought any relaxation would imperil his personal supremacy.

Because of the Cold War and the expansion of Russian control of eastern Europe there was a concentration on producing armaments. In 1949 the first Soviet atomic bomb was tested, showing the USSR catching up on technical achievement, in part due to captured German scientists. With the focus on heavy industry and, apart from reparations from Germany and eastern Europe, no outside investment, resources came at the expense of consumer industries. Goods like clothes, shoes and furniture were in short supply. The details of the Fifth Five-Year Plan, which was meant to have begun in 1951, were not announced until 1952. The plan followed similar lines to the Fourth and had not progressed very far before Stalin's death in 1953.

Agriculture

Agriculture was in a terrible state at the end of the war:

- Whole rural districts had been wrecked. Nearly 100,000 collective farms or *kolkhozy* had stopped functioning. Many peasants had returned to farming the land privately.
- There was a shortage of agricultural labour since most of the Red Army had been peasants and there had been a heavy loss of life. In addition, many peasant soldiers had learned skills in the army and went into industry rather than return to the villages.
- A large amount of arable land had not been cultivated for some time and had to be brought back into operation.
- There was a shortage of tractors, horses, fuel and seeds.
- Livestock had been slaughtered and stock levels were low.

Pressure on the peasantry was fierce. There was a major drive in 1946 to tighten discipline on the *kolkhozy* and reverse wartime trends, particularly the expansion of private plots. It was a dreadful year. Grain procurements to feed the people in the cities and towns took up to 70 per cent of a much reduced yield, leaving barely enough to feed the peasants and keep the animals alive, and there was a drought too. In 1946–47, 1 to 1.5 million people died from starvation and related diseases, with Ukraine hit particularly hard.

During 1947 delivery targets and taxes on income arising from private plots were raised to a new height. Extra taxes were invented, for example, on each fruit tree in a peasant household's garden. Retail outlets and consumer goods were in short supply in the countryside and currency reform was designed to devalue drastically the savings the more entrepreneurial peasants had made during the war. Derisory prices were paid to the peasants for their produce and for the work days served on the *kolkhoz*. By the end of 1952 the number of *kolkhozy* was reduced by nearly two-thirds to 94,800 to increase production but an even more important reason was to increase Party control.

Since top priority had been given to industry, the villages were not allowed electricity from state power stations and not provided with building materials to rebuild their houses. With few incentives, motivation was at rock bottom and agricultural production suffered as a result. In the Fifth Five-Year Plan there were announcements of large projected increases in grain and meat production but nothing was done to facilitate this. The peasants were perpetually squeezed under Stalin, and his successors sought to ease the pressure on them; but in 1954, a full year after Stalin's death, the average pay of a *kolkhoznik* remained lower than one-sixth of the earnings of the average factory worker.

1940	95.6
1945	47.3
1946	39.6
1947	65.9
1949	70.2
1952	92.2

▲ **Figure 5** Grain production (million tons). This shows how bad a year 1946 was, but also how grain production was back up to pre-war figures by 1952.

Stalin's personalised and centralised control

How far did Stalin's style of government and policies change between 1945 and 1953?

Stalin's personal dominance was unchallenged, but in his eyes the military leaders constituted a threat. Zhukov (formerly Deputy Supreme Commander of the Soviet Armed Forces) was banished to an obscure command in the Urals. His name disappeared from the press and Stalin was celebrated as the architect of victory. As the personality cult scaled fresh heights a film was made on the fall of Berlin. It showed no staff, no generals, just Stalin attended by his loyal secretary directing the great battle. Between 1946 and 1948 senior commanders were executed on trumped up treason charges.

Cult of personality

Success in the Second World War fed the cult, which reached its height at the end of the 1940s. Paintings show Stalin in god-like solitude or with Lenin, sometimes even appearing to tell Lenin what to do. Stalin had lost his role as a disciple; now he was an equal or even the master. The omnipresent images of Stalin said to the Soviet people: 'Stalin is everywhere present and watching over you; he understands your hopes and has your best interests at heart.' The celebrations of his 70th birthday were extremely elaborate with galas and greetings almost every day from 21 December 1949 (actually his 71st birthday) to August 1951. A giant portrait of Stalin was suspended over Moscow and lit up at night by a battery of searchlights.

NOTE-MAKING

Using pages 245–253 make notes to show how Stalin tried to reassert his authority over:
- the military
- the Politburo
- the Party
- the security forces
- society in general.

▲ *Glory to Great Stalin*, 1950 by J.P. Kugach. A picture which captures the adoration of Stalin and the celebration of his 70th birthday.

The Politburo and the Party

The Soviet Union was a one-party state, but the Party was not significant in initiating policies and actions. Just as before the war, its main role was co-ordinating economic activity. It supervised the agencies of government and chose and scrutinised their personnel. Stalin fostered tensions between Party and government to stop either undermining his personal power. The Politburo rarely met and a Party Congress was not convened until 1952. Stalin preferred to rule more informally, sending out his orders by telegram or convening small groups to discuss key policy issues. Stalin told them no more than they needed to know and only when they needed to know it; Martin McCauley reminds us of Khrushchev's recollection, 'if you were not told you presumed you were not supposed to know. Under no circumstances did you ask'.

The Politburo in 1945 was almost the same as it had been in 1939, with key roles for Molotov, Kaganovich, Khrushchev, Zhdanov, Malenkov and Mikoyan. Stalin controlled decision-making although he left the details to others. He used the same pre-war technique of playing people off against each other and encouraging rivalry between contenders for the leadership and Party influence. He did this to protect himself, but also to make sure that the members of the Politburo worked hard to produce the outcomes he wanted. It was bear-pit politics. Malenkov and Zhdanov were fierce rivals. Zhdanov was regarded as Stalin's favourite. He had led the defence of Leningrad when it had been besieged by the Germans during the war. He fronted the campaign against Western bourgeois influences. Beria, Stalin's secret police chief and enforcer, appears to have sided with Malenkov. In the post-war period the MVD (formerly the NKVD) exercised enormous and terrifying power.

During the Second World War the Party had grown from 4 to 6 million members, with a large number under the age of 45. Many of the new intake had little knowledge of the outside world, old revolutionary history or traditions, and tended to follow directives without question. Stalin may have been even more in control than ever but he still remained suspicious. Dmitry Shepilov, editor of *Pravda* and a protégé of Zhdanov, wrote in his memoirs, 'For Stalin in the final period of his life, the exposure of "terrorists", "poisoners", and "conspirators" became as vital as vodka to a hardened alcoholic'.

In 1952, at the 19th Party Congress, Stalin took little direct part and contented himself with sitting and watching the proceedings. But at a meeting of the Central Committee after the conference he made his last speech, in which he attacked Molotov and Mikoyan. A Presidium of 25 replaced the Politburo of 11. This could be interpreted as an indication that Stalin was contemplating another purge at the top level in the Party and bringing up his reserves in preparation. A new generation of leadership was introduced. Beria felt he was at risk and Molotov was certain he was in danger. Nobody felt safe.

Stalin's increasing paranoia: the destruction of 'supposed' opposition

With age, Stalin became even more suspicious of those around him. Although he had made them, he seems to have felt they were potentially dangerous to his political authority. To keep them in their place, purges and terror remained as much a part of Stalin's system of government as before the war, though it was used more selectively. In Extract C on page 259 Chris Ward examines this idea.

The Leningrad affair, 1949

Zhdanov, a heavy drinker, died suddenly in 1948 of a heart attack, although rumours spread that he had been killed by his doctors. There followed a savage purge of the Leningrad Party organisation engineered by Beria and Malenkov, probably to gain influence and deal with potential rivals. Voznesensky and Kuznetsov were widely tipped as Stalin's successors. Voznesensky, a member of the Politburo, was responsible for planning the Soviet war economy which was so successful after 1942, and by 1948 was second only to Stalin in the Council of Ministers. Stalin did not like war heroes and it is also likely that he thought that the Leningraders were becoming a little too confident and independent. Leading Leningrad Party and government officials, including Voznesensky and Kuznetsov, were arrested, forced to confess, 'tried' in secret and executed. Before the secret 'trial', Politburo members had signed the accuseds' death warrants. The Leningrad affair, as it is often called, made everybody at the top feel insecure. This feeling was heightened by the arrest of Molotov's wife.

Mingrelians – an ethnic division of the Georgian nation. It was no coincidence that Beria was a Mingrelian. The arrests have been interpreted as a dress rehearsal for an accusation against Beria. Interrogators were told not to forget about 'the big Mingrelian'. Stalin, always anxious to break up client networks, was sending a clear signal here.

1 How accurate is it to compare Stalin to a gangster boss? Use Source G and your own knowledge to answer the question.

2 Can you give examples of Stalin behaving towards those around him in such a way as described in Source G?

Continued purges

In Georgia in 1951 Stalin ordered the arrest of a number of **Mingrelian** Party and governmental officials who were accused of being involved in a Mingrelian nationalist plot. Beria was a Mingrelian and the victims were all close to him. Beria was compelled to carry out the purge. This added to his sense of insecurity.

Stalin's health deteriorated after the war. He appeared much less frequently in public and retreated to his private residences. His meals were tasted for poison and his routes of travel regularly changed. Some contemporaries and historians claim that he was becoming more detached from reality and paranoid, seeing enemies everywhere. His 'hysterical' antisemitism seeing Jewish people as American fifth columnists, seems to bear this out. It is unclear whether Stalin planned a mass deportation of Soviet Jews to Siberia and Central Asia.

Party leaders feared his mood swings. Bulganin, a member of the Politburo, returning from Stalin's *dacha* confessed to Khrushchev, 'It happened that a man goes to Stalin on his invitation as a friend. And when he sits with Stalin he does not know where he will be sent next, home or to gaol'. Voznesensky was arrested after a cordial supper with Stalin. The parties at Stalin's *dacha* involved heavy drinking and making his guests seem ridiculous by, for example, forcing them to sing and dance. He used these events to test them, get information out of them and inspire jealousy. Some historians have suggested that he was displaying the same personality traits that he had had throughout his life. However, most agree that he had become more morose, vindictive and unpredictable, and that his health was deteriorating.

The historian T. H. Rigby writes that Stalin employed the 'rational political calculation of the "mafia boss"'.

Source G T. H. Rigby quoted in *The Rise and fall of Communism* by Archie Brown, (Bodley Head), 2009, p 200.

Stalin wanted to be obeyed, he wanted to be secure against conspiracy, and he believed that instilling fear was essential to winning and maintaining that obedience and security. Having achieved this by egregious [shocking, remarkable] display of his power to kill, he thenceforth avoided the obvious mistake of so abusing his power as to drive his entourage to collective desperation. The prudent despot or gangster boss will seek to ensure that those around him, those on whom he depends for information and for executing his will, are men whose unqualified subservience and sensitivity to his needs has been tested out over many years, and whose strengths and weaknesses he knows inside out.

The Doctors' plot

Stalin grew more suspicious towards the end of his life, even turning against his daughter, personal bodyguards and loyal retainers. The Doctors' plot is further evidence of his increasingly suspicious nature. In January 1953, *Pravda* announced that thirteen doctors, several of whom were Jewish, who treated top Party officials, were accused of conspiring with the USA and killing Zhdanov and other high-ranking officials. It was said that they planned to wipe out the top Soviet leadership. Confessions were obtained under torture, during which two of the doctors died. But before they could be executed, Stalin died. Subsequently, the plot was declared a fabrication and MVD officers were executed.

Recent work by the Russian historians Yoram Gorlizki and Oleg Khlevniuk has argued that to focus exclusively on paranoia as an explanation for Stalin's behaviour is an oversimplification. While they accept that his behaviour displayed 'high drama' and obsession, and a compulsion to preserve his dictatorial rule, they also insist that his machinations were ideologically driven. Stalin wanted to consolidate a 'separate, respected, and powerful socialist system'. To do this he promoted younger specialists who would staff expert commissions and committees to which Stalin delegated responsibility. He could and did intervene decisively though, if he felt he needed to do so.

Tightening of control on culture

Stalin intervened directly in the ideological, cultural and scientific life of the Soviet Union. It shows that he was intellectually alert and as keen as ever to keep the Soviet intelligentsia in line, especially after the relaxation during the war. Stalin treated questions of theory very seriously and his writings were saturated with Marxist–Leninist language. For Stalin no subject was beyond politics. Furthermore, in the atmosphere of rising Cold War tensions, this strong element of patriotism bordered on xenophobia. Soviet culture was to be seen as superior to liberal, Western culture. This drive for ideological and cultural purity was known as the *Zhdanovshchina*, but Zhdanov was only Stalin's mouthpiece.

This anti-Westernism can be seen in Stalin's policy towards the arts. The State Museum of Modern Western Art was closed down. Hundreds of writers, condemned for kow-towing to the West, were expelled from the Writers' Union, which meant their works could not be published. This included Anna Akhmatova, the famous poet, whom Zhdanov denounced as 'half-nun, half-whore'. Akhmatova's status as a symbol of Leningrad's spirit of endurance during the war did not help her. Stalin was always suspicious of Leningrad and, as Orlando Figes points out, wanted to underline the subordination of the Leningrad intelligentsia to the Moscow-based regime.

Theatres were attacked for staging too many Western plays. Soviet composers were attacked because their work was supposedly corrupted by bourgeois values and did not reflect Soviet virtues and musical traditions. Shostakovich's symphonies could no longer be performed; musicians needed a special pass to listen to Stravinsky. Painters and film directors had to follow the regime's dictats. Stalin himself intervened in Eisenstein's film about Ivan the Terrible, urging the director to show 'that it was necessary to be ruthless'. Stalin added that Ivan's great strength as a leader was that he 'championed the national point

Writers and musicians and the war

For Boris Pasternak the war seemed 'an omen of deliverance, a purifying storm'. The struggle for survival did bring a sense of community; writers were involved and valued. Pasternak himself worked for a time as a fire watcher, if necessary dislodging incendiary bombs from the roof of the twelve-storey apartment in which he lived. Some of his work was published again and he started writing again. The poet Anna Akhmatova silenced in the 1930s (see page 221) was treated with honour for the first time and allowed to publish and, as we have seen (page 242), to broadcast. The composer Shostakovich publicly attacked in 1936 (see page 219) was now celebrated. Shostakovich had worked by candlelight in Leningrad on his seventh symphony which he dedicated to the city. On 9 July 1942, it was performed by a motley collection of musicians in the bombed Great Hall of the Leningrad Philharmonia and piped through loudspeakers into the streets of the still besieged city. It had an overwhelming emotional effect. The novelist Vasily Grossman was a war correspondent reporting vividly from the front line in the battle of Stalingrad. Pasternak hoped that, 'So many sacrifices cannot result in nothing. A presage of freedom was in the air'. He was to be bitterly disappointed.

of view … he safeguarded the country against penetration of foreign influences'. Stalin took a particular interest in linguistics. In his *Marxism and the Problems of Linguistics*, written in 1950, he dismissed class theories of linguistics and the development of the Russian language, tracing its origins to places in the RSFSR (Russian Republic) rather than Kiev in Ukraine where academics had previously located it. Anti-Westernism had a broader purpose too. If the Soviet population was to be galvanised into great efforts to rebuild the economy, all unfavourable comparisons with the outside world had to stop. The briefest contact with a foreign person could bring an arrest.

Science

In this atmosphere absurd claims were made for the achievements of Soviet science. Ethnic Russians seemed to have invented almost everything from the steam engine to the aeroplane. Scientists, though, had to adhere to the guidelines set down by the state if they wanted to survive. Crude interventions were made into science. Stalin worked closely with Lysenko in 1948 to impose the latter's view of genetics on the USSR. Lysenko was a biologist and agronomist who claimed heritable changes in plants could be achieved by changes in the environment, rather than by genetic factors alone. So, wheat subjected to refrigeration would produce seeds that could be sown in colder climates. This was just not the case and held back progress in Soviet biology and led to the arrest of renowned geneticists who did not agree with his theory. Chemistry also suffered. Physics was different. Although Einstein's theory of relativity was dismissed as it did not fit with Marxism–Leninism, Russian scientists could not ignore it or quantum mechanics if they wished to develop the atom bomb. Working under the pressure of the Stalinist regime, whose leadership knew no science, Soviet scientists developed the bomb in only a little more time than the American team had taken and helped only slightly by espionage.

Russian nationalism

Stalin mounted a drive to emphasise the superiority of ethnic Russians over other nationalities, despite the fact that he was a Georgian. He had been called a 'Great Russian chauvinist', by Lenin. Stalin was a genuine believer in Russian nationalism, but this policy sat well with ethnic Russians and helped to secure their support for the regime. It was also an effective way of controlling other nationalities. In the non-Russian republics the top jobs, particularly Party secretaries and police chiefs, went to Russians. Soviet central planning, collective farms and other institutions and practices were imposed on the newly annexed countries. In the Baltic states there were deportations to Siberia and Kazakstan. In all, 142,000 people from these new Soviet Republics were deported in 1945–49, notably peasants resisting the imposition of collectivisation in 1948. Russian migrants took over their homes. Deportations took place in western Ukraine and tens of thousands of Russian migrants and migrants from Russian-speaking eastern Ukraine moved in. The cultures of nationalities like the Latvians and Lithuanians were denigrated. The Moldavian language had Russian words added and it had to be written in Cyrillic letters. Ukrainian was decreasingly taught to Ukrainian-speaking children in the Russian Republic. Stalin was as keen on Russification as the tsars (see page 46).

Antisemitism

Stalin reserved particular venom for Jewish people, initiating a vicious campaign of antisemitism. In 1948, the Jewish anti-Fascist committee, which had helped send thousands of Russian Jews to fight the Nazis, was closed down, its leaders arrested and thirteen of them executed. Jewish Soviet politicians disappeared and others in important positions lost their jobs.

Jewish writers and artists were arrested. Jewish schools and synagogues closed. Textbooks did not refer to the fact that Karl Marx was Jewish. Stalin talked about setting up a special area for Jewish people in the Soviet Union in eastern Siberia. There were a series of trials in which Zionist conspiracies were exposed, culminating in the Doctors' plot just before Stalin died. The reason for the campaign lay in Jewish connections to the West. Many Jewish people had relatives in the USA, other Western countries and the new state of Israel, which was heavily backed by the Americans. Stalin called them 'rootless cosmopolitans' who owed more loyalty to Jewish internationalism and Israel than to the Soviet state. They were suspected of being agents for the West and particularly America, Stalin's main enemy in the Cold War.

The nature of High Stalinism

Some historians call the period after the war up until Stalin's death High Stalinism because it contained all the features that define Stalinism:

- personalised and centralised control
- the command economy focused on heavy industry
- stifling bureaucracy
- the cult of personality
- the use of terror and an enhanced role for the secret police
- effective propaganda and cultural uniformity.

But was there anything new about this? The American historian Robert Daniels has written that it is extraordinary that the Stalinist system came through the ordeal of war so little changed. Disappointed Soviet citizens were likely to think that the post-war world was a lot more of the same.

Three main factors contributed to this:

- Stalin had been given an entirely new legitimacy by victory and his system had been triumphant in the ultimate test of total war. He was immovably entrenched. As he grew older he was unlikely to change things.
- There was the urgent task of reconstruction after the terrible devastation of the war.
- The 'imperialist danger,' the Cold War, had been used to justify the emphasis on heavy industry in the Five-Year Plan and to stamp out potential discontent and dissent at home. It contributed to the strident anti-Westernism and nationalism associated with Zhdanov. Interestingly while Zhdanov opened up a war against bourgeois influences in the USSR, a few years later the anti-communist frenzy of McCarthyism gripped the USA.

There may not have been terror on the scale of 1937–38, but the population of the gulags certainly swelled. However, just as before the war, the level of totalitarian control implied by High Stalinism should not be exaggerated. There was even unrest in the gulags with strikes and an armed uprising in the winter of 1949–50. In 1952, according to the gulags' own statistics, 32 per cent of prisoners had not fulfilled their work norms. Robert Service argues there is something wrong when a totalitarian state cannot keep order in detention centres. There was a gulf between the centre and the periphery: cliques in regions far away from Moscow ran their own fiefdoms for their own interests while paying lip service to the central government. Outwardly there was obedience to orders, but under the surface there was often considerable disorderliness.

Zionist – one who supports Zionism, the idea of creating a Jewish national homeland in Palestine.

McCarthyism – a term coined in 1950 to describe the anti-communist witch-hunts of Senator Joseph McCarthy. McCarthy claimed that there were large numbers of communists and Soviet spies and sympathisers inside the United States, notably in the federal government, Hollywood, education and trade unions.

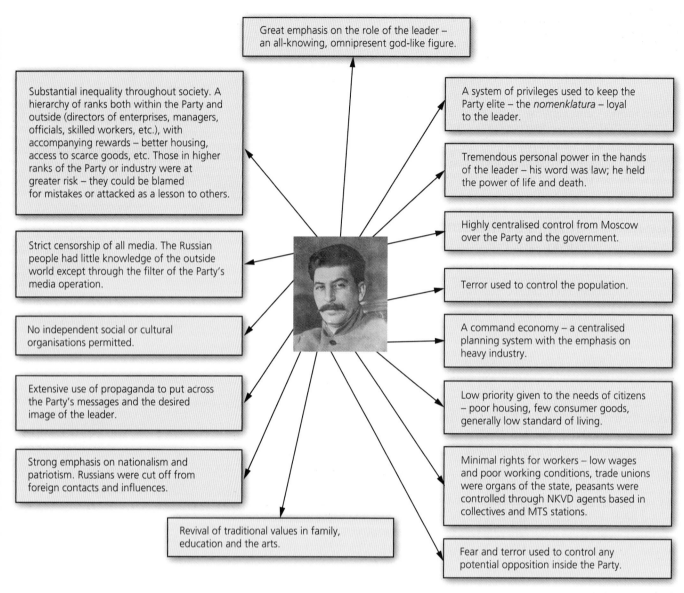

Great emphasis on the role of the leader – an all-knowing, omnipresent god-like figure.

Substantial inequality throughout society. A hierarchy of ranks both within the Party and outside (directors of enterprises, managers, officials, skilled workers, etc.), with accompanying rewards – better housing, access to scarce goods, etc. Those in higher ranks of the Party or industry were at greater risk – they could be blamed for mistakes or attacked as a lesson to others.

A system of privileges used to keep the Party elite – the *nomenklatura* – loyal to the leader.

Tremendous personal power in the hands of the leader – his word was law; he held the power of life and death.

Strict censorship of all media. The Russian people had little knowledge of the outside world except through the filter of the Party's media operation.

Highly centralised control from Moscow over the Party and the government.

Terror used to control the population.

No independent social or cultural organisations permitted.

A command economy – a centralised planning system with the emphasis on heavy industry.

Extensive use of propaganda to put across the Party's messages and the desired image of the leader.

Low priority given to the needs of citizens – poor housing, few consumer goods, generally low standard of living.

Strong emphasis on nationalism and patriotism. Russians were cut off from foreign contacts and influences.

Minimal rights for workers – low wages and poor working conditions, trade unions were organs of the state, peasants were controlled through NKVD agents based in collectives and MTS stations.

Revival of traditional values in family, education and the arts.

Fear and terror used to control any potential opposition inside the Party.

▲ **Figure 6** The features of High Stalinism.

Stalin's death

Stalin died in a way that fitted the atmosphere of fear he had created. After a night of heavy drinking he did not come out of his rooms the following day, 1 March. Eventually his security guards found him conscious but unable to speak. He had had a stroke. When Politburo members arrived they were equally reluctant to act; possibly the leaders hoped he would die before he could act against them. There was a long delay before the doctors were called. Paradoxically, Stalin's personal physician was in prison because of the Doctors' plot (page 248). Stalin died four days later. At his deathbed, the Politburo leaders were mostly sad, although relieved. But Beria appeared 'radiant' and 'regenerated' as he saw an opportunity to become the power broker in the USSR.

There was a genuine outpouring of grief when Stalin's death was announced to the wider Russian public. People were shocked and wept openly in the streets. He had been their saviour in the Second World War and represented stability and order in a changing and confusing world. Crowds flocked into Moscow to see his body and pay their respects, some being crushed to death in an eerie echo of Nicholas II's coronation disaster at Khodynka Field. Of course, not everybody felt sorry, particularly in the gulag and the countryside, but it was better not to express negative views about Stalin. Stalin's body was embalmed and laid in the mausoleum next to Lenin's.

LOOK AGAIN

To what extent did Stalin become a Red tsar?

At the beginning of this book we looked at the tsarist regime in pre-revolutionary Russia. The Stalinist state that emerged in the 1930s and 1940s had many features in common with its tsarist predecessor. The system of personalised control in Stalin's dictatorship was very similar to that of the tsar: the notion of a god-like leader, the chief benefactor and protector of the people, who knows the right course to follow and can lead the Russian people out of darkness into the light; the culture of blaming officials for problems instead of the person at the top. The icons of tsarism and Stalinism – the pictures, statues and imagery – are very similar in the way they portray the leader.

There is a strong case for arguing that the traditions of Russian history played an important role in determining the shape and characteristics of Stalinism. One school of thought sees Stalin as a Red tsar who pursued some of the tsars' traditional goals such as promoting nationalism and Russification and extending the boundaries of the empire. Stalin certainly saw himself as a moderniser in the tradition of Peter the Great. It is reported that in 1935 Stalin himself said that ordinary people needed a tsar to worship.

In small groups, work out the main similarities between the tsarist state and the Stalinist state. Then compare your findings with other groups and decide whether calling Stalin a Red tsar is justified.

In carrying out the comparison you could use the three guiding principles of tsarism: autocracy, orthodoxy (the equivalent in Stalin's Russia being Marxism–Leninism) and nationalism as a basis, along with aspects of economic policy.

KEY DATES: HIGH STALINISM

1946 Zhukov removed from position of influence.

1948 Death of Zhdanov.

1949 Purge of the Leningrad Party.

1951 Mingrelian case.

1952 Politburo replaced by a Presidium of 25.

   19th Party Congress.

   Plans to resettle many Jewish people in Siberia.

1953 January Doctors' plot announced in *Pravda*.

March Death of Stalin

NOTE-MAKING

Draw a spider diagram to make notes on the four areas of Stalin's legacy:
- terror and repression
- foreign relations and the Cold War
- the command economy
- the Stalin political system and the Stalin image.

The power vacuum on Stalin's death and his legacy

What major problem areas did Stalin leave for his successors?

Stalin's death 'left a crucial, Stalin-shaped hole at the centre of the system', as Christopher Read has written. This hole was made all the more significant because of the vast cult of personality, 'which had become a central prop of national politics'. There seems to have been a determination to prevent the emergence of another personal dictatorship. A leading group of Politburo members met regularly during Stalin's long absences from Moscow between 1950 and 1952, acting in the manner of the collective leadership of the 1920s (although decisions of this group were sent to Stalin for approval). This prepared the way for a collective leadership in the political transition after Stalin's death.

In four important areas Stalin left a difficult legacy.

Terror and repression

A high level of fear and repression pervaded Stalin's Russia. It was paralysing and affected everyone, the leadership included. It stifled initiative and creativity, and kept out new ideas, including desirable technical information from the West. It kept the camps full with many inmates of above-average education whose talents it failed to utilise fully. Stalin's possible successors agreed that the level of terror and repressions was counter-productive. The whole labour camp system did not make economic sense. Inmates working with insufficient food and medical care did not operate as efficiently as free men and women would have done. Timber, gold and uranium could have been obtained in more cost-effective ways. However, Stalin believed in the economics of slave labour. He gave the MVD (Ministry of Internal Affairs, the secret police in charge of gaols and camps in the post-war era) increasing economic power so that by 1952 they controlled 9 per cent of the capital investment in Russia, more than any other ministry. The Five-Year Plan for the years 1951–55 doubled this. Unsurprisingly, Beria told Stalin what he wanted to hear, thus in 1940 he had reported, 'The entire system of camps and labour colonies is fully paying its way and no subsidy for prisoners (1,700,000 persons), their guards or the camp apparatus is needed'. Beria knew this was not true. The cost of maintaining the camps far exceeded any profits made from prison labour and by 1953 the numbers in the gulags had doubled to over 2.5 million. Gulag construction projects were among Stalin's pet projects. Some were pointless: an inspection carried out in 1951 revealed that an entire 83 kilometres of far northern railway track, constructed at the cost of many lives, had not been used for three years.

Foreign relations and the Cold War

It is beyond the scope of this book to examine the origins of the Cold War and the extent of Stalin's responsibility for it. Stalin's foreign policy after the war had involved some miscalculations just as it had done before. The Berlin blockade was the greatest and completely counter-productive. It accelerated the move towards the North Atlantic Treaty Organisation, a defensive alliance linking the United States, Canada and ten western European nations, established in April 1949. It lessened the prospects of a collaborative settlement of the German problem and speeded progress to the formation of a West German state that would gradually become part of the Western world.

Soviet military power had undoubtedly grown and, although there was a bitter quarrel with Yugoslavia, control of eastern Europe had been achieved. However, this did not bring lasting security; if anything it brought the reverse. In Asia, the Korean War dragged on. The USSR needed to increase its influence in

The Berlin blockade

Following the war, Berlin was well within the Soviet zone of Germany but was itself divided into four occupational zones: Soviet, American, British and French. In August 1948, in an attempt to prevent Western reform of the German currency, the USSR blockaded the land routes to the Western zones of Berlin. It was seen in the West as an attempt to drive them out of Berlin and in response they organised an airlift of necessary supplies. It was a massive undertaking. It was so successful that by the time Stalin called off the blockade in May 1949 the supplies coming in by air were greater than those brought in by rail before the blockade began. It was seen as a major test of strength and determination and hardened attitudes on both sides.

developing countries, if only to challenge pro-American governments and to reduce the threat from American bases. By 1953 two hostile military camps faced each other and this had major consequences. There could only be one winner of an arms race – the West.

In Russia, rather than building up the civilian economy, the best scientists and engineers were creamed off to work in the defence sector and a very large army meant that industry and agriculture were deprived of young, fit men. Stalin's determination to catch up with the Americans in turn made the latter nervous; they stepped up their defence spending which in turn forced the USSR to do the same. It was a vicious circle. The notion of 'the inevitable war' would have to be rethought by Stalin's successors.

The command economy

Work and production were at the heart of the Soviet system with the aim to catch up and overtake capitalism. In 1953 this seemed a long way away for Soviet citizens living in overcrowded, poorly maintained housing and accustomed to long queues for very poor quality consumer goods. Christopher Read has summed up the situation (Source H).

Something would have to be done for consumers, and Stalin's successors were bound to seek the credit for doing so.

The planning system was over rigid, over centralised and excessively bureaucratic. Meeting the target was the key. Even the official press featured a cartoon depicting a factory worker joyfully unveiling a completely useless 2 million-watt light bulb with the caption 'Plan fulfilled'. Innovation and initiative were stifled and the centrally planned system was ill-equipped to compete in a world which was seeing increasingly rapid product and technological development. There was a concentration on the old staples such as solid fuels rather than oil and natural gas. Little attention was given to synthetics and plastics.

Agriculture remained the weakest element. Poverty-stricken villages and miserably low productivity were Stalin's agricultural legacy. In the post-war years he had continued to neglect the interests of agriculture. Payments for mandatory deliveries were so low that peasants sold their output for much less than the cost of production. To the very end, even in the context of worsening food shortages, Stalin had blocked any talk of serious policy reform in agriculture. His successors were to vie with each other to do something about this.

The Stalin political system and the Stalin image

De Tocqueville, a famous nineteenth-century French political thinker and historian, wrote that the most dangerous moment for a bad government was when it begins to reform. Stalin's possible successors all saw the need to reform; their dilemma was how far could any relaxation go without endangering the Soviet state?

The Russian tradition was one of firm rule as the one alternative to anarchy and confusion. What would a sniff of reform bring? The Party had a monopoly of power and many vested interests benefited from this, not just materially. They looked to their own comfort and privileges rather than the drive to build socialism, and had much to lose by real change.

Stalin was the infallible embodiment of the repressive system. If his successors criticised his errors and crimes would they not open themselves up to the question, why had he been tolerated for so long? On the other hand, if parts of the structure were dismantled without any criticism of Stalin it would be neither very convincing nor effective.

All in all it was a very difficult set of problems. The historian William Taubman, looking back in 2005 over the 50 years that followed Stalin's death, writes of 'the terrible legacy that Stalin's heirs faced and eventually defeated them all'.

Source H *The Making and Breaking of the Soviet System* by Christopher Read, (Palgrave), 2001, p 149.

The system was at its best in focusing vast resources on a relatively narrow range of options – war production, for instance, or basic post-war recovery – and at its worst in providing quality consumer goods. Stories of grotesque waste surfaced in the first post-Stalin years. 'Pairs' of shoes both of which were left-footed; coats all in one extremely small size because it was economical with material ...

LOOK AGAIN

Were the features mentioned in Source H present in the working of Stalin's economic system in the 1930s?

Chapter summary

- The war began disastrously for the Soviet Union, but the Germans were checked outside Leningrad and Moscow. By 1943 the Red Army had developed into an effective modern army. Victory at Stalingrad was a turning point in the war.
- Stalin emerges after early mistakes as an effective war leader who learned and listened to his generals. He was utterly ruthless, casualties were huge, repression continued and ethnic minorities were deported.
- The economy was seriously hit by early territorial losses but the command economy came into its own during the war, enabling it to produce more military hardware than Germany.
- Patriotism and readiness for self-sacrifice were key factors in Soviet success. The loss of life – up to 27 million Soviet citizens – and physical damage done to the USSR during the war was on an unimaginable scale.
- Stalin dashed hopes of any relaxation after the war. In order to counter the imperialist threat the country would have to endure at least three or four more Five-Year Plans with the emphasis once more on heavy industry.
- Stalin's position as the all-powerful leader of the one-party state was strengthened by the war. The cult of Stalin reached new heights. He used the same manipulative politics to maintain his grip on power and control contenders for the leadership.
- Stalin mounted a campaign of nationalism and anti-Westernism to help unite society and prevent contamination by any democratic ideas. Zhdanov led a drive for ideological and cultural purity (the *Zhdanovshchina*), which included a clampdown on the arts and sciences.
- Post-war terror, the Leningrad affair, the arrest of the Mingrelians and the Doctors' plot show that Stalin was ever more suspicious, paranoid and antisemitic.
- The period from 1945 to 1953 has been called High Stalinism. Its main features were nearly all present before the war.
- Stalin left a difficult legacy and his successors had to decide what to do about: terror and repression, foreign relations and the Cold War, the command economy and the Stalin political system and the Stalin image.

▼ Summary diagram 1: The Great Patriotic War, 1941–45

The course of the war	The impact on the USSR
Phase One: June–December 1941, Operation Barbarossa catches Stalin unprepared; all-conquering German army halted outside Leningrad and Moscow. **Phase Two:** January 1942–January 1943, German offensive resumes but Stalingrad is a decisive victory. **Phase Three:** February 1943–August 1944, Battle of Kursk begins process of chasing the Germans out of Soviet territory. **Phase Four:** August 1944–May 1945, The drive to Berlin.	• In a savage war of annihilation and attrition the USSR lost 27 million people but probably played the major role in defeating Hitler. • The Russian people showed tremendous resilience whether in the Red Army or on the home front, where the contribution of women was very important. • The Soviet economy responded impressively and in 1942–43 was out-producing Germany in armaments. Lend-Lease was important too. • Repression continued with mass deportations of nationalities and an increase in the size of the NKVD. • Stalin was to claim and be given much of the credit. Victory made his position virtually impregnable.

▼ Summary diagram 2: Stalin's Russia, 1945–53

Stalin and political developments	Economy, culture and society
The cult of personality reached new heights, especially in Stalin's 70th birthday celebrations.	Post-war reconstruction showed the same strengths and weaknesses as the pre-war economy. Heavy industry recovered very well, but there was a famine in 1946 and the peasants were squeezed. There were consumer goods shortages.
Stalin was firmly in control. The Politburo rarely met. Stalin favoured informal meetings with its members and stirred up rivalries between them.	The *Zhdanovshchina* saw tight control over culture and an anti-Western policy in the arts. The work of Akhmatova and Shostakovich was banned.
At the Party Congress of 1952 (the first since 1939) Presidium of 25 replaces Politburo of 11.	Soviet science was tightly controlled too, and distorted by Stalin's own preferences, such as Lysenko. However, the atomic bomb was developed quickly.
Stalin becomes increasingly suspicious. Renewed purges: Leningrad affair 1949, the Mingrelians 1951, the Doctors' plot 1953.	Russification policies continued as a means of controlling non-Russian republics within the USSR.
There was a genuine outpouring of grief when Stalin died. His body was embalmed and laid in the mausoleum next to Lenin's.	The Doctors' plot was just one example of Stalin's antisemitism. At the time of his death no Jewish person in Russia could feel safe.

Working on essay technique

So far, in the advice given, the skills being developed could help a student to write a good essay.

To write an outstanding essay, all the same skills are needed. In addition:

- All those skills should be shown at a high level.
- There should be a good understanding shown of issues and concepts (which might on this breadth paper include showing awareness of longer-term perspectives).
- The conclusion should contain a well-substantiated judgement.

Try to demonstrate these skills in answering the following A-level practice question:

How far was Stalin's USSR between 1928 and 1953 a totalitarian state?　　　　　　　　　　　　　　　　**(25 marks)**

There is scope for investigation of **key question 1: How was Russia governed and how did political authority change and develop?**

Working on interpretation skills

The extracts and A-level practice question which follow are designed to lead you towards your own judgement on how far Stalin's regime was totalitarian in the years 1928–53. The situation was not necessarily the same all through the period and Extract C homes in on the post-war years.

Using your understanding of the historical context, assess how convincing the arguments in these three extracts are in relation to the extent of Stalin's power in the USSR between 1928 and 1953.

(30 marks)

Extract A

Stalin's power was not based on control of the government or the party or the political police. It involved exploiting all three. It was vital to Stalin that he should maintain several independent sources of information; in that way he hoped to judge which source was misleading. After 1934 he successfully prevented any body, be it the Politburo or the CC of the party or the government, meeting as a group and taking counsel together independent of him. He preferred to consult individuals or small groups, and here his tactics were based on setting one person against another. This explains why there were only two Party Congresses between 1934 and 1953. Was the USSR a totalitarian state under Stalin? It all depends what is meant by totalitarian. If it is insisted that totalitarianism demands that all institutions have to be controlled, that the ruling ideology has to be totally pervasive, that control over the population has to be complete, then no state on earth will qualify. Yet even on this definition Stalin came nearer to creating the model totalitarian state than anyone before or since.

Stalin and Stalinism by Martin McCauley, (Longman), 1983, p 44.

Extract B

The notion of contradiction is central to my argument. The contradictions are legion: Stalin as 'Leader, Teacher, Friend' of the Soviet people, and yet the oppressor of millions; Stalin as 'omnipotent dictator', and yet dependent on provincial cliques to carry out his will; the image of material abundance in Stalinist culture and propaganda compared to the dire shortages, rationing and poverty experienced by millions of Soviet citizens; the 'most democratic' constitutional state in the world in 1936 descends into the bloodbath of the Great Terror in 1937–8; and the 'all-powerful' modernising communist state finds itself constrained and undermined by the political culture of a 'backward' peasant society. This contradictory essence of Stalin and Stalinism clashes head on with the popular image of Stalin controlling all aspects of Soviet public and private life by means of a totalitarian grip on power and mass repression.

Adapted from *Stalin* by Kevin McDermott, (Palgrave), 2006, p 5.

Extract C

While the structures and predilections of pre-war Stalinism resurfaced after 1945 – party purges, the command-administrative system, the emphasis on heavy industry, the re-imposition of collective farming – the attempt to reassert control over an economy and society, profoundly transformed by the experience of 1941–45, looks more haphazard and less successful than was once thought. Moreover, it now seems that whilst the Russo-German conflict strengthened the regime and legitimized the Generalissimo as a symbol of the will to victory, Stalin's personal power was threatened. The Red Army's commanders' prestige was very high and new client-patron relationships had crystallised during the war e.g. in Leningrad. Stalin seems to have tried to reassert his authority in several spheres – over the military (Zhukov's demotion), the party (the Leningrad Affair), the security apparatus the Mingrelian Case), the upper reaches of the Presidium (the Doctors' plot) and society at large (the *Zhdanovshchina*). The success or otherwise of these projects, however, is open to question.

Adapted from *Stalin's Russia*, 2nd edition, by Chris Ward, (Arnold), 1999, pp 225–26.

8

Khrushchev and de-Stalinisation, 1953–64

This chapter covers the years from the death of Stalin until the fall of Khrushchev in 1964.

It deals with the following areas:

- Khrushchev's rise to power; policies and ideology; de-Stalinisation; political and Party change
- Changes in industrial organisation from Stalin to Khrushchev; agriculture and the Virgin Lands scheme; social and cultural change from Stalin to Khrushchev
- Opposition: cultural dissidents, communist divisions, hardliners and reformers, opponents of Khrushchev and his fall from power
- The political, economic and social condition of the Soviet Union by 1964

The chapter covers all the key questions and the main issues in it can be phrased as a question:

How successful was Khrushchev in changing the Soviet Union between 1953 and 1964?

This question will look at changes in politics, the economy, culture and society, and the role Khrushchev and his ideas played in these developments.

CHAPTER OVERVIEW

Rather to the surprise of his rivals, Khrushchev emerged victorious in the power struggle which followed Stalin's death. Khrushchev was a very different man from Stalin. He was an extrovert who, through his initiatives and schemes, sought to humanise and modernise a system which cried out for change. His speech at the 20th Party Congress in 1956, in which he denounced Stalin's crimes, proved to be a turning point in the history of the regime. These were the years of the thaw. There was some easing in cultural life and living standards did improve, although not as spectacularly as Khrushchev boasted they would. There were successes and failures: the dramatic developments in the space programme enhanced Soviet prestige in the world, while his much vaunted Virgin Lands scheme was ultimately damaging to agriculture. In foreign affairs he believed in peaceful co-existence and travelled to the USA but he also triggered the Cuban Missile Crisis – the most serious crisis of the Cold War. By 1964 he had alienated many interest groups within the ruling elite and was ousted. However, he was allowed to retire, a mark of the changes he had encouraged. The extent to which Khrushchev had succeeded in changing the Soviet Union will be assessed at the end of the chapter.

1 The emergence of Khrushchev and de-Stalinisation

This section will look at how Khrushchev emerged from the collective leadership as Stalin's successor and at the process of de-Stalinisation, and in particular at Khrushchev's 20th Party Congress speech in 1956 and its impact.

Khrushchev's rise to power

How did Khrushchev ditch his rivals?

Khrushchev was a clever operator and we shall see that his actions and policies between 1953 and 1957 were designed to strengthen his position and weaken his rivals.

Collective leadership

The five-man collective leadership of Malenkov, Beria, Molotov, Voroshilov and Khrushchev, who took over the Party on Stalin's death, pledged themselves to collective leadership, but there was a fierce power struggle going on behind the scenes. They decided quickly to cut the size of the Presidium down to ten. Malenkov, who had ranked second on the eve of Stalin's death, succeeded Stalin as Prime Minister and Party Secretary. He remained Party Secretary for only a week. It is unclear whether this was his decision, but if a collective leadership was to be viable no one should stand out. All the collective leaders were members of the Presidium and their names were printed in the order below (their positions have been added):

- Malenkov, Prime Minister
- Beria, Minister of the Interior and Head of the Secret Police (arrested June)
- Molotov, Foreign Minister
- Voroshilov, Head of State (a ceremonial role)
- Khrushchev, First Party Secretary (from September)

Malenkov may well have believed that being Prime Minister was a more important role than that of Party Secretary. Lenin had been Prime Minister as had Stalin from 1941.

Khrushchev was the only member of the collective leadership who did not have a top government job, but he was also the only person who was in the Secretariat and the Presidium. The Party was now his power base and he was determined to exploit it fully, as Stalin had done in the 1920s.

Beria makes the early running

Beria rushed from Stalin's deathbed to ransack Stalin's office and empty the safe in which he kept evidence of colleagues' personal foibles (which Beria himself planned to use) and damning reports on the state's excessive violence. Beria (see page 246), ambitious, head of the secret police and personally odious, was feared and disliked by the other leaders. He was quick to grasp the initiative and appeared initially to overwhelm his competitors, adding to their fears. He put forward a reform programme. An amnesty brought the release of about 1 million prisoners, mainly criminals on shorter sentences, and he talked of dismantling the gulags. Beria knew better than anyone how uneconomic they were and how innocent most of the inmates were. He reversed the policies of Russification, in particular in west Ukraine and the Baltic states. He appeared ready to accept a unified, neutral non-communist Germany and imposed reforms on the East German leadership. But when there was a rising in East Berlin, Beria was blamed. This helped Khrushchev to gain support for his removal.

Khrushchev takes the lead in the removal of Beria

Beria was hard to move against since he had control of the secret police and he had bugged the Kremlin and the telephones and homes of his rivals. Surprise and the support of the army were essential. Khrushchev took the lead at the Presidium meeting on 26 June; several members were carrying arms in case things got out of hand. Marshall Zhukov and an armed squad were in the next room. Khrushchev, Malenkov and others accused Beria of many crimes and at a given signal Zhukov rushed in and arrested him. Two weeks later his disgrace was endorsed by the Central Committee who, with Khrushchev as the dominant figure, blamed him for the worst excesses of Stalinism. Beria was denounced in *Pravda*, in the old Stalinist style, as an enemy of the people and an enemy agent. Implausibly he was accused of having been a British agent for 30 years. He was kept in custody for six months and after a secret trial, was executed along with six of his colleagues.

Khrushchev outmanoeuvres Malenkov

Malenkov, as Prime Minister, was the leading reformist. His rivalry with Khrushchev produced the first open policy debates in the Soviet Union since the 1920s. The economy was a crucial battleground and Malenkov embarked upon a New Course in which the output of consumer goods was to expand even faster than that of heavy industry. He also announced that agricultural taxes would be halved, the prices paid for produce were to be raised and the size of private plots was to be increased – all measures popular with peasants.

In this chapter test Crankshaw's judgement (Source A) on Khrushchev's attitude to Stalin, his colleagues and his recklessness.

The career of Khrushchev up to 1953

Khrushchev was extrovert, boorish, overbearing and full of energy. He was born to a peasant family in 1894 and had only four years of schooling. He became a metal worker in Yuzovka (later Stalino, now Donetsk).

He joined the Party in 1918 and after the civil war worked for it either in Ukraine or Moscow. He worked closely with Kaganovich on the Moscow metro and succeeded him as Party Secretary for the Moscow region. He was complicit in the Terror but was not a full member of the Politburo until 1939. Khrushchev hero-worshipped Stalin and was thrilled that Stalin liked him and wrote proudly in his memoires that 'several Politburo members virtually considered me his pet'. He spent the war as a political officer and was at Stalingrad. Afterwards he was Party Secretary in Ukraine and then in Moscow where he was part of Stalin's inner circle. He had a particular interest in agriculture which became more pronounced when he came to power and, completely the opposite of Stalin, he liked to get mud on his boots and visit collective farms.

Source A From *Khrushchev Remembers Vol 1* by Edward Crankshaw, (Penguin), 1977, p 13.

... a determinedly ambitious Party professional, sycophantic towards his master, bullying towards his subordinates, manoeuvring around his rivals with deep peasant cunning, he was simply a thug among other thugs, visibly distinguished from the others only by a certain liveliness of imagination, a warmth of feeling, a sturdy self-reliance, and at times the recklessness of a born gambler.

The career of Malenkov up to 1953

The historian Roy Medvedev described Malenkov as 'a man without a biography' whose life was so tied to bureaucratic duty that 'he had no image of his own, not even his own style'. He was more educated and intelligent than many of his colleagues, a loyal Stalinist who benefited from the purges. During the war he was a member of the all-powerful State Defence Committee with responsibility for aircraft production. The sharpest rivalry in the immediate post-war years was between Malenkov and Zhdanov. The Leningrad affair in 1949 (see page 247) was engineered by Beria and Malenkov, probably to gain influence, deal with potential rivals and reclaim the power positions they had lost to Zhdanov. Malenkov's close involvement in the Leningrad affair and his connection with Beria would be used against him later. However, in 1952 Malenkov began to be looked upon as Stalin's successor and had given the chief report at the 19th Party Congress with the ageing Stalin looking on.

However, the harvest in 1953 was poor and Malenkov got the blame. In foreign affairs Malenkov believed that now that the Soviet Union had nuclear weapons war would be disastrous for both communists and capitalists; therefore, peace could be achieved.

Khrushchev counter-attacked. He resented Malenkov taking the initiative on agriculture, which he regarded as his area of expertise. Early in 1954 he launched his Virgin Lands campaign in Kazakhstan and Siberia (see page 270), promising a quick end to the grain shortage. Khrushchev got the Party behind his campaign and its early success gave him momentum. He saw better than Malenkov the importance of the role of Party organisation. He became known as First Secretary in September. He asserted the clear supremacy of the Party bureaucracy over that of the secret police – the new Committee for State Security (KGB) – and the Council of Ministers.

Khrushchev had strengthened his own position and weakened that of Malenkov. The military, who wanted to match US defence spending, said Malenkov was unbalancing the economy. The economy was indeed overstrained and Malenkov was not in a strong enough position politically to adjudicate between conflicting claimants on resources. Khrushchev had made allies with heavy industry, planners and the military men, and on this issue he could count on the support in the Presidium of the Stalinist hardliners Molotov and Kaganovich. As a result, Malenkov was forced to resign as Prime Minister in February 1955. Bulganin, who was not a threat, took over with Khrushchev's support.

	Malenkov	Khrushchev
Personality	Intelligent, sophisticated, steady but rather colourless	Cunning, impulsive, down-to-earth, energetic, extrovert
Position	Prime Minister	First Secretary
Power base	Government	The Party
Policies		
Industry	Raise living standards. His New Course focused on consumer goods at the expense of the military – industrial complex and heavy industry.	Sided with heavy industry and planners who said Malenkov was unbalancing the economy. After Malenkov's defeat favoured raising living standards.
Agriculture	Halved taxes on agriculture. Increased prices paid to collective farms. Increased size of private plots allowed. More mechanisation and use of chemical fertilisers.	Attacked Malenkov's proposals as a retreat from the collective principle. Virgin Lands campaign began in Kazakhstan and Siberia in 1954, an ideologically pure alternative.
Cold War	Malenkov argued that now the USSR had the H-bomb a state of deterrence existed between East and West. Resources could be diverted from defence to consumer goods.	Soviet service chiefs rejected Malenkov's policies. Khrushchev backed their view to gain their support against Malenkov. Once Malenkov was defeated, Khrushchev adopted this policy.

▲ **Figure 1** Malenkov outmanoeuvred by Khrushchev.

LOOK AGAIN

A comparison with the struggle over power in the 1920s

Just as Stalin had been underestimated by rivals who were rather disparaging about his intellect, there is evidence that both Beria and Molotov thought that Khrushchev was second rate. However, Khrushchev, like Stalin, was cunning and able to outmanoeuvre his rivals.

● Like Stalin, he was ready to change policies for tactical reasons and take over rivals' policies once they had been defeated. He put forward his doctrine of peaceful co-existence having previously attacked Malenkov when he stated that an all-out war between communism and capitalism was out of date in the nuclear age.

● It was Malenkov who first called for a higher standard of living for the people and a higher priority for consumer goods long before Khrushchev did.

● Like Stalin, Khrushchev exploited his position in control of the Party Secretariat with wide power over appointments and thus over elections to both the Central Committee and the Presidium. He often placed former colleagues in the Moscow and Ukrainian Party organisations in key positions. He built up his support among the regional Party Secretaries. Like Stalin he could win crucial votes in the Central Committee.

KEY DATES: KHRUSHCHEV'S RISE TO POWER

1953

March Death of Stalin.

June Arrest of Beria.

December Execution of Beria.

1955 Malenkov resigns as Prime Minister.

Later events which increased Khrushchev's power:

1956 Khrushchev's 20th Party Congress speech.

1957 The defeat of the Anti-Party group.

De-Stalinisation

How should the Party leadership deal with Stalin's repressive policies?

There were grave dangers in denouncing Stalin. He had been placed on so high a pedestal that knocking him off could endanger the whole structure. The period from 1953 to 1956 has been called a time of silent de-Stalinisation since the revision of Stalin's repressive policies was done largely in secret, and without explanation. Silent de-Stalinisation saw the release of thousands who had been convicted of counter-revolutionary crimes, and some non-publicised rehabilitations. However, this could not continue with so many prisoners returning from the camps. William Taubman, Khrushchev's biographer, writes that, 'He had a naive faith that socialism, once purified of its Stalinist stain, would command ever more loyalty from its beneficiaries'.

At the end of December 1955 Khrushchev proposed that a commission be set up to look into Stalin's activities, paying particular attention to executed Party officials. The 70-page report, stated that of 1,920,635 persons arrested for anti-Soviet activities between 1935 and 1940, 688,503 had been shot. All the alleged plots and conspiracies had been fabricated; Stalin had personally sanctioned the torture that produced the confessions. Politburo members knew all about this. Khrushchev's reaction was, 'We've got to have the courage to tell the truth'. Molotov, Kaganovich and Voroshilov were totally against revelation. All of them had been Politburo members throughout the 1930s, Khrushchev not until 1938. Molotov wanted the Party Congress to recognise that 'Stalin was the great continuer of Lenin's work'. Khrushchev was absolutely determined to deliver his 'secret speech' condemning Stalin. The report provided him with much of the raw material.

What were Khrushchev's motives?

- According to his memoirs Khrushchev was plagued by his moral conscience and wanted to repent. He genuinely thought that the truth was the only way to restore Party faith and unity – and thus save the Party from a fatal loss of self-belief.
- The historian Martin McCauley argues that Khrushchev's purpose was to liberate Party officials from fear of repression. If the Party could become an efficient mechanism, stripped of the brutal abuse of power by any individual, it could transform the country and the world.
- Khrushchev was afraid that if they did not speak of Stalin's crimes there would be more radical debate, which the Party wouldn't be able to control and which could drown them all.
- By building support in those sectors of the Party and society that supported his ideas of reform and Leninist renewal, Khrushchev was working to undermine his rivals for the leadership. If his rivals, who were more at the heart of things in the 1930s than he had been, criticised him they might appear to be advocating a return to state terror.

The 'secret speech' and its limitations

Khrushchev's 'secret speech' at the 20th Party Congress was entitled, 'On the Personality Cult and its Consequences'. The speech is one of praise for the Party and Martin McCauley calls it 'a cry of anguish at its suffering'. The speech lasted nearly four hours, with an intermission, and was delivered to delegates at an unscheduled secret session at the end of the Congress.

The problematic nature of the term 'de-Stalinisation'

The term was never used publicly in the Khrushchev era. The phrase 'the overcoming/exposure of the cult of personality' was used. Before the 20th Party Congress speech there was no overt admission that the cult was linked with Stalin. Gradually the expression 'the era of the cult of personality' came to be used for Stalin's authoritarian regime. 'De-Stalinisation' was used widely in journalism and scholarship in post-Soviet Russia as well as in the West. The historian Polly Jones points out that there is a finality about the phrase which is at odds with the more hesitant reality of the situation. She argues that 'thaw' captures better the fragility and the potential for reversal (or 'freeze') which each tentative forward step carried. The historian Anne Applebaum agrees, and writes of 'an era of change of a particular kind: reforms took two steps forward, and then one step – or sometimes three steps – back'.

In the speech Khrushchev:

- attacked Stalin for what now became a cardinal sin – the 'cult of the personality' – and the way in which Stalin was given unquestioning adulation. He cited how Stalin was guilty of sickening self-glorification while maintaining a front of modesty in his amendments to his 1948 *Short Biography* (see Chapter 7, page 245);
- read out Lenin's testament emphasising the part criticising Stalin (see page 180) and letters about Stalin's rudeness to Krupskaya to demonstrate Lenin's doubts about him;
- focused on Stalin's attack on loyal Party members, notably the delegates to the 1934 Party Congress, projecting an aura of heroism about them and revealing shocking figures, for example, 98 out of the 134 members of the Central Committee had been arrested and shot;
- suggested that Stalin might have been complicit in the murder of Kirov. Kirov was a revered figure and this shocked the audience;
- stated that though Trotskyite and Bukharinist oppositions had been ideological and political enemies they had not deserved physical annihilation;
- criticised the role of the NKVD in the purges, especially the use of torture to extract confessions for which Stalin was personally responsible, giving instructions 'to beat, beat and, once again, beat';
- criticised the performance of Stalin during the war, holding him responsible for the disasters of 1941;
- denounced the mass deportations of the 'punished peoples' during the war as contrary not only to Marxism–Leninism but also to common sense;
- demonstrated that Stalin's 'grave abuse of power' continued after the war with the purge of the Leningrad Party and the Doctors' plot;
- told the delegates that Stalin apparently had plans to destroy old members of the Politburo 'to hide the shameful acts we are now reporting'.

What Khrushchev did not say in the speech:

- There was no criticism of the essential correctness of Marxism–Leninism, the viability of the Soviet system of rule or its superiority to every other form of government. Khrushchev went out of his way to stress that Stalin's 'grave abuse of power' was an aberration.
- There was no criticism of Stalin before 1934 and it accepted that rapid industrialisation and enforced collectivisation were necessary.
- It ignores the sufferings of non-Party members before the war. There was nothing on the repression of the *kulaks*, ethnic cleansing of the border regions before the war or the notorious NKVD Order 00447 ordering mass executions of former *kulaks* and criminals (page 212).

Khrushchev and the Terror

There can be no doubt about Khrushchev's complicity in Stalin's Terror. His actions show just how much destruction someone as keen to please Stalin as Khrushchev could wreak:

NKVD Order 00447 was dreadful enough as it was without people acting as zealously as Khrushchev. He over-fulfilled his quota for Moscow and Moscow province as you can see below.

	Criminal and *kulak* elements	
	Arrested	Shot
Quota	35,000	5,000
Khrushchev reported to Stalin	41,305	8,500

▲ **Figure 2** Number of people arrested and shot under NKVD Order 00447.

When Khrushchev presented long death lists, Stalin's response was, 'There can't be so many!' 'There are in fact more,' Khrushchev replied, 'You can't imagine how many there are'.

Only 10 out of 146 Party Secretaries in the Moscow region survived.

When he was moved to Ukraine in January 1938, Khrushchev was just as active. All members but one of the Ukrainian Party Politburo, *Orgburo* and Secretariat were arrested. Khrushchev could not, or would not, prevent even his closest and most trusted associates from being arrested and shot, and made violent speeches in favour of the purges.

The obvious defence for Khrushchev in retrospect would have been that to oppose Stalin would have been to invite his own death. But Khrushchev was unwilling to invoke this defence. Taubman argues that Khrushchev remained to the very end 'in denial' about his own complicity. Guilty of 'deception and self-deception', Khrushchev preferred to plead ignorance of what was happening.

The consequences of the 20th Party Congress speech

The 'secret speech' was sent to local Party organisations to be read to all rank-and-file members and even broader audiences of 'working collectives', in total 20–25 million people.

Immediate consequences at home

Khrushchev had, in historian Geoffrey Hosking's words, 'torn the veil away from the inner-sanctum and revealed a blood-stained torture-chamber'. The Party was thrown into confusion. Some blamed the leaders for failing to speak out earlier, while others criticised Khrushchev for raising all these questions. At Moscow State University, students boycotted the university canteen, notorious for its bad food, in a semi-intentional re-enactment of the revolt on the battleship *Potemkin* in 1905 (see page 94). In schools, students tore Stalin's portraits off the walls and trampled them underfoot. At public meetings to discuss the speech, Stalin was condemned as an 'enemy of the people'. There were calls for multi-party elections and real rights and freedoms to prevent the Terror from happening again.

The response was well beyond Khrushchev's expectations and he was worried by the Party's more radical critics. They were expelled from the Party and pilloried in the press as 'rotten elements'. Khrushchev had to perform a delicate balancing act, which meant that his de-Stalinisation was marked by retreats as well as advances.

The freeing of political prisoners accelerated. In the three years preceding the 'secret speech', 7,000 had been rehabilitated. In the ten months that followed, 617,000 were rehabilitated.

Immediate consequences outside the USSR

In the communist countries of eastern Europe which had only been under communist rule since 1945, an attack on Stalin's post-war conduct had a de-stabilising impact. A strike brought a change of government in Poland, but in Hungary in October 1956 there was a full-blown uprising. At first Soviet troops complied with the demand for them to leave, but when the new Hungarian prime minister denounced the Warsaw Pact and declared

Rehabilitation

Full social rehabilitation with complete reinstatement of job, apartment and pension was very rare. Less than half of those who demanded the restoration of their Party membership were granted it. Local authorities were still suspicious of former prisoners. Anne Applebaum offers an interesting insight (Source B).

Source B *Gulag* by Anne Applebaum, (Penguin), 2004, pp 461–62.

The return home of millions of people from camps and exile must have stunned the millions of other Soviet citizens they encountered upon their arrival. Khrushchev's secret speech had been a shock, but it was a remote event, directed at the Party hierarchy. By contrast, the reappearance of people long considered dead brought home the message of the speech in a far more direct way, to a far wider range of people. Stalin's era had been one of secret torture and hidden violence. Suddenly, the camp veterans were on hand to provide living evidence of what happened.

Warsaw Pact – a military alliance of east European communist states formed in 1955 as a response to the admission of West Germany into NATO (North Atlantic Treaty Organisation) – the association of European and North American states formed in 1949 at the height of the Cold War.

Hungary's neutrality, it was too much for Khrushchev and he decided to crush the uprising. There were 20,000 Hungarian casualties. The turbulence inside the Warsaw Pact strengthened the position of those in the Presidium who were critical of Khrushchev's de-Stalinisation.

In China, Mao Zedong was shocked by the betrayal of Stalin and later denounced Khrushchev as a 'revisionist' for watering down the tough revolutionary doctrine of Bolshevism never forgave Khrushchev for not revealing to him what he intended to do beforehand.

Longer-term consequences

The historian Orlando Figes argues that the Soviet system never really recovered from the crisis of confidence created by the speech:

The speech changed everything. It was the moment when the Party lost authority, unity and self-belief. It was the beginning of the end.

For the first time the Party was admitting it was wrong and in a catastrophic way.

Many of Khrushchev's colleagues never forgave him for the speech. Many years later, in 1984, when the Politburo decided to readmit Molotov to the Party, it reaffirmed its hostility to Khrushchev. According to Dmitrii Ustinov, the then Defence Minister, 'No other enemy brought us as much harm'.

Khrushchev deals with opposition

Molotov, Kaganovich and Voroshilov were hardliners and strongly opposed to Khrushchev's 'secret speech'. Malenkov, as we have seen, had been a reformer but bitterly resented his treatment by Khrushchev. They would look for their chance to oust him.

The Anti-Party group

The unrest in Poland and the Hungarian uprising were used by the hardliners to argue that Khrushchev's 'secret speech' had undermined the credibility, unity and strength of the international communist movement. Khrushchev was too liberal for them. But it was not just the hardliners who had been alienated. The Presidium majority were angered by his abolition of the central economic ministries, which weakened their power (see page 273). They were prepared to challenge Khrushchev whose style of leadership had become increasingly assertive. His unpredictable and ill-considered initiatives across foreign and domestic policy were cited as the reason for the need to remove him.

In June 1957, Khrushchev was outvoted seven to four, but he appealed to the Central Committee who had elected him First Secretary. He also had the support of the head of the army, Zhukov, and the head of the KGB, and they made sure that members of the Central Committee were assembled quickly, flying in members from all over the USSR. Khrushchev had promoted many of them, and he prevailed. He referred to his opponents as the 'Anti-Party group'. A Central Committee resolution expelling them denounced them for opposing Party policy on a whole range of issues over the previous three or four years, and Molotov was castigated for his long years as Stalin's Foreign Minister. They were condemned for factionalism. All this, and the carefully recorded unanimous verdict of the Central Committee, had echoes of the Stalin years. Their fate did not. Kaganovich feared for his life and he telephoned Khrushchev. This gave Khrushchev the chance to make clear the difference between his regime and Stalin's (see Source C).

Bulganin

Bulganin's greatest asset was that he was acceptable to everyone and not seen as a threat. He became a member of the Politburo under Stalin in 1948 and was made Minister of Defence shortly after Stalin's death. He was seen as a reformist ally of Khrushchev and replaced Malenkov as Prime Minister, but in 1957 he sided with Khrushchev's opponents. He was not removed until 1958 so as not to draw attention to the scale of opposition to Khrushchev in the Presidium.

You wanted the country to revert to the order that existed under the personality cult. You wanted to kill people. You measure others by your own yardstick. But you are mistaken. We apply Leninist principles with vigour and will continue to apply them. You will be given a job. You will be able to work and live in peace if you work honestly like all Soviet people.

Kaganovich and his colleagues were sent a very long way from Moscow and given humiliating jobs. Kaganovich was sent to manage a cement factory in the Urals, Molotov was made ambassador to Mongolia and Malenkov was sent to look after a hydroelectric plant in Kazakhstan. The fact that Khrushchev had been in a minority in the Presidium was not made public and he did not take over as Prime Minister from Bulganin, who had been one of the Anti-Party group, until 1958.

Khrushchev removes Zhukov

Marshall Zhukov had been a vital support to Khrushchev in the removal of Beria and the defeat of the Anti-Party group. After this Zhukov became more assertive; he had a big reputation and an even bigger ego. He had been Defence Minister from 1955 and in the summer of 1957 he introduced some military reforms without consulting the Party and clearly wanted to develop a purely professional army. This was seen as a direct threat to Party control. Zhukov was dismissed from the Presidium and the Central Committee. Khrushchev knew he had the other Soviet marshals on his side; they bitterly resented Zhukov's style. The new Minister of Defence, Marshal Malinovsky, was much more pliable. Khrushchev was determined to make the Party supreme and to strengthen his own position. The years 1957–60 were his best: he had more freedom of action than ever before but he also became more authoritarian and arrogant.

22nd Party Congress, 1961

Even after the defeat of the Anti-Party group Khrushchev still faced opposition to reform from inside the Party and did not push anti-Stalinism for a while. At the 21st Party Congress in 1959 the question of Stalinism was not raised. Khrushchev did, however, resume his attack on Stalin at the 22nd Party Congress in 1961. New information about the purges was given, along with emotionally charged assessments of Stalin. An old Bolshevik D. A. Lazurkina – a 77-year-old, active participant in the October Revolution who had joined the Party in 1902 and been imprisoned by the Tsar and Stalin – took to the platform. She informed the delegates that Lenin had appeared to her in a dream and made it clear that he did not like lying beside Stalin in the mausoleum. Ending Lenin's discomfort was only one of the measures taken as a result of this speech:

- Stalin's mummified body was removed from the Lenin Mausoleum and reburied in a simpler grave by the Kremlin wall.
- Places named after Stalin were renamed, for example, Stalingrad became Volgograd and Stalino became Donetsk.
- Monuments of Stalin were destroyed.
- Khrushchev proposed that a memorial to Stalin's victims be built in Moscow.

What does Khrushchev mean by 'the personality cult' and 'Leninist principles' (Source C)?

LOOK AGAIN

The circular flow of power

The American historian R. V. Daniels has drawn attention to the circular flow of power in relation to Stalin (page 183). The First Secretary (or General Secretary in Stalin's case) had great power in the appointment of key posts, especially Party Secretaryships at the all-union, republican and regional levels. Those people, by virtue of the offices they held, would become members of the Central Committee. There they could be expected to support the patron who had appointed them, thus completing the circle. Khrushchev benefited from this in 1957 and logically the leader should not lose power except by dying. However, the Central Committee voted Khrushchev out of office in 1964 (see pages 279–80). They did so because between 1961 and 1964 he pursued policies which went against their interests. This suggests that common interests rather than just an obligation of appointees to back him played their part in Stalin's rise to power.

KEY DATES: DE-STALINISATION

1956

February Khrushchev's 20th Party Congress speech.

October Hungarian rising.

1957 Malenkov, Molotov and Kaganovich removed from influence.

1961 Khrushchev's attack on Stalin at the 22nd Party Congress leads to the removal of Stalin from the Lenin Mausoleum.

Biological yield – the maximum possible yield of the standing crop in the field at moment of maximum ripeness. It was used from 1933 onwards to inflate harvest figures. It did so by between 15 and at least 30 per cent.

2 Economic and social developments, 1953–64

This section will look at Khrushchev's economic policies, in particular agriculture and the Virgin Lands campaign, his changes in industrial organisation and at social and cultural change.

Khrushchev's economic policies

How and with what success did Khrushchev try to reform the Soviet economy?

Once he had defeated Malenkov, Khrushchev focused on consumer goods and raising the standard of living. Increasing food production was always one of his aims and he came to regard himself as the agricultural expert.

Khrushchev and agriculture

In 1953, Khrushchev made the first honest assessment of the state of Soviet agriculture since collectivisation:

- Productivity was too low.
- Livestock numbers compared very unfavourably with 1928 and even 1916, and the number of cows was falling.
- Terms like 'biological yield' for the grain harvest were used to hide realities.
- Farmers' incomes were too low because state procurement prices were far too low.
- High taxes on private plots discouraged production.

A series of measures followed to change the situation. Procurement prices were raised. Taxes were cut. Investment in the needs of agriculture, such as the production of fertiliser and farm machinery was to go up. Costs to the collective farms for transport and hire of equipment were cut. Taxes and restrictions on private plots were reduced. Khrushchev's major initiative was his Virgin Lands campaign (the first harvest was in 1954). In Alec Nove's view, 'World history knows nothing like it'.

The Virgin Lands campaign

Whereas after the early 1930s Stalin never came nearer to the ordinary people than the reviewing stand on top of the Lenin Mausoleum, Khrushchev loved contact with peasants and workers.

The Virgin Lands campaign was a huge operation designed to plough up a vast tract of virgin and fallow land in Kazakhstan, the Urals and Siberia for grain cultivation. More than 300,000 *Komsomol* volunteers were mobilised to settle and cultivate this huge area – by 1956, 35.9 million acres, an area equal to the total cultivated area of Canada. They would be joined by even larger contingents of students, soldiers, and truck and combine-drivers who were transported to the virgin lands on a seasonal basis. Conditions were primitive and the climate harsh. Like the Five-Year Plans it was run like a military campaign with an emphasis on speed. There was much publicity and very little listening to advice.

▲ Khrushchev visiting a wheat field in the virgin lands of Kazakhstan in 1959.

Source D From 'Memoir of the "virgin lands" campaign' by Eduard Shevardnadze. Quoted in *The Soviet Union, A Documentary History, Volume 2* by Edward Acton and Tom Stableford, (University of Exeter Press), 2007, p 267. Shevardnadze was the long-time First Secretary in Georgia and later to become Gorbachev's Foreign Minister. In the 1950s he was in charge of the Georgian *Komsomol* contingent. His memoir both reflects the enthusiasm of the campaign and that it was ultimately disastrous. He recalled machinery brought from all over the country breaking down, crops left to rot and nowhere to store the grain.

There was a colossal waste of billions of roubles, machinery and labour. The virgin lands cost the country dearly. I now believe that all that expenditure could have brought large returns, had a different approach to solving the grain problem been adopted. But in those days a different approach was not possible.

> What do you think that, 'in those days a different approach was not possible' (Source D) means?

The harvest in 1956, announced as a great victory, was the largest in Soviet history up to that point: over half of the 125 million tons of grain produced came from the new regions. Results never quite reached that level again and by the early 1960s, reliance on single-crop cultivation had taken its toll on the fertility of the soil, and failure to adopt anti-erosion measures led to millions of tons of topsoil simply blowing away. In 1960 this happened to 13,000 square miles of land. By 1963 the grain harvest was disastrous and the Virgin Lands produced their smallest crop for years.

The maize obsession

Khrushchev believed that he had not only solved the grain problem, but also the fodder problem. With the Virgin Lands campaign underway, maize could now be grown in traditional grain-producing areas. It would provide cattle-feed and revive meat and dairy farming which was languishing. He wanted it grown everywhere, claiming, 'corn can produce high yields in all areas of our country', and 'that corn is unequalled by any other crop'. In fact, while it is a valuable crop in Ukraine, it barely ripens elsewhere. Whilst 85 million acres were planted, only about one-sixth was harvested ripe.

With typical impulsiveness Khrushchev claimed in 1957 that the USSR would catch up with the USA in per capita meat output by 1960. This required a threefold increase. One provincial Party boss did achieve such an increase and was much praised by Khrushchev. This had only been achieved by the slaughter of dairy cattle, rustling, false accounting of all sorts and even levying taxes on schools in meat! It could not be maintained and a mere one-sixth of the vaunted promise was delivered the following year. The Party boss shot himself.

Other agricultural changes

- In 1958 MTS (see page 195) were abolished. They had maintained and hired out machinery, now the *kolkhozy* had to buy the machinery. They had to pay too much and too quickly for machinery and there were not the barns on farms to store it. Mechanics from the former MTS tended to go to the towns where living standards were higher and so there was not enough expertise to maintain or repair the machinery properly and it was left to rust away.
- Khrushchev restricted the size of private plots putting pressure on peasants to sell their cows to the *kolkhoz*. Khrushchev interfered too much with different campaigns forced upon farms, often with little regard for local conditions and he reorganised things continually.

Industry

There were spectacular achievements in the space programme and more attention was given to consumer goods. Khrushchev, who could never be accused of lacking ambition, wanted to catch up and overtake the United States' standard of living! But his major interest always lay in agriculture rather than industry.

The Seven-Year Plan

Khrushchev introduced a Seven-Year Plan covering the years 1959–65. He wanted a rapid expansion of the chemical industry to provide more mineral fertilisers for agriculture. There was a large investment in oil and natural gas, and a focus on investment in areas east of the Urals. By 1961 Khrushchev, who was always in a hurry and now buoyed up by Soviet space exploits (see below) announced some upward amendments. Overall industrial progress was impressive and there was a major increase in consumer goods. However, the soaring expenses of the space and missile programme, and increased military expenditure placed a heavy strain on scarce skills and specialist equipment. Growth rates suffered, and in 1963 and 1964 fell to the lowest in peacetime since planning began.

The space programme

The Soviet Union under Khrushchev took the lead in space research and exploration. In August 1957 the first successful test of an inter-continental ballistic missile was carried out, and two months later that rocket was used to launch the first satellite – the *Sputnik* – into space to great excitement. There was even more when in 1961 Yuri Gagarin became the first man in space. It was a huge boost to Soviet prestige and coupled with Khrushchev's boasting

---

Inter-continental ballistic missile – a guided ballistic missile with a minimum range of more than 5,500 kilometres capable of delivering one or more nuclear warheads.

KEY DATES: KHRUSHCHEV'S ECONOMIC POLICIES

1954 First harvest in Virgin Lands campaign.

1956 Largest harvest in Soviet history up to this point.

1957 *Sputnik* launched.

1958 MTS were abolished.

1959 Seven-Year Plan began.

1961 Yuri Gagarin became the first man in space.

1963 Disastrous harvest.

about its military rocketry, led the outside world to overestimate Soviet progress. There was in fact no 'missile gap' with the United States in favour of the Soviet Union.

Khrushchev's reorganisations

Khrushchev's reorganisations had clear political motives, though it was hoped they would avoid waste and bring decision-making nearer the point of production. The Stalinist command economy concentrated great power in the central governmental ministries and this was where his main Presidium opponents had their power bases. Khrushchev's devolution of powers to the republics strengthened Party rather than ministry control and increased his power and influence.

- Between 1954 and 1955 about 11,000 enterprises were transferred from central to republican control.
- In 1956 factories run by twelve central governmental ministries were placed under the jurisdiction of republican governments.
- In May 1957, 105 regional economic councils were established to take the place of the central economic ministries. This was one of the factors which stirred up Khrushchev's Presidium opponents into challenging him.

Khrushchev overcame his opponents but the regional economic councils were abolished soon after Khrushchev was ousted.

Social and cultural change

How much did quality of life improve?

Once Khrushchev had secured the leadership he prioritised 'the good of the people': consumerism, housing and greater freedom to move jobs. Khrushchev positively invited comparison between American and Soviet material achievements as can be seen in the New Party Programme of 1961 (see below). Fridges, televisions and even washing machines appeared in Soviet homes and meat consumption rose by 55 per cent between 1958 and 1965. The differences between the social classes had been reduced, wage differentials were smaller and the differences between the town and the countryside, industry and agriculture were being reduced – but not by enough to stem the flow of young people, in particular, from the countryside.

The New Party Programme of 1961

Khrushchev was not very interested in abstract ideas but was eager to associate himself with movement to a new stage in the development of Soviet society. According to the testimony of those who knew him, Khrushchev always remained a 'true believer' in communism, which he interpreted as meaning a better life for ordinary people.

Khrushchev wanted to issue an effective summons to action and to revive the mood of the 1920s that there was 'no fortress a Bolshevik cannot storm'. The New Party Programme of 1961 was Khrushchev's contribution and was delivered at the 22nd Party Congress. It has been described as 'a remarkable combination of self-delusion, wishful thinking and utopianism'. Below are some parts of it:

- The Soviet Union had already built socialism and was on the way to creating communism.
- The Communist Party was now a party of the whole people; it was no longer the dictatorship of the proletariat.
- It was to be more accountable to the membership with limits on terms served and rotation of office (see page 279).
- The Communist Party was to be the key institution in the march towards communism.

Missile gap – the Soviet *Sputnik* launch in 1957 stunned people in the USA. John F. Kennedy who wanted to run in the 1960 presidential election seized on these fears and claimed that the United States was losing the satellite-missile race with the USSR and the Republicans were weak on defence. A missile gap was emerging. This was not the case and the US government knew this, but President Eisenhower did not want to refer to evidence gained by U2 spy planes to deny the claims.

- A communist society will be almost complete by 1980.
- By 1970 there will be no housing shortage and the Soviet Union will have overtaken the United States in per capita production.
- By 1980 the real income per head will have increased by more than 250 per cent.

These claims were made without any proper regard for the views of experts. A classic example of Khrushchev's bravado was this statement in the programme:

The achievement of Communism in the USSR will be the greatest victory mankind has ever won throughout its long history

Social change

In 1956 the minimum wage rose sharply and there was a major expansion of the pension scheme for the elderly, disabled and sick. This was important in a country where the ravages of the war had left many permanent invalids and one-parent families. In 1964 comprehensive cover was extended to collective farmers. The seven-hour day (six hours on Saturday) was introduced in 1960, the minimum wage was raised significantly and holiday pay was introduced. The fierce labour laws against absenteeism and changing jobs without permission were repealed.

Housing, education and medicine

Khrushchev's housing programme was one of the most important social and political changes of the post-Stalin years. In honour of the 40th anniversary of the October Revolution in 1957, Khrushchev launched a programme to end the housing shortage in the next ten to twelve years. It was a quick fix. The annual rate of housing construction almost doubled and between 1956 and 1965 approximately 108 million people moved into new apartments. Cheap, prefabricated and five storeys high, to cut out the need for lifts, the housing may have been of poor quality, but the change it made to people's lives was marked. Families who previously might have lived in one room in a communal apartment were liberated. They could now shut their own front door, they had privacy and they could acquire radios and televisions.

The numbers of doctors and hospital beds rose impressively, and Khrushchev gave maximum publicity to improvements in educational provision. The numbers in higher education almost trebled in his time in power. In 1958 the secondary school-leaving age was raised from fourteen to fifteen and fees both for senior classes of secondary and for tertiary education were abolished. He was particularly keen to make education available to the children of workers and peasants, and spoke out against the very high proportion of students from privileged families entering university. He noted a tendency to look down on manual work. Khrushchev's solution was to attempt to make entry to higher education conditional on the completion of two years' work experience. There was much resistance to this and the proposal was severely watered down, never fully implemented and dropped quickly after he was ousted.

Khrushchev's aggressive campaign against religion

During the war, Stalin had come to an accommodation with the Church and there was an attitude of relative tolerance after the war. Khrushchev sought to revive Lenin's spirit of Party activism and militant atheism. It was not an accident that it coincided with the preparation of the New Party Programme. It also appeased ideological purists in the Presidium. Anti-religious propaganda was strengthened, taxes on religious activity increased and churches and monasteries were closed. Between 1959 and 1964 about three-quarters of all

The Thaw

Ilya Ehrenburg's novel *The Thaw* published in 1954 caught the atmosphere of the time and gave a name to it. It was a metaphor for the arrival of spring, the spring that had to come after the Stalin era.

Christian churches and monasteries in the Soviet Union were closed down. Mosques and synagogues were under attack too.

Cultural change

There was a partial thaw in cultural life during the Khrushchev era stimulated by his 'secret speech'. Many writers who had been banned were rehabilitated, such as Anna Akhmatova. Writers tested the limit of state censorship, finding that prose or poems critical of Stalin were acceptable, but works that denounced the Party or belittled the present Soviet way of life were off limits. When the editor of *Novy Mir* asked Party bosses for permission to write a little bit of 'truth about realities in the country', he received the answer that 'literature must stay completely at the service of the Party'. When in 1956 Boris Pasternak offered the manuscript of *Dr Zhivago*, his only novel, to *Novy Mir* it was rejected. It was felt that the novel was against the revolution and that it portrayed the Soviet state in a very negative light. It was published in Italy in 1957 and in 1958 Pasternak was awarded the Nobel Prize for literature. Illegal copies circulated in the USSR, helped, we now know, by the CIA who believed it would have an effect and so gave out copies to Soviet visitors to the Brussels Universal and International Exposition in 1958. In Russia there was a huge campaign to denounce Pasternak. He was expelled from the Writers' Union and forced to renounce the Nobel Prize. His health gave out under the strain and he died of cancer in 1960. Thousands turned out for his funeral.

In October in the same year Vasily Grossman submitted to an official literary journal *Life and Fate*, his great novel about the Second World War, and acknowledged to be the twentieth century's *War and Peace*. He clearly believed that the novel could now be published. The authorities did not agree. In February 1961 three KGB officers came to his flat and confiscated the manuscript and any other related material, even carbon paper and typewriter ribbons. It was regarded as even more damaging than *Dr Zhivago* and Grossman was told that his novel could not be published for two or three hundred years. This in its own way acknowledged the book's lasting literary value. Grossman tried to appeal against 'the arrest of his book' to Khrushchev personally. It was to no avail. Grossman died in 1964 and the book was not published in the West until 1980 and in the USSR until 1988.

Khrushchev was able to see how poets and novelists could further his own ends. He tended to favour works that discomforted the diehards like Molotov, but could take a violent dislike to modern art. When the editor of *Novy Mir*, Tvardovsky, received the manuscript of a short novel, *One Day in the Life of Ivan Denisovich*, he was excited by it and determined to publish it. He offered it to Khrushchev to be used as a weapon against his enemies. Khrushchev praised the book as being written 'in the spirit of the 22nd Party Congress'. He compelled his colleagues on the Presidium to read the manuscript, and then authorised its publication in 1962. Its author was Aleksandr Solzhenitsyn, then completely unknown. While serving in the Red Army in 1945 he had written a letter critical of Stalin which resulted in nine years in prisons and labour camps and then exile in Kazakhstan. The book deals with a single day in one prisoner's long sentence. Tvardovsky said that the story had 'not a drop of falsehood in it'. For the first time, the full truth of what went on in the camps had been revealed in Soviet literature. The book, though, neither probed the roots of Stalinism nor did Ivan Denisovich blame the Soviet system, he simply marveled that such a fate should befall him and his fellow citizens. One million copies were sold in its first six months. The readership was vastly greater as it was passed from hand to hand. It made a particular impact on former camp inmates who were overjoyed to read something which reflected their own feelings and experience.

LOOK AGAIN

Anna Akhmatova

(See pages 221 and 242.) Anna, her family and friends suffered in the Great Terror and her poetry cycle *Requiem* written between 1935 and 1940 was eventually published in 1963. She also remarked to a friend in 1956, 'Now the arrested are returning, and two Russias stare each other in the eyes: the ones who put them in prison and the ones who were put in prison'.

Novy Mir – a literary journal in which *One Day in the Life of Ivan Denisovich* and other work representative of the thaw was published.

CIA – United States Central Intelligence Agency, active in the Cold War.

Boris Pasternak and *Dr Zhivago*

During the war Pasternak (see page 221) worked on his semi-autobiographical novel *Doctor Zhivago*. The novel's central figure is a doctor and poet. He is already married when he falls in love with another woman, Lara – who is married herself, to a committed Bolshevik – and the plot follows the progress of their doomed relationship, as their lives are caught up in Russia's three revolutions and the civil war. In 1965 it was made into a very popular British film directed by David Lean, starring Omar Sharif and Julie Christie.

NOTE-MAKING

In parallel columns note the reasons why *Dr Zhivago* was not published and *One Day in the Life of Ivan Denisovich* was.

On 21 October 1962, *Pravda* published Yevgeny Yevtushenko's poem 'The Heirs of Stalin'. The poem attacked Stalin and his followers and warned against a resurgence of Stalinism. It began with the removal of Stalin's coffin from the Lenin Mausoleum for reburial and contained the lines:

And I appeal to our government with the request:

to double,

to treble the guard at this tombstone,

So that Stalin may not rise,

and together with Stalin –

the past.

Along with *One Day in the Life of Ivan Denisovich*, the publication of the poem marked the high watermark for reform; conservatives were outraged. They rallied and the criticisms of Solzhenitsyn began.

Source E *Gulag* by Anne Applebaum, (Penguin), 2004, p 470.

If the Soviet Union's elite were to accept that the portrait of Ivan Denisovich was authentic, that meant admitting that innocent people had endured pointless suffering. If the camps had really been stupid and wasteful and tragic, that meant that the Soviet Union was stupid and wasteful and tragic too.

Solzhenitsyn was unable to publish his next novels and Yevtushenko's poem was not printed again for a quarter of a century.

Khrushchev's views on modern art were caustic. Some of it he regarded as decadent and irrelevant to popular needs. In a row with a sculptor reported in *Pravda* he condemned pictures 'that make you wonder whether they were painted by the hand of a man or daubed by the tail of a donkey'.

How does Source E illustrate the difficulties associated with the process of de-Stalinisation?

KEY DATES: SOCIAL AND CULTURAL CHANGE

1954 *The Thaw* published.

1956 Minimum wage rose sharply, expansion of pension scheme.

Dr Zhivago rejected by *Novy Mir*.

1957 Housing programme launched.

1958 School-leaving age raised to fifteen, fees abolished.

Pasternak forced to renounce the Nobel Prize for Literature.

1960 Seven-hour day introduced.

1961 New Party Programme announced at 22nd Party Congress.

1962 *One Day in the Life of Ivan Denisovich* published.

1964 Comprehensive pension cover was extended to collective farmers.

3 Opposition and the fall of Khrushchev

This section will first examine dissent in Khrushchev's Russia, which was rather more widespread than once thought. It will then look at why and how Khrushchev's opponents within the leadership removed him and will conclude by looking at the state of the country in 1964.

Dissent and repression

How much dissent was there and how was it dealt with?

In the past historians have focused on cultural dissent when looking at opposition in the Khrushchev era. Recent research from Robert Hornsby and others makes it clear that dissent at this time was not solely, or even primarily, a matter for the intelligentsia. Hornsby has analysed the case files of the Soviet Procuracy and these reveal that in the late 1950s and early 1960s workers came to dominate the 'underground', which the Procuracy targeted.

> **Soviet Procuracy** – the government bureau concerned with pursuing dissenters accused of anti-Soviet agitation and propaganda.

The most important example of dissent came at Novocherkassk. In this solidly working-class town in Ukraine an uprising took place on 1 June 1962. The previous day the price of butter had been increased by 25 per cent and meat by 30 per cent – cheap food prices had been taken for granted. These sharp price rises coincided with the announcement of a cut in wages at the large electrical works. The crass insensitivity of the works director when confronting the crowd of workers inflamed the situation, and unrest spread rapidly across the town. A passing train was stopped and a placard was hung on it, which read 'cut up Khrushchev for sausages'. The Party headquarters were occupied. In response, troops were brought in, opened fire and killed 28 people and wounded over 80. The uprising was dealt with swiftly with a few ring leaders executed, the area was given the highest priority for food supplies, and local officials were blamed for letting the situation get out of hand and placed under strict orders to ensure there would be no repetition. The square where the shootings took place was covered in asphalt overnight to hide the blood, and the bodies were buried, unmarked, in existing graves in five different cemeteries. Unlike in the Stalin era there were no claims that the unrest was the product of spies and counter-revolutionary agitation. Instead there was a very successful news blackout and the full story only came out 30 years later.

The Novocherkassk uprising was exceptional only in its number of casualties. The reasons for it, and the fact that it was workers who were involved, was typical. There was no dissident movement, but it has been estimated that 500,000 Soviet citizens participated in mass disorders, disturbances, demonstrations, protest meetings and strikes between 1953 and 1964. The view of Ludmilla Alexeyeva that these years were 'an incubation period when people began to learn to talk about the problems of Soviet life' does not go far enough. There were significant differences between dissent in different eras:

- Stalin era, 1928–53: largely spontaneous and volatile and often centred on angry peasants and workers.
- Khrushchev era, 1953–64: involved both workers and peasants and a few members of the intelligentsia. However, they did not act together.
- Brezhnev years 1964–82: more legalistic and sober criticism mainly from a small proportion of the intelligentsia in the big cities.

Workers and peasants focused on increases in the price of food, restrictions on private plots and specific abuses of power rather than questions of political reform. Dissent among the intelligentsia focused on the uneven progress of de-Stalinisation and restrictions upon cultural affairs.

Dealing with dissent

After Novocherkassk there was a decline in the frequency and scale of protests largely because the authorities took greater care to prevent unrest occurring in the first place. Working-class grievances were particularly worrying in an era of rising expectations. The workers' standard of living had to be raised with more consumer goods and above all food prices had to be kept down. From this time on food prices were held down however strong the case for bringing them more closely in line with the costs of production. It was another problem for the command economy.

The grievances of the intelligentsia were more fundamentally political and less easy to buy off by material improvements. Mass terror had been abandoned but there were new layers of social control, and peer-policing was employed to stifle the expression of political doubts and discontents. A dense network of informers was maintained which invaded every corner of society. It was still an extremely authoritarian state and there was to be no compromise with those considered to be anti-Soviet. Practically all of the foundations for the persecution of dissidents in the 1960s, 1970s and 1980s had been laid during Khrushchev's time in power. In a backlash after the Hungarian rising (see page 267) more dissenters were jailed during 1957 and 1958 than at any other time since Stalin's death. The forced commitment of dissenters to psychiatric hospitals also had its roots in the early 1960s. The extent to which Khrushchev was a liberal leader can be exaggerated.

Cultural dissidents

Historian Orlando Figes argues that:

In no other country did literature attain as much authority – as the voice and conscience of the People – as it did in Soviet Russia

Cultural dissidents were, by the 1960s, the most articulate opponents of communism and Solzhenitsyn became one of the chief of their number. The Khrushchev era saw the rapid development of *samizdat* (Source F).

Source F Vladimir Bukovsky quoted in *Rulers and Victims: The Russians in the Soviet Union* by Geoffrey Hosking, (Harvard University Press), 2006, p 273.

I would erect a monument to the typewriter ... It brought forth a new form of publishing, *samizdat* or self publishing; write myself, edit myself, publish, distribute myself, go to jail for it myself.

Initially a new way of circulating poetry and fiction, *samizdat* was not just an individual enterprise, it expanded into a true underground press. Retyping and redistributing, and sometimes reading the texts, was a collective endeavour. It became an important cultural activity and a subject of worry and investigation for the security services. It became a way of spreading political and factual information on internal events in the country. Poetry readings in Mayakovsky Square in Moscow expanded in scope to include controversial issues. The KGB intervened and broke them up. The young Vladimir Bukovsky was taken to a police station, beaten up, and warned: 'Don't ever go to Mayakovsky Square again. Next time we'll kill you!'. He became a leading dissident, best known for exposing the use of psychiatric hospitals against dissidents; he himself had been so confined between 1963 and 1965.

LOOK AGAIN
How well does Bukovsky's statement in Source F and the quotation from Figes above relate to what you have read about literature in tsarist Russia? Did literature play the crucial role in developing criticism of the regime in the years covered by this book?

Khrushchev's downfall

Why was Khrushchev overthrown so easily?

Khrushchev was seen as unpredictable and explosive and got into the habit of insulting colleagues, who neither forgot nor forgave him. Arrogance was one of the main charges against him when his colleagues deposed him in October 1964. Once committed to an idea he often pursued it without proper consultation. Hence the charge levelled against him of 'hare-brained scheming'. His weaknesses were highlighted in three areas between 1962 and 1964, all of which contributed to his downfall.

Cuban missile crisis

In his diplomacy Khrushchev was determined to show that the USSR was capable of defending its own interests vigorously. For years the existence of American nuclear missiles in Turkey on the USSR's border had been bitterly resented. A communist revolution in Cuba 90 miles (145 km) from the coast of the United States gave Khrushchev an opportunity to put similar pressure on the USA by placing Soviet missiles on Cuban bases. American spy planes detected the scheme before it was complete and President Kennedy placed a naval blockade around Cuba. The world stood on the brink of a nuclear war that Khrushchev never intended to launch. He drew back. The missiles were removed. In the compromise that defused the situation the USA had promised both to dismantle its nuclear facilities in Turkey and never to invade Cuba. However, part of the compromise was that this should remain secret so the Soviet Union appeared humbled in the eyes of the world. Although Khrushchev had consulted the Presidium throughout the crisis the missiles had been his idea and he alone was blamed.

Agricultural failures

In 1963, the dry summer, the problems of the Virgin Lands campaign and the effect of devoting too much land to maize, meant that the grain harvest was 107 million tonnes and was judged against Khrushchev's boasting and the planned target of 170–180 million tonnes. Khrushchev would take no risks after Novocherkassk. Precious gold and currency reserves were used to buy grain from the West. This was a humiliation for Khrushchev in what he regarded as his field of expertise. When in October 1964 Khrushchev was summoned to a meeting of the Presidium he was accused of gross mistakes in agricultural organisation.

The effect of reorganisations

Khrushchev's restlessness and his impatience can be seen in his many attempts to interfere with both the State and Party bureaucracies. He liked to shake up institutions but had no wish to use Stalin's methods of doing so; this left persuasion and the reshuffling of personnel as the only means available to him.

- Between 1956 and 1961 he replaced more than two-thirds of the members of the Council of Ministers, the Presidium and the local Party Secretaries, and half of the Central Committee.
- In 1961 he limited to three the number of times that leading officials could be elected to the same office. There was to be a turnover of at least half the members of Party committees at the lower levels, a third at the higher levels and a quarter of the members of the Central Committee and the Presidium at each Party Congress.
- In 1962 he divided the Party between parallel hierarchies responsible for agriculture and industry.

NOTE-MAKING

Draw a spider diagram to show the main factors which contributed to Khrushchev's overthrow.

Khrushchev upsets diplomats

Khrushchev was an enthusiastic traveller and he visited the United States in 1959. However, his international diplomacy could be marred by the most extreme boorishness. The most infamous example was when he banged his shoe on the table at the UN General Assembly in 1960. His interpreters and colleagues were appalled and humiliated at being represented on the world stage by such a leader. He upset the Foreign Office again in 1964 when he sent his son-in-law to negotiate with West Germany.

Contemporary joke

By this time Khrushchev was completely bald except for a white fuzz above each ear, prompting the joke:

What do you call Khrushchev's hairdo?

Harvest of 1963.

Soviet jokes are not side-splitting but they are historical sources; the clear association of Khrushchev and the harvest of 1963 is significant.

The last two moves in particular were bitterly resented by the officials affected and regarded by his opponents as part of his 'hare-brained schemes'. The division of the Party was especially unpopular with provincial Party Secretaries who had previously run the Party throughout the province. They were now being asked to choose between industry and agriculture thus drastically reducing their power. What is more, the Party Secretaries had great influence in the Central Committee whose members already resented the limits imposed on their time in office. These people had formed Khrushchev's main power base, and he would have to face the consequences in October 1964. All these changes were reversed very soon after Khrushchev was removed from power.

The Presidium	Resented his arrogance, his style, his policies. Some felt his anti-Stalinism had gone too far.
Provincial Party Secretaries and the Central Committee	Bitter resentment of his reorganisations.
The military	Resented cuts in military spending and the policy of relying on nuclear weapons, a policy refuted by the Cuban missile crisis.
Professional people/ managers	Resented the enhanced role of the Party and its interference.
Intelligentsia	Disappointed with the retreat from the thaw after 1962.
The diplomatic service	Appalled by some of his behaviour, and his use of his son-in-law on diplomatic missions.
Workers	Alienated by the rise in food prices in 1962.
Peasants	Resented disruptive and repeated interventions and the failure of his policies.

▲ Figure 3 Khrushchev alienates nearly everyone by 1964.

The blow falls

Khrushchev was on holiday in Georgia when a phone call from Brezhnev summoned him to an emergency meeting of the Presidium. When the meeting began it became immediately clear that Khrushchev was its subject. Starting with Brezhnev, the Presidium members condemned his behaviour and style: his 'explosiveness', 'acting unilaterally, ignoring the Presidium', 'the cult of Khrushchev', 'the rudeness of which Lenin had once accused Stalin'; and his policies, especially on agriculture and 'juggling the fate of the world' in Cuba. The meeting was adjourned until the next day. Khrushchev had put up little resistance, and that night called his friend and Presidium colleague Anastas Mikoyan, on a phone which was of course bugged, and told him:

I'm old and tired. Let them cope by themselves. I've done the main thing. Could anyone have dreamed of telling Stalin that he didn't suit us anymore and suggesting he retire? Not even a wet spot would have remained where we had been standing. Now everything is different. The fear is gone, and we can talk as equals. That's my contribution. I won't put up a fight.

The next day there was further criticism but the Presidium knew they had their man. The vote to oust him was unanimous. The Presidium demanded that Khrushchev should voluntarily retire 'in connection with his advanced age and deterioration of his health'. Later that day there was a meeting of the full Central Committee, the body which had saved him in 1957. Not this time. After a further condemnation the vote went unanimously against Khrushchev. Brezhnev was unanimously selected as Party First Secretary with Kosygin as Prime Minister.

LOOK AGAIN

Political authority

This activity will help you to compare the political authority of Stalin and that of Khrushchev.

In Chapter 6 (pages 222–4) you looked at the basis of Stalin's dictatorship. Revisit this. In small groups work out:
● How much of this was still there under Khrushchev?
● Had it become diluted?
● Does this help to explain why Khrushchev was overthrown?

Khrushchev was allowed to retire and ignored. When he died in 1971 there was a four-line announcement of his death in *Pravda,* without comment and no obituary. At his burial there were no official speeches and none of his successors and erstwhile colleagues attended, indeed it was made very difficult for anyone except his family to get to the cemetery. As Alec Nove puts it, 'Silence. An undeserved epitaph for this most talkative of Soviet leaders'.

The political, economic and social condition of the Soviet Union by 1964

Had Khrushchev succeeded in shaking up the Soviet Union?

The biggest change in the post-Stalin years was the ending of mass terror and the reduction in coercion. This was seen most dramatically in the numbers of people in the gulag. The gulag population fell fastest in the two years immediately after Stalin's death due to Beria's amnesty which affected mainly criminals on shorter sentences; the freeing of political prisoners accelerated after Khrushchev's 'secret speech'.

The 'secret speech' was the bravest thing Khrushchev did and the Soviet Union was never the same again. The move away from terror proved irreversible but for it to happen smoothly, support for the system had to be broadened and consolidated. This was sought by material incentives – there was a marked and general improvement in the standard of living. Cold War propaganda stressing the American threat encouraged patriotism and conformity. The message from the Party was that material progress and peace depended upon 'Soviet socialism'. It has been argued that Russia had become more stable than at any time since the days of Alexander I in the first quarter of the nineteenth century.

Khrushchev had shaken things up, or at least threatened to do so, in a way that worried the Presidium and Central Committee. He was succeeded by Brezhnev and an **oligarchy** determined to preserve the *status quo*. Khrushchev's reforms in agriculture, education, economic administration and the Party apparatus were speedily reversed. The rule about regular rotation of Party officials was dropped. Party Secretaries, a key position in the regions, could now regard themselves as having jobs for life.

Source G *Rulers and Victims, The Russians in the Soviet Union* by Geoffrey Hosking, (Harvard University Press), 2006, p 3054.

By the mid-1960s the Soviet Union had become a stable, hierarchical, and conservative society – and after the upheavals of recent decades, most people were content to see it that way. At the apex of the pyramid was Moscow, the Kremlin and the building of the Central Committee of the CPSU. From that focal point tentacles of appointment, control, and supplies extended outward to the Russian provinces and to the non-Russian republics. Every enterprise and institution had its place in the hierarchy, according to whether its work was deemed to be of 'all-Union significance', of 'republican significance' or lower. The salaries and perks of its managers and employees depended on that rating. The positioning of each town on the ladder would depend on the status of its enterprises, and on that in turn would depend the quality of its facilities and the supplies of its shops. Villages stood on the lowest rung.

	1953	1960
Number and percentage of political prisoners in the gulag	539,718 (22%)	9,596 (1.6%)
Total gulag population	2,467,893	582,717

▲ **Figure 4** Gulag population figures, 1953 and 1960.

Oligarchy – a state where a small group holds power.

How far does Source G illustrate the problems of bringing about change in the Soviet Union?

The economy and society

Reform of the planned economy had proved very difficult. Technical innovation was very slow because new equipment meant disrupting production lines and anything that reduced output, even temporarily, had the effect of reducing workers' pay. Most industries therefore relied on materials and techniques that had proved successful in the big push of post-war reconstruction. Only military and space technology kept up with the highest international standards, and under Khrushchev did so very successfully.

In spite of Khrushchev's emphasis on agriculture the Russian village remained a depressing place; the young sought the first opportunity to leave and many villages became the preserve of women and elderly men. From the mid-1950s urban dwellers outnumbered rural ones. The demographic impact of the war was still clear; in 1959 women still formed 55 per cent of the population. The burdens of society were overwhelmingly being borne by women. Russia had the world's highest rate of female employment and usually it was women who shouldered the domestic responsibilities, which still included much queuing for scarce items.

While there was a clampdown after 1962 on publishing the revelatory works associated with 'the thaw', *samizdat* still grew. The significant numbers of students receiving higher education posed a dilemma for the Soviet state. It needed highly qualified people with inquiring minds in all branches of science and technology, but, in time, such minds might also challenge the whole system. However, in 1964 the Soviet Union entered upon twenty years of stagnation.

Khrushchev had found that the bureaucratic apparatus of Party and State could distort policy and paralyse desired initiative. When Gorbachev tried major reform it brought about the collapse of the system.

LOOK AGAIN

Parallels have been drawn between the Khrushchev era and the Gorbachev years and between both periods and the political crisis of the early 1900s. In all three there were unsuccessful top-down reforms, poorly thought out and ill performed. In all cases the system's capacity for change from within proved limited, with inconsistent reforms leading to political catastrophe.

Chapter summary

- Khrushchev was very different from Stalin: extrovert, volatile and constantly out and about at home and abroad. He became increasingly arrogant and overbearing but initially, like Stalin, he was underestimated by his rivals.
- Khrushchev took the lead in getting rid of Beria. He used his position as Party Secretary and had support from the army and KGB. This allowed him to oust Malenkov and defeat the Anti-Party group.
- In his 'secret speech' Khrushchev focused on Stalin's treatment of loyal Party members, his conduct during the war, the cult of personality and the Leningrad affair and Doctors' plot after the war. He ignored forced collectivisation and the sufferings of non-Party members in the Terror.
- The speech had a profound impact at home and abroad. It shook faith in the communist system and sparked the Hungarian uprising. It led to the Anti-Party group's challenge of Khrushchev in 1957.
- The Virgin Lands campaign and maize growing were Khrushchev's main agricultural initiatives. His Seven-Year Plan focused on the chemical industry, oil, gas and consumer goods. Space exploration was a great success. His economic reorganisations alienated people and his policies were more successful in the 1950s than 1960s.
- The standard of living was raised. There were more consumer goods and improvements in housing, education, medicine and pensions. The boastful targets of Khrushchev's New Party Programme of 1961 were not achieved.
- This was the era of the 'thaw'. In literature some criticism of Stalin was acceptable but any perceived attack on the Party or the present Soviet way of life was not.
- There was no dissident movement in the Khrushchev era but there was dissent usually deriving from workers' material concerns, the Novocherkassk uprising being the most serious. Thereafter food prices were kept down.
- The Cuban missile crisis, the bad harvest of 1963 and exasperation with Khrushchev's constant reorganisations were key factors in his overthrow. His behaviour had alienated far too many in the Presidium and Central Committee and he was easily ousted.
- The most important legacy of the Khrushchev era was the ending of mass terror. The lives of people had improved but it was difficult to reform the system. Russia entered a twenty-year period of stagnation following Khrushchev's departure.

Year	Political developments and de-Stalinisation	Economic, social and cultural developments
1953	**March** Death of Stalin. **June** Arrest of Beria. **December** Execution of Beria.	Khrushchev and Malenkov clash on agricultural policy.
1954		First harvest in Virgin Lands campaign. *The Thaw* published.
1955	Malenkov resigns as Prime Minister.	
1956	**February** Khrushchev's 20th Party Congress speech. **October** Hungarian rising.	Bumper grain harvest and the Virgin Lands contribute over 50 per cent of the total. *Dr Zhivago* rejected by *Novy Mir.*
1957	Khrushchev defeats the attempt to oust him. Malenkov, Molotov and Kaganovich are removed from influence.	Khrushchev launches a programme to end the housing shortage in the next ten to twelve years. *Dr Zhivago* published in Italy. First satellite – the *Sputnik* – launched into space.
1958	Khrushchev replaces Bulganin as Prime Minister.	Pasternak was awarded the Nobel Prize for literature. Forced to renounce it.
1959	21st Party Congress. Khrushchev visits USA.	Seven-Year Plan launched.
1960	Khrushchev bangs shoe at the UN General Assembly.	
1961	Khrushchev's attack on Stalin at the 22nd Party Congress leads to the removal of Stalin from the Lenin Mausoleum.	Programme of the Communist Party launched: unrealistic goal of introducing a 35-hour working week and overtaking the United States in per capita production by 1970. Yuri Gagarin becomes the first man in space.
1962	Khrushchev divides the Party between parallel hierarchies responsible for agriculture and industry. Cuban missile crisis.	*One Day in the Life of Ivan Denisovich* published in *Novy Mir.* Novocherkassk strike in which 28 are killed.
1963		Disastrous harvest, grain and fodder imported.
1964	**October** Khrushchev deposed.	

Working on essay technique

'After the war Stalin consolidated his rigid system. Under Khrushchev there was real change.' Assess the validity of this view. (25 marks)

At the heart of your answer to this type of question will be your assessment of Khrushchev, which you need to work out. Robert Hornsby's essay (pages 286–7) is a balanced assessment of Khrushchev and valuable in helping you come to your own view.

Hornsby's essay includes material that you might want to use in any essay on Khrushchev because it supports your view of the era. You need to have your own view of what Khrushchev did, but you should not have a 'Khrushchev essay'.

- The question asks you to address the Stalin era as well as Khrushchev's. Your answer should be evenly balanced between Stalin and Khrushchev. 'Consolidated' requires some brief reference to the fact that pre-war Stalinism shaped post-war Stalinism, so this brings in an understanding of his system at the end of the 1930s.
- Do not be intimidated by being asked to assess quite a long statement. In fact it actually helps you to structure your answer as it tells you what you have to write about:
  - The consolidation of Stalin's rigid system after the war
  - Whether Khrushchev brought real change
  While the first area is not particularly controversial there is room for a range of views on how much real change there was under Khrushchev.
- You will need to establish some criteria for measuring change and how far what occurred could be seen as real change. Hornsby is very helpful here.

- The question requires you to look at how far Stalin's rigid system was changed and not a particular aspect. Political, economic, social and cultural life will need to be referred to even if some of the references will be very brief. You have limited time but you do need to show that you are aware of the broad scope of the question.
- In judging real change you need to be aware of the circumstances in which Khrushchev was operating and assess what was possible. Was Stalin's system 'unsuited to fundamental reform'?
- Make sure an argument runs through your essay and that you are able to substantiate it. Take a bit of time to write an effective conclusion.

ACTIVITY: PRACTICE QUESTION

The question above covers a range of breadth issues. Have a go at an A-level practice question that focuses on one issue: cultural change.

'The Khrushchev years (1953–64) saw significant cultural change when compared with the Stalin era (1928–53).' Assess the validity of this view. (25 marks)

The question states 'Khrushchev years' so it is not just Khrushchev's views you will be looking at. For example, you may want to show that there were different views both within the leadership and outside, particularly in the Khrushchev years.

Furthermore there are changes within the years under discussion. This is true of the Stalin era as well as Khrushchev's time. Thus for Stalin you will need to look at the impact of the cultural revolution, socialist realism, the war and post-war years.

There is certainly enough material to use for a good answer and by now you should have developed the skills to produce one.

Working on interpretation skills: extended reading

An assessment of Khrushchev

Dr Robert Hornsby assesses the extent of change brought about in Russia by Khrushchev's time in power.

When Khrushchev denounced Stalin in his Secret Speech it was telling that he insisted the Soviet system was essentially sound: it had merely been temporarily perverted by Stalin's rampant paranoia and dictatorial character. In this sense, he promised to 'correct flaws' and put the country back on the path that Lenin had originally marked out (and from which Stalin had strayed), rather than to overhaul the system entirely. The scale of political repression went into steep and permanent decline, living standards began to rise for ordinary citizens, the leader cult was scaled down, and the country became a little more open to the outside world.

It is important to remember that each of these improvements was relative to what had gone before: people still went to jail for political offences and living standards were generally not high. Numerous fundamental aspects of Stalinism, such as collectivised agriculture and tight control over the media, were judged entirely proper and so remained virtually untouched by Khrushchev's reform programme. Trotsky remained an 'enemy', criticism of the Communist Party was still forbidden, religious activity was suppressed, and the security apparatus (now known as the KGB) kept a close eye on what people said and did.

The system left behind at Stalin's death, though, was both unsustainable in the long term and unsuited to fundamental reform. There has hardly been a more suitable case to apply Alexis de Tocqueville's old maxim that 'the most dangerous moment for a bad government is when it begins to reform'. Like Gorbachev three decades later, Khrushchev had to tread a difficult path between those who supported reform and those who opposed it. There were plenty among both the Party leadership and the wider population who had thrived during the Stalin years and did not wish to see that period rubbished, or else they had plenty of skeletons in their own closet that they did not wish to be exposed to public scrutiny. For all those who denounced Stalin, it is important to remember that there were still plenty who viewed positively his achievements as Soviet leader.

However, Stalin's death undoubtedly changed the atmosphere in the country for the better. With his promise of a 'return to Leninism' Khrushchev even managed to reignite some of the old romance and idealism about building Communism. In regard to how daily life changed for ordinary Soviet citizens between the mid-1950s and mid-1960s there are a few points worth noting. Efforts at tackling the terrible shortage of housing, providing more consumer goods and providing more leisure facilities and opportunities all had a significant impact and were continued long after Khrushchev's departure. Millions were released from the *gulag* or else were pardoned and rehabilitated. For most people, life clearly became easier and less fraught with danger, even if all manner of basic political rights were still denied to them.

Khrushchev himself was by no means a consistent force for liberal reform, partly because of his volatile and unpredictable character and partly because he often faced pressure from more conservative colleagues in the Party leadership. When public discussion of controversial topics, like the Stalin-era *gulag*, threatened to grow beyond the authorities' control, it was quickly shut down. Khrushchev later recounted how he had feared the 'thaw' of post-Stalin reform turning into a flood and washing away everything. While the period is often known as 'the thaw', it is much more accurate to think of a series of 'thaws' and 'refreezes'.

Some years after he had been forced into an unwanted retirement, Khrushchev made the case in his memoirs that his greatest impact on Soviet political life could be seen in the fact that he had been voted out of power by his colleagues, rather than arrested and shot. This, of course, entirely overlooked the point that he had no intention of leaving power of his own accord and there was no way that 'the people' could or should have a say in the matter. Nonetheless, he was absolutely right to note that the country's political life was no longer deadly, and that no Soviet leader would again wield the kind of unchallenged power that Stalin had.

The extent to which Khrushchev managed to reform the Soviet system can perhaps be best demonstrated by what followed his removal in October 1964. More politically conservative than Khrushchev, the Brezhnev leadership ended all prospect for further reform and abandoned all criticism of Stalin and Stalinism. What they did not do – and most likely could not do, even if they so wished – was return to the unbridled brutality and deprivation that had been key hallmarks of full Stalinism.

Dr Robert Hornsby is a Research Fellow at the School of History, University of Kent.

ACTIVITY

Having read the essay, answer the following questions.

Interpretation

1 How convincing is Khrushchev's argument in his memoirs about his greatest impact on Soviet political life?

Evidence

2 Make a list of examples of:
- Khrushchev making a positive change
- the limitations of the changes made.

Evaluation

3 How much of a reformer does Dr Hornsby think Khrushchev was?

Key questions: The Soviet Union, 1917–64

The specification you have been studying on Russia highlighted six key issues. We reviewed these at the end of Part 1 (page 153), providing opportunities for you to think about themes that run through your study of the period. Now there is the opportunity for you to review this for Part 2 and the whole period of your study.

In the examination the essays will be focused on broad areas of the content and will reflect one or more of the six key issues. Therefore, this section should be of great help to you in your revision, both looking at themes and also revisiting the detailed content you have studied.

KEY QUESTION 1:
How was Russia governed and how did political authority change and develop?

Questions to consider

- How did the centralised state develop in Russia between 1918 and 1924?
- From where did the political authority of the communist regime come?
- How was the political authority of Lenin different from that of Stalin and Khrushchev?
- How did Stalin's power grow and develop? What was the nature of Stalinism?
- How much change was there in government and political authority under Khrushchev?

Working in groups

Taking the period as a whole:
1 How much did the Stalin revolution change the way the USSR was governed?
2 Compare the degree of political authority of the tsarist and communist states.
3 Both the tsars and the communist rulers were autocratic rulers:
   - Were the communists more effective?
   - If so, why was this?
4 There were six wars in these years: the Crimean War, Russo-Japanese War, First World War, Civil War, Second World War and the Cold War. There were three revolutions: the 1905 Revolution, the February and October Revolutions of 1917:
   - Consider the effects of these wars on the development of Russian government.
   - Which had the greater impact on the development of Russian government: wars or revolutions?
5 Discuss the view that Stalin was a 'Red Tsar'.
   - Look at the role of autocracy, nationality, orthodoxy/Marxism–Leninism in the systems of tsarism and Stalinism.
   - How similar were the aims of all the rulers of Russia in these years?

Why did opposition develop and how effective was it?

Questions to consider

- The peasants weren't Bolsheviks and the Bolsheviks weren't peasants.
  - How did the Bolsheviks perceive the peasants?
  - How did the peasants perceive the Bolsheviks?
- Do you agree with Christopher Read that 'the conflicts arising from the disparity between Bolshevik views and peasant reality were amongst the most severe in post-revolutionary Russia'?
- What do we learn of opposition within the Party in the 1920s? Think about: workers' opposition, ban on factions, struggle over power, Ryutin Platform.
- Were the Terror and the purges a response to genuine opposition either before or after the Second World War?
- How were things different under Khrushchev? Consider:
  - dissent and cultural dissidents
  - divisions and opposition within the leadership
  - Khrushchev's fall from power.

Working in groups

Taking the period as a whole:

1 Opposition to the tsarist regime appears to have been more effective than opposition to the communists. Consider whether this was because in communist Russia:
  - the opposition was weaker
  - suppression was more ruthless
  - propaganda was more effective.
  Discuss the relative importance of these three factors.

2 Draw a graph covering the years 1917 to 1964 and plot the ups and downs in the relationship between the communists and the peasants.

3 Discuss why it was that while wars contributed importantly to revolutionary outbreaks under Nicholas II, the much more disruptive Great Patriotic War was not so problematic for Stalin.

4 The people of Russia were consistently repressed whether ruled by the tsars or by the communists. Do you agree?

- -

How and with what results did the economy develop and change?

Questions to consider

- Why were there so many changes in Bolshevik economic policies in their first years in power?
- Why was economic policy such an important issue in the power struggle?
- How do you explain the ending of the NEP in Soviet Russia?
- Why was the Soviet wartime economy able to out-produce the Germans in spite of the huge losses of land, people and resources?
- Does the experience of Khrushchev show that the planned economy could not be effectively reformed?

Working in groups

Taking the period as a whole:

1 Discuss the question: Which brought the greater transformation in the lives of peasants: the emancipation of the serfs or collectivisation?

2 Compare the similarities and differences in the modernisation policies of Witte and Stalin. Which do you think was more successful?

3 Compare the impact of the First World War, the Civil War, the Second World War and the Cold War on the economy of Russia.

Questions to consider

- How had Russian society changed as a result of the revolution and Stalin?
  - Look at the impact on the class system, the family, youth and women.
  - Look at the Great Retreat and Khrushchev's policies.
- How successful was the attempt to create the New Soviet Person?
- How did Russian culture change as a result of Bolshevik rule? Look at the Russian avant-garde, socialist realism, the thaw.
- Examine the experiences of leading figures in the arts: Eisenstein, Gorky, Akhmatova, Pasternak, Solzhenitsyn.

Working in groups

Taking the period as a whole:

1 How different socially and culturally was tsarist Russia (1855–1917) from communist USSR (1918–1964)?
2 Who did more to improve the lives of the working class in the period 1855–1964: the communists or the tsars?
3 Compare the extent and nature of the control of literature and the arts between tsarist and communist Russia.

. . . .

KEY QUESTION 5:
How important were ideas and ideology?

Questions to consider

- Consider the importance of ideas and ideology for Lenin and the Bolsheviks:
  - How important was Lenin's view of the Party and its role?
  - How important was class war?
  - How important was the international dimension in Bolshevik thinking before and after October 1917?
- What was the role of ideology in the struggle over power in the 1920s?
- How far did ideology play a part in Khrushchev's policies?
- Did the three communist rulers have different attitudes to religion?

Working in groups

Taking the period as a whole:

1 Consider the similarities between Bolshevism and orthodoxy:
   - Dogma (the principles each group believed were true) must be protected at all costs.
   - Heretics must not be tolerated.
   Can you find examples of both of these?
2 Ideas and ideology come to the fore at times of political ferment. How much real influence did they have?
3 Was ideology more important for the Bolsheviks before or after they achieved power?
4 Compare and contrast the attitudes to religion of the three tsars and the three communist rulers between 1855 and 1964.

KEY QUESTION 6:
How important was the role of individuals and groups and how were they affected by developments?

Questions to consider

- E. H. Carr distinguishes between those great men who helped to mould the forces that carried them to greatness and those who rode to greatness on the back of already existing forces. Was Lenin one of the former and Stalin one of the latter?
- Who was the more important during the October Revolution and civil war: Lenin or Trotsky?
- How far was Khrushchev able to change the Stalinist system?
- Think of key groups, for example, the secret police; Kronstadt sailors; communist enthusiasts, such as *Komsomols*, 25,000ers, Stakhanovites; *kulaks* and Nepmen. How important was their contribution?

Working in groups

Taking the period as a whole:

1 Did Stalin change the nature of Russia more than any other ruler between 1855 and 1964?
2 Compare and contrast the impact of the secret police in tsarist and communist Russia.
3 Examine the experience of Gorky both before and after the revolution.
4 The results of a poll to find Russia's greatest historical figure taken in Russia at the end of 2008 placed Stalin third, Lenin sixth and Stolypin second. The winner was Alexander Nevsky who rallied the Russians against foreign invaders in the thirteenth century and was the subject of a famous Eisenstein film.
   - What do you think of this result?
   - Does it tell us more about Russia in 2008 than the historical figures involved?

Further research

There are scores of excellent books on Russian history in the period covered by this book. It is impossible for most students to consult more than a few of these. However, it is vital that you read some. It is a common complaint of all history examiners that candidates do not read widely enough. The following suggestions are meant to serve as a guide.

Also listed throughout are novels and films to extend your overall sense of the period.

General recommendations

Endurance and Endeavour 1812–2001 by J. N. Westwood (Oxford University Press), 5th edition, 2002.

The standard book on the period, it has a great deal to offer students.

Revolutionary Russia, 1891–1991 by Orlando Figes (Pelican), 2014.

The book's aim 'to chart one hundred years of history as a single revolutionary cycle' makes it particularly well suited to a breadth study like this.

Russia and the Russians: A History by Geoffrey Hosking (Harper Collins), 2001.

This book combines Hosking's work on Imperial Russia and the USSR and is very accessible.

Natasha's Dance, A Cultural History of Russia by Orlando Figes (Allen Lane), 2002.

If you really want to get inside cultural developments through the whole of this period then this is the book to read. It is full of fascinating detail about individuals, customs and beliefs as well as literature and art.

Articles geared to AS and A-level students are well worth reading too. They can be found in:

New Perspective through the Sempringham eLearning History Resources website.

History Today which has a good website and also published *History Review* which had useful articles which are available on the website.

Modern History Review published by Hodder Education.

General recommendations for Part 1

The End of Imperial Russia, 1855–1917 by Peter Waldron (Macmillan), 1997.

Excellent analysis of this period, setting events and development in a wide context.

The Romanovs, Ruling Russia 1613–1917, by Lindsey Hughes (Bloomsbury), 2008.

Lively, engaging and scholarly account of the last three Romanov tsars.

Russia: People and Empire, 1552–1917, by Geoffrey Hosking (Harper Collins), 1997.

First class general book, good on ideology underpinning autocracy, particularly orthodoxy, nationalism and national minorities.

Chapter 1

Alexander ll has not received much attention from historians in recent years. Lindsey Hughes (see general section) is good on his personality and provides an overview.

Russia in the Age of Reaction and Reform 1801–1881 by David Saunders (Longman), 1992.

Chapters 8 and 9 are relevant on the emancipation of the serfs and other reforms, good assessment and interpretation. Chapter 11 is good on Populism.

Alexander II, Emancipation and Reform by Maureen Perrie (Historical Association), 1993.

Excellent overview of emancipation and assessment of reforms in general.

The Abolition of Serfdom in Russia, by David Moon, Seminar Studies in History (Pearson Education), 2001.

Detailed account of the reasons for, the process and the impact of the emancipation of the serfs. Also considers historians' interpretations.

Russia 1815–81, by Russell Sherman and Robert Pearce (Hodder & Stoughton), 2nd edition, 2002.

Good on background for the period as well as the emancipation and reforms themselves.

The Great Reforms: Autocracy, Bureaucracy, and the Politics of Change in Imperial Russia by W. Bruce Lincoln (Northern Illinois University Press), 1990.

W. Bruce Lincoln has written extensively and interestingly on this period.

Alexander ll and the Modernisation of Russia, by W. Mosse (English University Press), 1970. Paperback 2nd revised edition (I. B. Tauris), 1995.

Written some time ago but still a standard work.

There are a number of articles on Alexander ll available on the History Today/History Review website at www.historytoday.com. Three very useful ones are:

- *The Reforms of Tsar Alexander II*, by Carl Peter Watts, History Review, 1998.
- *The Emancipation of the Russian Serfs, 1861: A Charter of Freedom or an Act of Betrayal?* by Michael Lynch, Issue 47, December 2003.
- *Milyutin and the Russian Serfs* by W. Bruce Lincoln, History Today, Vol.19, Issue 7, 1969.

Alexander ll, The Last Great Tsar by Edward Radzinsky (Free Press), 2006.

Highly personalised account of Alexander ll, told almost in story form.

Chapter 2

The year 1881 is a dividing line for Russian history. Many books and general accounts start from this date in describing the period before and leading up to the revolutions of 1917. Some of these are included below. Books which specifically cover the economic development of Russia in the late tsarist period are not covered as the books that have been written are highly detailed and difficult for students to access. Many of the books that are often listed are over thirty years old. Students are best served by reading the sections on the Russia economy in the main texts that are listed in the general section and here, for example, Hans Rogger (see below).

Russia in the Age of Modernisation and Revolution 1881–1917, by Hans Rogger (Longman), 1986.

Good overall account of the period. Strong on economy, agriculture and industry, workers and peasants and the nationalities.

A People's Tragedy, The Russian Revolution 1891–1924, by Orlando Figes (Pimlico), 1997.

Comprehensive coverage in an absorbing, engaging and accessible form which manages to bring in the private lives and experience of Russians into the wider narrative.

Russia Under the Old Regime, by Richard Pipes (Penguin Books), 1995.

Chapters 9, 10 and 11 are relevant here.

Land Reform in Russia 1906–1917 by Judith Pallot (Oxford University Press), 1999.

A detailed examination of Stolypin's land reforms and their impact.

Alexander lll by W. Bruce Lincoln, *History Today*, Volume 26, Issue 10, October 1976.

Good article giving clear overview of Alexander lll, available online.

Novels

There are a vast number of novels from this period that you could read from the great writers of all time like Tolstoy, Dostoyevsky and Gorky. You could pick one or two novels like the ones listed below or a collection of short stories. Many of these are available on the internet. You can also read short stories and plays by Chekhov.

My Childhood by Maxim Gorky (Penguin Books), 1966, many available editions.

An evocative description of Gorky's early life in a poor and brutal family.

Anna Karenina by Leo Tolstoy (Penguin classics), many available editions.

Great background reading to get a sense of Russian society in the second half of the nineteenth century.

Russian Short Stories (CreateSpace Independent Publishing Platform), 2014.

Stories by Tolstoy, Turgenev, Gorky and Dostoyevsky.

Chapters 3 and 4

The books for Chapters 3 and 4 can be considered together because most of them are concerned with the February and October Revolutions in 1917 and the period immediately after them. There are an enormous number of books on this period. The ones below have been selected for accessibility or because they offer a different approach to the period.

The Russian Revolution, A Very Short Introduction by S. A. Smith (Oxford), 2002.

Very accessible and clear overview from before the revolution to the end of NEP.

The Russian Revolution by Sheila Fitzpatrick (Oxford University Press), 3rd edition, 2008.

Good narrative, clear analysis from a top Russian historian. Required reading for students.

Nicholas ll, Emperor of all the Russias by Dominic Lieven (John Murray), 1993.

Highly regarded biography of Nicholas ll setting the issues facing Nicholas in a wider context.

Nicholas ll: The Last of the Tsars by Marc Ferro (Viking), 1991.

A straightforward, easy-to-read account.

Conspirator, Lenin in Exile, The Making of a Revolutionary by Helen Rappaport (Hutchinson), 2009.

Covers Lenin's early life and his years in exile, the creation of the Bolshevik Party and his relationships with other revolutionaries.

For biographies of Lenin, see those listed in Chapter 5.

The Revolution of 1905 by A. Ascher (Stanford), 2004.

Authoritative read.

The Russian Revolution 1917–21 by Beryl Williams, Historical Association Studies (Blackwell), 1995.

Clear account of the revolutionary year of 1917 and the Bolshevik take-over.

The Russian Constitutional Experiment: Government and Duma 1907–1914 by Geoffrey Hosking (Cambridge), 1973.

Richard Pipes is an eminent scholar in this field and has written several books which put his particular interpretation on events including:

A Concise History of the Russian Revolution by Richard Pipes (Harvill Press), 1995.

Three Whys of the Russian Revolution by Richard Pipes (Pimlico), 1998.

Rethinking the Russian Revolution by Edward Acton (Edward Arnold), 1990.

Considers different interpretations of the February and October Revolutions in 1917.

Ten Days that shook the World, by John Read (Penguin Books), 1977.

The classic contemporary account of the Bolshevik revolution by a committed American socialist in St Petersburg.

Witnesses of the Russian Revolution by Harvey Pitcher (Pimlico), 2001.

Eye-witness accounts of events during 1917. These are western observers, including diplomats and journalists. Very accessible and gives a sense of the times.

The Eastern Front 1914–1917 by Norman Stone (London), 1975.

Good book for the Russian army during the First World War.

Cathy Porter has written a number of books about women in the Russian Revolution including:

Alexandra Kollontai by Cathy Porter (Merlin Press), 2013.

Kollontai was a revolutionary Marxist who became a member of the Bolshevik Government in 1918.

Novels

Dr Zhivago by Boris Pasternak (Vintage), 2011. First published 1957, many different editions.

A love story conducted during the period around the Russian Revolution by a writer living and working in Russia during 1917 and who stayed after the October Revolution. It has evocative scenes describing the revolution and the ensuing civil war. It was refused publication in the Soviet Union but was published in Italy in 1957. In 1958 Pasternak was awarded the Nobel Prize for literature.

Films

There are many dreadful films to do with the last days of the Tsar which are hopelessly inaccurate and largely sympathetic to the Tsar. Much better are:

Dr Zhivago David Lean (dir.), 1965 (PG).

Epic film of the book

Battleship Potemkin Sergei Eisenstein (dir.), 1925 and ***October*** Sergei Eisenstein (dir.), 1928.

Both of these films have provided classic images of the revolutionary period. In the famous 'Odessa steps' scene from ***Battleship Potemkin*** Eisenstein's radical new filming techniques of editing together different images build tension and produce a dramatic climax. The filming of the storming of the Winter Palace in ***October*** caused more damage than the actual event.

General recommendations for Part 2

As well as the books mentioned at the beginning which cover both parts, three very good studies covering the whole period are:

The Making and Breaking of the Soviet System by Christopher Read (Palgrave), 2001.

Another book which is particularly well-suited to a breadth study.

The Penguin History of Modern Russia: From Tsarism to the Twenty-First Century by Robert Service (Penguin), 2009.

The third edition of Service's much praised history, very useful for all chapters.

The Rise and Fall of the Soviet Union by Martin McCauley (Routledge), 2007.

Another good breadth study.

Two good economic histories:

An Economic History of the USSR, 1917–91 by A. Nove (Penguin), 1992.

Still an excellent and accessible economic history.

Soviet Economic Development from Lenin to Khrushchev by R. W. Davies (Cambridge), 1998.

A brief history by one of the experts in the field.

Two collections of documents. The very helpful commentary by Edward Acton is a history of these years in itself.

The Soviet Union: A Documentary History, Vol. I 1917–1940 by Edward Acton and Tom Stableford (University of Exeter Press), 2005.

The Soviet Union: A Documentary History, Vol. II 1939–1991 by Edward Acton and Tom Stableford (University of Exeter Press), 2006.

The two books in the popular Access to History series are well established and geared towards A-level students:

Reaction and Revolution: Russia 1894–1924 by Michael Lynch (Hodder Education), 3rd edition, 2005.

Stalin's Russia, 1924–53 by Michael Lynch (Hodder Education), 4th edition, 2008.

The A-level History magazines mentioned at the beginning are packed with useful articles on Lenin and Stalin in particular and well worth consulting.

Chapter 5

Lenin and the consolidation of power have received plenty of attention from historians.

There are the books on the Russian Revolution by Sheila Fitzpatrick and S. A. Smith which go beyond 1917 and are mentioned under Chapters 3 and 4.

Revolutionary Russia, 1891–1991 by Orlando Figes (Penguin), 2014.

Chapters 7, 8 and 9 are relevant to this chapter and there is of course his big book, *A People's Tragedy: The Russian Revolution 1891–1924* (Pimlico), 1997, which is very readable.

There are many biographies of Lenin, three of the best are:

Lenin, A Biography by Robert Service (Macmillan), 2000.

Lenin by B. Williams (Longman), 2000.

Lenin: A Revolutionary Life by Christopher Read (Routledge), 2005.

All three biographers have written books on the revolution and the Bolshevik consolidation of power:

The Russian Revolution 1900–1927 by Robert Service (Macmillan), 3rd edition, 2009.

The Russian Revolution 1917–21, by Beryl Williams, Historical Association Studies (Blackwell), 1987.

War and Revolution in Russia: 1914–22 – The Collapse of Tsarism and the Establishment of Soviet Power by Christopher Read (Palgrave), 2013.

A book which stretches A-level students, but Read's latest thinking.

The two economic histories by Alec Nove and R. W. Davies mentioned earlier are very useful in this chapter where economic matters are very important.

Stalin's Russia by Chris Ward (Edward Arnold), 2nd edition, 1999.

A very stimulating summary of all the key historiographical debates, excellent on the power struggle.

Stalin Vol 1 Paradoxes of Power 1878–1928 by Stephen Kotkin (Allen Lane), 2014.

The long, first volume of a major work which promises to be a definitive biography of Stalin. It deals with Stalin's times as well as his life.

Trotsky by Ian Thatcher (Routledge), 2003.

A good short study of Trotsky's political life.

Two articles which look at the power struggle from a different perspective are:

Zinoviev and Kamenev by Chris Corin in *History Review*, March 2006.

Bukharin: No match for Stalin by Chris Corin in *New Perspective*, March 2014.

Novels

We by Yevgeny Zamyatin (Vintage), 2007.

A short novel written in 1924 and banned in the USSR for sixty years, this was the forerunner of Huxley's *Brave New World* and Orwell's *1984*. In this Dystopia (a nightmare Utopia) the people are robot-like, known by numbers and have lives programmed in every detail.

Red Cavalry by Isaac Babel (Penguin), 2005.

Written in the 1920s, a collection of short stories of Babel's experiences with the Red Cavalry during the Civil War and Russo-Soviet War.

Films

Battleship Potemkin Sergei Eisenstein (dir.), 1925 and *October* Sergei Eisenstein (dir.), 1928.

These films are available as DVDs. They were mentioned under Chapters 3 and 4 but are relevant here for giving the 1920s' perspective on the events.

Chapter 6

This period has seen a great deal of research over recent decades.

Stalin by Kevin McDermott (Palgrave Macmillan), 2006.

This book is an excellent guide to current debates on Stalin's Russia. Clear, concise and strong on all aspects of Stalin's rule. Particularly helpful on the Terror.

Stalin and Stalinism by Martin McCauley (Routledge), revised 3rd edition, 2013.

Seminar series, updated and still a good survey.

The Stalin Years by Evan Mawdsley (University of Manchester Press), 1998.

Another good study on all aspects of the era, with sources and a useful chapter on Socialist Realism.

Stalin, A Biography by Robert Service (Macmillan), 2004.

A highly praised and very thorough biography.

The Russian Revolution by Sheila Fitzpatrick (Oxford University Press), 3rd edition, 2008.

More than the title suggests, Fitzpatrick takes the story from 1917, through to the great purges of the 1930s; particularly useful on the Cultural Revolution.

Stalin's Peasants by Sheila Fitzpatrick (Oxford University Press), 1994.

Detailed, but examines resistance and survival in the villages after collectivisation.

Everyday Stalinism by Sheila Fitzpatrick (Oxford University Press), 1999.

The pioneering account of everyday life under Stalin.

Stalin's Russia by Chris Ward (Edward Arnold), 2nd edition, 1999.

A very stimulating summary of all the key historiographical debates, so very helpful for this chapter.

The Great Terror: A Reassessment by Robert Conquest (Oxford University Press), 1990.

The classic account, though the emphasis has shifted in work on the terror.

The Road to Terror: Stalin and the Self-Destruction of the Bolsheviks, 1932–39 by J. Arch Getty, and Oleg Naumov (Yale University Press), 1999.

A comprehensive collection of documents on the Terror, with Getty's commentary. Getty was the leading revisionist but modifies his views somewhat here.

The Soviet Union: A Documentary History, Vol. I, 1917–1940 by Edward Acton and Tom Stableford (University of Exeter Press), 2005.

Particularly useful for the Terror.

Art under Stalin by Matthew Cullerne Brown (Phaidon Press), 1991.

An analysis of the art of the Stalin era, from 1932 to 1953.

Stalin: A New History edited by Sarah Davies and James Harris (Cambridge University Press), 2005.

A series of essays ranging across the political, economic, social, cultural, ideological and international history of the Stalin era.

Rethinking the Soviet Experience, by Stephen Cohen (Oxford University Press), 1985.

A series of essays and strong on historiography and the debate on the degree of continuity between Lenin and Stalin.

The Stalin-Kaganovich Correspondence 1931–36 edited by R. W. Davies, et al. (Yale University Press), 2003.

Dipping into these letters gives a real insight into how Stalin communicated his political will and his angry and vindictive nature.

Novels

Virgin Soil Upturned by Mikhail Sholokhov (Penguin), 1935.

A novel about the experience of collectivisation and much quoted by historians. Sholokhov was a socialist realist author and acceptable to the regime, but also a Nobel Prize winner – he was allowed to accept his!

Chapter 7

The Making and Breaking of the Soviet System by Christopher Read (Palgrave), 2001.

This book is very helpful on the war and post-war years.

Stalin by Kevin McDermott (Palgrave), 2006.

Good on the war and helps to clarify the post-war years, which can be a bit difficult to understand.

The biographies of Stalin, notably Service, and the other studies of the whole Stalin era are all relevant.

Russia's War by Richard Overy (Penguin), 1998.

A fine study of the war, with interesting final chapters on its legacy for Stalin and the country, and Russia's war: myth and reality.

Ivan's War by Catherine Merridale (Faber and Faber), 2005.

A book in which the experience of the ordinary Russian soldier is at the heart of the narrative.

Victory at Stalingrad by Geoffrey Roberts (Longman), 2002.

Short and more than just the battle of Stalingrad, the text of Stalin's orders 270 and 227 is there in full.

The Soviet Home Front: A Social and Economic History of the USSR in World War II by John Barber and Mark Harrison (Longman), 1991.

The best book on the home front, Harrison is the leading expert on the war economy.

Stalin's Russia by Chris Ward (Edward Arnold), 2nd edition, 1999.

A very stimulating summary of all the key historiographical debates, looks at the post-war years a little differently.

Stalinism and After by Alec Nove (Allen and Unwin), 1975.

Good on Stalin's legacy and the problems he left his successors.

Novels

Life and Fate by Vasily Grossman (Vantage), 2006.

A long but immensely powerful novel – the twentieth-century *War and Peace*.

Chapter 8

Khrushchev has not attracted as much attention as Lenin and Stalin, but there is still plenty of material available.

Revolutionary Russia, 1891–1991 by Orlando Figes (Penguin), 2014.

Chapter 17 is particularly useful, Figes believes that the USSR never recovered from Khrushchev's 1956 speech.

The Penguin History of Modern Russia: From Tsarism to the Twenty-first Century by Robert Service (Penguin), 2009.

The third edition of Service's much praised history, very useful for the Khrushchev era.

Khrushchev The Man and his Era by W. Taubman (W. W. Norton), 2003.

The definitive biography, and although it is long it is easy to read.

Martin McCauley has written extensively on Khrushchev. The following two short books are good, but are no longer in print.

The Khrushchev Era 1953–1964 by Martin McCauley (Longman), 1995.

Khrushchev by Martin McCauley (Cardinal), 1991.

You are more likely to find McCauley's longer general histories:

The Rise and Fall of the Soviet Union (Routledge), 2007, which is a 3rd edition of *The Soviet Union 1917–1991* (Routledge), 1993.

Rulers and Victims: The Russians in the Soviet Union by Geoffrey Hosking (Harvard University Press), 2006.

There is a very useful chapter on the Khrushchev years.

Stalinism and After by Alec Nove (Allen and Unwin), 1975.

A good chapter on Khrushchev.

An Economic History of the USSR, 1917–91 by A. Nove (Penguin), 1992.

This is useful on Khrushchev's agricultural policy, one of his top priorities.

Khrushchev and Stalin by Ian Thatcher, History Review, March 2009.

The Soviet Union: A Documentary History, Vol. II, 1939–1991 by Edward Acton and Tom Stableford (University of Exeter Press), 2006.

Good on Khrushchev and some useful documents.

Khrushchev Remembers translated and edited by Strobe Talbott, Vol. 1 (Penguin), 1977.

Khrushchev on the Twentieth Party Congress and the full text of the speech.

Gulag by Anne Applebaum (Penguin), 2004.

Chapter 25 is good on the Thaw and the publication of *One Day in the Life of Ivan Denisovich*.

Novels

One Day in the Life of Ivan Denisovich by Aleksandr Solzhenitsyn (Penguin), new edition 2000.

Short very readable, the most famous of all gulag novels.

Dr Zhivago by Boris Pasternak (Vintage), 2002.

Interesting to read to see why it was banned, it also captures the atmosphere of the three revolutions and the Civil War.

Red Plenty by Francis Spufford (Faber and Faber), 2010.

A novel about a brief era when, under Khrushchev, the USSR 'looked forward to a future of rich Communists and envious capitalists'. Uses a lot of genuine historical material and captures the time.

Films

One Day in the Life of Ivan Denisovich Caspar Wrede (dir.), 19709 (G).

Dr Zhivago David Lean (dir.), 1965 (PG).

Glossary

Agronomist The profession concerned with applying science and technology to use plants for food, fuel and fibre.

Anarchy The absence of government or authority, usually leading to disorder.

Annexation Taking over the territory of other countries and joining it to own country.

Artel Co-operative association of craftsmen living and working together.

Autocracy System of government where there are no constraints on the power of the ruler, absolute rule by one person.

Biological yield The maximum possible yield of the standing crop in the field at moment of maximum ripeness.

Bourgeoisie Owners of capital, industrialists, manufacturers, wealthy merchants; also the wealthy middle classes.

Burzhooi **(bourgeois)** This term did not only apply to the middle classes. It was a form of abuse used against employers, officers, landowners, priests, Jewish people, merchants or anybody seemingly well-to-do after 1917.

Calendar Tsarist Russia used the Julian calendar while most of Europe had adopted the Gregorian calendar. There was a difference between the two calendars of thirteen days. The Bolshevik government adopted the Gregorian calendar on 31 January 1918; the next day was declared to be 14 February.

Capitalism Economic system based on private enterprise and the profit motive in which the market determines the price of goods, the supply of raw materials and the distribution of products.

Cheka The All-Russian Extraordinary Commission for Combating Counter-Revolution and Sabotage; the Soviet secret police from 1917–22.

CIA United States Central Intelligence Agency, active in the Cold War.

Cold War Post-1945 hostility between the democratic West and the Soviet Union; a war of threats and propaganda, rather than actual conflict in a war between the two sides.

Comintern Communist International, set up in March 1919 to support worldwide revolution.

Commissar Russian word for a minister.

Communism Last stage in Marx's notion of the evolution of history: everybody would be equal and people would take what they needed from a central pool of goods, people would have more leisure time.

Communist Party of the Soviet Union (CPSU) New name adopted by the Bolshevik Party in 1919.

Constituent Assembly An elected parliament whose main job is to write a constitution which sets out a new system of government including the relationships between the different organs of government, the legal system, and the checks and balances in the system.

Corpus Body or collection of writings.

Counter-revolution When the supporters of the old system of government try to take back power.

Desyatina **(plural,** *desyatiny***)** Russian measurement of land, equivalent to 2.7 acres.

Dues Payments in cash or kind (for example, produce) made by serf to nobles.

Duma Russian parliament after 1906.

Factionalism Forming of 'factions' or groups in the Party which argue about policy and ideology.

Fifth column A term used to describe enemy sympathisers.

GPU (sometimes OGPU) The *Cheka* was renamed the GPU (Main Political Administration) in 1922.

Greens Peasant armies, often made up of deserters from the Whites or Reds. Some of these armies fought for the Bolsheviks, some against.

Gulag An acronym for the Main Administration of Corrective Labour Camps and Colonies.

Haemophilia Condition in which blood does not clot and may cause internal bleeding.

Historiography The study of history writing, talking about the different schools of thought on a historical subject; how the circumstances in which history is written affect what historians say about a subject.

Icon A religious painting, usually of a holy figure, often on wood and used as an aid to devotion.

Institutions The formal structures on which a society depends, e.g. the government, administrative system, the law, education, the economy.

Intelligentsia Educated and more enlightened section of Russian society.

Kolkhoz **(plural,** *Kolkhozy***)** Collective farm the peasants who lived on the farms were called *Kolkhozniks*.

Komsomol Party youth organisation open to those aged between 14 and 28.

Kulak Better-off peasant who owned animals and hired labour.

Lend-Lease This was US aid in the first place to Britain in March 1941, but extended later to the USSR.

Mir The peasant commune.

MTS Machine and tractor stations, as well as providing machinery and advice the 2,500 MTS were also used to control the countryside.

MVD (Ministry of Internal Affairs) The secret police in charge of gaols and camps in the post-war era.

Nationalise To take industries and banks out of private ownership and put them under the control of the state.

Neopatriarchal A new form of male domination.

Nepmen Traders during the NEP period.

Nihilism From the Latin *nihil* meaning nothing. A philosophy which takes different forms, often denying the notion of absolute morality.

NKVD The name for the secret police between 1934 and 1943.

Novy Mir A literary journal in which *One Day in the Life of Ivan Denisovich* and other work representative of the thaw was published.

Okhrana Secret police established in 1881.

Oligarchy A state where a small group holds power.

Orgburo Short for Organisation Bureau, which turned Politburo policies into practice.

Plebian apparatchiki Working-class communist officials.

Pogrom Organised, violent attack on the homes and businesses of Jewish people.

Politburo Short for Political Bureau, top body of the Communist Party making key decisions about policy.

Poll tax Tax on all men of the lower orders. Nobles and clergy exempt. Abolished 1883–7.

Popular revolution One that is accepted and welcomed by the majority of the people in a country. Many of the people may have been involved in carrying out the revolution.

Populists (Narodniks) Revolutionary group in 1870s who believed in peasant-based socialism.

Proclamation of the Abolition of Serfdom (also referred to as Emancipation Manifesto) Document in which Alexander ll announced the reform to the people, read out by parish priests March–April 1861.

Productionism Production at any price. Maximising economic output had to be the first priority in the conditions of 1918–22, but it also had a vital ideological dimension.

Proletariat Industrial workers.

Real wages Wages in terms of the amount of goods and services that can be bought.

Redemption payments Payments made by peasants to the government to redeem the land they had been allocated in the emancipation.

Red Guards Armed militia trained by Bolsheviks.

Reds The Bolsheviks and their supporters.

Samizdat System of clandestine publication of banned literature in the USSR.

Serfs Peasants bound to the estates of nobles.

Slavophiles Wanted to preserve Slav culture and the autocratic system of government, saw western values and institutions as unsuited to Russia.

Smychka The alliance between the working class and the peasantry.

Socialism Workers' control of state. Means of production – factories, machines, etc. – owned collectively and run by state, everybody equal, wealth and goods shared out fairly.

Socialist realism The ideological philosophy that guided literature and the arts after 1934; creative writing and art had to celebrate the achievements of the proletarians and leaders building the new Soviet vision.

Soviet Russian word for council of representatives.

Soviet Procuracy The government bureau concerned with pursuing dissenters accused of anti-Soviet agitation and propaganda.

Sovnarkom Council of the People's Commissars; the top Bolshevik governing body (30–40 members) set up after the October Revolution in 1917.

Statutes of 19 February 1861 Statutes which abolished serfdom.

Third Section Secret police set up by Nicholas l, closed down in 1880.

Three-field rotation system Crops would be grown in two fields while one field was left fallow each year to recover.

Total war A war which is not restricted to the warfront and where the economy and lives of citizens are bound up in prosecuting the war.

Totalitarian state One in which power is concentrated in the hands of one man or small group, exercising excessive control of individuals and denying them fundamental civil and political liberties; monitoring and control of aspects of individuals' lives carried out by secret police who are accountable only to the political élite.

Troika (plural, troiki) A three-man commission set up in all regions and territories to consider the cases of those subjected to 'punitive measures'.

Union of Liberation Liberal organisation, established in 1903, pressing for constitutional change and social and political evolution along European lines.

Union of Russian People Right-wing supporters of the Tsar who organised paramilitary groups to attack socialists and Jewish people.

Vesenkha Supreme Council of National Economy.

Vozhd Russian term for a supreme leader.

Warsaw Pact A military alliance of east European communist states formed in 1955 as a response to the admission of West Germany into NATO (North Atlantic Treaty Organisation)

Wehrmacht The German army.

Westernisers Believed Russia should adopt certain western values, e.g. the rule of law, and develop institutions along lines of those in Western Europe.

Whites The opponents of the Bolsheviks in the civil war including monarchists, nationalists, liberals, moderate socialists and Socialist Revolutionaries and other groups.

White Russians People who live in the area we now call Belorussia.

Zemgor Joint organisation of *zemstva* and towns to organise care of wounded and provide hospitals but also played part in supplying military equipment.

Zemstva (singular zemstvo) Elected district and provincial councils.

Zionist One who supports Zionism, the idea of creating a Jewish national homeland in Palestine.

Index